Professional Conduct

Professional Conduct

Inns of Court School of Law

Institute of Law, City University, London

OXFORD
UNIVERSITY PRESS

OXFORD

UNIVERSITY PRESS

Great Clarendon Street, Oxford OX2 6DP

Oxford University Press is a department of the University of Oxford.
It furthers the University's objective of excellence in research, scholarship,
and education by publishing worldwide in

Oxford New York

Auckland Cape Town Dar es Salaam Hong Kong Karachi
Kuala Lumpur Madrid Melbourne Mexico City Nairobi
New Delhi Shanghai Taipei Toronto

With offices in

Argentina Austria Brazil Chile Czech Republic France Greece
Guatemala Hungary Italy Japan Poland Portugal Singapore
South Korea Switzerland Thailand Turkey Ukraine Vietnam

Oxford is a registered trade mark of Oxford University Press
in the UK and in certain other countries

Published in the United States
by Oxford University Press Inc., New York

British Library Cataloguing in Publication Data

Data available

Library of Congress Cataloging in Publication Data

Data available

Typeset by Newgen Imaging Systems (P) Ltd., Chennai, India
Printed in Great Britain
on acid-free paper by
Ashford Colour Press, Gosport, Hampshire

ISBN 0–19–928156–4   978–0–19–928156–5

1 3 5 7 9 10 8 6 4 2

FOREWORD

It is a privilege to write this Foreword, following the tradition set by my predecessor, the Hon. Mr Justice Elias.

The Bar Vocational Course (BVC) bridges the gap between completion of a university degree and the start of a professional working life, whether by way of pupillage preliminary to a career at the Bar, or otherwise. These Manuals are geared to the practical and professional approach that is central to the BVC. Updated and revised, the Manuals form an integral part of the student's vocational training; as such, they are an important ingredient in the constant drive to raise standards in the public interest.

The Manuals are written by staff at the Inns of Court School of Law (ICSL). The range and coverage of the Manuals have grown steadily. They are intended to provide a useful resource for all concerned in the training of legal skills, hopefully at whichever validated institution such training takes place.

Legal vocational training does not stand still; the ICSL and authors would welcome feedback from any source, which may assist to improve the Manuals in the future. Any such comments should be addressed to the BVC Course Director at the ICSL.

Finally a word of thanks is appropriate to the publishers for their enthusiasm and efficiency in arranging production and publication of the Manuals.

The Hon. Mr Justice Gross
Chairman, Advisory Board of the Institute of Law
City University, London
October 2004

OUTLINE CONTENTS

DETAILED CONTENTS

PREFACE

'Ethics — a small county east of London?'

The main reason you will read this Manual is because as an intending barrister, your understanding and application of professional conduct and ethics will be the foundation of all you achieve at the Bar. This Manual represents the guidance you will require as a barrister to steer you through these sometimes problematic areas of practice.

Of course the focus of this Manual is on the development of your skills to effectively deal with professional conduct matters as the intending practitioner. You can never work in isolation at the Bar. You will come into contact with and represent a variety of individuals from all walks of life and the way in which you choose to carry out your dealings is under increasing public scrutiny. It is important, therefore, that this Manual contains practical advice and guidance from those at the 'coal-face' of practice and from others such as the National Consumer Council, who can help your understanding of the relationship with your clients, as well as setting out the Code of Conduct (see **Appendix 1**) and other key practical texts such as the Equality Code for the Bar.

You are a member of a professional body whose reputation is linked to each and every one of its members. The need to maintain the highest standards is an ongoing obligation for the Bar. As an intending member you will soon recognise how helpful other members of the Bar are with regard to professional conduct matters and of the support the Bar Council itself will give you. However, you will not be able to draw upon the support of others if you are unable to identify potential areas of difficulty. To help you to develop these crucial skills you must first identify the fundamental principles set out in the Code of Conduct and question the application of the spirit of the Code based on these fundamental tenets when no express provision can be found. This Manual will help you to develop these skills by discussing situations that frequently arise during the differing assessment areas you will undertake during the Bar Vocational Course, where the application of the Code and its spirit is paramount.

Furthermore, the guidance set out in this Manual will then encourage you to think further about your obligations towards helping to 'protect individuals and groups from the abuse of public and private power' (The Lord Chancellor's Advisory Committee on Legal Education and Conduct, 1996). This concept, know as the 'ethical challenge' should ensure that your understanding of professional conduct and ethics reaches further than a simple familiarisation with the Code of Conduct and of the complaints procedure for dealing with transgressions. Indeed, in meeting this challenge the Manual will also encourage you to think carefully about your own moral standpoint and how this could impact upon your response to the ethical dilemmas you will meet in practice. After all, as an intending practitioner, the recognition of your own subjective personal morality should then ensure that it does not interfere with your practice as a lawyer.

The approach this Manual takes towards your development of a disciplined way of working will be of great value throughout your career at the Bar. It will help to ensure that you become a respected member of the profession and in time you may be giving advice to junior members of the Bar, as to the most suitable approach to professional conduct problems.

Kate R Stead LL.B (Hons), M.Phil (Cantab)
Barrister
Lecturer in Law, ICSL

1

Introduction

Paragraph 301 of the Code of Conduct states that:

A barrister ... must not:

(a) engage in conduct whether in pursuit of his profession or otherwise which is:
   (i) dishonest or otherwise discreditable to a barrister;
   (ii) prejudicial to the administration of justice; or
   (iii) likely to diminish public confidence in the legal profession or the administration of justice or otherwise bring the legal profession into disrepute.

You are hoping to join this profession at a time of change. The courts, for example, are no longer the exclusive adversarial platforms of barristers, but are now open to solicitor advocates, in-house solicitors and the employed Bar. The Bar is therefore focusing on opportunities such as Licensed Access, the Human Rights Act and quality standards. The Bar is increasing in size and income, there is an increased number of female practitioners and an increasing representation among ethnic minority groups. However, even in these changing times there is nothing more important to practice at the Bar than the way in which barristers conduct themselves, and the regard in which they are held by their peers, judges they appear before, their instructing solicitor and members of the public with whom they come into contact during their professional lives.

1.1 The Code of Conduct

Underpinning the profession is the Code of Conduct (the Code) and no matter what challenges you will face individually or as part of a profession, your comprehension and application of the Code must be thorough. Without this solid foundation the Bar's efforts in the face of change would crumble to nothing. The way you conduct yourselves in practice and towards those whom you meet in your professional lives is rightly under scrutiny. Barristers never work in isolation. Ignoring the application of the Code not only affects an individual's reputation and career at the Bar, it can have far reaching implications to those affected by such oversights and thus the behaviour of the Bar as a profession is brought into question. Consequently, the Code set out in **Appendix 1** is perhaps the most important text to comprehend and then apply throughout your career at the Bar.

1.2 The ethical challenge

It would be comforting to think that at this stage of your legal training the Code will expressly deal with all professional conduct situations. Of course during the BVC and in early practice it becomes apparent that not only does the letter of the Code need to be understood, but also the application of its spirit to many situations is crucial. **Chapter 4**, 'the letter and spirit of the Code', prompts you to think carefully about they way in which you choose to interpret the Code and it also suggests that you recognise the 'underpinning values' of the Code. This approach is vital if as a barrister you are to operate within the spirit of the Code, where there is no letter, albeit that this is so often based on an interpretation of the combination of the fundamental tenets. Indeed, the chapter also advises that you are wise to be aware of your own personal morality and that it does not cloud your objective professional judgment in dealing with the ethical difficulties you will meet in practice.

Accepting that the Code is designed to ensure ethical practice at the Bar, your analysis of professional conduct issues must also take place within the context of an important principle identified by the Lord Chancellor's Advisory Committee on Legal Education and Conduct (ACLEC). The committee in its first report on Legal Education and Training (April 1996) identified 'the ethical challenge' (para 1.21):

> From the earliest stages of education and training, intending lawyers should be imbued not only with the standards and codes of professional conduct, but also more generally with the obligations of lawyers to help protect individuals and groups from the abuse of public and private power.

ACLEC recognised therefore that 'familiarisation of the professional codes of conduct and the machinery for enforcing them' (p 17) was not enough. Trainee lawyers must be made aware through effective training of their wider obligations to society.

Fair treatment of individuals is a factor which Lady Justice Hale comments upon in a speech to the Bar Council (December 2002):

> . . . the public perception should not be of a profession fighting hard to keep things as they are, which the public will see as mainly for its own benefit rather than for the public good, but of a profession fighting hard for equal protection of the laws, and equal access to justice, most needed by the powerless rather than the powerful.

1.3 A profession under scrutiny

Popular perceptions about the Bar are often wrong. Conclusions portrayed in the media about alleged 'fat cat' lawyers overlook the £2.5 million worth of pro bono work the Bar undertakes or the many lawyers struggling to make ends meet. Michael Scott CBE DSO, the Lay Complaints Commissioner (LCC) to the General Council of the Bar in his 5th Annual Report (2001) recognises the difficulties faced by some in practice and states:

> Members of the public who think a barrister's life begins at 10 am by alighting from the Rolls and gently easing into a large lunch, should see the serious financial difficulties many face at the unglamorous end of, say, magistrates' courts and the like.

You may be puzzled as to why it is necessary to mention such problems. The answer is simple — whatever difficulties are encountered, financial or otherwise, the application of the Code of Conduct remains paramount. Cutting corners, being rude to a difficult professional client or not being aware of a client's specific needs are not options.

Every day the way in which you choose to conduct your affairs is rightly under scrutiny by all parties you come into contact with. For example, in the context of criminal trials, recent case law has highlighted defence counsel's professional duties with regard to procedural errors by the prosecution. The judiciary has clearly set out that such matters should be identified and dealt with at the earliest opportunity and not left until the last minute because criminal proceedings are not a game (*R v Gleeson* The Times, 30 October 2003 and *Hughes v DPP* [2003] EWHC 2470).

As you become fully versed in the letter of the Code and its application, it is useful to read a list recently compiled by Mark Stobbs (General Council of the Bar, former Head of Professional Conduct) setting out the main reasons for complaints against barristers.

Principal Reasons for Complaints Against Barristers

Poor Services to Clients
This can cover a wide variety of circumstances but typical examples are:

- arriving late at court or for a conference without reasonable excuse;
- behaving rudely or abruptly to the client — no matter how difficult the client may be;
- failing to ensure that the client properly understands advice or the consequences of any decision or settlement;
- giving negligent advice or failing to take steps to protect the client's interest;
- double-booking and other clerks' room errors.

Misconduct
All of the above cases can amount to misconduct as well if the facts are sufficiently serious. The following types of action will also amount to misconduct:

- breach of confidence;
- expressing personal opinions in the press in matters which are continuing and in which you have been instructed;
- acting where you have an interest or where another client has an interest which is opposed to that of your client;
- bullying your client and threatening to withdraw if your client does not accept a settlement or plead guilty;
- making allegations of fraud without a proper basis for so doing no matter how hard your client may press you to do so;
- coaching or rehearsing a witness in their evidence;
- holding yourself out as a barrister when offering legal advice if you have not completed pupillage or complied with the other practising requirements;
- misleading the court or continuing in a case where your client has misled the court or failed to disclose a document that the law requires to be disclosed.

Personal Problems
Generally, the Bar Council does not seek to make judgements about individuals' personal lives, but there are times when conduct outside practice can call a person's suitability to remain a barrister into question. Particular examples include:

- being convicted of a criminal offence or being charged with a serious criminal offence — both must be reported to the Bar Council;
- being adjudicated bankrupt or made subject to an Individual Voluntary Arrangement or a Directors Disqualification Order which must, again be reported to the Bar Council;

- using the qualification to obtain an advantage that would not otherwise be given or to intimidate another person;
- failing to comply with the order of a court;
- other dishonest or disreputable behaviour which is likely to bring the Bar or the administration of justice into disrepute.

Breaches of the Practising Rules
- Failing to pay the insurance premium to the Bar Mutual Indemnity Fund or practising certificate fee;
- not complying with compulsory continuing education scheme.

Given the number of complaints stemming from the relationship between a barrister and the lay client, it is worth noting that the Professional Conduct and Complaints Committee of the Bar Council have commented in the General Council of the Bar Annual Report 2001 that:

It is clear from a number of the complaints considered by the PCC that some members of the Bar could place client care more at the forefront of their professional behaviour — by ensuring, for example, that their lay client understands the reasons for a particular outcome.

1.4 Fair treatment

The Bar is committed to equal opportunities. An integral part of good professional conduct is the attitude which you adopt and display towards the variety of people with whom you come into contact in your professional life. These range from colleagues in chambers, opponents, the judiciary, professional clients, lay clients, witnesses and court staff, to other professionals such as police officers, doctors, probation officers and social workers. You will be dealing with people from every walk of life, every socio-economic group, with differing mental abilities, customs, religions and expectations. It is crucial that you treat people courteously and fairly and that you are scrupulous to avoid discriminating directly or indirectly against any person on grounds of race, colour, ethnic or national origin, nationality, citizenship, sex, sexual orientation, marital status, disability, religion or political persuasion (see the Code para 305.1). Such discrimination is not only a breach of the Code; it is also a breach of the Bar's Equality Code (see Miscellaneous Guidance in Section 3 of the Code in **Appendix 1**).

Your success at the Bar will depend more than anything upon the way that you treat other people. **Chapter 3**, 'working at the Bar today', sets out how you can develop your awareness of and approach to treating people fairly. As such, the chapter contains information on the sources of guidance relating to fair treatment, harassment and discrimination and sets out invaluable advice for your practice at the Bar today. **Chapter 2** which deals with 'professional relationships' is also a very useful source of guidance in ensuring that you behave towards others with the courtesy, respect and sensitivity that the Bar requires of its members. It draws upon the experience of barristers, solicitors, judges, clerks and organisations to which the lay client turns, such as the National Consumer Council and the Bar Council's professional conduct department. It also contains key practical texts such as the Code for Crown Prosecutors in an attempt to ensure that whatever your role is in proceedings you will know the sources of guidance that an intending barrister needs.

1.5 The consequences of misconduct

Barristers who choose the approach of keeping their head in the sand when faced with professional conduct issues in practice will inevitably meet problems. They will fall down the path of sleepless nights; their reputation will be soiled and because any failure to comply with the Code will constitute professional misconduct and may result in liability for disciplinary proceedings (see para 901 of the Code), they may find, at worst, that they are disbarred from practice or suspended for a period of time. Consequently, because the Code of Conduct has a 'remorseless grip' and the 'disciplinary system of the Bar is very strong' (LCC 5th Annual Report 2001) barristers who choose to ignore the early warning signs in a case do so at their peril. Disciplinary proceedings are the most obvious consequence following a transgression of the Code, not to mention the possibility of a wasted costs order. If you gain a reputation as a sharp practitioner, your life in practice will become very difficult. Your fellow practitioners will treat you suspiciously, judges will give you a hard time, solicitors will no longer brief you and you will lose the trust of your clerk. If you cannot command the respect of those you regularly come into contact with, it becomes readily apparent that you will not have a career at the Bar. Remember the Bar is a small profession and the 'grapevine' is extremely effective. Your reputation at all times must be untarnished. **Chapter 6** is a useful guide to the Bar Council's complaints procedure.

1.6 Practical advice

In his keynote speech to the Inns of Court School of law (2001, 2002) Michael Pooles QC, a member of the Bar Council's Professional Conduct and Complaints Committee, reminds all trainee lawyers that, 'If you have to ask yourself whether a matter constitutes a professional conduct difficulty, then the answer to this question is inevitably yes and the matter must then be dealt with'.

Chapter 7, 'BVC, practice and professional conduct', is designed to help further with your analysis of professional conduct and ethical difficulties. It provides you with a central source of reference of specific problem areas which can occur frequently in practice and which you will meet during your participation in the key skill areas on the BVC and may well be examined upon. It therefore focuses on professional conduct problems pertinent to the following skills: conference, advocacy, negotiation, opinion writing and drafting. The chapter refers to relevant sources of guidance to ensure that intending barristers are fully aware of why a certain approach to these issues is necessary. It includes, for example, Bar Council guidance on dealing with previous convictions. Additionally, **Chapter 5** is a useful overview of court etiquette and takes you through many of the customs you will meet in practice. **Chapter 8** provides guidance on issues raised by the Proceeds of Crime Act 2002 for the practitioner. These issues are important due to their complex interplay with obligations to the client under the Code.

It is hoped as you read the specific provisions of the Code and of the discussions relating to the potential areas of difficulty in practice, your skills in the following areas will develop:

- the *identification* of potential professional conduct issues;
- the *sources* of guidance on particular issues;
- the necessity of applying the *spirit* of the Code where there is no letter;

- the need to recognise obligations towards *fair treatment*; and
- how you would deal *practically* with the matter.

1.7   BVC, pupillage and professional conduct

Throughout the ICSL Bar Vocational Course you will be able to monitor the development of these skills set out above. The professional conduct course begins with an introductory Keynote speech given by a member of the Professional Conduct and Complaints Committee. This is followed by two panels of practitioners of differing call who will discuss the problems set out in **Chapter 9**. During the BVC, in both large and small groups, professional conduct teaching continues with PTX's deliberately containing areas of ethical difficulty. In addition to this, you will also attend a number of small group sessions, which deal with a number of conference scenarios devised to increase your awareness of professional conduct and ethical difficulties and to think through how best to approach these issues. It is during these sessions that you are encouraged to use the Bar Council's web site as a source of the most current version of the Code (www.barcouncil.org.uk) and to make use of the ethical guidance contained therein. You are advised to keep a separate note of all professional conduct matters arising on the course and your approach to them, together with a note of the suggested response. As part of the professional development course you should reflect upon the way in which you are approaching these issues and keep a note of the sources of information used to help with your response. Very importantly you will be examined on professional conduct during your undertaking of the skills assessments. Hence, by keeping a note for the purposes of reflection, you will also have a central reference source setting out the likely areas you will be examined upon. This approach to professional conduct issues will also be useful in pupillage when the Bar Council expects that you will continue with the monitoring of this area of practice with the use of the pupillage checklist.

1.8   Conclusion

In conclusion, taking the right approach to professional conduct and ethical difficulties from the outset of your professional training is crucial. One word sums up all that has been set out above. That word is '*Awareness*'. Being alert to professional conduct and ethical difficulties and knowing both the Code and its application will hold you in good stead throughout your career at the Bar and you will, in time, inspire others through your professionalism, to join this respected profession. This commitment to a disciplined way of working, no matter the breadth and depth of our practices, no doubt underpins Matthias Kelly QC's comments in his role as chairman of the Bar (Inaugural Speech December 2002):

We prove our value as specialist advocates and advisers on a daily basis in courts and tribunals across the country to all clients be they ordinary citizens, trade unions, governments or major commercial organisations in difficulty. For hundreds of years the Bar has been there to advise, represent and advocate the client's cause. That's what makes us the fiercely independent profession we are today. That's why we survive and grow. Governments come and go. Clients with a need for our services are always there. The Bar is strong and determined to continue to deliver high quality services to all who need those services.

2

Professional relationships

Whether instructed for the prosecution or defence, claimant or defendant, applicant or respondent, as counsel you must consider a number of responsibilities beyond those to your client. Of course everything possible must be done on behalf of the client, but counsel has a number of wider duties. Miscarriages of justice can and do occur when counsel forget or ignore their duties to the court, to their professional client and the Crown Prosecution Service, and to other members of the profession. There is even a duty to the Legal Services Commission. A barrister should be concerned in the administration of justice, and **not** to win at all costs.

It is not uncommon for these duties to conflict, eg, over the disclosure of some evidence or an authority harmful to your case. Frequently the question is not straightforward. It is important that from the earliest days you can at the very least recognise that there is a potential problem so that you can then take steps, eg, discussion with a senior barrister or telephoning the Professional Conduct and Complaints Committee, to ensure that the right answer is reached.

In this chapter we consider a number of ways in which the duty to one's client is, and must be, fettered, so that ultimately justice is achieved. More broadly we consider the range of professional relationships that the barrister will enter into in the course of practice and the duties and obligations that are owed in conducting each relationship successfully and to the appropriate ethical standard. In addition there is practical advice from some of those on the other side of the various relationships with counsel. A senior solicitor, a senior clerk and the National Consumer Council to whom dissatisfied lay clients can turn, all contribute practical guidance and advice which, if heeded, will provide you with a sense of how to make your professional relationships work effectively in day-to-day practice.

2.1 Relationship with the court

2.1.1 Duties and responsibilities owed to the court

Time and again, the judiciary have stressed the paramount duty of counsel to the court. In *Rondel v Worsley* [1969] 1 AC 191, 227 Lord Reid put it in this way:

Every counsel has a duty to his client fearlessly to raise every issue, advance every argument, and ask every question, however distasteful, which he thinks will help his client's case. But, as an officer of the Court concerned in the administration of justice, he has an overriding duty to the Court, to the standards of his profession, and to the public, which may and often does lead to a conflict with his client's wishes or with what the client thinks are his personal interests.

In the same case, Lord Denning MR explained the nature of the duty to the court in these terms:

[Counsel] must accept the brief and do all he honourably can on behalf of his client. I say 'all he honourably can' because his duty is not only to his client. He has a duty to the Court which is paramount. It is a mistake to suppose that he is the mouthpiece of his client to say what he wants: or his tool to do what he directs. He is none of these things. He owes allegiance to a higher cause. It is the cause of truth and justice. He must not consciously misstate the facts. He must not knowingly conceal the truth. He must not unjustly make a charge of fraud, that is, without evidence to support it. He must produce all the relevant authorities, even those that are against him. He must see that his client discloses, if ordered, the relevant documents, even those that are fatal to his case. He must disregard the most specific instructions of his client, if they conflict with his duty to the court. The code which requires a barrister to do all this is not a code of law. It is a code of honour. If he breaks it, he is offending against the rules of the profession and is subject to its discipline. But he cannot be sued in a Court of law. Such being his duty to the Court, the barrister must be able to do it fearlessly. He has time and time again to choose between his duty to his client and his duty to the Court. ([1966] 3 WLR 950, 962.)

2.1.1.1 Examples of duties and responsibilities

Your overriding duty to the court to act with independence in the interests of justice incorporates many separate responsibilities. These are set out in the Code of Conduct and include a duty:

(a) To assist the court in the administration of justice, and not to deceive or knowingly or recklessly mislead the court (para 302). Note that ss 27 and 28 of the Courts and Legal Services Act 1990 are amended by s 42 of the Access to Justice Act 1999. This imports an overriding duty on advocates to the court to act with independence in the interests of justice. This would include, eg, correcting any misleading information which is incorporated in your client's affidavit and which on your instructions, is inaccurate. In *Abraham v Justsun* [1963] 2 All ER 402, 404 Lord Denning MR explained this duty further:

[It is an] advocate's duty to take any point which he believes to be fairly arguable on behalf of his client. An advocate is not to usurp the province of the judge. He is not to determine what shall be the effect of legal argument. He is not guilty of misconduct simply because he takes a point which the tribunal holds to be bad. He only becomes guilty of misconduct if he is dishonest. That is, if he knowingly takes a bad point and thereby deceives the court.

(See also, *Memory Corporation and Another v Sidhu and Another* [2000] 1 WLR 1443.)

(b) To act with due courtesy to the court (Section 3, Miscellaneous Guidance, Written Standards, para 5.5).

(c) To bring to the attention of the court all relevant decisions and legislative provisions of which you are aware, whether or not their effect is favourable to your case (para 708(c)). (See *Copeland v Smith and Another* [2000] 1 All ER 457.)

(d) To bring any procedural irregularity to the attention of the court during the trial (para 708(d)). (See *R v L (Glen Bernard)* The Times, 12 January 2001 and *R v B (Appeal: lack of reasons)* [2003] EWCA Civ 881; [2003] 2 FLR 1035.)

(e) To advise that all relevant documents be disclosed and withdraw from the case if such advice is not followed (para 608(d) and (e)).

(f) To record the proceedings. You have a duty to take a note of the judge's reasons for his decision and have it typed as soon as there is any question of an appeal (see *Letts v Letts* The Times, 8 April 1987).

(g) Not to devise facts which will assist in advancing your lay client's case or settle a groundless statement of case or other document (para 704). In *Steamship Mutual Underwriting Association Ltd v Trollope & Colls Ltd* The Times, 31 March 1986, May LJ put it in these terms:

> . . . To issue a writ when there was no evidential basis upon which a statement of claim could be founded and without any intention to serve one was an abuse of the process of the court.

(h) Not to allege fraud in any statement of case or other document without clear instructions to do so and without reasonably credible material which as it stands establishes a prima facie case of fraud (para 704(c)). (See *Medcalf v Mardell (Wasted Costs Order)* [2001] Lloyd's Rep PN 146.)

(i) Not to assert a *personal* opinion of the facts or the law to the court unless invited to do so by the court (para 708(b)).

(j) Not to make statements or ask questions which are merely scandalous or intended or calculated only to vilify, insult or annoy either a witness or some other person (para 708(g)).

2.1.1.2 Wasted costs orders: civil and criminal

The barrister is also under a duty to take all reasonable and practicable steps to avoid unnecessary expense or waste of the court's time (Section 3, Miscellaneous Guidance, Written Standards for the Conduct of Professional Work, General Standards, para 5.11); this includes a duty not to waste an appellate court's time. In *Ainsbury v Millington* The Times, 13 March 1987, Lord Bridge stated that it was:

> . . . the duty of counsel and solicitors in any pending appeal in publicly funded litigation whenever an event occurred which arguably disposed of the matter in contention, either to ensure that the appeal was withdrawn by consent or, in the absence of agreement, to bring the facts promptly to the attention of the appellate court and to seek directions.

Note that counsel could be made liable personally for costs thrown away (see Supreme Court Act 1981, s 51(6) and CPR, Part 48, r 48 and PD 48). Similar orders could follow under CPR, Part 44, r 44 (assessment of costs). Section 19 of the Prosecution of Offences Act 1985, gave the magistrates' courts, the Crown Court and the Court of Appeal power, where satisfied that one party to criminal proceedings has incurred costs as a result of an unnecessary or improper act or omission by, or on behalf of, another party to the proceedings, to make an order as to the payment of those costs. Section 19A, which was inserted by the Courts and Legal Services Act 1990, gives similar powers to disallow or (as the case may be) order the legal or other representative concerned to meet the whole of any wasted costs or any part of them. 'Wasted costs' means any costs incurred by a party:

- as a result of any improper, unreasonable or negligent act or omission on the part of any representative or any employee of a representative; or
- which, in the light of any such act or omission occurring after they were incurred, the court considers it is unreasonable to expect that party to pay.

There have been a number of cases in which courts, including the Court of Appeal, have made wasted costs orders against barristers. In *Re A Barrister (Wasted Costs Order No 1 of 1991)* [1992] 3 WLR 662, the Court of Appeal recommended a three-stage test:

- Had there been an improper, unreasonable or negligent act or omission?
- If so, had any costs been incurred by any party in consequence thereof?

- If so, should the court exercise its discretion to disallow, or order the representative to meet, the whole of any part of the relevant costs and, if so, what specific sum was involved?

In the Court of Appeal case of *Ridehalgh v Horsefield* [1994] 3 WLR 462 Sir Thomas Bingham MR made it clear that the judgment was applicable to criminal as well as civil courts, and made the following points.

(a) 'Improper' covered, but was not confined to, conduct which would ordinarily justify serious professional penalty. It was not limited to significant breach of the relevant code of professional conduct. It included conduct which was improper according to the consensus of professional, including judicial, opinion, whether it violated the letter of a professional code or not.

(b) 'Unreasonable' described conduct which was vexatious, ie, designed to harass the other side rather than advance the resolution of the dispute. Conduct could not be described as unreasonable simply because it led to an unsuccessful result, or because other more cautious legal representatives would have acted differently. The acid test was whether the conduct permitted of a reasonable explanation. If it did, the course adopted might be regarded as optimistic and reflecting on a practitioner's judgment, but it was not unreasonable.

(c) 'Negligent' should be understood in an untechnical way to denote failure to act with the competence reasonably expected of ordinary members of the profession. It was not a term of art and did not necessarily involve an actionable breach of the legal representative's duty to his own client.

(d) A legal representative was not acting improperly, unreasonably or negligently simply because he acted for a party who pursued a claim or defence which was plainly doomed to fail.

(e) However, a legal representative could not lend his assistance to proceedings which were an abuse of process, and was not entitled to use litigious procedures for purposes for which they were not intended, eg, by issuing proceedings for reasons unconnected with success in the action, pursuing a case which was known to be dishonest or knowingly conniving at incomplete disclosure of documents.

(f) Any judge considering making a wasted costs order must make full allowance for the fact that an advocate in court often had to make decisions quickly and under pressure.

(g) Legal professional privilege might be relevant. If so, the privilege was the client's which he alone could waive. Judges should make full allowance for the inability of respondent lawyers to tell the whole story. Where there was room for doubt, the respondent lawyers were entitled to the benefit of it. It was only when, with all allowance made, a lawyer's conduct of proceedings was quite plainly unjustifiable that it could be appropriate to make the order.

(h) When a solicitor sought the advice of counsel, he did not abdicate his own professional responsibility. He had to apply his mind to the advice received. But the more specialised the advice, the more reasonable it was likely to be for him to accept it.

(i) A threat to apply for a wasted costs order should not be used as a means of intimidation. However, if one side considered that the conduct of the other was improper, unreasonable or negligent and likely to cause a waste of costs, it was not objectionable to alert the other side to that view.

(j) In the ordinary way, such applications were best left until after the end of the trial.

(k) As to procedure, the respondent lawyer should be told very clearly what he was said to have done wrong. No formal process of discovery would be appropriate. Elaborate statements of case should in general be avoided. The court could not imagine circumstances in which the applicant could interrogate the respondent lawyer or vice versa. The legal representative must have opportunity to show cause why an order should not be made (Rules of the Supreme Court 1965, Ord 62, r 11(4)), but this did not mean that the burden was on the legal representative to exculpate himself. (Note that this was written before the introduction of the Civil Procedure Rules 1998.)

In *R v Ullah* The Times, 11 November 1999, the Court of Appeal held that it was only a significant fault by trial counsel or a solicitor that could found a challenge to a jury's verdict. The proper and convenient approach was to apply the *Wednesbury* test.

In *Re A Barrister (Wasted Costs Order No. 4 of 1992)* The Times, 15 March 1994, the Court of Appeal held that a barrister who practised at home without a clerk must not rely wholly on instructing solicitors to notify him of the dates and times of cases. He was responsible for keeping abreast of listing details and should have adopted a system which enabled him to do so.

In *Re A Barrister (Wasted Costs Order No. 4 of 1993)* The Times, 21 April 1995, the Court of Appeal held that a judge should not impose such a Draconian penalty as a wasted costs order without taking into account the daily demands of practice and the difficulties associated with time estimates.

2.1.1.3 Problems

(1) In the course of legal argument, your opponent advances a proposition of law to the court in support of their client's case, but fails to produce a particular reported decision of which you are aware and which would plainly be of assistance. Without it you are likely to win; with it you may well fail. What do you do? Does your answer depend upon for whom you are acting and whether in civil or criminal proceedings?

(2) Whilst sitting in court waiting for your case to be called, you listen to the previous case. Counsel for the claimant is seeking to persuade the judge that the maximum time that the judge can allow the defendant to vacate the claimant's premises is 14 days. The defendant is unrepresented. The judge is an assistant recorder with clearly little experience of landlord and tenant law. You are aware that the judge has a discretion to allow the defendant a maximum period of six weeks. Do you do anything?

(3) You start to cross-examine a prosecution witness about matters which you consider to be vital to your client's case. The judge, having heard argument on the matter, disallows your line of questioning. You are convinced the judge is wrong and that your client will thereby be convicted. What, if anything, can you do?

2.1.2 Specific responsibilities of prosecuting counsel

Prosecuting counsel plays a very important role within the criminal justice system to ensure that the system operates openly and fairly. You must be familiar with a number of sources of guidance. See also **2.3.2.1** which sets out the Code for Crown Prosecutors and **2.3.3** which includes a source for the CPS instructions for prosecuting advocates.

The role and responsibilities of prosecuting counsel are fully set out in Section 3, Miscellaneous Guidance, Written Standards for the Conduct of Professional Work (Standards Applicable to Criminal Cases, para 10) including guidance to counsel on the role of the prosecution in relation to the sentencing process. Although those provisions are not repeated here, it is important to be familiar with their content. The following paragraphs merely highlight some further aspects of those responsibilities, and are not a comprehensive guide in themselves.

2.1.2.1   The relationship between prosecuting counsel and the judge

This relationship was considered in the Farquharson Committee Report in 1986. The following passage is reproduced from Archbold's *Criminal Pleading, Evidence and Practice*, paras 4–76 to 4–80, Vol 1, 1995 by kind permission of Sweet & Maxwell (an abbreviated version of this passage appears at 4–96 of the 2003 edition of *Archbold*). You should note that since February 2002 the Farquharson Committee's guidance has been updated and reissued as 'The Farquharson Guidelines: The Role and Responsibilities of the Prosecution Advocate'. The new guidance builds upon the principles summarised at the end of the passage reproduced here in order to provide a framework for the Bar and Crown Prosecution Service to work within. It is reproduced in full at **2.3.2** below, and you should make specific reference to it. The committee stated:

It is a matter of curiosity that the respective rights and duties of the Judge and Prosecution Counsel have never been clearly defined. The most likely explanation is that whenever a difference has arisen between the two as to which course to take in particular circumstances, it has usually been resolved by discussion. Such authority as there is suggests that there has been some change of view on the topic by the Court of Appeal over the last thirty years.

In 1948 in the case of *Soanes* 32 Cr App R 136 Prosecution Counsel in an Indictment for murder agreed with defence Counsel to accept a plea of guilty to infanticide. The Judge, Singleton J refused to accept it on the grounds that there was nothing on the depositions which could justify such a course. As a matter of history the trial proceeded on the charge of murder and the jury convicted of infanticide. In the Court of Criminal Appeal Goddard LCJ said this:

> '. . . it is impossible to lay down a hard and fast rule in any class of case in which a plea for a lesser offence should be accepted by counsel for the Crown — and it must always be in the discretion of the Judge whether he will allow it to be accepted — in the opinion of the Court, where nothing appears on the depositions which can be said to reduce the crime from the more serious offence charged to some lesser offence for which a verdict may be returned, the duty of Counsel for the Crown would be to present the offence charged in the Indictment . . .'

In 1980 in *R v Coward* 70 Cr App R 70 at 76 Lawton LJ said:

> 'It is for Prosecuting Counsel to make up their own minds what pleas to accept. If the judge does not approve he can say so in open Court and then the Prosecution will have to decide what course to take.'

We approach the problem by considering whether Counsel acting on behalf of the Prosecution may or should decide to offer no evidence on any particular count in an Indictment or on the Indictment itself, without the approval of the Judge. When taking such a decision it is usual for Counsel to explain his reasons for doing so to the Judge. It is open then to the Judge to express his own views and if he disapproves of the course taken by Counsel he will no doubt say so. In those circumstances, Counsel is under an obligation to reconsider the matter, both personally and with his junior, if he has one, and his Instructing Solicitor. Whilst great weight should be given to the Judge's view, if Counsel still feels that the Prosecution's decision is the correct one then he must persist in the course he originally proposed. He will have much more information about the background and weight of the case than the Judge who will only have the depositions and exhibits. Counsel is therefore in the best position to make the decision and although one would expect that Counsel would rarely have to take the course of offering no evidence in defiance of the opinion of the Judge, in the final analysis the decision must be his.

There is now no doubt that where Counsel for the Prosecution wishes to proceed on a properly laid Indictment the Judge cannot prevent him doing so because he is of the opinion that the evidence is too weak for the Prosecution to succeed. See *R v Chairman of London County Sessions, ex p Downes*, 37 Cr App R 148. Nor may the Judge refuse to allow the Prosecution to proceed on an Indictment on the grounds that he disapproves of the course being taken unless it amounts to an abuse of the process of the Court. The explanation must be that Counsel for the Prosecution has the carriage of the proceedings and it is for him to decide in a particular case whether to proceed or not to proceed.

In accepting a plea of guilty to a lesser offence or offences Counsel for the Prosecution is in reality making a decision to offer no evidence on a particular charge. It follows in our opinion that if Counsel is entitled to decide whether he should offer no evidence on the Indictment as a whole, as we think he is, then correspondingly, it must be for him to decide whether or not to proceed on a particular count in an Indictment. This is subject to three important qualifications:

(a) It is sometimes the practice when Prosecution Counsel decides to accept a plea to a lesser count for him to invite the approval of the Judge. Counsel may feel it appropriate to do so in cases where it is desirable to reassure the public at large that the course proposed is being properly taken, or when he has been unable to reach agreement with his Instructing Solicitor.

As we have already said, Counsel is not bound to invite the Judge's approval but if he does so, then he must of course abide by the Judge's decision. 'When Counsel for the Crown invites the Judge to give approval to some course which he wishes to take the seeking of that approval is no idle formality. The Judge in such circumstances is not a rubber stamp to approve a decision by Counsel without further consideration, a decision which may or may not be right.' *R v Broad* 68 Cr App R 281, *per* Roskill LJ.

(b) While the Judge will not have all the information available to Counsel he will have derived considerable knowledge of the case from the depositions and exhibits; certainly enough to enable him to decide upon the right sentence after receiving the appropriate report and hearing any mitigation. There may well be cases where the Judge so disapproves of the decision taken by Prosecution Counsel to accept a plea to a lesser offence that he cannot consistently with his duty, as he sees it, proceed to sentence on that basis. The Judge may take the view that Counsel's decision proceeds from caprice or incompetence, or simply that he entirely disagrees with the decision however carefully Counsel has arrived at it. The Judge cannot in such circumstances be expected to lend himself to a process which in his judgment amounts to an abuse or to injustice. While for the reasons already given the Judge cannot insist on Prosecution Counsel proceeding on the major charge he may decline to proceed with the case without Counsel first consulting with the Director of Public Prosecutions, on whether he should proceed in the light of the comments the Judge will have made. In an extreme case he may think it right to invite Counsel to seek the advice of the Attorney-General. In the final analysis, when these steps have been taken, the Judge has no power to prevent Counsel proceeding. Indeed any attempt by him to do so would give the impression that he was stepping into the arena and pressing the Prosecution case. However, we are of the opinion that the occasions when counsel felt it right to resist the Judge's views would be rare.

These views are in accordance with the Guidelines to Prosecution Counsel given by the Bar Committee of the Senate of the Four Inns of Court and the Bar (dated 9 May, 1984) to the following effect:

'Counsel may in his discretion invite the trial Judge to assist him in his decision (whether to offer no evidence or to accept or to refuse pleas tendered by the accused) but he is never under a duty to do so nor should he do so as a means of avoiding his personal responsibility.'
'Counsel should in any case be ready to explain his decision in open Court and to reconsider it in the light of any observations made by the trial Judge.'

This guidance has recently received the approval of the Court of Appeal and must now be taken to be the proper approach for a Judge when he is informed by Prosecuting Counsel that he does not intend to proceed. See *R v Jenkins* (1985) 83 Cr App R 152.

(c) Sometimes a decision has to be made to offer no evidence during the course of the trial; and similarly pleas of guilty may be tendered to lesser counts. While the Prosecution case is being presented the decision as to what course to take in these circumstances remains with Counsel.

After the prosecution case is completed, once the Judge has ruled that there is a case to answer or where he has not been invited to do so but the case is proceeding, then in our view the prosecution cannot be discontinued nor pleas of guilty to lesser charges be accepted without the consent of the Judge. *Ex hypothesi* there is at this stage a case to answer and it would, in our view, be an abuse of process for the Prosecution to discontinue without leave. In such a situation while the Judge may rule that the case shall proceed and be considered by the Jury it would not be the duty of Counsel to cross-examine the defence witnesses or address the Jury if he was of the view that it would not be proper to convict.

The only exception to this rule is when the Attorney-General enters a *nolle prosequi* which can be done at any stage of the proceedings.

4. *Prosecuting counsel in the Court of Appeal*

In the event of an Appeal against conviction or a reference by the Secretary of State Prosecution Counsel's view can be no more than persuasive. Section 2 of the Criminal Appeal Act 1968 expressly provides that:

> 'The Court of Appeal should allow an Appeal . . . if they think that . . .'

In other words by Statute the decision is vested exclusively in the Court of Appeal.

If Prosecution Counsel has formed the view that the Appeal should succeed he should acquaint the Court with the view and explain the reasons for it. If the Court disagrees with him Counsel is entitled to adhere to his view and is not obliged to conduct the Appeal in any way which conflicts with his own judgment. At the same time it remains Counsel's duty to give assistance to the Court if requested to do so.

5. *In summary it is our opinion that:*

(a) It is the duty of Prosecution Counsel to read the instructions delivered to him expeditiously and to advise or confer with those instructing him on all aspects of the case well before its commencement.

(b) A solicitor who has briefed Counsel to prosecute may withdraw his instructions before the commencement of the trial up to the point when it becomes impracticable to do so, if he disagrees with the advice given by Counsel or for any other proper professional reason.

(c) While he remains instructed it is for Counsel to take all necessary decisions in the presentation and general conduct of the prosecution.

(d) Where matters of policy fall to be decided after the point indicated in (b) above (including offering no evidence on the Indictment or on a particular count, or the acceptance of pleas to lesser counts) it is the duty of Counsel to consult his Instructing Solicitor/Crown Prosecutor whose views at this stage are of crucial importance.

(e) In the rare case where Counsel and his Instructing Solicitor are unable to agree on a matter of policy, it is, subject to (g) below, for Prosecution Counsel to make the necessary decisions.

(f) Where Counsel has taken a decision on a matter of policy with which his Instructing Solicitor has not agreed, then it would be appropriate for the Attorney-General to require Counsel to submit to him a written report of all the circumstances, including his reasons for disagreeing with those who instructed him.

(g) When Counsel has had the opportunity to prepare his brief and to confer with those instructing him, but at the last moment before trial unexpectedly advises that the case should not proceed or that pleas to lesser offences should be accepted, and his Instructing Solicitor does not accept such advice, Counsel should apply for an adjournment if instructed so to do.

(h) Subject to the above, it is for Prosecution Counsel to decide whether to offer no evidence on a particular count or on the Indictment as a whole and whether to accept pleas to a lesser count or counts.

(i) If Prosecution Counsel invites the Judge to approve the course he is proposing to take, then he must abide by the Judge's decision.

(j) If Prosecution Counsel does not invite the Judge's approval of his decision it is open to the Judge to express his dissent with the course proposed and to invite counsel to reconsider the matter with those instructing him, but having done so, the final decision remains with Counsel.

(k) In an extreme case where the Judge is of the opinion that the course proposed by Counsel would lead to serious injustice, he may decline to proceed with the case until Counsel has consulted with either the Director or the Attorney-General as may be appropriate.

2.1.3 Further duties

There are further duties of prosecuting counsel which are not expressly included in the Code.

2.1.3.1 To inform the defence of any known previous convictions of any prosecution witness

See *R v Collister and Warhurst* (1955) 39 Cr App R 100. It should be noted that previous convictions include any disciplinary offences/findings and criminal cautions against police witnesses.

2.1.3.2 To call or tender witnesses at trial

The general rule is that the prosecution must call (or tender for cross-examination) all the witnesses whose evidence was used in the committal proceedings. The exceptions are those set out in the cases of *R v Russell-Jones* [1995] 3 All ER 230 and *R v Armstrong* [1995] 3 All ER 831:

- the defence has consented to the written statement of that witness being read to the court;
- counsel for the prosecution takes the view that the evidence of that witness is no longer credible; or
- counsel for the prosecution takes the view that the witness would so fundamentally contradict the prosecution case that it would make more sense for that person to be called as a witness for the defence.

There remains a limit to the prosecution's discretion, namely that it must be exercised in the interests of justice, so as to promote a fair trial.

2.1.3.3 To adduce all the evidence upon which you intend to rely to prove the defendant's guilt before the close of your case

This is provided that such evidence is then available.

2.1.3.4 To disclose not only all of the evidence that will be called at trial, but also information of which the defence may be unaware and which will not be part of the prosecution case

This duty is dealt with mainly in the Criminal Procedure and Investigations Act 1996. The statutory scheme is covered in the *Criminal Litigation and Sentencing Manual*.

In essence, there is a duty on the police officer investigating the offence to record and retain information and material gathered during the investigation. The prosecution must inform the defence of certain categories of that material that it does not intend to rely on at trial. The defence then has a duty (or for summary trial, the option) to inform the prosecution of the case that it intends to present at trial (the 'Defence Statement'). The prosecution then has a duty to present further material to the defence which might be reasonably expected to assist the accused's defence as disclosed by the defence. After this, applications can be made to the court where there is a dispute as to whether the prosecution should disclose certain material. Where public interest immunity is involved, the 1996 Act expressly preserves the existing common law.

The prosecutor remains under a continuing duty to review questions of disclosure.

The prosecution's duty of primary disclosure applies to summary trial where the accused pleads not guilty. The defence may make voluntary disclosure. In such a case, the prosecution will be obliged to make secondary disclosure.

It should be noted that para 10.2 Standards Applicable to Criminal Cases in Section 3, Miscellaneous Guidance, Written Standards for the Conduct of Professional Work, provides:

Prosecuting counsel should bear in mind at all times whilst he is instructed:

. . .

(ii) that he should use his best endeavours to ensure that all evidence or material that ought properly to be made available is either presented by the prosecution or disclosed to the defence.

2.1.3.5 To consider whether witness statements need to be edited

See *Practice Direction (Criminal Proceeding: Consolidation)* [2002] 1 WLR 2870, pt III, para 24 for the relevant considerations and practice on editing witness statements.

2.1.3.6 To be familiar with the *Practice Direction: Crown Court (Plea and Directions Hearings)* [1995] 1 WLR 1318

The purpose of a Pleas and Directions Hearing (PDH) is to ensure that all necessary steps have been taken in preparation for trial and to provide sufficient information for a trial date to be arranged. The *Practice Direction* stresses that 'it is expected that the advocate briefed in the case will appear in the PDH wherever practicable'. With the demands of a busy practice this will not always be possible. Pupils and junior tenants should be very conscious of the fact that it is regarded as a serious dereliction of duty for counsel to turn up at a PDH and say 'Sorry, this isn't my brief and I can't provide the information required'. If you are going to appear at a PDH in the place of counsel who will be appearing in the case, go armed with all the relevant information, and there is a lot of it to gather together! Information required includes informing the court of the issues in the case, number of witnesses and the form their evidence will take, exhibits and schedules to be admitted at trial, points of law and admissibility of evidence that will arise at trial, applications for evidence to be given via television links etc, witness availability, length of witness testimony, counsel availability.

2.1.3.7 Problems

(1) You are instructed to prosecute a case in which the allegation is that the defendant and associates burst into the victim's flat intent on causing injury. The victim, seeing the group arrive, tried to escape by jumping off the fifth floor balcony. He fell and was seriously injured. The defendant was charged with causing grievous bodily harm with intent. After the victim has given evidence, you are shown a note by the officer in the case which the officer says was written by the victim about ten days before these events. It shows that at that time the victim was threatening suicide. You do not think that that is the reason why he jumped that day and it certainly does not accord with the evidence the victim has just given. What do you do, if anything, about the note?

(2) In the course of a ruling given following argument by counsel for both prosecution and defence, the judge gives reasons which are based on a case cited in argument. The ruling is favourable to you, the prosecution. It is, however, clear that the judge has misunderstood the passage quoted. What do you do?

(3)   You arrive in court to prosecute a defendant. You realise that the defendant was a client of a solicitor's firm for which you worked during the holidays. You learnt details about the defendant which might well help you in prosecuting the case. The defendant does not appear to recognise you. Do you do anything?

2.1.4   Specific responsibilities of defence counsel

You are referred to the Written Standards, Standards Applicable to Criminal Cases, para 11 **Appendix 1**, (see Section 3, Miscellaneous Guidance) and to Guidance on Preparation of Defence Case Statements in Section 3, Miscellaneous Guidance, for a full consideration of these responsibilities. It is not proposed to repeat them here. The most common ethical problems associated with defending, other than those which involve a (potential) conflict of interest, tend to arise in the following circumstances where:

- a client confesses his or her guilt. Coping in this situation is dealt with in para 12 of the Standards Applicable to Criminal Cases 'Confessions of Guilt';
- a client changes his or her instructions;
- a client insists upon you conducting the case in a manner which you consider detrimental to his or her interests, eg, by calling unhelpful witnesses; or
- you find yourself in the position of being a material witness.

These points will be considered in detail during the Professional Conduct Course classes (see **Chapter 9** for professional conduct problems).

Although the primary responsibility of defence counsel in a criminal case is to endeavour to protect the client from conviction except by a competent tribunal and upon legally admissible evidence sufficient to support a conviction for the offence charged (para 11.1 of the Standards Applicable to Criminal Cases), this does not displace the overriding duty to the Court. It is important, however, to bear in mind the duty of confidentiality owed to the lay client which must not be breached (para 702). As with prosecuting counsel, defence counsel should be familiar with the duties and obligations imposed by the *Practice Direction: Crown Court (Pleas and Directions Hearings)* [1995] 1 WLR 1318.

2.1.4.1   Problems

(1)   You represent a defendant in a trial at the Crown Court having advised and appeared (without your instructing solicitor having been present) at the magistrates' court. The defendant, having been given the new caution, did not answer any question in his or her police interview. During your client's cross-examination by the prosecution, it is suggested that the account he or she is giving has been thought up recently. You know that he or she gave that account to you on the first remand date. You were alone with him or her at the time. What should you do?

(2)   There is crucial prosecution evidence of your client's presence at the scene of the crime at a material time. Your instructions are that your client was present but merely an onlooker, not a participant in the crime. You conduct your cross-examination on that basis and do not challenge the evidence of your client's presence at the scene. When he or she gives evidence, the defendant denies his or her presence at the material time by saying that he or she had just left the scene. The judge points out the difference and demands that you clarify the situation.

(3)   Your client is pleading guilty in the magistrates' court. Your instructions are that he or she has a number of previous convictions. The police antecedents given to the court show him or her as a person of good character. How do you mitigate? Would your

approach be different if the omitted previous conviction had involved the imposition of a suspended sentence of which the defendant was in breach by virtue of the instant conviction?

2.1.5 Access to the judge

2.1.5.1 Indications on sentence

In certain circumstances it is possible to seek an indication on sentence from the judge. Until very recently, the guidance on this area was to be found in the decision of the Court of Appeal in *R v Turner* [1970] 2 QB 321. However, the Court of Appeal in *R v Goodyear* [2005] EWCA Crim 888 considered that the modern practice of criminal litigation required a fresh approach to indications on sentence. Whilst you should read the judgment in *Goodyear* for yourself, there follows a summary of the guidance issued by the Court of Appeal in that case:

- The fundamental starting point remains that the defendant is exclusively responsible for his plea. He must enter it voluntarily and without improper pressure.

- Provided that the defendant seeks the indication of sentence, there is no automatic assumption that responding to that request with an indication of sentence constitutes improper judicial pressure in respect of the defendant's decision on plea.

The role of the judge

- The judge should not give an advance indication of sentence unless one has been sought by the defendant.

- As recognised in *Turner*, the judge remains entitled to indicate that the sentence, or type of sentence, for the defendant would remain the same whether the defendant pleaded guilty, or on conviction following trial. The Court of Appeal considered that this situation would now be unusual given that a guilty plea will normally attract credit.

- The judge is entitled in an appropriate case to remind the defendant's counsel that the defendant is entitled to seek an advance indication of sentence.

- The judge has an unfettered discretion to refuse to give an indication. The Court of Appeal recognised that there may be cogent reasons why a judge would not want to give an indication for fear of creating additional pressure on the defendant. Paragraph 57 of the judgment contains a number of examples of situations where a judge may feel unable to indicate sentence. The judge would not be obliged to give his reasons for refusal.

- A judge should also be able to reserve his position on sentence until such time as he feels able to give an indication. In such circumstances the judge would normally explain why he wished to postpone the indication, together with an indication of the circumstances in which he would be prepared to give an indication in future.

- Any advance indication of sentence should normally be <u>confined to the maximum sentence if a plea of guilty were tendered at the stage at which the indication is sought</u>.

- The judge should <u>not</u> then indicate the maximum possible sentence following conviction by the jury.

- <u>An indication, once given, is binding upon both the judge giving the indication and any other judge who becomes responsible for the case.</u>

- However, if the defendant does not then plead guilty, after a reasonable time and opportunity in which to consider his plea, the indication ceases to have effect.

Obligations upon counsel for the defence

- Counsel for the defence should not seek an indication of sentence without written authority, signed by his client, that the client wishes to seek an indication.
- The advocate is personally responsible for ensuring that his client understands:
  1 he should not plead guilty unless he is guilty;
  2 any sentence indication given by the judge remains subject to any entitlement in the Attorney General to refer an unduly lenient sentence to the Court of Appeal;
  3 if the judge does give an indication, it reflects the situation at the time it is given and will cease to have effect if a guilty plea is not tendered after a reasonable opportunity for consideration;
  4 the indication relates only to the matters on which it is sought. Therefore, certain steps which follow automatically, such as confiscation proceedings, remain unaffected.
- The basis of the plea must be clear, agreed between prosecution and defence, and reduced into writing. There should be no disagreement about acceptable plea or pleas to the indictment, nor disagreement about the factual basis of the plea.
- The judge should never be asked to indicate levels of sentence depending on possible pleas — for example, asking the judge to indicate sentence depending on whether the plea was to s 18, or s 20, or s 47 as alternatives. This would be to involve the judge in plea bargaining.

Role of the prosecution

- The prosecution can only react to, not initiate the process of requesting an indication.
- Prosecution counsel is responsible for reminding the judge of this guidance where the defence seek an indication although the basis of the plea is not agreed.
- The prosecution is also obliged to check that the judge has had access to all prosecution evidence, including personal impact statements from any victims and the relevant previous convictions of the defendant.
- Prosecution counsel will normally draw to the judge's attention, prior to an indication being given, any minimum or mandatory sentencing requirements, together with any guideline cases or views of the Sentencing Guidelines Council if appropriate. Further, where it applies, to remind the judge that the power of the Attorney General to refer any sentencing decision as unduly lenient is unaffected by the indication process.
- Counsel should not say anything which gives the impression that the sentence indication has the support or approval of the Crown.

Procedural points

- The Attorney General's power to refer unduly lenient sentences to the Court of Appeal under s 36 of the Criminal Justice Act 1988 is unaffected by the sentence indication process provided that prosecution counsel has followed the above guidance.
- Equally, the defendant's entitlement to apply for leave to appeal against sentence is unaffected.

- Any sentence indication should normally be sought at the plea and case management hearing, although the possibility of seeking an indication at a later stage is available.

- In a complex or difficult case, the judge is unlikely to be able to give an indication unless the basis of the plea and related issues are resolved as between prosecution and defence. Therefore, in such cases, at least 7 days' notice in writing of an intention to seek an indication should be given to the prosecution and the court. A failure to do so might result in an unnecessary adjournment and reduction of the credit for a guilty plea accordingly.

- Hearings should normally take place in open court, fully recorded, in the defendant's presence.

- The fact that notice of intention to seek an indication has been given in a complex case, and the request for indication itself, would be inadmissible in any subsequent trial. Additionally, reporting restrictions would apply until the defendant pleads, or is found, guilty.

- The procedure does not apply in the Magistrates' Court. These are covered by Schedule 3 of the Criminal Justice Act 2003.

2.1.5.3   Situations where it is permissible to see the judge

Although most judges will refuse to see counsel on a matter of sentence, there are a variety of other situations in which it is permissible and indeed advisable for counsel to ask to see the judge. These include:

- if your client is thinking of pleading guilty but, for instance, wants to discuss the matter with your instructing solicitor who is not present at court that day, counsel may see the judge and ask for an overnight adjournment. To mention that the client is thinking of pleading guilty in these circumstances is sensitive information that ought not to be mentioned in open court;

- if the defendant has given information or assistance to the police he or she may not wish details to be given to the judge in open court. His or her safety or that of his or her family may be at risk;

- any matters that would be embarrassing to the defendant if mentioned in open court, for instance, if he or she is suffering from an illness that may make him or her appear drowsy or uninterested whilst in court;

- any matters that are personal to counsel and would be embarrassing to mention in open court, eg, illness, a bereavement necessitating an adjournment etc.

2.2   Relationship with the lay client

2.2.1   Duties and responsibilities owed to the lay client

First and foremost, the profession requires strict observance of the 'cab-rank' rule: see paras 601 and 602 of the Code of Conduct. You must accept any instructions or brief to represent any client, at a proper professional fee (para 604(b)), in the field(s) in which you profess to practise irrespective of the nature of the case or any belief or opinion which you may have formed as to the character, reputation, cause, conduct, guilt or innocence of that person. The cab-rank rule applies whether your client is paying privately or is publicly funded.

Note that any instructions in a publicly funded matter shall, in specified circumstances, be deemed to be at a proper professional fee (para 604(b)), although the Bar Council has decided that cases subject to family graduated fees or criminal graduated fees are no longer deemed to be at a proper professional fee for the purposes of para 604(b).

Many of the duties and responsibilities you owe to the lay client are dealt with in the Code of Conduct. Before you accept any brief or instructions, you must satisfy yourself that you are competent and have adequate time to prepare and do the particular case (para 603). If at any time in any matter you consider it would be in the best interests of any client to have different representation, you must immediately so advise the client (para 607). You have an added obligation to consider whether the best interests of the client would be served by instructing or continuing to instruct you (para 606.1). You must also consider the best interests of the client and whether it is suitable for them to instruct more than one advocate (para 606.2); and whether in the interests of the lay client or the interests of justice, to instruct a solicitor or other authorised litigator or other appropriate intermediary either together with or in place of you (para 606.3); and how several parties are represented or advised (para 606.4). If, however, the client insists that you do the case, you are bound by the 'cab-rank' rule subject to it being the sort of work you are competent to undertake. It is also obviously important to determine in any case whether a conflict of interest exists or arises which prevents you from acting/continuing to act for that client.

Your duties to the lay client include a responsibility:

(a) To promote fearlessly and by all proper and lawful means the lay client's best interests and to do so without regard to your own interests or to any consequences to yourself or to any other person (including any other professional client or other intermediary or another barrister) (para 303(a)).

(b) To owe your primary responsibility as between the lay client and any professional client or other intermediary to the lay client and not to permit the intermediary to limit your discretion as to how the interests of the lay client can best be served (para 303(b)).

(c) To preserve the confidentiality of your client's affairs (para 702).

(d) To act with reasonable competence and maintain professional independence.

(e) To keep your lay client informed of the estimate and likely impact of costs. In *Singer (formerly Sharegin) v Sharegin* [1984] FLR 114, 119, Cumming-Bruce LJ expressed the duty in this way:

> I conclude by emphasising the immense importance of the obligation upon solicitors and counsel in all these cases (financial disputes) to form accurate estimates as to costs, to inform their lay client what the impact of costs is likely to be, to inform the lay client of the probable estimate of the totality of costs on both sides so that the lay client can fully understand the enormous financial risks they may incur if they insist on sticking to what they regard as their own sensible point of view and so refuse to make or accept an offer involving much compromise on both sides.

(f) To advise your lay client, when a conflict of interest arises between your lay client and a professional client or other intermediary, that it would be in his or her interests to instruct another professional adviser or representative (para 703).

(g) To owe your primary duty to your lay client, in cases funded by the Legal Services Commission, subject only to compliance with para 304 (see para 303(c)).

(h) To advise your client (and professional client) where it becomes apparent that funding in any case by the Legal Services Commission has been wrongly obtained by false or inaccurate information, and to withdraw from the case where action is not taken by the client to remedy the situation immediately (para 608(c)).

In order to provide a practical and objective insight into the relationship between counsel and the lay client, the then chairman of the National Consumer Council, David Hatch CBE, JP, and Marlene Winfield, the then Acting Head of Policy Research and Strategy at the National Consumer Council, wrote the following essay on barristers and their lay clients.

Barristers and their Lay Clients

> We believe that the excellence of the Bar will not simply be judged by the quality of its advice and advocacy. The Bar, like other professions and businesses, needs to display a wider, more all-round excellence: value for money and good client communications are an essential part of the modern profession.
> *Report of the Bar Standards Review Body*, September 1994

> In future a solicitor will increasingly need to have a reason to instruct counsel rather than to do the work himself, or to refer it to his in-house advocacy department or to an agency solicitor. Moreover, he will need to have a reason which can be explained to the client.
> *The Work of the Young Bar*, November 1993

A changing world
When today's fledgling barristers enter pupillage and practice, they will enter a world very different from that of their predecessors. The young barrister of today will face new types of work requiring different relationships with lay clients. Examples might include: providing or participating in alternative methods of dispute resolution such as mediation, arbitration and neutral case evaluation; coaching lay clients to be their own advocates; developing expertise in areas of social welfare law in order to take direct referrals from advice agencies operating under legal aid contracts.

Even in the traditional forms of work, things are changing. There is increasing specialisation by both barristers and solicitors. In areas such as personal injury and medical negligence, the harm that 'dabblers' can do is being recognised. Anecdotal evidence suggests that in all areas of the law lay clients are less content to take a passive role than they once were. Increasingly they want to be informed and consulted, to participate in decision-making. And they are more ready to complain if they feel they are not getting a good service.

Other changes to the nature of the traditional work of barristers are coming about as a result of the new Civil Procedure Rules 1998. New procedures have been introduced for dealing with multi-party actions, medical negligence, housing cases, and more generally with cases involving sums of money under £10,000. New procedures are streamlined, less adversarial and cheaper. A large share of the savings should be made on legal fees.

At the same time, competition is hotting up. Increased rights of audience and a desperate search for new sources of work, have driven solicitors into court in increasing numbers. Even that traditional training ground for new barristers, the magistrates' court, is equally likely these days to feature showdowns between salaried prosecutors and young solicitors.

Meanwhile, the size of the Bar has increased rapidly, by nearly a quarter in recent years. This means that more people are chasing fewer briefs. And as if that were not enough, the 1993 joint working party on the young Bar discovered other worrying trends: an apparent decline in levels of fees in the early years and increasing debt arising from barristers' training.

The many changes afoot pose threats, but they also offer opportunities for young barristers. What they all have in common is that they call for new ways of working with lay clients and their lay advisers. Those most likely to succeed in the brave new streamlined world of Woolf reforms and alternatives to trial will be those least afraid to explore new types of working relationships. It might be as well to start that exploration by learning from the mistakes of the past.

Working with lay clients
To a certain extent, barristers are shielded from the criticism of lay clients by solicitors. When something goes wrong, the solicitor is usually the first port of call. However, Action for Victims of Medical Accidents, AVMA, with over 19,000 medical negligence clients having passed through its

doors, has experienced the highs and the lows of barristerial performance in an area of the law where sensitivity is perhaps most needed.

AVMA staff make the following observations about client care, based on their experience of accompanying lay clients on visits to counsel:

> Inexperienced lay clients need to be adequately prepared by the solicitor for conferences with counsel. Clients need to know what to expect from the barrister and what the barrister expects from them. They also need to know what they are and are not allowed to do, for example, if they can speak directly to the barrister.

> Lay clients need to be given a clear idea of who is making the decisions, the solicitor or barrister, and who is ultimately responsible for the conduct of the case.

> Clients should be asked at an early stage what they hope to achieve by legal action. Thereafter, they should be asked their opinions.

> It is essential that at the outset the client is given a clear idea about the difficulties of the case, the likely outcome and the potential costs.

> Some clients are left feeling that their concerns were not addressed. If the client's concerns are not considered relevant, the reasons should be explained to them.

> When a solicitor and barrister talk in legal jargon, it often excludes the client from the discussion.

> If the solicitor and barrister wish to speak without the lay client being present, the purpose should be made clear.

> Both solicitors and barristers should consider the client's needs as well as their own when determining the time and place of meetings. Factors such as ease of access for people with disabilities and availability of lavatories should be considered when fixing venues. Consideration should be given to where the client will feel most comfortable and thus best able to participate: chambers can be difficult to find and daunting places. Clients might prefer to meet in the solicitor's office, particularly if they have been there before. Wherever the meeting, clients should be given good directions.

> When meetings are not well-organised or structured, clients can be left feeling that the barrister was not familiar with the case.

> Simple kindnesses should not be forgotten. One AVMA staff member told of a stressful five hour conference during which the clients, who had travelled a long way and started very early in the morning, were not even offered a cup of coffee.

The above comments represent a mixture of good client care, common sense and basic courtesy. Lapses would be particularly out of place in medical accident cases, an area of the law where people can be extremely vulnerable. But, arguably, going to law for any reason is potentially stressful for lay clients, who will always benefit from sensitivity on the part of the barrister.

At a time of fierce and increasing competition between barristers, and between barristers and solicitors, those barristers — young and old — offering a high standard of client care will have a competitive edge.

. . .

Looking to the future
The future is by no means all gloom and doom. The young Bar can look forward to new opportunities in areas such as alternative dispute resolution, new civil justice fast track procedures, social welfare law, and the burgeoning area of public policy. But if young barristers are to compete with the new generation of solicitors, increasingly trained in both client care and advocacy skills, they too must adopt a more client-centred approach. A fine line has to be walked between providing good client care and retaining the objectivity that is the Bar's hallmark. The training of young barristers needs to grapple with how the changing expectations of lay clients can best be met within the Code of Conduct of the Bar and its working practices.

David Hatch CBE JP
Chairman [to December 2000]
National Consumer Council
and

Marlene Winfield
Acting Head of Policy Research and Strategy [to October 2000]
National Consumer Council

2.2.1.1 Problems

(1)   Your client bombards you with instructions, both before and during the trial. He or she insists you put each one to the various witnesses, who are all children your client is said to have abused. Your client insists on giving evidence even though he or she has previous similar convictions. He or she is also adamant that you call a witness that you suspect will destroy his or her case. How do you conduct the trial?

(2)   Whilst discussing with your client his or her witness statement outside court, you query his or her explanation of a certain event. The client tells you that is not what really happened but 'it was what the solicitor told me to say'. The solicitor is not present but has sent an articled clerk. What, if anything, do you do?

(3)   Your client loses his claim for the sale and a share of the proceeds of a house owned by his former girlfriend. Upon leaving court, he mumbles 'She'll be sorry, I'll make sure she doesn't live to enjoy it'. How do you react?

2.3   Relationship with the professional client and other intermediaries

2.3.1   Duties and responsibilities owed to the professional client and other intermediaries

You may now accept instructions from professional clients (see paras 401 and 1001) and from members of approved professional bodies, for example, accountants and surveyors. You must comply with the Licensed Access Rules and Recognition Regulations and the Public Access Rules reproduced in Annexes F1 and F2 of the Code of Conduct (see para 401).

With regard to your relationship with those who instruct you, problems can arise in circumstances where they seek to limit the way in which you present the case; where they take a different view of the lay client's prospects of success; where you consider they have been remiss/negligent in their handling of the client's affairs, or where they consider you have 'let them down' by not being available to do a case or have been guilty of delay. Many of these problems are due to poor communication, lack of control of your clerk or an unjustifiable attitude that you are somehow superior to them.

It is important that you foster good relations with those who instruct you, discuss any differences of opinion, and ensure that he or she is kept fully informed of any potential difficulties or conflicting dates in your diary. Your clerk should always inform any person who seeks to instruct you on a case if there is likely to be a conflicting engagement. Watch the chambers diary yourself to ensure this is being enforced. Do not delay your paperwork. If some delay cannot be avoided due to other pressing work, telephone them and explain the position so that he or she is free to instruct other counsel.

Do not criticise your solicitor or those who instruct you in front of the lay client without first discussing your view with the solicitor or the person who instructs you. Do not criticise your solicitor or those who instruct you in court unless they agree that some fault lies with them and they accept that the court must be told to prevent the lay client suffering the consequences.

A further area in which the relationship with a solicitor, in particular, may become problematical, arises out of the growth of the number of solicitors with rights of audience in the higher courts. This can lead to a variety of difficulties — not least if you are co-defending with a solicitor whose firm is acting for your defendant too, and who may be more likely to go to him or her than you. Be tactful.

The Legal Services Committee of the Bar Council has provided guidance on the area of solicitors acting as juniors to silks, which it quaintly describe as 'mixed doubles'. The committee stressed the importance of ensuring that the right amount of advocacy expertise is properly used, and in particular:

- if a case requires both a leader and junior, it is inappropriate for a solicitor advocate to try to perform both roles;
- the junior in any case (whether he or she be a barrister or solicitor advocate) must have appropriate skills and experience for the roles he or she is to perform and must be competent and available to perform the junior work required by the leader including examination of witnesses, the preparation of skeleton arguments and chronologies, the drafting of statements of case etc as the case may require;
- if a case is suitable for a silk to conduct alone, there should be no junior. But, if a junior is genuinely necessary, it would be manifestly inappropriate for a solicitor without rights of audience to seek to dispense with a junior on the basis that he or she will carry out the junior work, excluding advocacy, whilst also acting as a solicitor.

Guidance upon your main duties to the professional client and other intermediaries can be found in paras 603, 610, 701(e), 703, 706 and 707 of the Code. Remember that your primary duty is to the lay client (para 303(b)). Note also Annexe G which covers the Terms of Work on which Barristers Offer their Services to Solicitors and the Withdrawal of Credit Scheme 1988.

2.3.1.1   Making the relationship work

A barrister's practice will depend largely upon the way in which he or she behaves towards and works with those who instruct him or her, particularly with his or her instructing solicitors. The relationship requires counsel to understand clearly what it is that solicitors expect from them. It also requires counsel to understand what is likely to alienate a solicitor. In order to provide a practical insight into the relationship between solicitor and counsel, there follows an essay by a senior solicitor on making the relationship work. It is written from the perspective of civil work (specifically medical negligence).

A Solicitor's View on the Barrister's Relationship with the Professional Client

Preface
The author specialises in claimant medical negligence litigation funded predominantly by legal aid. At the time of writing, he was a partner at Bolt Burdon, a firm that holds a legal aid franchise, and was in charge of supervising the firm's policy on the use of 'approved sub-contractors', which includes barristers.

The starting premise for this article was the general myth that traditionally the relationship between solicitors and barristers has been an uneasy alliance. Do barristers really think that they are the intellectual superiors of solicitors, who are always having to look to counsel to sort out ill-prepared cases? Do solicitors really think that barristers are arrogant snobs who blame solicitors when well-prepared cases fall apart because they have not bothered to read the papers properly? The reality, I think, is that at the extremes both are true, but for most of the time barristers and solicitors work very well together, and lay clients benefit from the combination of skills.

Preparation for court
Competent solicitors will ensure that the case has been prepared thoroughly from the outset, and by the time of trial will normally have met with counsel and experts on two or three occasions. On each

of those occasions counsel will have had very full instructions, and will have been encouraged to think forward to ensure that at the pre-trial conference there are no glaring omissions in the evidence. So, the first piece of advice is that you should always think ahead — both in practical terms and legal terms. On a number of occasions I have sat in conferences with counsel knowing that the papers have not been read properly, and with the sinking feeling that I will get poorly drafted statements of case that will need amendment, and that in the weeks before trial counsel will suddenly want information that he or she could have asked for at the first conference. This is very annoying and does little to inspire confidence in the lay client.

In the weeks leading up to a trial I expect to work fairly closely with counsel. Typically we arrange a pre-trial conference for two or three weeks before the trial, and even with the best prepared case there will always be further work to be done before the brief is delivered. I expect and welcome telephone conversations about particular aspects of the case, and I am always encouraged as the questions become more complex, as it indicates that counsel is making a proper analysis of the papers. If there are to be settlement negotiations I expect to conduct them, unless we are at court, and I would not expect counsel to speak with opposing counsel without first discussing the prospect with me. Generally I think settlement negotiations are better conducted by solicitors. It is difficult to rationalise why this is so, as it has to be acknowledged that counsel will have a better understanding of the law and evidential strengths and weaknesses of the case. I think that it is partly because the solicitor manages the case for a long time and should have a better 'feel' for the case and understanding of how the opposing legal team behave, and partly because solicitors are not constrained by the thought that they may have to present the case in court, which enables us to be tougher in negotiation.

I expect a barrister to have a thorough knowledge of matters of law and procedure. I will happily defer to counsel's views on these matters, but I expect a reasoned discussion of why a particular course of action is being taken. A competent solicitor will not be happy to spend three to four years preparing a case, only to abdicate responsibility for it when it comes to trial.

An uneasy alliance?

Most of the solicitors and barristers that I know are specialists in their fields. They are confident of their abilities, and do their respective jobs very well. For many it was not ever thus. I trained in a very general practice, where I was expected to carry out all types of contentious and non-contentious work. When working with counsel I invariably had only a very superficial understanding of the case. In some instances this did not really matter, because I was the clerk sent along to sit behind counsel at trial, and make no more contribution than to take notes. In other cases it did matter, because I was dealing with cases that were beyond my competence and experience. Mostly the barristers I worked with were very kind about this, but I would have forgiven any of them for thinking that he or she was the real lawyer, because on those occasions they undoubtedly were. I think much has changed in the training of solicitors since then and certainly in my firm we try to make sure that trainees have a proper and appropriate role to play in the preparation of cases.

When done properly, the solicitor's job is a complex and demanding one. We gather a great deal of information, narrow it down, and fashion it into a well-prepared and well-thought-out case that can then be finished off by counsel. Appropriate metaphors are elusive. Clients often ask if we are like GPs and barristers are like hospital specialists, but I think of the process more in terms of the case being a large cargo ship, perhaps an oil tanker, with the solicitor as its captain. As it approaches port a pilot comes on board to guide it through the treacherous rocks and shallows. The pilot is the barrister. Without him or her the ship will not get through the treacherous rocks and shallows, but he or she should still remember that the captain has managed to bring the vessel all the way from Africa. Which metaphor brings me rather neatly to my first anecdote which comes from the time when I was a shipping lawyer. I admit that I was not very interested in shipping law, and consequently was not a very good shipping lawyer. However, I was reasonably competent, and the barrister I was instructing, although very intelligent, was not much more experienced than me. He was a nice man, and during the conference he sympathised with me as he knew what it was like to be a solicitor 'standing at the photocopier all day'. Now I know that the mysteries of a solicitor's office can sometimes be difficult for counsel to understand, but to clear any doubt that is in your minds I can honestly say that the person who stands at a photocopier all day is a copying clerk, not a solicitor.

Returning to my main theme, I have no doubt that some solicitors still allow their cases to be 'counsel driven', but they are increasingly a thing of the past. It may interest you to know that there is a strong financial incentive for this. When my costs are taxed I can claim a higher hourly rate if I can show that as a specialist solicitor I was able to run the case with minimal use of counsel. As your career progresses, and you are able to move into a specialist area of law, you will start to get instructions from solicitors who also specialize, and when that happens the relationship can be a very good one.

So, I hope that I have now firmly established that solicitors are real lawyers, and that we have no doubts about the value of our work being equal to the value of the work performed by counsel. Now I will tell the truth, or at least the rest of the truth in so far as it applies to me, and, I suspect to quite a lot of solicitors. In a small corner of our minds we have a lingering jealousy of barristers — jealous because they spend more of their time thinking about interesting legal points, jealous because all of the drama attaches to the final days in court, rather than the three years of preparation, jealous because there are more television dramas about barristers than there are about solicitors, and jealous because barristers have more opportunity to dress up as eighteenth-century clergymen. Of course we are not jealous of the barrister's responsibility as the final presenter and advocate of the case, or jealous of the red eyes and tobacco-reeking breath that evidence the Sunday nights spent preparing for the Monday morning trial.

Ironically we still think that our job is harder. Your job may be intellectual and occasionally very stressful, but ours is continually stressful, often very frustrating, frequently intellectual, and above all never-ending. At the end of the conference or trial you give the papers back to us, but we have to carry on dealing with them, along with dozens of other cases. Too much drudgery and too little drama. Thus it was that I was very surprised to learn that barristers apparently think that they have the more difficult job. This revelation came to me only recently, when a very complicated medical negligence case settled just before trial. There was an enormous amount of paperwork, my expert witnesses were brilliant, but slightly eccentric, my client was nice, but near hysterical. My counsel was very able, but was delaying really getting to grips with the papers until the last possible moment. When the case settled, everyone concerned with it, including the defendant's lawyers, breathed a huge sigh of relief. When I spoke with counsel on the telephone, I was very surprised to find that he had anticipated that his task would be more difficult than mine. Did he not realise that all he had to do was turn up at court and present the case, whereas I had to orchestrate the whole thing, and make sure that papers and people (him included) were matched up and sent to the right place at the right time?

Behaviour towards the lay client

Most clients are scared of lawyers. It is scary for them to telephone a solicitor, and scary for them to walk into a solicitor's office for the first time. Happily most of them soon overcome that fear and build up a relationship of trust with their solicitor. However, the experience of litigation is still a stressful one, particularly when it involves professionals looking into very personal matters, as is often the case in a medical negligence claim.

Barristers are even scarier for the clients. The first meeting is usually a conference with counsel, and beforehand I reassure them that the purpose of the conference is to have a friendly, informal discussion about the case. Mostly the barristers I instruct never let me down. They are polite and do everything they can to put the clients at ease. One of the things I think about when selecting a barrister is how he or she will meet the needs of the case, and the client. If I have an exceptionally timid client I choose an exceptionally nice barrister. Occasionally I have very bullish clients who can be quite aggressive and difficult to control. In those circumstances I tend to choose a barrister who is more concerned with getting to the point than being charming. Having said that, on one notable occasion when I did that, within about 20 minutes the conference had turned into an all-out argument between the barrister and my client.

The only time when I have had cause to complain about a barrister arose out of a conference attended by my assistant. The client was a single woman in her late forties who had sustained gynaecological injuries as a result of medical negligence. The conference was with a male barrister, and was to be attended by two male medical experts. Inevitably it had to involve a detailed discussion of very intimate matters for my client, and as she was a rather shy woman, I knew she would be very apprehensive. I chose the barrister because he was recommended to me by some colleagues as being exceptionally intelligent, and very clear in his understanding of medical matters. I assumed that he would read the papers and realise that the client would have to be dealt with sensitively. He did just the opposite. First, he had a male pupil sitting in with him. Of course I have no objections to people training by observation, but it would have been courteous for him to ask my assistant, or indeed the client if she was happy to have yet another strange man discussing her very personal life. Secondly, he opened the conference not by talking about the weather, or the many general questions that had to be discussed, but by asking her if she was sexually active, and when was the last time that she had a sexual partner. Apparently the poor client tried her best to answer, but was clearly humiliated and uncomfortable.

I will never instruct that barrister again, although I should emphasise that it was an exceptional experience. Generally the barristers I use are very nice to my clients, and indeed that is one of the reasons why I use them. Perhaps I am in the fortunate position of using mostly very senior barristers who have had many years to practise their communication skills.

For any young professional starting out on his or her career, communicating with clients can be an area of weakness, and that is completely understandable. You will be working in a complicated field, uncertain about your ability to do the job, and the client may think that you look so young that you can't possibly be a properly qualified barrister. Therefore the temptation may be to prove that you are, by making everything sound so complicated that the client will think that you must be clever because he or she cannot understand a word you are saying.

Also, there is the all-embracing atmosphere of the legal profession, particularly in the Temple, where the centuries of wisdom will permeate your being, and you may find yourself acquiring the habits, dress and speech of a Chancery judge. That may make you seem and feel like a real barrister, and whilst to some extent we all have to act out our chosen role in order to placate our clients, remember that not all clients are stupid, and that solicitors in particular will not be terribly patient if very young barristers become too theatrical in presenting their professional selves.

Do you call your lay client/your solicitor by their first name, or address them formally? With lay clients you should always start by calling them Mr, Mrs or Ms. As you get to know them better you may move on to first name terms, but it is important to establish the professional relationship from the outset. It is always easy to get more friendly, but very difficult to withdraw from familiarity when, for example, you have to give unpalatable advice to an angry client. As for your instructing solicitors, I am sure that practice varies. I believe that it is probably sensible to address your instructing solici-tors formally at first, particularly if they are older than you. If there is a substantial age difference you should continue to do so until invited to do otherwise. If there is not a big age difference I think you should move on to first name terms fairly soon, and in fact I find it rather odd when a barrister, particularly one of similar age to me, insists on calling me Mr Donovan. As far as I am concerned we are working in a team together, and it would concern me if I thought that my barrister would prefer to keep me at arm's distance — just like the potentially difficult lay client.

With all of this there is a substantial element of human nature, and ordinary social skills, and really the best person that you can be is yourself. (Although in saying that, I assume that you are intelligent, confident and charming. If you are not it will be necessary for you to act as much as possible, and it may even help to dye your hair grey!)

Behaviour at court

You now take centre stage. To a certain extent the case is yours, and it will sink or swim with you. However, do not forget that your lay client is the true owner, and that your solicitor has had custody of the case for much longer than you. You must involve the lay client, particularly if there is a possi-bility of settlement. Clients become very emotionally involved in their cases, and although many of them will be terrified on the day, and may just want you to sort it all out for them, I think it is much healthier for a client to be involved fully in the reasoning behind a settlement. That way when he or she goes home, and the fear disappears and friends and relatives start to give the client advice about the damages that they would have insisted upon, there is less scope for the client to feel cheated.

Many solicitors send a trainee clerk to court. This generally makes financial sense because a senior solicitor's costs will not be recoverable in full where counsel is instructed. Thus it is that sometimes the person sitting behind you will have only a superficial knowledge of the case. That will mean more work for you, but if that person is a trainee solicitor it presents a golden opportunity for you to make a friend and do some marketing. Solicitors, particularly junior solicitors, prefer to instruct barristers that they like.

Like barristers, solicitors have considerable egos, and it is important that you remember this if you wish to be instructed again. I recently had a very complicated case listed for a two week trial in the High Court. Half-way through, the defence began to collapse, and the judge rose to allow the three parties to negotiate a settlement. By that stage counsel for all sides had become deeply involved in the case. There was much debate about case law, and I was relying heavily upon the skills of my QC and junior counsel. However, having had conduct of the case for four years it was important that I be involved in discussions, both for the client's sense of security, and proper conduct of the case. Happily my own counsel appreciated that, but counsel for one of the defendants clearly did not. We were having one of those court corridor conversations where all of us were huddled into a close group. The defendant's barrister wanted to make a remark to one of my counsel, who was standing to one side of me. Instead of facing all three of us when speaking, he walked into the centre of the circle, stood with his back to me (the frayed tail of his wig was literally six inches away from my nose) and began discussing terms with my counsel. Possibly this was just bad manners, but such behaviour does perpetuate myths about barristers' views of the worth of solicitors, and once again, if you want to get instructions it is best to avoid doing things like that.

Delay and incompetence

Reading through the professional conduct rules of the Bar I find that paragraphs 501 [now 603] and 601 [now 701] stipulate that a barrister should not take on work if he or she does not expect to carry it out within a reasonable time, and that if he or she finds himself or herself too busy to complete work already taken on, he or she must inform the professional client.

I am sorry to say that in my experience these rules are continually flouted. With one or two exceptions, the barristers that I work with are all very pleasant and intelligent people who never let me down in conference or at court. However, time and again I have to wait and wait for written work. My reminder letters go unanswered, and my chasing telephone calls are met with promises that are made to be broken. My clients wonder why their cases stop, directions orders have to be ignored; experts do not get the draft statements of case that they really needed to read whilst the conversation from the conference was fresh in their mind, and defendants' solicitors apply to strike me out for want of prosecution. If you chose to take note of only one thing in this paper, let it be this. Solicitors are very busy people who have to juggle many things in order to keep their large case loads moving along. A slow barrister is just one more thing to worry about, and it is a bitter irony indeed when your own barrister's involvement in a case can cause more problems than the opposing solicitors.

On at least two occasions in the last year I have had good cases that have moved along very well until counsel was instructed. In each case the barristers were experienced people, chosen because of their many excellent qualities. The conferences went very well, and finished with promises that the draft statements of case would be with me within a week. The weeks and months then slipped by, and despite reminder letters, faxes and phone calls, the statements of case did not come. Eventually there were applications to strike out by the defendants. This involved me in a great deal of work, for which I will not be paid, and even threats of personal costs orders against my firm. In my clients' eyes I became incompetent, and the cases having come from important referral sources, the reputation of my firm suffered. Fortunately in each case we were able to salvage the situation, but had we not done I might also have been facing a professional negligence claim.

Quality standards applied by solicitors to barristers

My firm has a legal aid franchise ['contract' under the Community Legal Service]. This means that we have to set quality standards for our clients, and ensure they are stuck to. As the partner in charge of the 'Register of Sub-Contractors' I am responsible for monitoring the performance of the other professionals that we use on behalf of our clients, most notably counsel. When staff in the firm have good or bad experiences with counsel, they send a note to me, and I report on those notes at our weekly fee earners' meetings. This is not a matter of choice. If we want to keep the legal aid franchise we have to show that the people that we instruct will do a good job. Thus it was that I recently had to send a fax to a barrister that I like very much, to say that six months was too long to wait for a written advice, and that if it was not supplied within two weeks, I would have to ask him to return the papers and no further instructions would be sent to him. I thought about adding that under his own rules of professional conduct he should probably have returned them a long time ago in any event, but decided that he should know that.

Quality control standards such as the legal aid franchise are part of modern business culture. The solicitors that instruct you have to be increasingly accountable to their clients; we in turn are your clients and it is much better for you to say that the papers will be with us in three months, and for us to know that that is true, rather than for you to say that the papers will be with us next week, when there is no real expectation that they will arrive before next year.

This is, of course, very tough on a young barrister who is trying to build up a following. When you eventually start to get some work you will not wish to turn cases away for fear of losing your professional clients, and indeed solicitors operate in exactly the same way. We might be too busy now, but we are worried about whether we will have enough work to do next year. Nevertheless, in my firm we have made a policy decision not to take on work if we cannot progress the work that we have reasonably quickly, and I would have no difficulty with a barrister saying that he or she is too busy to take on any work at present, but will be taking cases in two months' time. That would suggest to me that he or she is reliable and sensible, and I would at least have certainty when I did instruct him or her. You should also be working towards building up a long-term relationship with your instructing solicitor, and being honest about how busy you are will not harm that. In fact in some respects being busy can enhance your reputation, and I would be happy to say to a client that I am instructing a certain barrister because although he or she is busy now, he or she will give his or her whole attention to the work when the time comes.

Fees

As most of my work is legally aided it is seldom that I have to agree fees with counsel's clerk. However, when I do, I expect to be given an hourly rate for the barrister I want to instruct. Once again, I now work in an environment where I have to give very precise costs information to my clients, and thus I need counsel's chambers to operate in a similar way. I would not instruct a barrister on behalf of a private client on the basis of an oldfashioned style of valuation of the case by counsel's clerk upon receiving the papers. I need to be able to say to my clients that they can either have barrister X for £150, or barrister Y for £160.

The barrister's clerk

Much has been written recently about how barristers' chambers are acknowledging that they are modern businesses. This is all to the good. From the outside it seems that traditionally the clerks have observed a veneer of deference and respect towards barristers, whereas in reality they have controlled much of the power and of the wealth within chambers. A junior barrister is not a young aristocrat, and his or her clerk is not his or her trusty family retainer. They are both there to do a job in what should be a modern business environment, and I think it would be better for all concerned if that was acknowledged. In modern business good manners and respect are enough. Dickensian deference, particularly if it is false, can only breed resentment and poor working relationships.

It is difficult to give advice on how you can get the best out of your clerks, but from a solicitor's point of view the following points are helpful. Encourage them to adopt a professional attitude towards marketing. Obviously this will not be your decision as a pupil, or a new tenant, but every chambers should have a brochure giving details of its barristers, their experience and specialisation. The clerks should be ready to send that out very quickly. You should also try to ensure that they know where your areas of interest lie, so that if an opportunity does come up they will be able to mention your name. Some of the barristers that I use most regularly were originally introduced to me when a clerk suggested that they take over a case where my original choice had to drop out. Make sure that your clerk is rigorous about passing on telephone messages, and prompt in delivering fee notes. If he or she is not doing so, let your instructing solicitors know that the fault does not lie with you.

Getting work

Referring once more to my firm's policy on sub-contractors, part of our quality control system is only to use counsel that come recommended by a suitable source — for example, another solicitor who has worked with the barrister. Unfortunately specialist medical negligence solicitors are not a very good source of work for newly qualified barristers. We tend to use only very experienced counsel who have also taken the trouble to attend the same medical courses as we do in order to learn about medicine. Moreover, we do not have many hearings, and if you go into medical negligence work too early you will spend too much of your time drafting statements of case, and not enough time on your feet in court, and it seems to me that the best thing that a young barrister can do is to spend as much time in court as possible, learning how to be an effective advocate.

When you do start to specialise it will be a good idea to market yourself to the solicitors who have the work that you want. You do this partly by cross-referrals between solicitors, but also by turning up at places where they tend to congregate, and getting your face known. For example, if you were to specialise in medical negligence you would be able to meet the solicitors who control most of the work by attending medical courses run by AVMA (Action for Victims of Medical Accidents, the medico-legal charity) or any of the numerous medico-legal conferences that take place. Those courses are expensive, but in addition to showing that you are committed to the work, and that you are taking steps to acquire the necessary medical knowledge, you will also have the opportunity to meet the solicitors from whom you want instructions. However, if you have only just finished your pupillage, your efforts might be wasted, because most of those specialist solicitors will be dealing only with the more complex cases, and they will not wish to send them to a newly qualified barrister. In contrast, if you wait until you can display the scars and experience of a few years experience as an advocate, and no longer look like a school leaver, specialist solicitors will be more likely to consider instructing you when you show an interest in their field.

Summary

If my contribution had been limited to a few exhortations, which it probably should have been, they would be as follows. Make sure that you know the law. Read your papers very thoroughly. Be professional but be yourself. Work with your solicitor as a team. Be well-organised. Be well-organised. Be well-organised.

Postscript

The day after I wrote this article I had a meeting with a client. I was very pleased about her case, because she was a nice woman, and I had used all my skills and experience to help her get her claim off the ground. I believed in the case when no-one else would, and I guided her through the system, and even waited a very long time for her to pay my bills. The case is now looking very strong indeed, and she will soon get a fairly large award of damages. Counsel has been involved, but only very minimally. Thus at the end of the meeting I was sitting back, modestly thinking about how lucky she was to have a solicitor who was not only a wonderful human being, but also a very shrewd and experienced lawyer. And what did she say to me? She said, 'Wasn't our counsel good and will you go on to be a barrister?' I said, 'No, I wouldn't want to be away from my photocopying'.

Terence Donovan
Litigation Solicitor
Bindman & Partners

2.3.1.2   Problems

(1)   You are asked to advise on quantum in a personal injuries case where the defendants have offered to negotiate a settlement. It is clear that the claimant's general damages will be substantial but their assessment is not straightforward. In conference you state that in your opinion the case is worth £30,000 to £35,000 on full liability. Your solicitors (who value the case more highly) ask you for an opinion in writing that the bracket is £40,000–£45,000 in order to support their negotiations and to achieve a settlement at £35,000. What should you do?

(2)   You act for the claimant in civil proceedings. Unlike your client, the defendant has the benefit of a full legal aid certificate. You arrive at court on the day fixed for the hearing to find that the defendant's solicitor has forgotten to warn any of his or her witnesses. The judge accedes to the defendant's request for an adjournment. The defendant's solicitor is in fact well known to you and briefs you on a regular basis. What application, if any, do you make for costs?

2.3.2   Relationship with the Crown Prosecution Service

The Crown Prosecution Service has kindly allowed reproduction of a number of materials in this chapter. The material is Crown Copyright.

Since 2002, 'The Farquharson Guidelines: The Role and Responsibilities of the Prosecution Advocate' have provided important guidance on the relationship between the Prosecution Advocate and the Crown Prosecution Service. It is now reproduced:

The Role and Responsibilities of the Prosecution Advocate

1   **Pre-trial preparation**

Farquharson

(a) *It is the duty of Prosecution Counsel to read the Instructions delivered to him expeditiously and to advise or confer with those instructing him on all aspects of the case well before its commencement.*

1.1   The Crown Prosecution Service (CPS) will deliver instructions at a stage in the proceedings that allows sufficient time for the prosecution advocate adequately to consider, prepare and advise on the evidence before the court hearing or draft/agree the indictment.

1.2   Where a CPS Higher Court Advocate represents the prosecution at a Plea and Directions Hearing (PDH), the CPS will deliver instructions to the trial advocate no later than 10 working days after the date of the PDH.

1.3   The CPS will deliver instructions which:

i   address the issues in the case including any strategic decisions that have been or may need to be made;

ii   identify relevant case law;

iii   explain the basis and rationale of any decision made in relation to the disclosure of unused material;

iv   where practical, provide specific guidance or indicate parameters on acceptable plea(s); and

v   where a case is an appeal either to the Crown Court from the magistrates' court or is before the Court of Appeal, Divisional Court or House of Lords, address the issues raised in the Notice of Appeal, Case Stated, Application for Judicial Review or Petition.

Action on receipt of instructions

1.4   On receipt of instructions the prosecution advocate will consider the papers and advise the CPS, ordinarily in writing, or orally in cases of urgency where:

i   the prosecution advocate forms a different view to that expressed by the CPS (or where applicable a previous prosecution advocate) on acceptability of plea;

ii   the indictment as preferred requires amendment;

iii   additional evidence is required;

iv   there is an evidential deficiency (which cannot be addressed by the obtaining of further evidence) and, applying the *Code for Crown Prosecutors*, there is no longer a realistic prospect of conviction; or the prosecution advocate believes that it is not in the public interest to continue the prosecution;

v   in order to expedite and simplify proceedings certain formal admissions should be made;

vi   the prosecution advocate, having reviewed previous disclosure decisions, disagrees with a decision that has been made; or is not satisfied that he or she is in possession of all relevant documentation; or considers that he or she has not been fully instructed regarding disclosure matters;

vii   a case conference is required (particularly where there is a sensitive issue e.g. informant/PII/disclosure etc);

viii   the presentation of the case to the court requires special preparation of material for the jury or presentational aids.

1.5   The prosecution advocate will endeavour to respond within five working days of receiving instructions, or within such period as may be specified or agreed where the case is substantial or the issues complex.

1.6   Where the prosecution advocate is to advise on a specific aspect of the case other than 1.4(i–viii), the advocate should contact the CPS and agree a realistic timescale within which advice is to be provided.

1.7   The prosecution advocate will inform the CPS without delay where the advocate is unlikely to be available to undertake the prosecution or advise within the relevant timescale.

1.8   When returning a brief, the advocate originally instructed must ensure that the case is in good order and should discuss outstanding issues or potential difficulties with the advocate receiving the brief. Where the newly instructed advocate disagrees with a decision or opinion reached by the original advocate, the CPS should be informed so that the matter can be discussed.

Case summaries

1.9   When a draft case summary is prepared by the CPS, the prosecution advocate will consider the summary and either agree the contents or advise the CPS of any proposed amendment.

1.10 In cases where the prosecution advocate is instructed to settle the case summary or schedules, the document(s) will be prepared and submitted to the CPS without delay.

Case Management Plan

1.11 On receipt of a Case Management Plan the prosecution advocate, having considered the papers, will contact the Crown Prosecutor within seven days, or such period as may be specified or agreed where the case is substantial or the issues complex, to discuss and agree the plan. The plan will be maintained and regularly reviewed to reflect the progress of the case.

Keeping the prosecution advocate informed

1.12 The CPS will inform the prosecution advocate of developments in the case without delay and, where a decision is required which may materially affect the conduct and presentation of the case, will consult with the prosecution advocate prior to that decision.

1.13 Where the CPS is advised by the defence of a plea(s) of guilty or there are developments which suggest that offering no evidence on an indictment or count therein is an appropriate course, the matter should always be discussed with the prosecution advocate without delay unless to do so would be wholly impracticable.

Victims and witnesses

1.14 When a decision whether or not to prosecute is based on the public interest, the CPS will always consider the consequences of that decision for the victim and will take into account any views expressed by the victim or the victim's family.

1.15 The prosecution advocate will follow agreed procedures and guidance on the care and treatment of victims and witnesses, particularly those who may be vulnerable or have special needs.

Appeals

1.16 Where the prosecution advocate forms a different view to that expressed by the CPS on the conduct/approach to the appeal, the advocate should advise the CPS within FIVE working days of receiving instructions or such period as may be specified or agreed where the case is substantial or the issues complex.

PDH and other preliminary hearings

1.17 The principles and procedures applying to trials as set out in the following paragraphs will be equally applicable where the prosecution advocate is conducting a PDH or other preliminary hearing.

2   **Withdrawal of instructions**

Farquharson

(b) *A solicitor who has briefed Counsel to prosecute may withdraw his instructions before the commencement of the trial up to the point when it becomes impracticable to do so, if he disagrees with the advice given by Counsel or for any other proper professional reason.*

2.1   The CPS will consult and take all reasonable steps to resolve any issue or disagreement and will only consider withdrawing instructions from a prosecution advocate as a last resort.

2.2   If the prosecution advocate disagrees with any part of his or her instructions, the advocate should contact the responsible Crown Prosecutor to discuss the matter. Until the disagreement has been resolved the matter will remain confidential and must not be discussed by the prosecution advocate with any other party to the proceedings.

'Proper Professional Reason'

2.3   The prosecution advocate will keep the CPS informed of any personal concerns, reservations or ethical issues that the advocate considers have the potential to lead to possible conflict with his or her instructions.

2.4   Where the CPS identifies the potential for professional embarrassment or has concerns about the prosecution advocate's ability or experience to present the case effectively to the court, the CPS reserves the right to withdraw instructions.

Timing

2.5   It is often difficult to define when, in the course of a prosecution, it becomes impracticable to withdraw instructions as circumstances will vary according to the case. The nature of the case, its complexity, witness availability and the view of the court will often be factors that will influence the decision.

2.6   In the majority of prosecutions it will not be practicable to withdraw instructions once the judge has called the case before the court as a preliminary step to the swearing of the jury.

2.7   If instructions are withdrawn, the prosecution advocate will be informed in writing and reasons will be given.

2.8   Instructions may only be withdrawn by or with the consent of the Chief Crown Prosecutor, Assistant Chief Crown Prosecutor, Head of a CPS Trials Unit or, in appropriate cases, Head of a CPS Criminal Justice Unit.

2.9   In relation to cases prosecuted by the CPS Casework Directorate, the decision may only be taken by the Director Casework or Head of Division.

3   **Presentation and conduct**

Farquharson

(c) *While he remains instructed it is for Counsel to take all necessary decisions in the presentation and general conduct of the prosecution.*

3.1   The statement at 3(c) applies when the prosecution advocate is conducting the trial, PDH or any other preliminary hearing, but is subject to the principles and procedures relating to matters of policy set out in section 4 below.

Disclosure of material

3.2   Until the conclusion of the trial the prosecution advocate and CPS have a continuing duty to keep under review decisions regarding disclosure. The prosecution advocate should in every case specifically consider whether he or she can satisfactorily discharge the duty of continuing review on the basis of the material supplied already, or whether it is necessary to inspect further material or to reconsider material already inspected.

3.3   Disclosure of material must always follow the established law and procedure. Unless consultation is impracticable or cannot be achieved without a delay to the hearing, it is desirable that the CPS and, where appropriate, the disclosure officer are consulted over disclosure decisions.

4   Policy decisions

Farquharson

> *(d) Where matters of policy[1] fall to be decided after the point indicated in (b) above (including offering no evidence on the indictment or on a particular count, or on the acceptance of pleas to lesser counts), it is the duty of Counsel to consult his Instructing Solicitor/Crown Prosecutor whose views at this stage are of crucial importance.*

> *(e) In the rare case where Counsel and his Instructing Solicitor are unable to agree on a matter of policy, it is, subject to (g) below, for Prosecution Counsel to make the necessary decisions.*

Policy issues arising at trial

4.1   The prosecution advocate should alert the CPS at the first opportunity if a matter of policy is likely to arise.

4.2   The prosecution advocate must not give an indication or undertaking which binds the prosecution without first discussing the issue with the CPS.

CPS representation at Crown Court

4.3   Whenever possible, an experienced Crown Prosecutor will be available at the Crown Court to discuss and agree any issue involving the conduct or progress of the case.

4.4   When it is not possible to provide a Crown Prosecutor at court, an experienced caseworker will attend and facilitate communication between the prosecution advocate and the Crown Prosecutor having responsibility for the case.

4.5   In exceptional circumstances where it is not possible to contact a Crown Prosecutor, the prosecution advocate should ask the court to adjourn the hearing for a realistic period in order to consult with the CPS. Where an adjournment is refused, the prosecution advocate may make the decision but should record his or her reasons in writing.

Referral to senior CPS representative

4.6   Where an issue remains unresolved following consultation with a Crown Prosecutor; or where the case/issue under consideration is substantial, sensitive or complex; or the prosecution advocate disagrees with the advice of the Crown Prosecutor, the matter may be referred to the Chief Crown Prosecutor, the Director Casework or to a senior Crown Prosecutor with delegated authority to act on their behalf.

4.7   In order to ensure consultation takes place at the highest level appropriate to the circumstances and nature of the case, the court should be asked to adjourn if necessary. When an adjournment is sought, the facts leading to the application should be placed before the court only in so far as they are relevant to that application.

4.8   Where a Chief Crown Prosecutor has been directly involved in the decision making process and the issue remains unresolved, the matter may be referred to the Director of Public Prosecutions.

Farquharson

> *(f) Where Counsel has taken a decision on a matter of policy with which his Instructing Solicitor has not agreed, then it would be appropriate for the Attorney General to require Counsel to submit to him a written report of all the circumstances, including his reasons for disagreeing with those who instruct him.*

4.9   It will only be in exceptional circumstances that the Attorney General will require a written report. The prosecution advocate will first discuss the decision with the Chief

---

[1] *'policy' decisions should be understood as referring to non-evidential decisions on: the acceptance of pleas of guilty to lesser counts or groups of counts or available alternatives: offering no evidence on particular counts; consideration of a re-trial; whether to lodge an appeal; certification of a point of law; and the withdrawal of the prosecution as a whole.*

Crown Prosecutor or the Director, Casework. Where, by agreement, the issue remains one that either party considers should be drawn to the attention of the Director of Public Prosecutions the prosecution advocate will, on request, provide a written report for submission to the Director of Public Prosecutions. If he considers it appropriate to do so, the Director of Public Prosecutions may refer the matter to the Attorney General.

4.10 Where there has been a disagreement on a matter of policy, provided that the CPS is satisfied that the prosecution advocate followed the principles set out in this document, the professional codes of conduct and was not *Wednesbury* unreasonable, the CPS will not apply sanctions in respect of any future work solely as a result of the decision in a particular case.

5 Change of advice

Farquharson

(g) When Counsel has had the opportunity to prepare his brief and to confer with those instructing him, but at the last moment before trial unexpectedly advises that the case should not proceed or that pleas to lesser offences should be accepted, and his Instructing Solicitor does not accept such advice, Counsel should apply for an adjournment if instructed so to do.

5.1 The CPS and the prosecution advocate should agree a period of adjournment that would allow a newly instructed advocate to prepare for trial. The period should be realistic and acknowledge that in such circumstances a case conference will usually be required.

5.2 The facts leading to the application for the adjournment should be placed before the court only in so far as they are relevant to that application.

6 Prosecution advocate's role in decision making at trial

Farquharson

(h) Subject to the above, it is for Prosecution Counsel to decide whether to offer no evidence on a particular count or on the indictment as a whole and whether to accept pleas to a lesser count or counts.

6.1 The prosecution advocate may ask the defence advocate whether a plea will be forthcoming but at this initial stage should not suggest or indicate a plea that might be considered acceptable to the prosecution before a plea is offered.

6.2 Where the defence advocate subsequently offers details of a plea, the prosecution advocate may discuss the matter with a view to establishing an acceptable plea that reflects the defendant's criminality and provides the court with sufficient powers to sentence appropriately.

Responsibility of prosecution advocate to consult

6.3 Where the prosecution advocate forms the view that the appropriate course is to accept a plea before proceedings commence or continue, or to offer no evidence on the indictment or any part of it, the prosecution advocate should:

i   whenever practicable, speak with the victim or victim's family attending court to explain the position;

ii   ensure that the interests of the victim or any views expressed by the victim or victim's family are taken into account as part of the decision making process; and

iii keep the victim or victim's family attending court informed and explain decisions as they are made.

6.4 Where appropriate, the prosecution advocate may seek an adjournment of the court hearing in order to facilitate discussion with the victim or victim's family.

6.5 The prosecution advocate should always comply with paragraph 6.3 and, where practicable, discuss the matter with the CPS before informing the defence advocate or the court that a plea is acceptable.

6.6 Where the defendant indicates an acceptable plea, unless the issue is simple, the defence should reduce the basis of the plea to writing. The prosecution advocate should show the CPS any written record relating to the plea and agree with the CPS the basis on which the case will be opened to the court.

6.7 It is the responsibility of the prosecution advocate to ensure that the defence advocate is aware of the basis on which the plea is accepted by the prosecution and the way in which the prosecution case will be opened to the court.

6.8 It will not be necessary for the prosecution advocate to consult the CPS where the plea or course of action accords with the written instructions received from the CPS, although paragraph 6.3 may still apply.

Prosecution advocate's role in sentencing

6.9 The prosecution advocate should always draw the court's attention to any matters, including aggravating or mitigating features, that might affect sentence. Additionally, the advocate should be in a position to assist the court, if requested, with any statutory provisions or sentencing guidelines and should always draw attention to potential sentencing errors.

6.10 Where a discussion on plea and sentence takes place, the prosecution advocate must adhere to the Attorney General's *Guidelines on The Acceptance of Pleas* published on 7 December 2000.

7   Seeking judicial approval

Farquharson

(i) *If Prosecution Counsel invites the Judge to approve the course he is proposing to take, then he must abide by the Judge's decision.*

7.1 A discussion with the judge about the acceptability of a plea or conduct of the case should be held in the presence of the defendant unless exceptional circumstances[2] apply.

7.2 In exceptional circumstances, where the prosecution advocate considers it appropriate to communicate with the judge or seek the judge's view in chambers, the CPS should be consulted before such a step is taken.

7.3 Where discussions take place in chambers it is the responsibility of the prosecution advocate to remind the judge, if necessary, that an independent record must always be kept.

7.4 The prosecution advocate should also make a full note of such an event, recording all decisions and comments. This note should be made available to the CPS.

Farquharson

(j) *If Prosecution Counsel does not invite the Judge's approval of his decision it is open to the Judge to express his dissent with the course proposed and invite Counsel to reconsider the matter with those instructing him, but having done so, the final decision remains with Counsel.*

7.5 Where a judge expresses a view based on the evidence or public interest, the CPS will carry out a further review of the case.

---

[2] *For the purposes of these guidelines, 'exceptional circumstances' would include the following:*

i   *Where there is material or information which should not be made public, eg a police text, or for some other compelling reason such as a defendant or witness suffering, unknown to them, from a serious or terminal illness; or*

ii *There are sensitivities surrounding a prosecution decision or proposed action which need to be explained in chambers with a view to obtaining judicial approval. Such approval may be given in open court where it is necessary to explain a prosecution decision or action in order to maintain public confidence in the criminal justice system.*

7.6   The prosecution advocate will inform the CPS in a case where the judge has expressed a dissenting view and will agree the action to be taken. Where there is no CPS representative at court, the prosecution advocate will provide a note of the judge's comments.

7.7   The prosecution advocate will ensure that the judge is aware of all factors that have a bearing on the prosecution decision to adopt a particular course. Where there is a difference of opinion between the prosecution advocate and the CPS the judge will be informed as to the nature of the disagreement.

Farquharson

(k)   *In an extreme case where the Judge is of the opinion that the course proposed by Counsel would lead to serious injustice, he may decline to proceed with the case until Counsel has consulted with either the Director or the Attorney General as may be appropriate.*

7.8   As a preliminary step, the prosecution advocate will discuss the judge's observations with the Chief Crown Prosecutor in an attempt to resolve the issue. Where the issue remains unresolved the Director of Public Prosecutions will be consulted. In exceptional circumstances the Director of Public Prosecutions may consult the Attorney General.

Note that these Guidelines are not legally binding unless and until expressly approved by the Court of Appeal. However, they represent the standards to which you will be expected to adhere by all involved in the criminal justice system.

2.3.2.1   Code for Crown Prosecutors

The Phillips Royal Commission emphasised the need for those who prosecute to follow clear and consistent criteria when deciding whether or not to bring a prosecution. Since 1986 these have been set out in the Code for Crown Prosecutors issued pursuant to s 10 of the Prosecution of Offences Act 1985. It is important for both prosecuting and defence counsel to ensure that they have an up-to-date Code, and to be familiar with it. It will be highly relevant to the decision not just of whether or not to carry on with a case, but also the acceptability or otherwise of proposed pleas. The Code is reproduced below from sources provided by the Crown Prosecution Service.

The Code for Crown Prosecutors

1 Introduction

1.1   The decision to prosecute an individual is a serious step. Fair and effective prosecution is essential to the maintenance of law and order. Even in a small case a prosecution has serious implications for all involved — victims, witnesses and defendants. The Crown Prosecution Service applies the Code for Crown Prosecutors so that it can make fair and consistent decisions about prosecutions.

1.2   The Code helps the Crown Prosecution Service to play its part in making sure that justice is done. It contains information that is important to police officers and others who work in the criminal justice system and to the general public. Police officers should take account of the Code whenever they are responsible for deciding whether to charge a person with an offence.

1.3   The Code is also designed to make sure that everyone knows the principles that the Crown Prosecution Service applies when carrying out its work. By applying the same principles, everyone involved in the system is helping to treat victims fairly while prosecuting cases effectively.

2 General principles

2.1   Each case is unique and must be considered on its own facts and merits. However, there are general principles that apply to the way in which Crown Prosecutors must approach every case.

2.2 Crown Prosecutors must be fair, independent and objective. They must not let any personal views about ethnic or national origin, disability, sex, religious beliefs, political views or the sexual orientation of the suspect, victim or witness influence their decisions. They must not be affected by improper or undue pressure from any source.

2.3 It is the duty of Crown Prosecutors to make sure that the right person is prosecuted for the right offence. In doing so, Crown Prosecutors must always act in the interests of justice and not solely for the purpose of obtaining a conviction.

2.4 Crown Prosecutors should provide guidance and advice to investigators throughout the investigative and prosecuting process. This may include lines of inquiry, evidential requirements, and assistance in any pre-charge procedures. Crown Prosecutors will be proactive in identifying and, where possible, rectifying evidential deficiencies and in bringing to an early conclusion those cases that cannot be strengthened by further investigation.

2.5 It is the duty of Crown Prosecutors to review, advise on and prosecute cases, ensuring that the law is properly applied, that all relevant evidence is put before the court and that obligations of disclosure are complied with, in accordance with the principles set out in this Code.

2.6 The CPS is a public authority for the purposes of the Human Rights Act 1998. Crown Prosecutors must apply the principles of the European Convention on Human Rights in accordance with the Act.

3 The Decision to Prosecute

3.1 In most cases, Crown Prosecutors are responsible for deciding whether a person should be charged with a criminal offence, and if so, what that offence should be. Crown Prosecutors make these decisions in accordance with this Code and the Director's Guidance on Charging. In those cases where the police determine the charge, which are usually more minor and routine cases, they apply the same provisions.

3.2 Crown Prosecutors make charging decisions in accordance with the Full Code Test (see section 5 below), other than in those limited circumstances where the Threshold Test applies (see section 6 below).

3.3 The Threshold Test applies where the case is one in which it is proposed to keep the suspect in custody after charge, but the evidence required to apply the Full Code Test is not yet available.

3.4 Where a Crown Prosecutor makes a charging decision in accordance with the Threshold Test, the case must be reviewed in accordance with the Full Code Test as soon as reasonably practicable, taking into account the progress of the investigation.

4 Review

4.1 Each case that the Crown Prosecution Service receives from the police is reviewed to make sure that it is right to proceed with a prosecution. Unless the Threshold Test applies, the Crown Prosecution Service will only start or continue with a prosecution when the case has passed both stages of the Full Code Test.

4.2 Review is a continuing process and Crown Prosecutors must take account of any change in circumstances. Wherever possible, they should talk to the police first if they are thinking about changing the charges or stopping the case. Crown Prosecutors should also tell the police if they believe that some additional evidence may strengthen the case. This gives the police the chance to provide more information that may affect the decision.

5 The Full Code Test

5.1 The Full Code Test has two stages. The first stage is consideration of the evidence. If the case does not pass the evidential stage it must not go ahead no matter how important or serious it may be. If the case does pass the evidential stage, Crown Prosecutors must proceed to the second stage and decide if a prosecution is needed in the public interest. The evidential and public interest stages are explained below.

The evidential stage

5.2 Crown Prosecutors must be satisfied that there is enough evidence to provide a 'realistic prospect of conviction' against each defendant on each charge. They must consider what the defence case may be, and how that is likely to affect the prosecution case.

5.3 A realistic prospect of conviction is an objective test. It means that a jury or bench of magistrates, properly directed in accordance with the law, is more likely than not to convict the defendant of the charge alleged. This is a separate test from the one that the criminal courts themselves must apply. A jury or magistrates' court should only convict if satisfied so that it is sure of a defendant's guilt.

5.4 When deciding whether there is enough evidence to prosecute, Crown Prosecutors must consider whether the evidence can be used and is reliable. There will be many cases in which the evidence does not give any cause for concern. But there will also be cases in which the evidence may not be as strong as it first appears. Crown Prosecutors must ask themselves the following questions:

Can the evidence be used in court?

(a) Is it likely that the evidence will be excluded by the court? There are certain legal rules which might mean that evidence which seems relevant cannot be given at a trial. For example, is it likely that the evidence will be excluded because of the way in which it was gathered? If so, is there enough other evidence for a realistic prospect of conviction?

Is the evidence reliable?

(b) Is there evidence which might support or detract from the reliability of a confession? Is the reliability affected by factors such as the defendant's age, intelligence or level of understanding?

(c) What explanation has the defendant given? Is a court likely to find it credible in the light of the evidence as a whole? Does it support an innocent explanation?

(d) If the identity of the defendant is likely to be questioned, is the evidence about this strong enough?

(e) Is the witness's background likely to weaken the prosecution case? For example, does the witness have any motive that may affect his or her attitude to the case, or a relevant previous conviction?

(f) Are there concerns over the accuracy or credibility of a witness? Are these concerns based on evidence or simply information with nothing to support it? Is there further evidence which the police should be asked to seek out which may support or detract from the account of the witness?

5.5 Crown Prosecutors should not ignore evidence because they are not sure that it can be used or is reliable. But they should look closely at it when deciding if there is a realistic prospect of conviction.

The public interest stage

5.6 In 1951, Lord Shawcross, who was Attorney-General, made the classic statement on public interest, which has been supported by Attorneys-General ever since: 'It has never been the rule in this country — I hope it never will be — that suspected criminal offences must automatically be the subject of prosecution'. (House of Commons Debates, volume 483, column 681, 29 January 1951.)

5.7 The public interest must be considered in each case where there is enough evidence to provide a realistic prospect of conviction. Although there may be public interest factors against prosecution in a particular case, often the prosecution should go ahead and those factors should be put to the court for consideration when sentence is being passed. A prosecution will usually take place unless there are public interest factors tending against prosecution which clearly outweigh those tending in favour or it appears more appropriate in all the circumstances of the case to divert the person from prosecution (see section 8 below).

5.8   Crown Prosecutors must balance factors for and against prosecution carefully and fairly. Public interest factors that can affect the decision to prosecute usually depend on the seriousness of the offence or the circumstances of the suspect. Some factors may increase the need to prosecute but others may suggest that another course of action would be better.

The following lists of some common public interest factors, both for and against prosecution, are not exhaustive. The factors that apply will depend on the facts in each case.

Some common public interest factors in favour of prosecution

5.9   The more serious the offence, the more likely it is that a prosecution will be needed in the public interest. A prosecution is likely to be needed if:
   (a)   a conviction is likely to result in a significant sentence;
   (b)   a conviction is likely to result in a confiscation or any other order;
   (c)   a weapon was used or violence was threatened during the commission of the offence;
   (d)   the offence was committed against a person serving the public (for example, a police or prison officer, or a nurse);
   (e)   the defendant was in a position of authority or trust;
   (f)   the evidence shows that the defendant was a ringleader or an organiser of the offence;
   (g)   there is evidence that the offence was premeditated;
   (h)   there is evidence that the offence was carried out by a group;
   (i)   the victim of the offence was vulnerable, has been put in considerable fear, or suffered personal attack, damage or disturbance;
   (j)   the offence was committed in the presence of, or in close proximity to, a child;
   (k)   the offence was motivated by any form of discrimination against the victim's ethnic or national origin, disability, sex, religious beliefs, political views or sexual orientation, or the suspect demonstrated hostility towards the victim based on any of those characteristics;
   (l)   there is a marked difference between the actual or mental ages of the defendant and the victim, or if there is any element of corruption;
   (m)   the defendant's previous convictions or cautions are relevant to the present offence;
   (n)   the defendant is alleged to have committed the offence whilst under an order of the court;
   (o)   there are grounds for believing that the offence is likely to be continued or repeated, for example, by a history of recurring conduct; or
   (p)   the offence, although not serious in itself, is widespread in the area where it was committed; or
   (q)   a prosecution would have a significant positive impact on maintaining community confidence.

Some common public interest factors against prosecution

5.10   A prosecution is less likely to be needed if:
   (a)   the court is likely to impose a nominal penalty;
   (b)   the defendant has already been made the subject of a sentence and any further conviction would be unlikely to result in the imposition of an additional sentence or order, unless the nature of the particular offence requires a prosecution, or the defendant withdraws consent to having an offence taken into consideration during sentencing;
   (c)   the offence was committed as a result of a genuine mistake or misunderstanding (these factors must be balanced against the seriousness of the offence);
   (d)   the loss or harm can be described as minor and was the result of a single incident, particularly if it was caused by a misjudgement;
   (e)   there has been a long delay between the offence taking place and the date of the trial, unless:
      • the offence is serious;
      • the delay has been caused in part by the defendant;
      • the offence has only recently come to light; or
      • the complexity of the offence has meant that there has been a long investigation;

(f)   a prosecution is likely to have a bad effect on the victim's physical or mental health, always bearing in mind the seriousness of the offence;

(g)   the defendant is elderly or is, or was at the time of the offence, suffering from significant mental or physical ill health, unless the offence is serious or there is a real possibility that it may be repeated. The Crown Prosecution Service, where necessary, applies Home Office guidelines about how to deal with mentally disordered offenders. Crown Prosecutors must balance the desirability of diverting a defendant who is suffering from significant mental or physical ill health with the need to safeguard the general public;

(h)   the defendant has put right the loss or harm that was caused (but defendants must not avoid prosecution solely because they can pay compensation); or

(i)   details may be made public that could harm sources of information, international relations or national security.

5.11   Deciding on the public interest is not simply a matter of adding up the number of factors on each side. Crown Prosecutors must decide how important each factor is in the circumstances of each case and go on to make an overall assessment.

The relationship between the victim and the public interest

5.12   The Crown Prosecution Service does not act for victims of the families of victims in the same way as solicitors act for their clients. Crown Prosecutors act on behalf of the public and not just in the interests of any particular individual. However, when considering the public interest Crown Prosecutors should always take into account the consequences for the victim of the decision whether or not to prosecute, and any views expressed by the victim or the victim's family.

5.13   It is important that a victim is told about a decision which makes a significant difference to the case in which they are involved. Crown Prosecutors should ensure that they follow any agreed procedures.

6 The Threshold Test

6.1   The Threshold Test requires Crown Prosecutors to decide whether there is at least a reasonable suspicion that the suspect has committed an offence, and if there is, whether it is in the public interest to charge that suspect.

6.2   The Threshold Test is applied to those cases in which it would not be appropriate to release a suspect on bail after charge, but the evidence to apply the Full Code Test is not yet available.

6.3   There are statutory limits that restrict the time a suspect may remain in police custody before a decision has to be made whether to charge or release the suspect. There will be cases where the suspect in custody presents a substantial bail risk if released, but much of the evidence may not be available at the time the charging decision has to be made. Crown Prosecutors will apply the Threshold Test to such cases for a limited period.

6.4   The evidential decision in each case will require consideration of a number of factors including:

• the evidence available at the time;
• the likelihood and nature of further evidence being obtained;
• the reasonableness for believing that evidence will become available;
• the time it will take to gather that evidence and the steps being taken to do so;
• the impact the expected evidence will have on the case;
• the charges that the evidence will support.

6.5   The public interest means the same as under the Full Code Test, but will be based on the information available at the time of charge which will often be limited.

6.6   A decision to charge and withhold bail must be kept under review. The evidence gathered must be regularly assessed to ensure the charge is still appropriate and that continued objection to bail is justified. The Full Code Test must be applied as soon as reasonably practicable.

7 Selection of Charges

7.1 Crown Prosecutors should select charges which:
   (a) reflect the seriousness and extent of the offending;
   (b) give the court adequate powers to sentence and impose appropriate post-conviction orders; and
   (c) enable the case to be presented in a clear and simple way.

This means that Crown Prosecutors may not always choose or continue with the most serious charge where there is a choice.

7.2 Crown Prosecutors should never go ahead with more charges than are necessary just to encourage a defendant to plead guilty to a few. In the same way, they should never go ahead with a more serious charge just to encourage a defendant to plead guilty to a less serious one.

7.3 Crown Prosecutors should not change the charge simply because of the decision made by the court or the defendant about where the case will be heard.

8   Diversion from prosecution

ADULTS

8.1 When deciding whether a case should be prosecuted in the courts, Crown Prosecutors should consider the alternatives to prosecution. Where appropriate, the availability of suitable rehabilitative, reparative or restorative justice processes can be considered.

8.2 Alternatives to prosecution for adult suspects include a simple caution and a conditional caution.

Simple caution

8.3 A simple caution should only be given if the public interest justifies it and in accordance with Home Office guidelines. Where it is felt that such a caution is appropriate, Crown Prosecutors must inform the police so they can caution the suspect. If the caution is not administered, because the suspect refuses to accept it, a Crown Prosecutor may review the case again.

Conditional caution

8.4 A conditional caution may be appropriate where a Crown Prosecutor considers that while the public interest justifies a prosecution, the interests of the suspect, victim and community may be better served by the suspect complying with suitable conditions aimed at rehabilitation or reparation. These may include restorative processes.

8.5 Crown Prosecutors must be satisfied that there is sufficient evidence for a realistic prospect of conviction and that the public interest would justify a prosecution should the offer of a conditional caution be refused or the offender fail to comply with the agreed conditions of the caution.

8.6 In reaching their decision, Crown Prosecutors should follow the Conditional Cautions Code of Practice and any guidance on conditional cautioning issued or approved by the Director of Public Prosecutions.

8.7 Where Crown Prosecutors consider a conditional caution to be appropriate, they must inform the police, or other authority responsible for administering the conditional caution, as well as providing an indication of the appropriate conditions so that the conditional caution can be administered.

YOUTHS

8.8 Crown Prosecutors must consider the interests of a youth when deciding whether it is in the public interest to prosecute. However Crown Prosecutors should not avoid prosecuting simply because of the defendant's age. The seriousness of the offence or the youth's past behaviour is very important.

8.9 Cases involving youths are usually only referred to the Crown Prosecution Service for prosecution if the youth has already received a reprimand and final warning, unless the offence is so serious that neither of these were appropriate or the youth does not admit committing the offence. Reprimands and final warnings are intended to prevent re-offending and the fact that a further offence has occurred indicates that attempts to divert the youth from the court system have not been effective. So the public interest will usually require a prosecution in such cases, unless there are clear public interest factors against prosecution.

9   Mode of trial

9.1   The Crown Prosecution Service applies the current guidelines for magistrates who have to decide whether cases should be tried in the Crown Court when the offence gives the option and the defendant does not indicate a guilty plea. Crown Prosecutors should recommend Crown Court trial when they are satisfied that the guidelines require them to do so.

9.2   Speed must never be the only reason for asking for a case to stay in the magistrates' courts. But Crown Prosecutors should consider the effect of any likely delay if they send a case to the Crown Court, and any possible stress on victims and witnesses if the case is delayed.

10 Accepting guilty pleas

10.1 Defendants may want to plead guilty to some, but not all, of the charges. Alternatively they may want to plead guilty to a different, possibly less serious, charge because they are admitting only part of the crime. Crown Prosecutors should only accept the defendant's plea if they think the court is able to pass a sentence that matches the seriousness of the offending, particularly where there are aggravating features. Crown Prosecutors must never accept a guilty plea just because it is convenient.

10.2 In considering whether the pleas offered are acceptable, Crown Prosecutors should ensure that the interests of the victim, and where possible any views expressed by the victim or victim's family, are taken into account when deciding whether it is in the public interest to accept the plea. However, the decision rests with the Crown Prosecutor.

10.3 It must be made clear to the court on what basis any plea is advanced and accepted. In cases where a defendant pleads guilty to the charges but on the basis of facts that are different from the prosecution case, and where this may significantly affect sentence, the court should be invited to hear evidence to determine what happened, and then sentence on that basis.

10.4 Where a defendant has previously indicated that he or she will ask the court to take an offence into consideration when sentencing, but then declines to admit that offence at court, Crown Prosecutors will consider whether a prosecution is required for that offence. Crown Prosecutors should explain to the defence advocate and the court that the prosecution of that offence may be subject to further review.

10.5 Particular care must be taken when considering pleas which would enable the defendant to avoid the imposition of a mandatory minimum sentence. When pleas are offered, Crown Prosecutors must bear in mind the fact that ancillary orders can be made with some offences but not with others.

11 Prosecutor' role in sentencing

11.1 Crown Prosecutors should draw the court's attention to:
- any aggravating or mitigating factors disclosed by the prosecution case;
- any victim personal statement;
- where appropriate, evidence of the impact of the offending on a community;
- any statutory provisions or sentencing guidelines which may assist;
- any relevant statutory provisions relating to ancillary orders (such as anti-social behaviour orders).

11.2 The Crown Prosecutor should challenge any assertion made by the defence in mitigation that is inaccurate, misleading or derogatory. If the defence persist in the assertion, and it appears relevant to the sentence, the court should be invited to hear evidence to determine the facts and sentence accordingly.

12 Re-starting a prosecution

12.1 People should be able to rely on decisions taken by the Crown Prosecution Service. Normally, if the Crown Prosecution Service tells a suspect or defendant that there will not be a prosecution, or that the prosecution has been stopped, that is the end of the matter and the case will not start again. But occasionally there are special reasons why the Crown Prosecution Service will re-start the prosecution, particularly if the case is serious.

12.2 These reasons include:

(a) rare cases where a new look at the original decision shows that it was clearly wrong and should not be allowed to stand;

(b) cases which are stopped so that more evidence which is likely to become available in the fairly near future can be collected and prepared. In these cases, the Crown Prosecutor will tell the defendant that the prosecution may well start again; and

(c) cases which are stopped because of a lack of evidence but where more significant evidence is discovered later.

12.3 There may also be exceptional cases in which, following an acquittal of a serious offence, the Crown Prosecutor may, with the written consent of the Director of Public Prosecutions, apply to the Court of Appeal for an order quashing the acquittal and requiring the defendant to be retried, in accordance with Part 10 of the Criminial Justice Act 2003.

2.3.3 Prosecuting Counsel and the Crown Prosecution Service

As well as being familiar with the Farquarson Guidelines and the Code for Crown Prosecutors referred to above, you will need to be aware of the policy and procedure for advocates prosecuting on behalf of the CPS. The CPS has produced a document entitled 'CPS Instructions for Prosecuting Advocates' which is incorporated into every prosecution brief. The full current version is available from the CPS website at www.cps.gov.uk and it provides extensive instructions on a wide area of prosecution issues. It is very important that you are familiar with its contents whenever you prosecute, and indeed you also need to be familiar with it as a defence advocate since it will provide you with information on the likely approach of the prosecution on such issues.

You may find, on occasion, that a dispute arises between you and your instructing solicitor as to whether or not to continue with a prosecution or whether to accept a proposed plea. This problem was addressed by the committee presided over by Farquharson J (May 1986) on the role of prosecuting counsel. The summary of the recommendations of the Committee, set out in para 10.6 of the Written Standards for the Conduct of Professional Work in Section 3, Miscellaneous Guidance to the Code of Conduct, is adopted as part of the Code. The full text of the Committee's Report is reprinted in *Archbold: Criminal Pleading, Evidence & Practice* 1995 Re-issue Volume 1 at paras 4-71–4-80. You should also note that since the publication of the Committee's findings, new Farquharson guidelines have been produced. They are reproduced above at **2.3.2** and can also be located at the CPS website at www.cps.gov.uk.

2.3.3.1 Problem

A jury fails to agree in a case in which you have prosecuted. Given the nature of the case and the evidence available to you, their inability to reach a verdict is wholly understandable. You take the view that on the customary retrial the prosecution is almost certain to fail. You also consider that a rehearing would cause considerable distress to the principal witness. You decide to offer no further evidence when the case is relisted. Your instructing solicitors do not agree. How do you deal with the situation?

2.4   Relationship with other members of the profession

2.4.1   Duties and responsibilities to the profession as a whole

The main obligations which you are bound to observe are set out in the Code of Conduct and include a duty:

(a) To uphold at all times the standards set out in the Code of Conduct and to comply with its provisions.

(b) Not to engage directly or indirectly in any other occupation if your association with that occupation may adversely affect the reputation of the Bar or prejudice your ability to attend properly to your practice (para 301(b)).

(c) To ensure that you are insured with Bar Mutual Indemnity Fund Limited against claims for professional negligence (paras 204; 402).

(d) To have a current Practising Certificate (para 202).

(e) To ensure your practice is efficiently and properly administered (para 403.2).

(f) To exercise your own personal judgment in all your professional activities (para 306).

(g) Not to permit your absolute independence, integrity and freedom from external pressures to be compromised or to compromise your professional standards in order to please your client, the court or a third party (para 307).

(h) Not to engage in any advertising or promotion in connection with your practice other than as may be permitted by the provisions of the British Codes of Advertising and Sales Promotion, and otherwise permitted under para 710.2 (paras. 710.1; 710.2).

(i) As a self-employed barrister, not to practise from the office of or in any unincorporated association with any person other than a barrister except as permitted by para 403.1 (para 403.1).

2.4.2   Duties and responsibilities owed to other members of the profession

The most important aspect of your relationship with other members of the Bar is to ensure that you never knowingly mislead or deceive them. It is equally important to treat them with courtesy (para 701). Your other responsibilities include a duty:

(a) To inform counsel previously instructed in the same matter that you have received a brief or set of instructions in place of that other barrister (this appears to be a custom rather than a duty under the Code).

(b) To return, unread, a document belonging to another party which has come into your possession other than by the normal and proper channels (para 608(f)); para 7.2 to the General Standards in Written Standards for the Conduct of Professional Work in Section 3, Miscellaneous Guidance).

(c) To pay, upon receipt of any fees in respect of work done by another barrister, the whole of that fee forthwith to the other barrister (para 406.1).

(d) To pay any pupil except where they are in receipt of an award or remuneration which is paid on terms that it is in lieu of payment for any individual item of work, for any work done for you which, because of its value to you, warrants payment (para 805).

In the course of negotiating with a view to a compromise, your relationship with your opponent is of particular importance. The ethics of negotiation are discussed further in **Chapter 7**.

2.4.3 Relationship with the clerks

In the early days of practice, it is quite common for members of the Bar to shy away from ever challenging the authority of the clerks in chambers. Whilst it is important to recognise the position of the clerks and build up a good rapport, trust and working relationship with them, it is vital that you remember you are responsible for ensuring that your practice is properly and efficiently administered. If your clerk makes an error, you must take the blame. Remember that you employ the clerks, they do not employ you. On occasions it may be necessary to 'have words with' the clerks. Do so in a polite manner and on a one to one basis. Do not embarrass the clerks in front of each other or other members of chambers. If you do not succeed in obtaining the clerks' co-operation, consider speaking to your head of chambers.

The following short essay is by Martin Griffiths, Chairman of the Institute of Barristers' Clerks and a senior clerk in the Chambers of David Phillips QC, and it provides a practical insight into the relationship between barrister and clerk.

Relations between Barrister and Clerk

One of the most important people in the personal and professional life of a barrister is the barrister's clerk. The title 'clerk' does little justice to the role that the barrister's clerk plays. The popular image remains one of a slightly rough and ready 'wide boy' who exerts an inordinate amount of control and influence over his or her barristers and without whom solicitors can get nothing done. Unfortunately, this image is perpetuated by the caricatures that frequently appear in TV dramas.

The modern clerk, however, is an experienced and skilful manager at the helm of what is often a multi-million pound business. He or she does much to guide the careers of the barristers in chambers and is the link between the barristers who supply a service and the solicitors who are the customers.

The clerk's role is unusual. He or she is the agent and business manager of the barrister, the ultimate manager of the support team within chambers and the personal adviser to the barrister on all aspects of his or her professional life. Of necessity the barrister may share many problems, both professional and personal, with the clerk and a real friendship may develop between the two.

When the barrister first starts in chambers the senior clerk may appear a remote and forbidding individual. This may be particularly true in a large set of chambers where the principal point of contact between the barrister and the clerks' room is a more junior clerk. However, as manager of the clerking team, the senior clerk will always be monitoring the development and progress of the new barrister. Initially, the new barrister is dependent upon the clerk for providing him or her with work and giving him or her introductions to appropriate solicitors. In the early years the barrister will be very dependent upon this supply of work. As the barrister gains experience and establishes a reputation with solicitor clients, he or she will hopefully develop a practice of his or her own. During this period the clerk is likely to advise the barrister on how to conduct himself or herself and tell him or her what he or she should or should not do.

Whilst the new barrister should, of course, respect the experience of his or her clerk, the clerk should not be regarded as unapproachable. A relationship needs to develop between the two so that there is easy communication; the barrister must be able to feel free to seek advice and to be able to raise concerns or indeed complaints about the management of his or her practice; the clerk needs to understand the strengths, weaknesses and interests of the barrister in order to be able to direct his or her career appropriately.

Communication is probably one of the most important aspects of the smooth running of the barrister's life. Without information the clerk cannot clerk.

- Tell the clerks what you think will happen to cases that you are booked for. Is the case likely to settle, is it listed for trial and you expect it to plead, is the time estimate too short?
- Be punctual and consistent. If you usually arrive in chambers at 9.00 am but tomorrow do not expect to be in until 10.00 am, say so. It is no good if at 9.05 am the clerk needs to send

somebody to court on an urgent matter and is waiting for you to walk through the door. Notify your clerk of any changes to your normal routine so that he or she can plan accordingly.

- Always ensure that you telephone chambers with a progress report from court. Ring to say that you are finished and are returning to chambers, ring at lunchtime to say that the case will finish today, or will not and will last until tomorrow lunchtime. The clerk cannot properly plan without adequate warning and up-to-date information.

- Provide prompt and accurate information regarding work done for the purposes of billing. Each chambers will have its own system of time sheets. Complete these and legal aid claim forms promptly on completing any piece of work. The sooner the bill is sent, the sooner you will get paid.

The level and collection of fees is often a subject of discussion between barrister and clerk. Some barristers have absolutely no idea of the fee that a particular case can command; some believe that the fee should be far higher than can realistically be obtained, others undervalue their services dramatically. With experience some have a good idea and can be of tremendous assistance to the clerk in assessing what a particular case is worth. It is important to tell your clerk what is involved in a particular matter for without this information he or she will be assessing or negotiating in the dark. If you have a problem with the level of fees that are being obtained for you, or with the speed with which the fees are being collected, discuss the situation with the clerk. You may have got hold of the wrong end of the stick and not understand the problem; alternatively, he or she may be unaware that a problem exists and only by discussing it can the situation be rectified. If you cannot resolve the difficulty, raise the matter with your pupil master or mistress, with whom you may still have a strong relationship even though you are well past pupillage, or raise it with the head of chambers who has a duty to ensure that the chambers are managed properly.

All chambers are different and will operate in a slightly different way. In some the members of chambers will always be addressed formally, eg, Mr Smith, Miss Jones, Mrs Brown. In others the senior clerk will be on first name terms with the barristers but will expect his or her staff to address members of chambers formally, in other sets everyone may be on first name terms. Each chambers is different and I would advise that you err on the side of caution until you establish the house style. Having said that, I doubt if any senior clerk would these days expect to be addressed by anything other than his or her first name by the barristers.

As I have said, each chambers operates in a slightly different manner and hopefully when you start your second six months, or upon your arrival as a practising barrister, the senior clerk will run through how the chambers function. A few golden rules may well be as follows:

- Stay out of the clerks' room unless you have necessary business there. It is often a crowded and certainly a busy room and you gossiping to another member of chambers, or a clerk who has other duties, is not helpful.

- Keep personal telephone calls in chambers to a minimum. Do not expect the clerks to take telephone calls for you to organise your busy social life, sort out the cricket team fixtures or arrange a holiday for a dozen people.

- Let the clerk know when you are contemplating going on holiday before making the booking. It won't be very helpful suddenly to find that the five most junior members of chambers are all on holiday at the same time.

- Ensure that bills for chambers' expenses and clerk's fees are paid promptly.

- Feed back to your clerks news and views that you pick up from other barristers and your solicitors at court.

Remember that at all times your clerk is monitoring the work that you do and your progress. He or she will have views as to your future development and hopefully will wish to discuss these with you. Do not hesitate to share your views with him or her because at the end of the day the pair of you are a partnership.

2.4.3.1 Problems

(1)   A colleague in chambers comes to your room to discuss with you a quantum in a case in which he or she is giving some preliminary advice. He or she gives you the outline of the medical report and after you have exchanged valuations of the level of general damages, leaves you with the words 'We have terrible problems on liability'. Some months later, you receive instructions to settle a defence and, having read the papers, you realise that it is the same case which you discussed with your colleague. Do you continue to deal with the papers?

(2)   You have a row with your clerks. During the following week, one of the pupils in chambers asks your advice upon a brief he or she has been given for the next day. You realise it is a case you advised upon last year, yet the clerks have informed you that you have no work for the following day. What do you do?

3

Working at the Bar today

3.1 Introduction

Britain in the 21st century is a richly diverse and multi-cultural society. Statistics from the 2000 census shows that 4.6 million people, 7.9% of the population, are from a non-white ethnic group. In certain urban areas such as London, West Midlands, Greater Manchester and West Yorkshire, the percentage figure is much higher. Surveys by local education authorities show that over 100 different home languages are spoken. This diversity is further reflected by the number of religious beliefs, changes in the nature of the family, positive changes with regard to gender roles and the rights of the disabled, children and the gay and lesbian community. However, despite many positive changes in attitude, it is a society in which discrimination still exists and in which access to justice for all remains a burning issue. Yet, it is also a society whose diversity adds to the dynamism, excitement and challenges that you face as lawyers, irrespective of the area of practice you choose to enter.

The First Report on Legal Education and Training published in April 1996, the Lord Chancellor's Advisory Committee on Legal Education and Conduct (ACLEC) stated:

From the earliest stages of legal education and training, intending lawyers should be imbued not only with the standards and codes of professional conduct, but also more generally with the obligations of lawyers to help protect individuals and groups from the abuse of public and private power.

In the spirit of this statement, the aims of this chapter are to consider how the Code of Conduct operates in the areas of discrimination, diversity and equality of opportunity and how it impacts on your responsibilities to all those you work with, whether as colleagues or clients. To simply understand the Code is not enough, if barristers working at the Bar today are to rise to the obligation 'to help protect individuals and groups from the abuse of public and private power'. To effectively represent individuals you need to have an understanding of the different views, beliefs and customs of all those that make up Britain's diverse and multi-cultural society. The second part of this chapter gives some general guidance and sources of information that will help you meet this challenge. The barrister that has this understanding will not only have risen to this challenge, but will have completed a vital step in having a vibrant and successful practice.

3.2   The Code of Conduct and discrimination

An act of direct discrimination by a barrister amounts to a breach of the Code of Conduct. Paragraph 305.1 of the Code states:

A barrister must not in relation to any other person (including a client or another barrister or a pupil or a student member of an Inn of Court) discriminate directly or indirectly or victimize because of race, colour, ethnic or national origin, nationality, citizenship, sex, sexual orientation, marital status, disability, religion or political persuasion.

The breadth of this provision means that it covers a barrister's relationship with all of those people with whom he or she comes into contact in the course of carrying out a professional practice.

3.2.1   Fair representation: the 'cab-rank' rule

Fair treatment under para 305 would include fair representation, though this concept is specifically enshrined in para 603 of the Code and is known as the 'cab-rank' rule.

A barrister in independent practice must comply with the 'cab-rank rule' and accordingly except only as otherwise provided in paragraphs 603, 604, 605 and 606, he must in any field in which he professes to practice in relation to work appropriate to his experience and seniority and irrespective of whether his client is paying privately or is publicly funded:

    (a) accept any brief to appear before a court in which he professes to practice;

    (b) accept any instructions;

    (c) act for any person on whose behalf he is instructed;

    and to do so irrespective of

        (i)   the party on whose behalf he is instructed

        (ii)   the nature of the case and

        (iii)   any belief or opinion which he may have formed as to the character reputation cause conduct guilt or innocence of that person.

(See also paras 104, 303 of the Code and para 2.2 of the Written Standards for the Conduct of Professional Work in Section 3, Miscellaneous Guidance.)

The only permissible exceptions to the 'cab-rank' rule are set out in paras 603–610 of the Code. The rule otherwise means that a barrister must accept a brief or instructions to represent a client, no matter how repugnant the client is to the barrister on political, religious or moral grounds. Consequently, if the system is correctly and properly adhered to at all times, whatever a barrister's individual views are, effective representation of an individual is rightly ensured.

3.2.2   The Equality and Diversity Code for the Bar

The new Equality and Diversity Code for the Bar was adopted by the Bar Council in 2004. The Code is designed to assist barristers to apply good equal opportunities practices in the development and running of chambers. The Code states that 'Equality of opportunity is *fair, commercially advantageous, necessary for compliance with non-discrimination law and constitutionally important*'. The Code is set out in **Appendix 1** at Section 3, Miscellaneous Guidance. For the Annexes to the Code, you will need to refer to the Bar Council's website at www.barcouncil.org.uk.

3.3   Effective representation in a diverse society

We cannot be a beacon to the world unless the talents of all the people shine through. Not one black high court judge; not one black chief constable or permanent secretary; not one black army officer above the rank of colonel. Not one Asian either. Not a record of pride for the British establishment.

Prime Minister Tony Blair, 1997

The Bar itself is slowly changing and gradually becoming more representative of the society it serves. In October 2000 of the 8,263 barristers recorded by the Bar Council, 2,263 (24.5%) were women and 784 (8.7%) were from ethnic minority and mixed backgrounds.

As the Equality Code points out, 'Direct discrimination may frequently be subconscious, based on stereotypical assumptions about particular minority ethnic groups or about the difference in capabilities, characteristics, personalities and motivation between women and men'. From whatever background a barrister comes, at some time all will need help and advice on the customs and beliefs of the individuals that they represent. The Judicial Studies Board (JSB), the body responsible for training all those who sit in a judicial capacity, have issued specific guidance on these matters in the Equal Treatment Bench Book. Whilst this book is aimed at those sitting in a judicial capacity, you are advised that it holds equally invaluable information for those who are representing others. The full text of the Equal Treatment Bench Book is available on the JSB website at www.jsboard.co.uk. In addition, an easy-to-use companion booklet has been produced dealing with fairness before the courts, 'Fairness in Courts and Tribunals'. This deals with racial issues, and other issues of general equality before the courts, and can be downloaded from the website at the web address given above. You are strongly advised to read this — it offers a general introduction to some of the matters dealt with in more detail in the Equal Treatment Bench Book.

3.4   Sources of useful information

3.4.1   The Bar Council

Equality and diversity work at the Bar is directed by three Bar Council Committees: the Equality and Diversity (Race and Religion) Committee set up in 1984, the Equality and Diversity (Sex, Sexual Orientation and Age) Committee set up in 1992 and the Equality and Diversity (Disability) Committee set up in 1991. There is a designated place on the General Management Committee for an equality and diversity representative

The post of Bar Council Equality and Diversity Adviser is job-shared by Pamela Bhalla and Kathryn Hamylton. They are based at 289–293 High Holborn, London WC1V 7HZ (tel: 020 7242 0082, email: equalopps@barcouncil.org.uk). If you wish to speak to the Equality and Diversity Advisers in confidence there is a confidential line (tel: 020 7611 1310). Their role is to provide advice on any equality or discrimination matter to chambers wishing to improve their equality and diversity practice, to barristers with equality and diversity problems or queries, Practice Managers, clerks, pupils, BVC or law students. They work independently of all other Bar Council departments and report direct to the Chief Executive.

3.4.2   Other useful contacts

The Commission for Racial Equality (CRE)
Mr Trevor Phillips
Chair
St Dunstan's House
Borough High Street
London SE1 1GZ
Tel: 020 7939 0000 (switchboard)
Fax: 020 7939 0001 (general)

The Equal Opportunities Commission (EOC)
Ms Julie Mellor
Chair
Arndale House
Arndale Centre
Manchester M4 3EQ
Tel: 0161 833 9244 (switchboard)
Email: info@eoc.org.uk (general)

The Disability Rights Commission (DRC)
DRC Helpline
FREEPOST MID02164
Stratford upon Avon
CV37 9BR
Tel: 08457 622 633
Textphone: 08457 622 644

Society of Asian Lawyers (SAL)
Society of Asian Lawyers
c/o Mr Aamir Khan
Richards Butler
Beaufort House
15 St Botolph Street
London EC3A 7EE
Tel: 020 7772 5994
Fax: 020 7539 5319

Association of Women Barristers (AWB)
c/o The General Council of the Bar
289–293 High Holborn
London WC1V 7HZ
Website: www.womenbarrister.co.uk

Association of Muslim Lawyers (AML)
Student officer
The Association of Muslim Lawyers
PO Box 148
High Wycombe
Bucks HP13 5WJ
Tel: 01494 526 955
Email: aml@aml.org.uk

Bar Lesbian and Gay Group (BLAGG)
Damien Lochrane
3 Pump Court
Temple
London EC4Y 7AJ
Email: blagg_uk@yahoo.co.uk

South East Circuit Minorities Committee
c/o Karl King
Hardwicke Building
New Square
Lincoln's Inn
London WC2A 3UP

The Society of Black Lawyers
c/o Peter Herbert
Tooks Court Chambers
Chambers of Michael Mansfield QC
8 Warner Yard
Warner Street
London EC1R 5EY
DX 68 Chancery Lane
Tel: 020 7841 6100
Fax: 020 7841 6199

3.5 Conclusion

The obligations of lawyers to help protect individuals and groups from the abuse of public and private power, has been identified by ACLEC as the 'ethical challenge'. The guidance set out in this chapter will help you to meet that obligation. However, unless you are prepared to seek guidance, if necessary, to understand the views, beliefs and customs of all those who appear before the courts, you will risk individuals, through their legal experiences, believing that justice and fair treatment are not options for them. You must therefore remember the advice set out in the JSB guidance on 'Race and the courts' that, 'the responsibility for ensuring equality and fairness of treatment rests on everyone involved in the administration of justice'. You are shortly to become part of this system, embracing this important aspect of your professional conduct is crucial if you are to gain the respect of all individuals you come into contact with at the Bar today and generate the necessary trust and confidence of all sections of the community.

The letter and spirit of the Code

4.1 The lawyer joke

A layperson, an accountant and a lawyer were all asked: 'What do two and two make?'
The layperson replied: 'Four, of course.'
The accountant replied: 'Four — or five.'
The lawyer replied: 'What do you want it to make?'

Lawyers are the butt of many jokes, many of which flow from a perception that lawyers are capable of acting quite unethically in pursuit of their client's interests. While this perception has, fortunately, never developed in the UK to the extent that it has in the USA, the characteristics of practice in common law jurisdictions exposes lawyers to many ethical dilemmas, and responses to these vary. This chapter (and indeed this Manual) will provide you with some answers, but in other areas it will simply provide you with a framework within which you will still have to make your own decisions. In these cases it should provide you with tools and ideas which may help you to arrive at conclusions which satisfy the ethical demands of practice.

The issues have been neatly presented by Ross Cranston:

An important policy issue is the extent to which the Code of Conduct ought to be infused by wider ethical notions. There are two aspects to this. One is encapsulated in the question: 'Can a good lawyer be a bad person?'. In other words, are the standards in the Code of Conduct untenable when laid alongside ethical thought or common morality? The second aspect is that if there is a discrepancy between the Code of Conduct and secular ethical thought, what is special about barristers that exempts them from the precepts of the latter? To put it another way, how is it that barristers can decide ethically on a course of action for a client which is different from that which they would adopt for themselves?

(Cranston, R (ed): *Legal Ethics and Professional Responsibility* (Oxford, Clarendon 1996) at p 5)

4.2 The Code of Conduct

The Bar Code of Conduct provides you with the rules and standards that should inform all aspects of your practice at the Bar. It looks, at first sight, very much like a statute and this recognition should lead you to approach it with respect, but also to consider carefully how you should use it. It is not a statute, but a Code of Conduct.

There is a risk that, if the Code is perceived as essentially like any other piece of legislation, you will approach it in the same way. Why should this be a problem? It stems from the underlying principle within UK substantive law that all actions are permitted unless they are forbidden. Thus Acts that regulate behaviour are to be construed in a restrictive manner and loopholes may properly be exploited.

For example, the Theft Act 1968, s 9 provides:

> (1) A person is guilty of burglary if:
>   (a) he enters any building or part of a building as a trespasser and with intent to steal anything in the building or part of a building in question, to inflict on any person in it any grievous bodily harm or to rape any woman in it, or to do unlawful damage to the building or anything in it; or
>   (b) having entered any building or part of a building as a trespasser, he steals or attempts to steal anything in the building or that part of it or inflicts or attempts to inflict on any person in it any grievous bodily harm.

Your client has entered a building as a trespasser but with no particular intention, and, once inside decides to do unlawful damage to property within the building. Your advice to him should be to plead not guilty to a charge of burglary. This is because his actions fall within neither paragraph of the subsection even though his actions have produced the same result as behaviour which would lead to guilt (had he formed the intention to cause the damage before, rather than after entering the building). This conclusion may be hard for a layperson to understand but would be natural to any lawyer versed in statutory interpretation.

To adopt the same approach to following the Code may enable you to avoid successful disciplinary proceedings by the Bar Council. In other words, in so far as it acts in an analogous manner to a criminal statute, the Code may be treated in the same way. However, to approach the Code in this way could carry dangers for the reputation of the profession. Your interpretation of the Code should be informed by ethical values and where the Code permits a variety of responses your choice between them should be similarly informed.

An example of how the Code regulates your professional response arises from para 704:

> **704**   A barrister must not devise facts which will assist in advancing the lay client's case and must not draft any statement of case, witness statement, affidavit, notice of appeal or other document containing:
>
> …
>
>   (c) any allegation of fraud unless he has clear instructions to make such allegation and has before him reasonably credible material which as it stands establishes a prima facie case of fraud; …

The concept of 'reasonably credible material' inherently carries a degree of subjectivity. Suppose that you have been instructed by your lay client that the opponent has been perpetrating a fraud. It is not uncommon for hostility between the parties to lead to all sorts of allegations which are discovered later to be impossible of formal proof. That being the case it would be unwise to incorporate such an allegation into any draft on the client's assertion alone. What, however, if the client (who has behaved in a temperate manner throughout) tells you that the opposing party has admitted to committing fraud, but no other independent evidence is available? What if, in addition, the client is prepared to make a statement of truth in respect of this allegation? Would such a statement be 'reasonably credible material' given that it is in essence no more than the original assertion presented formally in a way which is admissible in court? Should you still insist on some independent evidence?

In practical terms you would doubtless advise your professional client to seek independent evidence to corroborate your lay client's oral evidence before settling a statement of case which contained an allegation of fraud. If it is not forthcoming, should you pursue the allegation? The only guidance the Code offers is that the material must be credible and establish a *prima facie* case. The assertion of an intemperate client would clearly be inadequate (it is the mischief the rule is designed to avoid). To rely on a statement of truth may be sufficient to avoid a finding of misconduct (although if there were no other evidence the client should be advised of the dangers of pressing the matter in court: a wasted costs order may loom). However, to refuse to incorporate such an allegation in those circumstances will upset your client, and is likely to upset them more if the allegations are in fact well-founded. You must not let your independence be compromised (para 307(a) and (c)) yet you should act on your client's behalf (para 303(a)).

Note that the House of Lords decision in *Medcalf v Weatherill and another* [2002] 3 WLR 172 (for details see **7.5.4.2**) while addressing this area, does not resolve this issue. If you check the specific guidance on this matter on the Bar Council website you will find:

The Professional Standards Committee (PSC) takes the view that there is no litmus test for determining whether it is proper to allege fraud. As Lord Bingham made clear: 'Council is bound to exercise an objective professional judgment whether it is in all circumstances proper to lend his name to the allegation'. That decision will depend on the individual facts of each case.

It should be noted that although paragraph 704 refers specifically to fraud, the same principle would apply to any other allegation of serious misconduct.

No doubt you should err on the side of caution and advise that further evidence should be obtained if possible, but it may not be available. Moreover, if, after settling the statement of case, it becomes clear that there is no credible evidence of fraud (for example, the opposing party may have made the admission to provoke a reaction or as an act of bravado) or if other facts come to light showing that the allegation of fraud has no prospect of success, you will no doubt recognise that the fraud allegation should no longer be pursued. It is submitted that the proper approach is not to seek a 'way around' the provisions of the Code, but to consider underlying values, so that your response is likely to assist to maintain the Bar's reputation as a thoroughly ethical profession. Fortunately, problems as awkward as this should not be a daily occurrence, and you should remember that advice will be available from your Head of Chambers or from the Bar Council. (The Professional Conduct Hotline is 020 7242 0082.)

An understanding of the underpinning values will give you a basis for deciding ethical questions beyond what the Code provides. Remember that behaviour prohibited by the Code is not made acceptable by a contrary underpinning value, but an underpinning value might validate conduct upon which the Code is silent or in circumstances which generate conflict between its provisions. Ultimately, where, having thought through matters in this degree of depth, you remain uncertain as to the proper way of proceeding, you should contact the Bar Council hotline available for advice in emergencies.

4.3 Underpinning values

Here is a number of values which may be said to underpin the Code of Practice. It is not intended to be exhaustive.

- Justice.
- Respect for the law.
- Client autonomy.
- Confidentiality.
- Honesty.

4.3.1 Conflict in underpinning values

Conflict between values is inherent in legal practice. Lord Reid makes this clear in his opinion in *Rondel v Worsley* [1969] 1 AC 191, 227:

> Every counsel has a duty to his client fearlessly to raise every issue, advance every argument and ask every question, however distasteful, which he thinks will help his client's case. But, as an officer of the court concerned with the administration of justice, he has an overriding duty to the court, to the standards of his profession, and to the public, which may and often does lead to a conflict with his client's wishes or what the client thinks are his personal wishes.

Consider a concrete situation. If your client in a criminal matter has provided you with information which is relevant (but adverse) to your case you will be faced with a conflict between maintaining confidentiality and not misleading the court. A perusal of the Code will throw up relevant provisions.

104   The general purpose of this Code is to provide the requirements for practice as a barrister and the rules and standards of conduct applicable to barristers which are appropriate in the interests of justice and in particular:

(a) in relation to barristers in independent practice to provide common and enforceable rules and standards which require them:

  (i)   to be completely independent in conduct and in professional standing as sole practitioners;

  (ii) to act only as consultants instructed by solicitors and other approved persons;

  (iii) to acknowledge a public obligation based on the paramount need for access to justice to act for any client in cases within their field of practice; . . .

301   A barrister must have regard to paragraph 104 and must not:

(a) engage in conduct whether in pursuit of his profession or otherwise which is:

  (i)   dishonest or otherwise discreditable to a barrister;

  (ii) prejudicial to the administration of justice; or

  (iii) likely to diminish public confidence in the legal profession or the administration of justice or otherwise bring the legal profession into disrepute; . . .

302   A barrister has an overriding duty to the Court to act with independence in the interests of justice: he must assist the Court in the administration of justice and must not deceive or knowingly or recklessly mislead the Court.

702   Whether or not the relation of counsel and client continues a barrister must preserve the confidentiality of the lay client's affairs and must not without the prior consent of the lay client or as permitted by law lend or reveal the contents of the papers in any instructions to or communicate to any third person (other than another barrister, a pupil . . . or any other person who needs to know it for the performance of their duties) information which has been entrusted to him in confidence or use such information to the lay client's detriment or to his own or another client's advantage.

708   A barrister when conducting proceedings in Court: . . .

(e) must not adduce evidence obtained otherwise than from or through the client or devise facts which will assist in advancing the lay client's case; . . .

These rules are helpful in identifying what is expected in relation to each of the underlying values. However, they provide little guidance as to how conflicts should be resolved. In fact, the conflict identified occurs so regularly in practice that a proper way of responding is well-established. You will not necessarily be required to withdraw unless your client wishes you to present information you now know to be incorrect. Your precise duties will depend on the nature of the information being withheld. This may range from a full confession to dishonesty in obtaining public funding or an indication of past offences of which the prosecution appears to be unaware. You will find detailed guidance as to how to respond ethically to these different situations at **7.2** below.

Note that further guidance on the preparation of witness statements is available on the Bar Council website. This is expressly described as applying to civil matters only as barristers do not draft witness statements in criminal cases. Thus you should note that striking a balance between different values might produce different results in the criminal and the civil context.

This itself throws up an important value, associated with client autonomy and justice. Our adversarial system of justice requires as close as possible an approach to equality of arms. The assumption is that representation by competent and qualified lawyers achieves that equality. In a civil matter the parties are to some extent equal (although one may be able to spend more money than the other in preparing the case). In a criminal matter, however, it is normal to find individuals (often impecunious and possibly facing loss of liberty) with all the forces and resources of a powerful state arranged against them. This goes some way to explaining:

- the cab rank rule, which requires a barrister to accept any case which is within his competence and ability to undertake (there are exceptions — see Part VI of the Code), and
- the lesser expectations to disclose adverse factual information in criminal, as opposed to civil matters (given that the task is for the prosecution to prove the case, not for the defendant to prove his innocence).

So your response to a clash of underlying values may need to differ depending on the context.

You may find yourself in a situation where you face such a clash of values or where you are challenged by a client holding different values to your own. Consider the following situations.

EXAMPLE

What if my client is impecunious and facing a wealthy opponent?

For example, you are acting *pro bono* for an unemployed client who claims to have been unfairly dismissed for fighting at work. Your professional client instructs you to contact the respondent's lawyers in order to seek a settlement. The evidence from a number of witnesses and from personnel records suggests that your client had, indeed, been fighting, had done so on many occasions, and was only dismissed after proper warnings had been given. In conference, however, your client continues to deny the allegation while offering no explanation for the evidence against him. You are confident that should the matter proceed to trial your client will lose. You are, however, aware that many cases can result in a technical finding of unfair dismissal for procedural failings, even if the compensation in such cases is likely to be minimal. Your lay client has indicated that he is willing to accept £2,000 in settlement. You recognise, moreover, that for the employer to defend the claim, should you make many demands on them for disclosure or further questions, will cost them over £2,000.

Should you contact the employer, pointing out that the hearing will be a long one and that you will be requiring considerable disclosure of documents and answers to detailed questions about personnel practices in the firm, suggesting that your client will withdraw the case if they pay £2,000 in settlement? To do so would promote the value of client autonomy and (by subverting the normal consequences of inequalities in wealth) promote a particular view of social justice.

Should you, instead, avoid putting that pressure on the employer when negotiating, recognising that this might make it less likely that the employer will settle for £2,000? To do so would promote the values of respect for the law and a particular (but different) perception of justice.

The Code does not prevent either course, provided you are acting on your client's instructions after giving proper advice. This is thus one example where your own values may have an impact on your choice of whether to use the 'we'll make this expensive for you' tactic.

What if my client is seeking to achieve, by instructing me, a goal which I regard as immoral?
For example, your clients, who are a couple seeking to have an exceptionally bright child, wish to carry out genetic checks to screen out any foetuses which appear not to be intelligent. You feel strongly that this is an abuse of the genetic research which has been done. Although the motive appears to be one which is forbidden under the relevant legislation you understand that similar checks (which are permitted) can indirectly provide information which would enable them to screen for intelligence.

Should you simply advise them that their proposed course of action would contravene the law and that they should not therefore attempt to pursue it? To do so may promote the value of (your particular view of) morality. This itself will be based on a value such as the integrity of the individual (in this case the unconceived child).

Should you, instead, indicate how they might achieve their goal without technically breaking the law? To do so would promote the value of client autonomy.

When considering the propriety of your response you must remember that your duty is to act for your client and you should not make moral judgements about your client's actions. You should also consider what your client needs to know in order to make a properly informed decision. These principles are addressed in the Code and clearly prioritise the value of client autonomy.

What if my client is seeking to achieve, by instructing me, a goal which involves a breach of the law?
For example, you are instructed by solicitors to advise a corporate client which wishes to reduce some of its production costs. The proposed savings will increase the risk of a release of toxic chemicals into a river. Such a release will constitute a breach of regulations designed to protect the environment and expose the client company to the risk of fines. However, you are aware that the local authority with responsibility for enforcing those regulations is extremely short of finance and is unable to make regular checks. A minor release is therefore unlikely to be noticed.

Should your advice be to explain the legal situation and simply point out that the proposed cost reductions place the company at risk of committing an illegal action for which they might suffer a penalty? To do so may promote the value of respect for the law.

Should your advice extend to your assessment of the very small risk of discovery? To do so may promote the value of client autonomy.

Does the principle indicated in the previous example (that you should not make moral judgements about your client's actions) apply equally here, when the proposed action involves your client committing a criminal offence? The Code indicates that you must do nothing dishonest or bring the profession into disrepute. Incitement to break the law clearly falls within that concept. You can therefore protect yourself from breach of the Code by giving clear advice not to break the law. However you may be doing that in the realistic knowledge that your client may well ignore you and break the law. Note that if this has occurred to you it is probably your own sensitivity to ethical issues that alerts you to the risk that this may have the effect of indirectly inciting a breach of the law.

You will see that none of these three examples produce a single, clearly correct answer. Regrettably, this may well arise in practice. I have my personal preferences as to the most appropriate response, but you may well take a different view. Any such difference will flow in part from the personal values that you or I espouse. For this reason we need to be aware of those values and how they impact on our responses when faced with ethical dilemmas (as we undoubtedly will be). At the same time it is important that we remember that we must not apply our personal values unrestrained. As barristers we are bound by the Code and that recognition may assist when you are faced with a conflict of potentially-applicable values. You cannot justify a departure from the clear requirements of the Code by pleading an inconsistent personal value, no matter how strongly you espouse it.

4.4 Role morality

One concept which may assist in resolving conflicts of this sort is that of role morality. A lawyer may be required to do something for a client which she could not morally justify doing for herself. That proposition may initially appear to be wrong, or at least counterintuitive. However, it is explained to a degree by the recognition that the basis of litigation in the UK is adversarialism. The lawyer is the skilled partisan advocate of the client and is (in theory) opposed by a similarly skilled partisan advocate for the opponent. The neutral decision-maker is neither lawyer but the tribunal.

This concept only works if the lawyer is genuinely partisan and the parties are equitably resourced. A client whose lawyer adopts a neutral role will be severely disadvantaged if opposed by a client whose lawyer adopts a partisan approach. In order to shoulder this burden properly lawyers may well have to seek to achieve conclusions of which they disapprove, or carry out actions which they would not carry out on their own behalf. To justify this, many have introduced the idea of 'role morality'. This concept prioritises the value of client autonomy and is the source of the cab-rank rule (see Code, para 601). Many lawyers regard it as enabling them to do for their clients what they would not do for themselves.

It may have surprising consequences. As Boon and Levin point out:

> Paradoxically, whilst lawyers are expected to act co-operatively, altruistically and ethically when dealing *with* their clients, they are expected to be unco-operative, selfish and possibly unethical in pursuing the objectives *of* their clients, assuming that this is what the client wishes. This creates considerable moral strain.

(Boon, A and Levin, J, *The Ethics and Conduct of Lawyers in England and Wales* (Oxford, Hart 1999) at 165)

That moral strain will alert you to the fact that while the concept of role morality may justify your doing for your client what you would not do for yourself, it does not give you guidance as to how far you can go. Take an example.

It may well be that if you clearly owed a debt you would not take advantage of the limitation provisions to evade it. However, would you apply the same moral judgement if it were your client who owed the debt? Suppose, for example, your client is very short of money and had forgotten the debt, which is owed to a large corporation? Suppose, instead, your client is the large corporation and the person owed the debt is impecunious?

Your view may be identical in those two situations or you may regard their relative wealth as a key issue. That is a matter for you. However, identifying the issue should make it clear that role morality, while potentially justifying actions which you would feel uncomfortable about on your own behalf, does not resolve questions about whether a particular course of action is ethically acceptable. For that, once again, you need to follow the Code and, where necessary, consider your underlying values.

The underpinning principle here is client autonomy. The Code permits you to do whatever your client wants provided that it is not illegal, you are not dishonest and you give the court the full benefit of your knowledge of the law, whether helpful to your case or not. Equally, you must provide your client with advice that helps them to take an informed decision as to whether to pursue a case or not. It would be improper (as with the second example at **4.3.1**) to prioritise your views over those of your client. There is nothing to stop you identifying ethical considerations to your client, but the decision must remain theirs.

The adversarial nature of the UK legal system may be some justification for a barrister behaving differently in professional and personal contexts, but it also carries its own limits to professional behaviour. Because (unlike in an inquisitorial system) the court does not have the resources to explore the truth for itself, it relies on the honesty of advocates and their ability to research the law fully. This is the source of the requirements not to mislead the court and to cite authorities that go against your client's interests. This should identify two insights:

(a) A claim to role morality does not justify all behaviour. A balance between conflicting values must still be maintained. This is clear from the Marre Report (para 6.1):

> The client is frequently acting under physical, emotional or financial difficulties and may well wish to take every step he can, whether legal or extra-legal, to gain advantage over the other party. In this situation the lawyer has a special duty and responsibility to advise his client as to the legal and ethical standards which should be observed and not to participate in any deception or sharp practice.

(Lady Marre, CBE, *A Time for Change: Report of the Committee on the Future of the Legal Profession* (General Council of the Bar and Council of the Law Society, London 1998))

This is helpful guidance, but leaves much to the individual lawyer.

(b) No advocate will be able to meet the standards expected unless the requisite knowledge, understanding and skills have been mastered. The knowledge, understanding and skills that you have acquired in your undergraduate study and which you are now developing on your Bar Vocational Course are central to your effectively meeting the demands of an adversarial system. Competence itself is an ethical issue.

For further discussions of role morality, see Boon, A and Levin, J, *The Ethics and Conduct of Lawyers in England and Wales* (Oxford, Hart 1999) at 195–198 and Nicolson, D and Webb, J, *Professional Ethics: Critical Interrogations* (Oxford, OUP 1999) at 169–171.

4.5 Ethical behaviour and self-interest

It is often said that ethical behaviour is in the individual lawyer's best interest because 'the Bar is a small profession and your reputation will quickly get around'. Barely hidden behind this assertion is the suggestion that if you acquire a reputation for poor ethical standards opponents will not trust you and you will find it increasingly difficult to meet your clients' needs. This may be true. However, it is important to recognise that ethics and self-interest should not be equated.

Some help may be available from the recognition that taking a long-term view of self-interest is highly likely to be an ethically safer approach than taking a short-term view. Thus, an approach which ensures that you have a reputation for honesty is likely to enable you to represent many future clients in negotiation. It is also therefore likely to enhance your long-term income. Willingness to deceive an opponent may achieve something your current client values but will inhibit your ability to come to desirable solutions for future clients. Not only would this inhibit long-term income, it would involve a breach of the Code (para 301(a)).

One other aspect of self-interest is worth addressing here. You have an interest in your profession continuing to be perceived as in good ethical standing. If you comply with the provisions of the Code this will preserve you from the risk of disciplinary proceedings. However, where the Code provides a framework within which different courses of action are permitted you should be alert to maintain the highest possible ethical standards.

This insight helps us to identify those aspects of self-interest which will assist us to maintain high ethical standards, but relying on self-interest is altogether insufficient. It ignores most of the underpinning values which we have identified earlier and leaves the individual lawyer without ethical guidance. Thus it remains necessary to comply with the requirements of the Code and to consider its underpinning values in those situations where conflicts nevertheless arise.

4.6 The lawyer joke again

So which of the three was acting most ethically? I have no problem with the layperson's response and am sufficiently ignorant to accept that there may be justification for the accountant's response. However, to judge the lawyer I need to go back to my core values again. If I prioritise client autonomy this lawyer may be responding perfectly correctly. There are few situations in reality where one simple answer is the only one available. The lawyer here is seeking the client's instructions as to what the desired outcome is. It may be that that outcome is not legally available, in which case the lawyer should advise the client to that effect. It may be readily available, in which case the lawyer is in the fortunate position of giving the client good news. It is just as likely, however, that the answer is somewhere between the two. How far should you go to achieve the client's desired result? That is a matter of your professional responsibility. The Code of Conduct is your guide ('a barrister must not . . . compromise his professional standards in order to please his client the Court or a third party' — Code, para 307(c)) which makes it clear that you should never allow your personal values to override the requirements of the Code. Within the boundaries provided by the Code, however, the final decision is yours.

Court etiquette

5.1 Introduction

Each time you appear in court you are on a public stage, in full view of the judge, the client and, usually, the public at large. How you appear and conduct yourself in front of that audience is of great importance if you are to do the job of a barrister properly. If you are discourteous, inappropriately dressed or do not behave in the way that you ought to, you risk alienating the tribunal you are seeking to persuade. Remember that as a barrister you are always appearing on behalf of someone other than yourself: unfavourable views formed about you by the tribunal because of an unprofessional manner may rebound onto your client. Some of the requirements of the etiquette that you must observe are to be found in written sources, such as the Code of Conduct, or the occasional Practice Direction (e.g, *Practice Direction (Court Dress) (No. 2)* [1995] 1 WLR 648), but others have been established through custom, tradition and commonsense.

5.2 Courtesy

It should go without saying that in every sphere of practice you ought to be courteous, and this is reinforced by the Code of Conduct, which states '[a] barrister must at all times be courteous to the Court and to all those with whom he has professional dealings' (para 5.5 of the Written Standards for the Conduct of Professional Work in Section 3, Miscellaneous Guidance). You are, of course, required by the Code of Conduct to '. . . promote and protect fearlessly and by all proper and lawful means the client's best interests and do so without regard to [your] own interests or to any consequences to [yourself] or to any other person . . .' (para 303(a)), but this does not give you *carte blanche* to be as rude as you like to judges, witnesses or your opposing counsel. Ultimately, discourtesy by counsel in court could amount to a contempt.

5.3 Dress in court

The Code of Conduct requires that '. . . a barrister's personal appearance should be decorous, and his dress, when robes are worn, should be compatible with them.' (para 5.12 of the Written Standards for the Conduct of Professional Work in Section 3, Miscellaneous

Guidance). In practice, this means that you should dress conservatively. A courtroom is not the place to make an individual fashion statement: you may like wearing paisley waistcoats and bright orange socks, but save that for your own time. As a barrister you are a professional: dress like one. Dressing conservatively means, amongst other things:

(a) Men should wear a suit (the traditional black jacket and grey striped trousers is an alternative, although less common now amongst younger members of the Bar). Do not wear blazers or linen jackets in court, even in hot weather. Either single or double breasted suits are acceptable, but a waistcoat should be worn if the former is chosen. Suits and dresses should be dark in colour, ie, black, dark navy or grey, and of a traditional cut. In May 1995 the then Lord Chief Justice, Lord Taylor of Gosforth, decided that it was perfectly acceptable for women to wear trousers when appearing in court. These should be worn as part of a trouser suit.

(b) Dresses or blouses should be long sleeved and high to the neck, even in warmer weather.

(c) Shirts or blouses should be predominantly white; collars should be white. For men (when robes are worn) a separate wing collar is the norm: avoid, as has been seen in court, a dress evening shirt.

(d) Shoes should be black; avoid wearing boots in court.

(e) Jewellery should be discreet: avoid studs and rings through places other than ears. Men should avoid wearing an ear-ring in court.

(f) When a wig is worn, wear it so that it covers your hair as far as possible; avoid fringes showing at the front, and keep long hair neatly tied back.

The Professional Conduct Committee of the Bar Council has been asked about the propriety of a barrister who customarily wears a turban to do so in place of a wig. The Committee was of the view that such matters were properly determined by the court concerned rather than the committee itself. However, it expressed the view that it is entirely reasonable for a barrister who customarily wears a turban to do so in court in place of a wig.

5.4 Robes

For counsel, being robed means wearing wig, gown, and bands. You will be robed when you appear in open court in County Courts, the Crown Court, the High Court, the Court of Appeal, and the House of Lords.

It is unnecessary to robe when you appear before a judge in private, or generally in chambers or before a magistrates' court, tribunal or arbitrators.

It is generally unnecessary to robe when you appear before a Master or district judge, whether sitting in open court or in private. If, however, the district judge is sitting in robes in open court it is desirable that you also appear robed. For this reason it is always advisable, though rather inconvenient, to take your robes to court in case the district judge before whom you are appearing on a private matter chooses to take the matter robed and in open court.

Always turn up to your chambers prepared to appear in court in robes, even if you were planning a day on papers, ie, wear a suit, have your robes with you and a collarless shirt to hand. It is not at all unusual for you to arrive at chambers to be told by your clerk that you are in open court on an urgent matter, when you thought you were going to have a paper-work day!

5.5 Customs

Much of court etiquette is derived from custom. Some of the more common customs are:

(a) Do not move or speak whilst a witness is being sworn; you should stay completely still and silent whilst this is being done, even if you are not involved in the case.

(b) Do not enter or leave court whilst a verdict is being taken, or when a defendant is being sentenced.

(c) When the judge enters the courtroom you must stand; he or she will normally bow to counsel before being seated — you should return the bow. You should also bow to the judge when leaving court, and, if you have just come in to a court when the judge is already sitting, as you sit down.

(d) Do not stare (indeed try not to look) at members of a jury when they come into court to deliver their verdict. At this stage they have made their decision: you can no longer influence them one way or the other, and there is no reason why you should make them feel uncomfortable by trying to guess their verdict.

(e) You should not show your emotions at a verdict, or a judge's ruling.

(f) By convention, briefcases are not usually carried by counsel when robed. Do not take a bag into court (other than a handbag). If you have to, for whatever reason, ensure it is concealed as far as possible. Similarly, newspapers and other miscellaneous items should be kept from the view of the tribunal you are before.

(g) There is a courtesy known as 'dressing the judge' which should be observed. A judge in robes should never be left without a member of the Bar being in court, unless the judge has indicated that he or she can leave. If your case is over, and you are the only barrister in court, do not leave unless the judge has given such an indication. In virtually every case the judge will so indicate.

(h) If your opponent rises to object, sit down. Two barristers should never be on their feet at the same time unless being addressed directly by the judge.

(i) Sometimes you will go into court where leading counsel will be appearing; by convention junior barristers sit in the row behind leading counsel, rather than the same one. Constraints of space sometimes mean that this is not always observed.

In addition to the above customs there are also a number of less common situations where there is still an element of custom and etiquette, eg, on the death of a judge, it will usually fall to the most senior member of the Bar present in the robing room that day to perform some form of valediction before the business of the court is resumed.

5.6 Modes of address

Reference should be made to the *Advocacy Manual* which contains a guide to the appropriate modes of addressing the court and the use of the correct form of address.

5.7 Problems

(1) You are instructed to represent the defendant in a High Court case at 10.30 am, at the Royal Courts of Justice. You sleep through your alarm clock and, to your horror, wake up at 10 am. The Court is an hour's journey from your home. What do you do?

(2) You are the junior pupil in chambers. At 4.30 pm on Thursday your clerk tells you that you have two cases listed at Exeter Crown Court for the following day: one at 10 am in court one, and one at 10.30 am, in court two, and that no one else in chambers is available to do either of them. At 10.35 am you are still conducting the case in court one, when you are passed a note by the usher from court two that that court has convened and that the judge is waiting for you and furious to know that you are in a different court. What do you do?

Professional misconduct: the complaints procedure

6.1 General

As part of its regulatory role, the Bar Council has a duty to investigate and, where appropriate, prosecute complaints against barristers. The procedures that it follows in doing so are laid down, or repeated, in the Code of Conduct.

(a) The Complaints Rules — Annexe J.

(b) Disciplinary Tribunal Regulations — Annexe K.

(c) Hearings before the Visitors Rules — Annexe M.

(d) Summary Procedure Rules — Annexe L.

(e) Adjudication Panel and Appeals Rules — Annexe P.

The structure of the system is outlined in the diagram at **6.15** below. There are two important figures in the procedure: the independent Complaints Commissioner and the Professional Conduct and Complaints Committee (PCC).

6.2 The Complaints Commissioner

The Complaints Commissioner is responsible for overseeing the investigation of complaints against barristers. The Commissioner is neither a barrister nor a solicitor and has power to dismiss complaints which are clearly unmeritorious without referring them to the PCC. In addition, the Commissioner advises the PCC about issues of inadequate professional services and compensation and plays an important role in presenting the lay client's perspective.

6.3 Professional conduct and Complaints Committee (PCC)

Under the present system, the PCC comprises around 40 members of the Bar, two lay members (chosen by rota from a panel of lay representatives appointed by the Complaints

Commissioner) and the Chairman and Vice-Chairman of the PSC who are members ex-officio.

Apart from dealing with complaints, the PCC also deals with applications and queries from members of the Bar concerning Code of Conduct matters, in so far as these concern the exercise of discretion or questions of interpretation.

6.4   The nature of complaints

Under the present system about 500 complaints are received each year from a wide variety of complainants including members of the lay public, prisoners, judges, solicitors and other members of the Bar. In addition, the Bar Council raises approximately 200 complaints itself against its members for offences such as failure to have insurance or a practising certificate. Of the external complaints, about 60% are dismissed by the Commissioner. The remainder are considered by the PCC.

The nature of complaints can vary widely but the most common, in descending order of frequency, are probably as follows:

(a) Dissatisfied lay clients (especially prisoners) alleging:
  (i)   incompetence and/or negligence;
  (ii) undue pressure to accept a settlement or to plead guilty;
  (iii) poor advocacy, style or tactics.
(b) Misbehaviour in court, especially rudeness to other counsel or to the judge and failure to accept the latter's rulings.
(c) Failure to pay debts. These are normally accepted as being within the Committee's jurisdiction only if use of the status of barrister or a degree of moral turpitude is involved.
(d) Maladministration of, or misbehaviour in, chambers.
(e) Reports of driving, public order or criminal convictions. The last of these almost invariably result in reference to a disciplinary tribunal, often with the most severe consequences.

6.5   Present complaints procedure

When a complaint has been received (other than one made by the Bar Council of its own motion) it is referred to the Complaints Commissioner who will give initial instructions on how the complaint should be investigated. In a relatively small number of cases it is likely that it will be obvious that the complaint as it stands shows no evidence of misconduct or of inadequate professional service. In such cases the Commissioner is able to dismiss the complaint immediately. In other cases, the matter may be suitable for conciliation or should be adjourned (for example because an appeal is pending). In the majority of cases, however, the Commissioner will seek further information and at this stage the comments of the barrister concerned with the complaint will be sought.

It is likely that the Commissioner will also approach the instructing solicitor (if there is one) for comments, together with other relevant witnesses at the same time. All comments are then sent to the complainant for further comments. Once these have been received the papers are sent to the Commissioner for further consideration.

If, having considered the papers, the Commissioner is satisfied that there is no *prima facie* evidence of professional misconduct or of inadequate professional service on the barrister's part, the complaint may be dismissed. Otherwise, it will be referred to the PCC. A member of the PCC (a 'sponsor member') will be asked to examine the file and prepare a report on the complaint for the PCC to consider.

The report will summarise the background, the detailed nature of the complaint and the arguments for and against, and will recommend a decision. This is tabled at the first available Committee meeting which the Sponsor Member can attend when the complaint is discussed in full and a decision is reached.

The primary purpose of consideration by the PCC is to determine whether a *prima facie* case of misconduct or inadequate professional services has been disclosed. The Committee considers only documentary evidence and none of the parties attend. Having considered the evidence, the PCC may:

(a) with the agreement of the two lay representatives who must be in attendance at each meeting, dismiss the complaint or determine that no further action should be taken; or,

(b) adjourn the matter for further enquiries; or,

(c) require counsel to attend on the Chairman of the PCC or other person to receive advice as to his future conduct or to advise the barrister in writing as to his future conduct (this does *not* amount to a finding of professional misconduct);

(d) find a *prima facie* case of inadequate professional service, in which case the matter will be referred to an adjudication panel;

(e) find a *prima facie* case of professional misconduct (whether with or without inadequate professional service) whereupon, depending upon the seriousness of the matter and whether there is a significant dispute as to facts, the PCC may refer the matter to one of an informal hearing, a summary procedure panel or a disciplinary tribunal.

The complainant is informed of the Committee's decision and, if it is dismissed, if no further action is taken or if the matter is dealt with informally, is told the outline reasons for the Committee's decision and, if appropriate, the nature of the advice given.

6.6 Adjudication Panels

Adjudication Panels exist to consider complaints where the PCC has only found that there is a *prima facie* case of inadequate professional service. This is defined as:

... such conduct towards the lay client (or in the case of an employed barrister the person to whom he has supplied the professional service in question) or performance of professional service for that client which falls significantly short of that which is to be reasonably expected of a barrister in all the circumstances.

Their procedures are governed by the Adjudication Panel and Appeals Rules. The Panel may:

- dismiss the complaint;
- require the barrister to apologise to the lay client;
- require the barrister to repay or reduce the fee;
- require the barrister to pay compensation up to £5,000 to the lay client.

A finding of inadequate professional service may only be made where the person making the complaint is the lay client or their representative.

Adjudication Panels normally sit in private and reach their decisions on the papers in front of them. Both the complainant and barrister will have been invited to make further representations about the matter in writing and, in particular, any loss that has been suffered. A barrister may attend the panel and/or be represented there if he or she wishes.

6.7 Informal hearings

Where the PCC considers that there is a *prima facie* case of misconduct but that it is relatively trivial, it may refer the matter to a panel comprising three barristers (usually chaired by a QC) sitting with a lay representative. If the panel finds either misconduct or inadequate professional services to have been established, it may advise as to future conduct or reprimand the barrister. A panel making a finding of inadequate professional service may order the same remedies as an Adjudication Panel.

6.8 Summary hearings

Summary hearings are held under the authority of Summary Procedure Rules. Panels, each consisting of a silk as chairman, at least one and up to two lay representatives, and at least one and up to three barristers. Procedure is informal. Proceedings are based on an agreed statement of facts, although witnesses can, with the prior permission of the chairman of the panel, be heard. Hearings may be held in public or, if the barrister wishes and the chairman of the tribunal consents, in private. Both the defendant and the PCC can be represented by counsel (although the latter is unusual) and evidence, where applicable, is taken on oath.

6.9 Tribunals

Disciplinary tribunals are held under the authority of and are organised by the Council of the Inns of Court and consist of a Chairman (a High Court or Circuit judge) together with two practising members of the Bar and two lay representatives. Both oral and documentary evidence is taken. Hearings are normally held in public. Both the defendant and the PCC (as prosecuting authority) are represented by counsel and evidence is taken, where appropriate, on oath.

6.10 Penalties

If charges of professional misconduct are found proved, a summary hearing or a tribunal may sentence a barrister to be:

(a) disbarred (disciplinary tribunals only);

(b) suspended from practice for a prescribed period, with or without conditions (for three months only in the case of a summary hearing);

(c) ordered to pay a fine to the Bar Council of up to £5,000 (£500 in the case of summary hearings);

(d) ordered to forgo or repay fees;

(e) reprimanded;

(f) permanently or temporarily excluded from undertaking publicly-funded work;

(g) advised as to his or her future conduct.

A barrister may be reprimanded or be given advice as to his or her future conduct by the tribunal or summary hearing panel itself, or by attendance on a nominated person.

Summary Hearings and Disciplinary Tribunals may also make findings of inadequate professional service and order the same remedies as an Adjudication Panel.

6.11 Appeals

Findings of professional misconduct and subsequent sentences by summary hearings and disciplinary tribunals are subject to appeal under the Hearings Before the Visitors Rules 2002. Findings of inadequate professional service may be appealed to an Appeals Panel under the Adjudication Panel and Appeal Rules. The Bar Council may appeal against a lenient sentence of a disciplinary tribunal.

6.12 Publication of findings and sentence

The proceedings of, and decisions by, the PCC, informal hearings or adjudication panels are not published unless the barrister concerned so requests. All other findings of professional misconduct are published unless the tribunal or summary hearing panel decides otherwise.

6.13 Conciliation

In some cases, where it is clear to the Commissioner that misconduct is not involved, the Commissioner may consider that it is most appropriate for the barrister to attempt some informal conciliation with the complainant. This may arise, for example, in cases where it is clear that the complainant simply has not understood what has gone on or where some minor problem has arisen over delay or confusion in clerking which is not serious enough to amount to misconduct. It is often most satisfactory if such difficulties can be resolved between the parties rather than by formal findings and an investigation. It should be stressed, however, that in suggesting this the Commissioner has not reached any formal view as to whether an issue of inadequate professional service is involved.

In these circumstances, the Commissioner will suggest that the barrister should approach the complainant to see whether it is possible to resolve the difficulties informally. It is up to the barrister to decide what response to this is appropriate. It may, for example, be reasonable to offer some sort of explanation or financial compensation or to refer the matter to a Chambers complaints procedure (if one exists). It is equally open to the barrister to make no response at all but if it is not possible to resolve the dispute, the complainant may return the matter to the Bar Council for a formal investigation.

6.14 Legal Services Ombudsman

The Legal Services Ombudsman, who is neither a barrister nor a solicitor, is appointed under the Courts and Legal Services Act 1990 to oversee the handling of complaints against members of the legal professions. If complainants are dissatisfied with the way their complaints have been dealt with, they have the right to request the Ombudsman to examine the PCC's treatment of the complaint and decide whether it was investigated fully and fairly. The Ombudsman then asks to see the PCC's file. If, after considering the matter, the Ombudsman thinks the complaint was not dealt with properly, the Ombudsman can recommend or require further action including, in certain circumstances, reconsideration of the matter by the PCC or the payment of compensation by the Bar Council and/or by the barrister(s) concerned.

Complaints have to be referred to the Legal Services Ombudsman within three months of the letter notifying the complainant of the PCC's decision. The Ombudsman has no power to investigate the substance of a complaint that has been decided by a court or by a disciplinary tribunal or where an appeal is being, or could still be, made against the PCC's decision though the Ombudsman may look at the Bar Council's handling of the matter. He or she will also not normally intervene while the PCC is still investigating the matter and will in fact only do so if there appears to have been unreasonable delay or if other strong reasons exist.

6.15 Complaints system structure

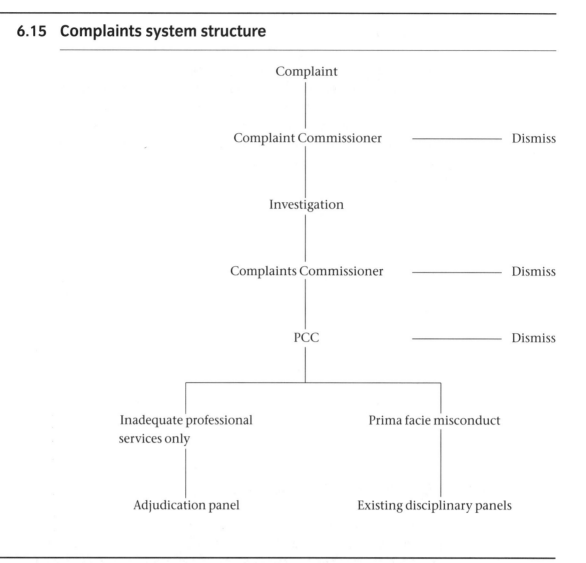

6.16 Advice to counsel who are the subject of a complaint

The number of complaints received by the Bar Council from lay clients and others has increased steadily over the last ten years and it is becoming increasingly likely that, at one stage or another, a barrister, particularly if he or she specialises in criminal or family work, will be required to respond to a complaint. Counsel will normally be informed of this in a letter from the Bar Council enclosing a copy of the material sent by the complainant to the Bar Council. That letter will indicate that counsel's comments are required within three weeks of its date.

It is worth making clear that, at this stage, the Bar Council or the Commissioner has not taken any view on the merits of the complaint. The majority of complaints are dismissed but in many cases the complainant will not have supplied sufficient information to allow the Commissioner to deal with the matter without seeking counsel's comments. The Legal Services Ombudsman oversees the working of the system and has power to refer matters back to the PCC for reconsideration. For this reason it is generally safer to seek counsel's comments where there may be any doubt about a particular complaint. Counsel should feel free to contact the Secretariat to discuss the handling of the complaint, the procedure generally or to seek advice. Clearly the Secretariat cannot advise on whether there is or is not a *prima facie* case of misconduct and cannot give a barrister advice on how to present his or her case. That said, the following questions arise frequently.

6.16.1   I am in a long case and cannot prepare my response adequately in time

The Secretariat is usually able to agree reasonable extensions for good reasons over the telephone. Generally it is most important that a barrister should at least make contact with the Secretariat even if he or she is not able to produce a full response by the deadline. Barristers should make every effort to produce their response as soon as is reasonably possible. The PCC can and does take action against barristers who are unreasonably dilatory in preparing their replies.

6.16.2   This matter took place many months ago and I have little recollection of the case

There is no reason why counsel cannot approach his or her instructing solicitors for a copy of the original instructions in the case and such other details as he or she may need in order to refresh his or her memory. It is certainly open to him or her to seek an extension of time in order to obtain such documentation.

6.16.3   May I approach solicitors and other witnesses for their views?

There is no reason why counsel should not approach instructing solicitors, judges, etc to provide statements or other information in support of counsel.

6.16.4   The client has issued/is likely to issue proceedings against me in negligence

Counsel should seek the advice of the BMIF on how to deal with the complaint. Normally consideration of such a complaint is adjourned until the matter has been considered by the civil courts. In any case if, on the advice of your insurers or for reasons of professional privilege, it is inappropriate for certain matters to be sent to the complainant which, nevertheless, it would be helpful for the Commissioner or the Committee to see, such material can be withheld from the complainant. If this is the case, counsel should make it clear which parts of the response should not be sent to the complainant.

6.16.5   What should I say in my response?

The content of the response to the complaint is very much a matter for the individual barrister to consider. There is nothing to stop him or her seeking advice from other colleagues or his or her head of chambers or a member of the Barristers' Complaints Advisory Service as to his or her reply. A good rule is to address specific allegations but not include comment or material 'just in case'. Simply refer to the further details or evidence which is available and can be supplied if required.

6.16.6   How will it affect my application for judicial appointment?

A complaint which has been dismissed is not at present required to be mentioned to the Department for Constitutional Affairs (DCA) in connection with any application for judicial appointment and the Bar Council will not disclose such a complaint, though the barrister may have to do so. The Bar Council will, however, disclose any finding of professional misconduct or any unresolved complaint. The exact effect of such disclosure is for the DCA to consider and will clearly depend on the circumstances of each case. It may be worth noting, however, that a finding of professional misconduct by one of the informal panels has not proved an insuperable barrier to preferment in the past.

6.16.7   Should I be represented at tribunals or panel hearings?

Barristers are almost invariably represented before disciplinary tribunals and may approach other counsel direct in order to be so represented. There is a long tradition at the Bar of very senior silks agreeing to act for no fee in such cases. It is, however, in each case, a matter for the individual concerned as to whom he or she seeks to approach and whether he or she needs to instruct solicitors on these matters. If a barrister has difficulty finding suitable counsel, then the Secretariat is usually able to assist. The individual should bear in mind that he or she will not always get his or her costs back even after a successful defence at a tribunal. Representation in front of panels and summary hearings is less common. There is, however, nothing to prevent a barrister from being represented if he or she wishes.

6.16.8   Is there any organisation that can help me?

The Bar Council recently established the Barristers' Complaints Advisory Service (BCAS) which consists of about 70 barristers of all levels of seniority and types of practice who are prepared to advise barristers on how to deal with complaints. A list of members and details of the scheme are included in the material sent to chambers when they are asked for comments on complaints. The London Common Law and Commercial Bar Association operates a similar scheme.

6.17   Legal Services Ombudsman: recommendations for compensation

As has been explained, the Ombudsman has power to consider the decisions of the Commissioner and the PCC and, on occasion, to recommend or require that the barrister concerned pay compensation direct to the lay client. The Bar Council is consulted about such recommendations but it is not its normal policy to make representations about the awards, unless those awards appear to it to be unreasonable. In dealing with the Ombudsman, barristers are recommended to contact the BMIF about any recommendations or requirements that they pay compensation.

6.18   Interim suspension and fitness to practise

Additionally, the Bar Council has rules to deal with cases where a barrister has been charged or convicted of a serious criminal offence or is medically unfit to practise. These rules essentially allow the Bar Council to suspend a barrister from practice pending a final decision on his or her future.

The provisions are contained at para 905(c) which requires a barrister to report to the Bar Council if he or she is charged with a serious criminal offence (as defined in s 116 of the Police and Criminal Evidence Act 1984) or a relevant criminal offence (which covers everything apart from fixed penalty or parking offences). Barristers who report themselves under these provisions will be considered under the Interim Suspension Rules in Annex N to the Code of Conduct. These effectively give the Bar Council power to suspend a barrister until the matter is dealt with by a disciplinary tribunal. It was thought inappropriate for members of the Bar to be able to continue practising while serious charges or convictions which might call into question their suitability to be barristers were over their heads. The rules empower the Bar Council to set early dates for hearings and to enable the barrister concerned to make appropriate representations.

The Fitness to Practice Rules are used where it comes to the attention of the Bar Council that a barrister may be unfit for medical reasons to practise. Essentially, the rules allow the Bar Council to require a barrister to attend on their appointed medical adviser for an examination. On receipt of a report from the medical adviser the panel can consider whether a barrister is unfit to practise by reason of medical incapacity (including addiction) and that a suspension is necessary for the protection of the public. The rules can be found at Annex O to the Code of Conduct.

7

The BVC, practice and professional conduct

7.1 General introduction

This chapter will focus on professional conduct problems pertinent to the key skills you will undertake during the Bar Vocational Course. It therefore concentrates on the following assessment areas: conference, advocacy, negotiation, opinion writing and drafting.

Undoubtedly the issues discussed will arise in practice. A sound understanding of these areas will ensure that when you are conducting a case you can identify these professional conduct points and, as a result, because you will be familiar with the fundamental tenets of the Code and of relevant statutory law (ref. the Proceeds of Crime Act 2002), the matters can be properly dealt with at the earliest opportunity, no matter in what context the problem arises.

All the contributors to this chapter are experienced lecturers, academic authors and subject co-ordinators at the ICSL and as such, are not only drawing on their own experiences of practice in these areas, but upon the types of professional conduct points which you will inevitably be examined upon as you complete your skills assessments. Consequently, it is particularly useful not only to use this chapter as a central source of reference for professional conduct difficulties, but also as you go through the BVC to take a note of your approach to the areas which have arisen in your small group discussions. You will then be in a position, as the course progresses, to check upon your development in handling these areas and how it compares to the advice set out below.

7.2 Conference skills

Conferences come in a variety of forms, most often involving the lay client, with or without the professional client in attendance. In some cases, for example, when you are prosecuting on behalf of a body such as the CPS, Serious Fraud Office or Customs and Excise, your conference may involve a number of other people. It would not be unusual, for example, to have a conference involving Crown Prosecutors, police officers and forensic scientists in a serious criminal case. At the other end of the range, you may be sent to the magistrates' court with little information and have to deal with finding your lay client and maybe even taking instructions through a wicket in a cell door or while standing in a corridor.

As stated in the *Conference Skills Manual*, these problems often arise without warning and in situations where you cannot readily seek advice. This means that you have to have a sound understanding of the principles which guide a barrister in practice, as well as the spirit of the Code. There are common duties which apply in all of these situations and they are discussed below.

7.2.1   Instructions from your lay client

With limited exceptions, the instructions that you receive from your lay client are to be treated in the strictest confidence. The Code states:

702 Whether or not the relation of counsel and client continues a barrister must preserve the confidentiality of the lay client's affairs and must not without the prior consent of the lay client or as permitted by law lend or reveal the contents of the papers in any instructions to or communicate to any third person (other than another barrister, a pupil ... or any other person who needs to know it for the performance of their duties) information which has been entrusted to him in confidence or use such information to the lay client's detriment or to his own or another client's advantage.

Clearly, you will expect to be able to use your client's instructions to cross-examine, draft statements of case or even draft witness statements. This will necessarily involve disclosing those instructions and the client will have given you permission to do so. A problem may, however, arise when the client makes a disclosure to you in conference, which he or she does not want to have revealed. A number of common disclosures are considered below.

7.2.2   Whether to disclose?

7.2.2.1   Disclosure to the National Criminal Intelligence Service (NCIS) under the Proceeds of Crime Act 2002 (POCA).

In practice you must be aware of how the POCA 2002 impacts on your disclosure obligations to NCIS, when as counsel you are concerned in an arrangement which you know or suspect relates to the proceeds of crime. Further, since 1 March 2004 barristers have been included in the 'regulated sector' by virtue of the Money Laundering Regulations 2003. **Chapter 8** considers these issues, with which you must be fully familiar.

7.2.2.2   Confessions

Every barrister has been asked by someone 'how can you represent someone when you know that they are guilty?' The answer that you may have given is that you are not the judge or a juror and if your client says that he or she is not guilty then those are the instructions you follow in presenting his or her case. So far so good. But what happens if the client actually tells you that he or she did commit the offence?

Using a criminal case as an example and assuming that the client's instructions to date have been that he or she wants to plead not guilty, what do you do when the client appears to admit to you in conference that he or she did commit the offence? In the first place do not panic. Recognise that there is a potential problem and continue your questioning to explore exactly what the client is saying—he or she is not a lawyer and may not appreciate what defences are avilable. If your questioning reveals that, without doubt, the client has told you that he or she does not have a defence, then you will need to advise on this clearly and advise him or her that the best course of action would be to plead guilty and make the most of the mitigation.

If the client tells you that, nonetheless, he or she wishes to continue to plead not guilty, you will need to consider your duty to the court. The Code expresses it as follows:

302 A barrister has an overriding duty to the Court to act with independence in the interests of justice: he must assist the Court in the administration of justice and must not deceive or knowingly or recklessly mislead the Court.

You may not make representations to the court that you know to be untrue — this would involve you in misleading the court. You will need to explain this to the client. He or she may well be concerned that this 'overriding' duty means that you will have to reveal his or her guilt to the court. You may well be concerned that your duty to the court appears to clash with your duty of confidentiality to your client.

The correct approach is that, first, you cannot reveal the client's instructions without his or her permission. However, you equally cannot put forward any positive case that he or she is not guilty as this would be knowingly misleading the court. You may, however, still test the prosecution evidence in cross-examination. This means that you can explore with a witness how reliable his or her evidence is, but you cannot put any positive case to him or her on behalf of your client. For example, if the issue were identification you might well question a witness about the conditions in which the identification was made, but if your instructions are that the identification was correct then you cannot put to the witness that he or she was mistaken in that identification. Practically, it makes it extremely difficult to run a successful case or to make any clear closing speech. You will have to explain all of this to the client and also remind him or her of the potential advantages of pleading guilty in terms of sentencing, reiterating your advice to plead guilty. If the client chooses to ignore that advice, as he or she is entitled to do, you may be wise to have the client endorse your brief to say that you have advised him or her of the consequences of his or her choice.

7.2.2.3 Information damaging to your client's case

Your lay client may reveal information in conference, which would be damaging to his or her case. For example, if the client discloses that he or she has previous convictions which the CPS do not seem to know about and wants to keep those secret at trial. In such a situation, you will advise the client that you have a duty of confidentiality and that, without his or her express permission, you cannot disclose the previous convictions to the court. However, you will also remind yourself that you have a duty not to mislead the court. While you do not have to volunteer information damaging to your client's case, if the judge were to ask you, for instance, whether your client wanted a good character direction in the summing up then you would be in an uncomfortable position.

In your conference, you will have to advise your client that this may happen and will need to ask whether he or she will allow you to disclose the previous convictions. If he or she says no, then when you are in court you will simply have to tell the judge that you are unable to answer any such direct question. The judge and prosecutor will easily work out why that is and the prosecutor will probably take the opportunity to have the client's record re-checked by police. You will certainly not get a good character direction. The effect, therefore, is the same as if you had revealed the previous convictions — but without the credit to your client of 'coming clean'. You should advise of this in your conference and may suggest that he or she would gain credit for being so honest.

The Bar Council has offered guidance to barristers on what they can and cannot say in such situations. The full text is available on the Bar Council website (www.barcouncil.org.uk), but some key points are extracted below:

In circumstances where counsel is aware of previous convictions, regardless of the nature of the case or potential sentence, counsel should give the defendant clear advice as to all the options. He should:

- Inform the defendant that the information as to the previous conviction will remain confidential unless the client specifically waives privilege;

- Inform the defendant that whilst the information remains confidential, he will be restricted in what he can say in mitigation;

- Advise the defendant that nothing can be said as to the defendant's record which expressly or impliedly adopts the position as outlined by the prosecution and in particular, that nothing can be said as to:
  - (a) the absence of convictions of the type or gravity of the undisclosed conviction;
  - (b) a period of time as being free from convictions if the undisclosed conviction occurred during that period;
  - (c) the absence of a particular sentence or disposal in the defendant's antecedents if such sentence or disposal was in fact imposed in respect of the undisclosed conviction; or
  - (d) an apparently good character of the defendant.

- Specifically advise the defendant as to the nature of the sentencing exercise if the court became aware of the undisclosed conviction, whether by virtue of the defendant's voluntary disclosure or by some other means.

- Advise the defendant as to the possibility of the prosecution subsequently discovering the undisclosed conviction;

- Advise of the real possibility that failure of counsel to refer to the defendant's antecedents would not go unnoticed by experienced prosecution counsel or judge. This could lead to an adjournment, to the matter being relisted for alteration of the sentence, or to a reference by the Attorney-General under section 36 of the Criminal Justice Act 1998.

The defendant should be told that the choice as to what course to adopt is his, but that if he decides to reveal the qualifying conviction, he would be entitled to expect significant credit from the court.

. . .

The Bar Council's guidance notes also make clear that this would not be an appropriate situation for counsel to withdraw.

7.2.2.4 Prosecutors

The Criminal Procedure and Investigations Act 1996 creates a positive duty for prosecutors to disclose information which undermines the Crown's case or which is helpful to the defendant's. Section 9 of the 1996 Act makes this a continuing duty to review information. This is a far heavier burden than that on defence counsel. The Code for Crown Prosecutors makes this clear:

2.5   It is the duty of Crown Prosecutors to review, advise on and prosecute cases, ensuring that the law is properly applied, that all relevant evidence is put before the court and that obligations of disclosure are complied with, in accordance with the principles set out in this Code.

This duty to disclose damaging information illustrates the different approach that defending and prosecuting counsel are obliged to take. The Code for Crown Prosecutors states clearly that the Prosecutor should not be primarily motivated by winning the case.

2.3   It is the duty of Crown Prosecutors to make sure that the right person is prosecuted for the right offence. In doing so, Crown Prosecutors must always act in the interests of justice and not solely for the purpose of obtaining a conviction.

If some piece of information (a disciplinary finding against a police officer, for example) were to come to light during a conference, your advice would have to be that it must be disclosed — even though it might expose your witness to cross-examination.

7.2.2.5 Civil cases

In civil matters, counsel is bound by the same duty of confidentiality to the lay client and the duty not to mislead the court. However, in fast track and multi-track cases, the parties are obliged to disclose any documents within their control which relate to the proceedings. This means that if counsel were told in conference about a relevant document which had not been disclosed, he or she would have to advise the client to disclose it to the other party. If the client refused, then counsel would have to advise that he or she could not continue to act for the client unless that disclosure were made. The Code of Conduct deals with this situation as follows:

608   A barrister must cease to act and if he is a self-employed barrister must return any instructions:...

> (e) if having become aware during the course of a case of the existence of a document which should have been but has not been disclosed on discovery the client fails forthwith to disclose it.

Before withdrawing from the case, counsel is obliged to consider whether he or she is prejudicing the client by the timing of that withdrawal. He or she is also obliged to explain why it is necessary to withdraw from the case. The Code says:

610   A barrister must not:

> (a) cease to act or return instructions without having first explained to the client his reasons for doing so;
>
> . . .
>
> (d) except as provided in paragraph 608 return any instructions or withdraw from a case in such a way or in such circumstances that the client may be unable to find other legal assistance in time to prevent prejudice being suffered by the client.

However, the wording of para 610 clearly suggests that the client's failure to make proper disclosure will be an overriding consideration — even if the revelation occurs during a trial. For guidance on disclosure of illegally obtained evidence refer to the Bar Council's web site, 'Guidance on Illegally Obtained Evidence in Civil and Family Proceedings'.

7.2.2.6   Public funding

It may well be that your lay client has the benefit of public funding through the Legal Services Commission (LSC). This adds another dimension to your duties in conference as the Code says that a barrister has a duty to the LSC in the following terms:

303   A barrister:

> . . .
>
> (c) when supplying legal services funded by the Legal Services Commission as part of the Community Legal Service or the Criminal Defence Service owes his primary duty to the lay client subject only to compliance with paragraph 304.

304   A barrister who supplies legal services funded by the Legal Services Commission as part of the Community Legal Service or the Criminal Defence Service must in connection with the supply of such services comply with any duty imposed on him by or under the Access to Justice Act 1999 or any regulations or code in effect under that Act and in particular with the duties set out in Annex E.

Annex E deals with counsel's obligations when drafting opinions on the suitability of cases for public funding by the LSC. At para 20, this states that:

Counsel acting under a funding certificate is under a duty to bring to the attention of the Commission any matter which might affect the client's entitlement to funding, or the terms of his or her certificate, at whatever stage of the proceedings that might occur.

In criminal matters, there is a similar duty to report abuse of the system. The relevant regulations under the Access to Justice Act 1999 are contained within the Criminal Defence Service (General) (No 2) Regulations 2001 (SI 2001/1437). This provides:

24.   Notwithstanding the relationship between or rights of a representative and client or any privilege arising out of such relationship, where the representative for an applicant or assisted person knows or suspects that that person:

    (a) has intentionally failed to comply with any provision of regulations made under the Act concerning the information to be furnished by him; or

    (b) in furnishing such information has knowingly made a false statement or false representation the representative shall immediately report the circumstances to the Commission.

If your publicly-funded lay client revealed facts in conference which would affect this entitlement, you would have to advise him or her to pass the correct information to the LSC immediately. If the client refuses to do this, then you will have to explain that you cannot continue to act:

608   A barrister must cease to act and if he is a self-employed barrister must return any instructions: . . .

    (c) if in any case funded by the Legal Services Commission as part of the Community Legal Service or Criminal Defence Service it has become apparent to him that such funding has been wrongly obtained by false or inaccurate information and action to remedy the situation is not immediately taken by the client;

    (d) if the client refuses to authorise him to make some disclosure to the Court which his duty to the Court requires him to make . . .

If you are forced to withdraw, para 610(a) of the Code obliges you to explain to your lay client why you are doing so, and, as far as possible, not to leave your client in a position where he or she will suffer prejudice (para 610(d)). However, as noted above, the wording of the Code makes clear that counsel cannot in any circumstances continue to act when he or she believes that one of the conditions within para 608 of the Code applies.

7.2.2.7   Sensitive information

The client may reveal information in conference that he or she wishes to be kept confidential, but which you believe would assist either at trial or in mitigation. For example, he or she may be able to assist the police by revealing the names of others involved in the same offence. This would assist the mitigation considerably. The duty of confidentiality to the client means that without his or her express permission you cannot reveal that information — even if you believe that it is in his or her interests to do so. You should advise clearly on how you believe that revealing the relevant information would assist him or her. However, if your client is clear that he or she will not reveal it, remember that it is your client's case and not yours. Only your client can say what is in his or her 'best interests', once he or she has been given the full picture by you.

In these circumstances, you may wish to invite the client to endorse your brief to say that you have advised him or her about the consequences of not revealing the relevant information and that he or she has nonetheless decided not to do so. This should protect you from any complaint that he or she might make about your advice if, for example, your client receives a more serious sentence than he or she was expecting.

7.2.3   The professional client

As a general rule you would expect your solicitor (or the firm's representative) to attend a conference between you and a lay client. He or she will take notes, record action points and, depending on how involved he or she is with the case, participate in talking to the lay client and clarifying points. The solicitor also acts as a witness to what is discussed. There may be times when you do not have this luxury — for example, in your early cases where you may meet the client for the first time at court and conduct your conference then and there. Solicitors, mindful of costs, may also not attend some court hearings simply to keep costs down for their clients. This raises a number of professional conduct issues:

706   A self-employed barrister who is instructed by a professional client should not conduct a case in Court in the absence of his professional client or a representative of his professional client unless the Court rules that it is appropriate or he is satisfied that the interests of the lay client and the interests of justice will not be prejudiced.

The Code does not make it mandatory that the professional client attends with you at court — indeed he or she will rarely attend at the magistrates' court. You will have to decide whether your lay client risks being prejudiced by this absence. Take a careful note of your instructions from your client and be prepared to explain to him or her, and, if necessary, the judge, why the solicitor is not there. The client may be unhappy that the solicitor (perhaps someone who deals with him or her regularly, or the only lawyer he or she believes is dealing with the case) is not there at court. It may also help to build your lay client's confidence if you can demonstrate your knowledge of the case and your skill in conference and as an advocate.

7.2.4   Witnesses

It is not prohibited for a barrister to meet and speak to witnesses. Extreme caution is, however, needed to avoid any suggestion of coaching witnesses. The Code says:

705   A barrister must not:

(a) rehearse practise or coach a witness in relation to his evidence; . . .

You must, of course, exercise care not to coach your lay client or suggest how the evidence should be given at any time. This caution extends to all witnesses of fact in a case. Remember also that interviewing witnesses includes not only sitting down in an interview room, but also chatting in the corridor or over a cup of coffee about the case. You need to be conscious of what you say about the case at all times. Clear guidance is given regarding counsel's obligations in respect of contact with witnesses in Pt 6 of the Written Standards for the Conduct of Professional Work. This is reproduced in **Appendix 1**, Section 3, Miscellaneous Guidance, in this Manual, and it is important that you are fully familiar with that guidance.

You may have a conference which involves an expert witness or someone giving character evidence on your client's behalf. The same rules apply — that you are not to seek to influence the way that the witness gives his or her evidence (save by your expertise in questioning in court). This does not prevent you from asking experts questions about matters within their expertise, or their view on the evidence given by other experts, only your suggesting the answers that they should give.

If a witness of fact attends court in a criminal matter and wants to give evidence on behalf of the defendant then you will want to know what he or she will say. If you have no proof from the witness and if you have a professional client in attendance then you will be able to leave it to him or her to take a proof from the witness. If you are alone then this leaves you in a more difficult position. The Code states that:

401   A self-employed barrister whether or not he is acting for a fee: . . .

(b) must not in the course of his practice: . . .

(iv) except as permitted by paragraph 707, take any proof of evidence in any criminal case . . .

If the only other option is to seek an adjournment of the case, then the best course of action may be to take the proof yourself. This Code says that this may be permissible if necessary:

707 A self-employed barrister who attends Court in order to conduct a case in circumstances where no professional client or representative of a professional client is present may if necessary interview witnesses and take proofs of evidence.

This situation is most likely to arise in the magistrates' court, where you may well be representing your client without your professional client in attendance. As the professional client will almost always be in attendance at the Crown Court, it will seldom be necessary to take a proof or interview witnesses in such matters.

You will have to take care not to lead the witness or coach him or her in any way. If the witness asks you what he or she should say then your advice must be to tell the truth. You would be very unwise to offer any more information than that. If you take a note of what the witness says to you, you may wish to have the witness sign it as an accurate record of what he or she told you.

At court you will never speak to or contact a witness while he or she is giving evidence, save by asking questions in examination-in-chief or cross-examination. The Code expressly prohibits such contact:

705 A barrister must not: . . .

    (c) except with the consent of the representative for the opposing side or of the Court, communicate directly or indirectly about a case with any witness, whether or not the witness is his lay client, once that witness has begun to give evidence until the evidence of that witness has been concluded.

This prohibition extends even to your client — for example, if the case is adjourned overnight while your client is still giving evidence you will not speak to him or her until the next day, after he or she has finished his or her evidence. If this situation is likely to arise, then you will need to explain this to your client before he or she goes into the witness box. If you are seen to be speaking to him or her (even if you are not discussing the evidence) it will appear that you are coaching your client and you can expect opposing counsel to protest to the judge in the strongest terms.

7.2.5 Fair treatment

It should hopefully come as no surprise that the Code of Conduct forbids you to discriminate in the following terms:

305.1 A barrister must not in relation to any other person (including a client or another barrister or a pupil or a student member of an Inn of Court) discriminate directly or indirectly or victimise because of race, colour, ethnic or national origin, nationality, citizenship, sex, sexual orientation, marital status, disability, religion or political persuasion.

What this means in terms of conference skills is that you must be sensitive to the differing needs of your lay client. The range of issues this may cover is necessarily wide. For example, you may be unfamiliar with the naming system of your client's culture, or you may find that your client has never learned to read — you may even find his or her lifestyle or personal views unattractive. Of course, whether or not you like your client or the way that your client lives his or her life — or any other of your personal prejudices — must not affect your dedication to conducting his or her case as effectively as possible. Equally, if you are unsure how to pronounce your client's name or how to address him or her, use your common sense and show your client the courtesy of asking.

Fair treatment goes beyond these obvious points. If your client could not read, for example, it would be up to you to do all you could to enable him or her to take a full part in proceedings. In consultation with your client, you would seek to find ways of overcoming that problem. Ignoring the problem would amount to discrimination.

Most importantly, your duty not to discriminate requires you to be aware of what discrimination is and the wide variety of circumstances where you might be found to be discriminating inappropriately. The examples above are merely the tip of the iceberg. It is recognising that there is a problem which is vital to dealing with a situation correctly. Once you know that there is a problem, you will then have to use your common sense and your sense of what is right, within the spirit of the Code, to deal with it depending on the individual circumstances. Remember, if you are in doubt, you can always consult another member of chambers or, in emergencies, the Bar Council's adviser on professional conduct problems.

7.2.6 What the lay client is entitled to expect from you

Finally, remember that your duty to the lay client includes giving full and accurate advice to him or her on all matters. This involves you in applying the spirit of the Code, as well as good business sense. Your function is to give information to your client on options and consequences, as well as your opinion on which line of action he or she should pursue and why. This enables your client to exercise informed choice. It is never your function to make choices for your client or to force him or her to do what you want.

Thinking back, for example, to the client who has information on others involved in his or her offending. Your duty to your client is to advise him or her on what might be done with that information, the consequences of what he or she decides to do and also your opinion on the best course of action to pursue. You will give your client the information that he or she needs to make a fully informed decision. Your opinion on the best course of action may be to reveal this information to the judge so that your client can receive maximum credit when being sentenced. You will explain to your client why you think that this best serves his or her interests, but make clear that the final decision is his or hers to make. If you have done your job in fully informing your client about the potential choices then he or she is ideally placed to make a decision. If the client decides not to follow your advice and you feel that this is a mistake, you may wish to have your client endorse your brief stating that he or she understands the consequences of the choice and that he or she still wishes to proceed in this way. As long as your client's choice does not involve your having to act unethically, then you will have to run the case as he or she instructs. It is, after all, your client's case.

Many trainee barristers seem to believe that the lay client's function is simply to listen respectfully to counsel's wise pronouncements, rather than play an active part in the conference. This is not correct. You are providing a service for which you are being paid and the lay client is entitled to expect professionalism and courtesy at all times rather than irritation or condescension. Remember that the most important person in any conference is your lay client.

7.3 Advocacy skills

The role of an advocate in court is very demanding and you will soon find yourself in challenging and highly stressful situations. Throughout, however, your conduct must meet the rightly demanding standards of the profession. If you do so you will avoid adverse criticism and know that you have acted to the best of your abilities in the interest of your client. For a recent example of unprofessional behaviour see *Boodram v State of Trinidad and Tobago* [2002] 1 Cr App R 12. In that case defence counsel conducting a trial for murder had failed to realise that it was in fact a retrial. This was described as 'the worst case of the failure of counsel to carry out his duties in a criminal case that their lordships have come across' (para 40).

This section will help you to identify the main duties of the advocate; it is not exhaustive and should be read in the context of the general guidance offered in the rest of this Manual. Many of the rules of professional conduct that are relevant to courtroom advocacy are longstanding, however, the precise wording of the rules and duties do change from time to time to adapt to the changing circumstances of modern life. It is therefore vital that you are up-to-date with any amendments to the rules. A full and up-to-date version of the Code is available on the Bar Council web site www.barcouncil.org.uk.

In the context of advocacy, the main areas of the Code for BVC students to concentrate on are:

(a) Part III which contains the Fundamental Principles, including the duty not to act dishonestly or bring the profession into disrepute and the particular duties to the court and to act in the best interests of the client. It also includes the duties to the Legal Services Commission and not to discriminate on grounds of race, sex and so forth and the duties which safeguard a barrister's independence.

(b) Part VII which sets out the duties of barristers when conducting work including the general duties to act courteously and promptly, the duty of confidentiality, duties where there is a conflict between clients, duties when drafting documents and appearing in court, the rules concerning contact with witnesses, media comment and advertising.

One of the main concerns for practising barristers is striking the balance between the overriding duty to the court and promoting the client's case:

(a) A barrister has an overriding duty to the court to act with independence in the interests of justice: he must assist the court in the administration of justice and must not deceive or knowingly or recklessly mislead the court. (Code para 302)

(b) A barrister must promote and protect fearlessly and by all proper and lawful means the lay client's best interests and do so without regard to his own interests or to any consequences to himself or to any other person (including any professional client or other intermediary or another barrister). (Code para 303(a))

See *R v McFadden* (1976) 62 Cr App R 187, where James LJ at page 190 offered the following stark observation on the competing considerations of duty to the court and the status of the Bar Council's guidance.

The Bar Council issues statements from time to time to give guidance to the profession in matters of etiquette and procedure. A barrister who conforms to the Council's rulings knows that he cannot be committing an offence against professional discipline. But such statements, although they have strong persuasive force, do not bind courts. If therefore a judge requires a barrister to do, or refrain from doing, something in the course of a case, the barrister may protest and may cite any relevant ruling of the Bar Council, but since the judge is the final authority in his own court, if counsel's protest is unavailing, he must either withdraw or comply with the ruling or look for redress in a higher court.

In this section we will discuss some of the duties that should help inform your decision about how to act in the face of such significant competing interests. Before doing so you will be advised to know where else you can find guidance on your duties and conduct in court.

7.3.1   Guidance on duties and conduct in court

7.3.1.1   The Crown Prosecutors' Code

The Crown Prosecution Service (CPS) is a public service for England and Wales headed by the Director of Public Prosecutions (DPP) and is answerable to Parliament through the Attorney-General. While the police are responsible for investigating crime, the CPS are the public prosecutors; however, they co-operate closely with the police whilst remaining independent of them.

The DPP is empowered under s 10 of the Prosecution of Offences Act 1985, to give guidance on the general principles to be applied when making decisions about prosecutions and this is the main function of the Code for Crown Prosecutors. For the purposes of this Code, 'Crown Prosecutor' includes members of staff in the Crown Prosecution Service who are designated by the DPP under s 7A of the Act and are exercising powers under that section. The code sets out the basic principles Crown Prosecutors should follow when they make case decisions. The Code helps the Crown Prosecution Service to play its part in making sure that justice is done. It contains information that is important to police officers and others who work in the criminal justice system and to the general public. The Code is also designed to make sure that everyone knows the principles that the Crown Prosecution Service applies when carrying out its work. By applying the same principles, everyone involved in the system is helping to treat victims fairly and to prosecute fairly but effectively.

The Code is a public document. It is set out in full in **Chapter 2** and is available on the CPS web site: www.cps.gov.uk. Translations into other languages are available, as are audio and braille copies.

7.3.1.2   Guidance for prosecuting counsel

In the mid-19th century Crompton J said that prosecuting counsel 'are to regard themselves as ministers of justice, and not to struggle for a conviction' (*R v Puddick* (1865) 4 F & F 497). Nearly a century and a half later the Court of Appeal repeated the concept of ministers of justice in *R v Gonez* [1999] All ER (D) 674. The role of the prosecuting counsel was also the focus of the Farquharson Committee in 1986. It concluded that such counsel have wide duties to the court and the public at large. Prosecuting counsel, it said, are under a duty to present cases for the prosecution fairly to the jury and that they have a greater independence of those instructing them than that enjoyed by other counsel. Prosecuting counsel should not strive unfairly to obtain convictions; they must not press a case beyond the limits that the evidence permits. The Written Standards for the Conduct of Professional Work, appended to the Bar's Code of Conduct at para 10.6 remind prosecuting counsel at all times to have regard to the Farquharson Committee report. Further and more detailed discussion of the conclusions of the committee can be found in *Blackstone's Criminal Practice*, 2005, para D13.5. Additionally, the Farquharson guidelines have recently been produced and although the principles established by the Farquharson Committee will continue to apply, this new guidance can be found in Chapter 2 or on the CPS website.

Paragraph 10 of the Written Standards of the Bar's Code of Conduct sets out the responsibilities of prosecuting counsel in detail. These standards and principles apply as appropriate to all practising barristers, whether in independent practice or employed and whether appearing as counsel in any given case or exercising any other professional capacity in connection with it (para 10A). Paragraph 10.1 encapsulates the spirit of Mr Justice Crompton's statement:

Prosecuting counsel should not attempt to obtain a conviction by all means at his command. He should not regard himself as appearing for any party. He should lay before the Court fairly and impartially the whole of the facts which comprise the case for the prosecution and should assist the Court on all matters of law applicable to the case.

For example, a prosecutor should take special care not to prejudice the defendant's trial by engendering inappropriate amounts of sympathy for the alleged victim of an assault.

7.3.1.3 Equal Treatment Benchbook

When working as an advocate in court you will have your ability to deal with people regularly tested. One of the keys to being effective in court is to know and understand the people you deal with and address. The trial process rests on the presumption that everyone in court has an ability to follow and understand oral communication and nowhere is this presumption more significant than in the oral testimony of the witnesses. The advocates and the judge will all have highly developed skills in questioning witnesses, analysing their evidence, and communicating their arguments to the jury. If at any point the witnesses or jury fail to comprehend the questions, answers or arguments (ie the oral communications) the trial system begins to fail justice. The Judicial Studies Board's Equal Treatment Benchbook (ETB) has identified what it labels 'cross-cultural misunderstanding' as one way in which oral communication can fail the justice system. Guidance is offered on all aspects of interpersonal communication in a multi-cultural and multi-faith society. Not only is helpful guidance offered on technical matters such as oaths and affirmations but also on interpreting how people answer questions and display respect in court. In addition there are sections on disability, gender and sexuality. The full text of the ETB is available on the web site: www.jsboard.co.uk.

7.3.2 Advocacy and professional conduct

7.3.2.1 General

In the context of civil practice it has been said that a barrister has complete authority over the conduct of litigation and all that is incidental to it, but not over matters which are collateral to the case: *Swinfen v Lord Chelmsford* (1860) 5 Hurl & N 890. Lord Esher MR stated (at 143) in *Matthews v Munster* (1888) LR 20 QBD 141:

... When the client has requested counsel to act as his advocate ... he thereby represents to the other side that counsel is to act for him in the usual course, and he must be bound by that representation so long as it continues ... The request does not mean that counsel is to act in any other character than that of advocate or to do any other act than such as an advocate usually does. The duty of counsel is to advise his client out of court and to act for him in court, and until his authority is withdrawn he has, with regard to all matters that properly relate to the conduct of the case, unlimited power to do that which is best for his client.

Under the Civil Procedure Rules 1998, r 1.3 the parties are required to help the court to further the overriding objective, that is to enable the court to deal with cases justly. The Access to Justice Act 1999, s 42 has inserted a new provision into the Courts and Legal Services Act 1990, s 27 (rights of audience), that any person exercising a right of audience before any court has a duty to the court to act with independence in the interests of justice and that duty shall override any other obligation with which it is inconsistent (other than an obligation under the criminal law). Should you receive instructions that are in conflict with these requirements you may find yourself to be professionally embarrassed and need to withdraw from the case.

As a barrister you have a duty to the court to ensure that it is informed of all relevant decisions and legislative provisions of which you are aware whether they are favourable or unfavourable to the contention which you are arguing (Code para 708(c)). Similarly any procedural irregularity must be brought to the court's attention during the hearing — you must resist the temptation to reserve the matter for an appeal (Code para 708(d)). These provisions are reiterated in the Written Standards at para 5.10(c).

7.3.3   Submissions

It is well known that counsel should not give evidence personally in court. However, inadvertent attempts to do so do occur. You should avoid statements that personalise your submissions, so avoid 'I think', 'I feel' and 'I believe'. If you remember that your role in court is to speak on behalf of your client and the judge will only accept your submissions you should be able to avoid this pitfall.

Similarly when appearing in a case you should maintain a professional detachment. Do not attempt to impose your own personality onto the application. So, avoid expressions of personal opinion, do not thank judges for administering justice in your client's favour and likewise, resist the temptation to express disappointment when they do not! (In any event the hearing may not be the end of the matter — are there meritorious grounds of appeal?) You should also avoid visible or audible reactions to your opponent's case as it is presented in court — wait until you have an opportunity to reply. And if the judge's questions are inconvenient or unhelpful to your case maintain a poker face and attempt to turn your answer to your client's advantage.

The following provisions of the Code are of direct relevance to submissions and applications, but most of them equally apply to trial advocacy. Remember that these duties apply to both oral advocacy and written advocacy (for example skeleton arguments).

(a) Preservation of *confidentiality* of lay client's affairs (para 702). Clients sometimes give their lawyers information on the understanding that it will not be communicated to others — including the court. Occasionally this information would be of assistance to their case. In such circumstances you must get the lay client's express permission to disclose the fact. It is often wise to have the client endorse your brief to confirm his or her permission — this is particularly advisable if the professional client is not present. If the court or an opponent attempts to draw you on a point that your client has identified as confidential you must still respect your client's wishes. Neither the court nor an opponent is in a position to require you to make a disclosure, though of course both are at liberty to draw their own conclusions. In civil proceedings the court can use its wide powers to stay proceedings until the information is disclosed. This may be a wholly consistent manoeuvre by the judge in order to meet the overriding objective of the rules of enabling the court to deal with cases justly, see CPR, r 1.1.

(b) Counsel must not deceive or knowingly or recklessly *mislead* the Court (para 302). Fortunately few barristers would countenance the former, but the latter can occur often through poor preparation and sheer carelessness. Note that recklessness will leave you on the wrong side of the line — hence the importance of finding adequate time for thorough preparation, marking your brief in such a way that you can find relevant facts readily and giving yourself adequate time to answer questions. If your brief or the pre-hearing client conference is unable to supply the answer do not speculate as to what it might be. The court will be sympathetic that you are not in possession of all the facts in a case (so long as you are not personally at fault) especially at the interim stage.

(c) A barrister must not adduce *evidence* obtained otherwise than from or through the client or devise facts which will assist the lay client's case (para 708(e)).

(d) A barrister must not devise facts which will assist in advancing his lay client's case (Written Standards para 5.8).

This follows on from what has just been said about avoiding speculation and filling in gaps. It also reminds us that a barrister cannot (in the ordinary run of events) give evidence in open court. (For the extraordinary circumstances when it is appropriate for counsel to give evidence see the Court of Appeal's guidance to the Bar Council and Law Society in *R v Jaquith* [1989] Crim LR 563.) Whilst you should do everything in your legitimate powers to promote the cause of your client there are limits and this is one of the most significant.

7.3.3.1 Full and frank disclosure

In civil applications that are without notice there is a duty to give full and frank disclosure. This means that adverse facts and potential arguments that the other side either does intend to raise or may raise should be brought to the attention of the judge. The Civil Procedure Rules require parties to address in their evidence 'all material facts of which the court should be made aware' (PD 25, para 3.3). However, it is not sufficient to assume that the judge is aware of an adverse fact simply because it is in the witness statement or your skeleton argument. You have a duty to draw the court's attention to such facts orally. This is a continuing duty, so if something material subsequently comes to light before the return date the court must be informed of it. Failure to disclose will usually result in an order being set aside as of right and would additionally be a breach of the Code of Conduct, in particular the duty not mislead the court (para 302).

7.3.4 Trial advocacy

Before conducting — indeed before planning — a trial you need to be aware of the limits placed on contact with witnesses within the Code. Basically witness coaching is not permitted in England and Wales (see para 705(a)). In most cases the solicitor is the main conduit for instructions and can relay important messages to the lay client. These and other points that are relevant to client conferences are dealt with in **7.2** above and discussed at length in the *Conference Skills Manual* (**Chapter 9**).

The special guidance for prosecuting counsel has been discussed, that for defence counsel is given in the Written Standards at para 11. The essence of this guidance is found at para 11.1:

When defending a client on a criminal charge, a barrister must endeavour to protect his client from conviction except by a competent tribunal and upon legally admissible evidence sufficient to support a conviction for the offence charged.

The rest of para 11 and the following paragraph on confessions of guilt should be read carefully before preparing the case, making any contact with the prosecutor, offering advice to clients in conference and attending court to represent them.

Attendance of counsel at court is considered in para 15 of the Written Standards. These should be read with care, as some of the guidance is complex. However one point is clear:

Defence counsel should ensure that the defendant is never left unrepresented at any stage of his trial. (Written Standards para 15.2.1)

7.3.4.1 Formulating a theory of the case and witness handling

One of the most important aspects of trial preparation is the theory of the case — a reasoned explanation of your side's case that will form the basis of your closing speech. Your sources are the uncontested evidence in the case and your client's version of the matters that are in issue. Naturally there are professional conduct considerations attached to the formulation of case theories. First and foremost of these is the duty to limit your theory to the facts in the case (according to your client's instructions and those facts that are not in issue) and any reasonable inferences that can be drawn from those facts. There are special limits for prosecutors, as has been set out previously under para 10.1 of the Written Standards.

On the other hand a defence barrister:

Must not suggest that a victim, witness or other person is guilty of crime, fraud or misconduct or make any defamatory aspersion on the conduct of any other person or attribute to another person the crime or conduct of which his lay client is accused unless such allegations go to a matter in issue (including the credibility of the witness) which is material to his lay client's case and which appear to him to be supported by reasonable grounds.
(Code of Conduct para 708(j) and Written Standards para 5.10(h))

When appearing for either the defence or prosecution you:

must not make statements or ask questions which are merely scandalous or intended or calculated only to vilify insult or annoy either a witness or some other person;
(Code of Conduct para 708(g) and Written Standards para 5.10(e))

must if possible avoid the naming in open Court of third parties whose character would thereby be impugned;
(Code of Conduct para 708(h) and Written Standards para 5.10(f))

With these very significant caveats your theory of the case will lead you to formulating a short explanation of why the events took place and why your client's version of the events is the preferable one. Not only will this form the basis of your closing address but it will also suggest themes that will run through your examination of your own witnesses and cross-examination of those of your opponent. Thus checking that your theory does not offend any of the rules of professional conduct is an essential stage in its formulation.

You will have to exercise personal judgement upon the substance and purpose of questions asked and statements made, since you are personally responsible for the conduct and presentation of your case. See Code of Conduct para 708(a) and Written Standards para 5.10(a). This is in keeping with para 306 of the Code of Conduct:

A barrister is individually and personally responsible for his own conduct and for his professional work: he must exercise his own personal judgement in all his professional activities.

7.3.4.2   Cross-examination

After the other side has brought out evidence from its witness in chief examination, or in civil trials has tendered the witness statement as evidence, you are given the opportunity to question that witness to advance your client's case. You can achieve this in ways that are positive or negative:

Positively:

- seek or emphasise agreement between your client's case and what this witness has just said or can say;
- elicit additional information from the witness that did not come out in examination-in-chief.

Negatively:

- undermine the evidence of this witness;
- undermine this witness.

The rule against unnecessary unpleasant statements and insults that applied to formulat-ing a theory of the case and examination-in-chief is perhaps even more pertinent to cross-examination, so it is worth repeating it. Code of Conduct para 708(g) and Written Standards para 5.10(e) states:

A barrister when conducting proceedings at Court: . . .

must not make statements or ask questions which are merely scandalous or intended or calculated only to vilify insult or annoy either a witness or some other person.

Tempting as it may be to get carried away during a particularly successful cross-examination it will in all likelihood damage rather than advance your client's case. Judicial reprimands in open court not only embarrass counsel they can also potentially jeopardise the lay clients' case.

7.3.4.3   Putting your case

A crucial feature of cross-examination is the obligation to put your case. You must put your client's version of a particular event to a witness who is in a position to dispute that ver-sion. You may not want to do so, because the witness will disagree with your version of events, but you must. Indeed, if the denial or disagreement is unconvincing this will have an impact in the jury: they may not believe the witness. Even if you strongly suspect that the witness will deny your case convincingly, you must still put the relevant questions to that witness. You cannot merely leave the point and deal with it in your closing speech — the Code prevents you from following this route. Code of Conduct para 708(i) and Written Standards para 5.10(g) states:

A barrister when conducting proceedings at Court: . . .

must not by assertion in a speech impugn a witness whom he has had an opportunity to cross-examine unless in cross-examination he has given the witness an opportunity to answer the allegation.

So, if you fail to put your case to the witness:

(a) You are acting incompetently at best, unethically at worst.

(b) You run a danger that you will not be allowed to deal with that point in your closing speech.

(c) When your client goes into the box and gives his or her evidence, and adduces evidence that the jury has not heard put to the other side's witnesses, it may conclude that the defendant has recently invented it.

If through your own fault you have failed to put the client's case; you will have to explain to the judge that it is your fault and not your client's. Witnesses may need to be recalled, the trial delayed and all parties inconvenienced. The consequences therefore are likely to be embarrassing in the extreme.

7.3.4.4   Conclusion of the trial and sentencing

At the conclusion of the judge's summing up the prosecuting counsel is under a duty to draw to the judge's attention any apparent omissions or errors of fact or law (Written Standards para 10.7). If you are acting as defence counsel you would not appear to be under such a duty (except in the case of provocation in a murder trial: *R v Cox* [1995] 2 Cr App R 513). However, if you were not to assist the court at this stage you could jeopardise any sub-sequent appeal raised by your client.

In relation to sentence, prosecuting counsel should not attempt by advocacy to influence the court with regard to sentence. Indeed if a defendant is unrepresented it is proper for prosecuting counsel to inform the court of any mitigating circumstances about which he or she is instructed (Written Standards para 10.8(a)). The prosecutor also should assist the court with sentencing guidelines and statutory provisions and other technical matters relevant to compensation, forfeiture and restitution (Written Standards para 10.8(b)–(d)). Further the prosecutor should draw the attention of the defence to any assertion of material fact made in mitigation which the prosecutor believes to be untrue. If the defence persists with the assertion prosecuting counsel should invite the court to have the matter determined in a Newton hearing (Written Standards para 10.8(e)).

There are also duties for defence counsel in the sentencing process. If a barrister acting for the defence is instructed to submit in mitigation anything which casts aspersions on the conduct or character of a victim or witness in the case, you must notify the prosecution in advance so as to give prosecuting counsel sufficient opportunity to consider the requirement for a Newton hearing (Written Standards para 11.2(k)).

It is sometimes appropriate for counsel — both for the prosecution and the defence — to see the judge prior to sentencing. Specific guidance is offered on this in the Consolidated Criminal Practice Directions, as amended and reissued, 29 July 2004, iv. 45. It is essential that you understand the limits on such contact and what you can expect judges to indicate about the sentence and perhaps more importantly what they will not indicate. See 2.1.5.

7.3.4.5 Appeals

When deciding whether to appeal the outcome of a case and especially when settling ground of appeal you must remember the guidance offered in the Code of Conduct. This includes the dogmatic statement that counsel should not settle grounds of appeal unless they consider that such grounds are properly arguable (para 704(b) and Written Standards para 16.3). Further if at any stage you are of the view that the appeal should be abandoned, you should at once set out your reasons in writing and send them to your professional client (Written Standards para 16.6). Naturally you should not devise facts which will assist in advancing the lay client's case and a barrister must not draft grounds of appeal or any other document containing:

(a) any statement of fact or contention which is not supported by the lay client or by their instructions;

(b) any contention which he does not consider to be properly arguable;

(c) any allegation of fraud unless he has clear instructions to make such allegation and has before him reasonably credible material which as it stands establishes a prima facie case of fraud; . . .

provided that nothing in this paragraph shall prevent a barrister drafting a document containing specific factual statements or contentions included by the barrister subject to confirmation of their accuracy by the lay client or witness. (Code of Conduct para 704)

7.4 Negotiation

Professional conduct is as important in negotiation as in any other aspect of a barrister's work. The Code of Conduct applies equally to your conduct as a negotiator as it does to your conduct as an advocate. Of particular relevance to negotiation are those paragraphs which are applicable to all practising barristers (paras 301–307) and those under Part VII relating to the conduct of work by practising barristers. Note in particular the duty in para 701(a) to be courteous, in para 702 the duty of confidentiality, in para 703 the duties in respect of conflicts between lay client and intermediaries, and para 704 the duty not to mislead which although headed 'drafting documents' is of more general application. You should also have regard to the Written Standards for the Conduct of Professional Work of the Code of Conduct, under the Conduct of Work at paras 5.5 and 5.11.

As with other aspects of your work as a barrister, the Code can only give general guidance on ethical rules when negotiating, it cannot deal specifically with every situation that may arise. Although negotiations are conducted privately with only those involved knowing what happened, it is as important to act as ethically as when you are acting in the public eye (eg as an advocate in court). Your reputation is based on how you conduct yourself in practice whether in public or private. The Bar is a small profession!

This section highlights the more common professional conduct issues that arise where a barrister is instructed to negotiate a settlement on behalf of his or her client. It focuses on the general duties when negotiating a settlement in a civil case, as negotiating in a criminal case (or plea bargaining) has very specific rules which are beyond the scope of this Manual. When instructed to negotiate a settlement, a barrister needs to be aware of his or her duties to a variety of people: the professional client, the lay client, the opposing lawyer (whether barrister or solicitor) and the court (when negotiating a settlement within the litigation process). The section is divided into four parts, each one dealing with one of these four relevant relationships.

7.4.1   The professional client

Both the solicitor and counsel may become involved in seeking to negotiate a settlement in a case. The division of roles should be kept clear. You might be asked to advise the solicitor on possible terms of settlement, in which case the solicitor will proceed with any negotiation. Alternatively, you might be instructed to try to settle a case, in which case you must keep the solicitor informed.

(a) Keep your professional client informed of developments. If such a client is present, listen to his or her views on the merit of any proposal that has been made.

(b) Be courteous and even-tempered in your dealings with your professional client. Do not argue in front of the lay client. If there is a difference of opinion between you, discuss it out of the lay client's hearing.

(c) Do not, however, keep your professional client happy at the expense of your lay client's interests. For example, do not advise your client to reject a fair offer of compromise merely because your solicitor insists that his firm, rather than the one proposed, handles the conduct of the sale of the property in dispute. The Code states:

303(b)   A barrister owes his primary duty as between the lay client and any professional client or other intermediary to the lay client and must not permit the intermediary to limit his discretion as to how the interests of the lay client can best be served . . .

703   If a self-employed barrister forms the view that there is a conflict of interest between his lay client and a professional client or other intermediary (for example because he considers that the intermediary may have been negligent) he must consider whether it would be in the lay client's interest to instruct another professional adviser or representative and, if he considers that it would be, the barrister must so advise and take such steps as he considers necessary to ensure that his advice is communicated to the lay client (if necessary by sending a copy of his advice in writing directly to the lay client as well as to the intermediary).

7.4.2   The lay client

A lawyer is negotiating for the client. The lawyer is the expert, the professional adviser and representative acting on behalf of the client. However, it is the client's case. The professional conduct issues which arise as a result are as follows.

7.4.2.1   Act only on instructions and within your client's instructions

As a lawyer, you act as your client's agent in a negotiation and general agency rules apply. You have actual authority to act only within the client's instructions and should never settle outside this actual authority. However, from the other party's point of view, you are acting for the client and have the apparent or ostensible authority to settle a case after proceedings have been issued. The extent of this apparent authority can of course be cut down by giving the other side notice of any limit on it. If you act outside your actual authority but bind the client because the agreement comes within your apparent authority you will be in breach of duty to your client and liable to him or her.

You must therefore only negotiate when your client instructs you to do so, and you can only negotiate within the authority given to you by your client. You must ensure that you really do understand the client's objectives, interests and needs and pursue these in the negotiation and that you have your client's clear authority to either propose or accept an offer of compromise.

Your brief will normally contain a lot of information which makes it clear what the client will or will not accept, ie, sets the parameters of your actual authority in negotiating a settlement. However, there may well be matters of detail on which it is not clear exactly what the client wants. Making it apparent to the other side that any negotiation is subject to the authorisation or approval of the client, leaves you open to agree detail on condition that the client does approve (ie, giving notice of the limited authority). By setting this parameter, it leaves you free to try to tie up the detail in the best way possible without binding the client.

7.4.2.2   Ensure that the client's claim is legitimate

Although it is the lay client's case, you have a duty not to knowingly allow yourself to be used as a tool to obtain settlement in respect of a groundless or fraudulent claim. If your client's case is without any foundation, you should not act for him or her. The Code sets out:

704   A barrister must not devise facts which will assist in advancing the lay client's case and must not draft any statement of case, witness statement, affidavit, notice of appeal or other document containing:

(a)   any statement of fact or contention which is not supported by the lay client or by his instructions;

(b)   any contention which he does not consider to be properly arguable;

(c)   any allegation of fraud unless he has clear instructions to make such allegation and has before him reasonably credible material which as it stands establishes a prima facie case of fraud;

(d)   in the case of a witness statement or affidavit any statement of fact other than the evidence which in substance according to his instructions the barrister reasonably believes the witness would give if the evidence contained in the witness statement or affidavit were being given in oral examination;

provided that nothing in this paragraph shall prevent a barrister drafting a document containing specific factual statements or contentions included by the barrister subject to confirmation of their accuracy by the lay client or witness.

7.4.2.3 Ensure your client's interests are protected

As counsel, it is also your duty to ensure your client's interests are adequately protected by the machinery of the compromise. For example, a judgment debt is likely to affect your client's prospects of obtaining future credit, whereas an agreement to pay the debt contained in a Tomlin order will not. For further guidance on enforcement of orders see the *Civil Litigation Manual*.

7.4.2.4 Advise the client clearly and fully on their case

You also have a duty, as counsel, to ensure that when the client decides whether or not to accept an offer or agree to settle, the decision is a fully informed one. You must advise the client both of your view of the case and of what, in your judgement, is the best course of action. Ensure that the client understands how the strengths and weaknesses of the case or any procedural or evidential matters affect the chances of achieving the objectives that he or she is seeking. Ensure that he or she is aware of the risks involved in making, accepting or rejecting an offer of compromise, for example, the incidence of costs, and that he or she understands the nature and effect of any agreement and/or any undertaking he or she is proposing to give to the court. The terms of the settlement must be fully explained as must the effect, in particular that settlement will mean the end of the matter and there will normally be no possibility of reopening it or seeking more.

Failing to advise the client properly or just accepting a decision where the client clearly does not understand his or her legal position or consequences of the decision is a breach of duty to the client.

7.4.2.5 It is the client's decision, not yours

Decisions about substantive matters, eg, whether or not to negotiate, what issues are open to negotiation and whether or not an offer should be accepted, must be made by the client. It is the client's case and you must ensure that any decision about whether to settle or not is that of the client and not yours. Whether the settlement is acceptable must be measured against the client's objectives, needs and interests. Having advised fully (see above), you must then accept the client's decision and abide by it. If the client is not prepared to accept a settlement, that is his or her prerogative. The only exception to this may arise if the client is funded by the Community Legal Service. The solicitor will be under a duty to report to the Regional Director of the Community Legal Service that the client has declined to accept an offer to settle (Funding Code Procedures, Section 12 Reporting Obligations, C43.2.vi.a Duties of the Solicitor). In such a case advice may have been required from a barrister on the merits of the case prior to funding being granted. You may have given that advice which included an assessment of quantum. If the settlement offer is within that which you advised, then you too may fall under the duty of any Legal Representative in the Funding Code Procedures (C44 i) to ensure that the Regional Director is informed, if it appears to you that the client has required the case to be conducted unreasonably, or so as to incur an unjustifiable expense to the Fund or has unreasonably required that the case be continued.

7.4.2.6 Conditional fee agreements

Barristers are increasingly entering conditional fee agreements whereby no fee is charged if the client loses the case but the barrister receives a 'success' fee if the client wins. These agreements raise novel practical problems and have significant potential pitfalls for the Bar. In particular, it is recognised that a conditional fee agreement could impact on the barrister/client relationship in respect of settling a case.

Guidance is given by the General Council of the Bar in its 'Conditional Fee Guidance' set out under Rules and Guidance on the Bar Council website (www.barcouncil.org). Part I deals specifically with Ethical Guidance. The paragraphs of particular relevance to negotiation are:

Conditional Fee Guidance

6. Form of agreement
In particular, the barrister should ensure that no term increases or tends to increase inappropriate pressure on the lay client to reach a settlement. . . .

9. Impartiality/conflict of interest
Having accepted instructions to act under a CFA, a barrister shall thereafter give impartial advice to the lay client at all times and take all reasonable steps to identify and declare to the lay client and to the instructing solicitor any actual or apparent conflict of interest between the barrister and the lay client.

10. Advice and interests of lay client
During the currency of a CFA, the barrister should use his/her best endeavours to ensure that:

  (a) any advice given by the barrister in relation to the case is communicated and fully explained to the lay client;

  (b) any offer of settlement is communicated to the lay client forthwith;

  (c) the consequences of particular clauses in the solicitor/lay client agreement and the solicitor/barrister agreement are explained to the client as and when they become relevant, particularly after an offer of settlement has been made.

This last obligation applies in particular to the financial consequences which may arise from the making of an offer to settle the case including consideration of (1) any increase in the offer of settlement; (2) 'conventional' costs consequences; and (3) the success fees which are or may become payable.

11. Advising on settlement
When advising on a settlement of the action the barrister should at all times have in mind his/her obligation under paragraph 303(a) of the Code to 'promote and protect fearlessly and by all proper and lawful means the lay client's best interests and do so without regard to his own interests or to any consequences to himself or to any other person (including any professional client or other intermediary or another barrister)'. The barrister's duty must be, when advising the client on a settlement or on a payment in or Part 36 offer, to advise as to the best course of action from the lay client's point of view only.

12. Disagreement over settlement
Difficulties may arise when the lawyers disagree about the wisdom of continuing the case or accepting an offer, whether that disagreement is:

  (a) between them on the one part and the lay client on the other; or

  (b) between solicitor and counsel; or

  (c) between leading and junior counsel.

In such event careful consideration must be given to the lay client's interests. Every effort should be made to avoid unfairly putting the lay client in the position where having begun proceedings s/he is left without representation. However, where, for example, counsel has been misled about the true nature of the evidence or the lay client is refusing to accept firm advice as to the future conduct of the case, the terms of the CFA may permit counsel to withdraw. Before taking this serious step the barrister will have to check carefully whether s/he is entitled to withdraw.

13. Withdrawal from the case
The barrister may withdraw from the case in any of the circumstances set out in the CFA agreement, but only if satisfied that s/he is permitted to withdraw pursuant to Part VI of the Code. In the event

that the CFA agreement does not contain a term that the barrister may withdraw from the case in particular circumstances, but the Code requires the barrister to withdraw in those circumstances, the Code takes priority over the agreement.

If you are acting under a CFA agreement you will need to ensure that your advice to your client satisfies these requirements, in particular that you advise the client on the best course of action for him or her regardless of your own position on any success fee. In addition, you must ensure that your advice on the offer of settlement and the consequences of the CFA agreement is clear to the client, in particular advising on the usual costs consequences of settlement and any success fee payable. You should also make clear the consequences of not accepting the settlement and ensure that the client is clear on the net gain of such action (the likely better sum/outcome, the prospects of getting it and the further costs consequences of continuing including any likely success fee).

7.4.2.7   Client confidentiality

Your duty not to divulge information entrusted to you in confidence by your client without his or her consent continues after the case, even if it has been dealt with by way of a negotiated compromise. If you are acting under a conditional fee agreement, the guidance of the Bar Council in para 14 states, 'The fact that the action is funded by means of a CFA, and the terms of a CFA, should not be disclosed to the other parties to the action without the express written permission of the lay client, or save in so far as such disclosure is required by the court, the CPR, statute, rule, order, or Practice Direction'.

7.4.3   The opponent

Negotiating with the other side raises the most difficult issues of professional conduct. These can be roughly divided between those matters which raise issues of confidentiality and/or privilege and those which raise issue of tactics and general behaviour in the negotiation.

7.4.3.1   Confidentiality/privilege

The first general principle is that you should avoid discussing a case without instructions. Remember you are acting for the client and must act on instructions whether express or implicit.

'Without prejudice'

Negotiations with a view to settlement should be conducted 'without prejudice' whether by letter, fax, phone or face-to-face meeting. This basically means that the contents of the negotiation cannot be revealed to the court to assist it to determine the case. While any negotiation with a view to compromise is impliedly without prejudice, the position is also frequently expressly stated, eg, by putting the words 'without prejudice' on a letter. Negotiations between counsel with a view to a compromise are impliedly made 'without prejudice'. Such discussions are in effect privileged and must not be repeated in court or in open correspondence. In the event of a failure to reach a satisfactory compromise, warn your client not to repeat in court what has been said during the negotiation. More detailed guidance on the evidential position of 'without prejudice' communications is contained in the *Evidence Manual*.

There are two exceptions to the rule that what was discussed in a negotiation is privileged and cannot be repeated. The first is where an admission of fact, which should properly have been openly disclosed, is made in the course of negotiations. For example,

'My client now admits he gave your client a gift of £500 although the balance of his claim for £2,000 was a loan.' The umbrella of 'without prejudice' does not protect such an admission. You may therefore use the admission if it is in your lay client's best interests to do so, though you should inform your opponent of your intention to do this. On the other hand, 'My client is prepared to waive £500 of his claim provided your client pays him the balance of £1,500 within 28 days' is not an admission. It is a concession made 'without prejudice' in the context of an offer of compromise.

The second is where agreement is reached. The phrase 'without prejudice' was discussed in *Guiness Peat Properties v Fitzroy Robinson Partnership* [1987] 2 All ER 716, where it was held to mean 'without prejudice to the position of the writer if the terms he proposes are not accepted'. If a 'without prejudice' offer is accepted it is a formal agreement to settle the claim, is immediately binding, and can be revealed. If the offer is not accepted it is ignored, and nothing said in a letter making the offer can be used as evidence (*Rush v Tompkins Ltd v GLC* [1988] 3 WLR 939).

Discussions between counsel about a possible settlement or how to assist the case to run smoothly frequently take place without either client being present. Both counsel may therefore be more informal than if the clients are present, using language and saying things which might not be said if the clients are present. However, you must always remember that your first duty is to your client; that you are negotiating on their behalf. Your duty of confidentiality means that you should not reveal anything to the other side that might be damaging to your client or their case. As a general rule, you should not disclose anything that your client would not wish the other side to know. If something is revealed to you by your opponent which it is in your client's interest to know or which may affect the way in which you conduct the case, you must disclose this to the client. You should also tell your opponent that you will inform your client.

Do not be persuaded to reveal matters which you feel you should not or not inform your client of things you feel you should by your opponent saying or implying that 'counsel to counsel' discussions exempt you from your duty to your client. There is no such thing within the Code of Conduct or professional ethics as 'counsel to counsel confidentiality'!

7.4.3.2 Behaviour/tactics in the negotiation

As counsel, you have a duty to conduct negotiations in a fair, honest, courteous and trust-worthy manner. You should never compromise your professional integrity. This does not mean that you should adopt an apologetic approach to negotiating. The importance of fair play should not detract from your duty to promote the interests of the lay client fearlessly. Frustration may tempt you on occasions to forget this: *don't let it*. A reputation for underhandedness or sharp practice will be retained long after the event. The old maxim 'you can fool some of the people all of the time' has little application at the Bar. The grape-vine is far too effective! You need to be conscious that, even if the behaviour comes within the ethical boundaries (which are often difficult to determine), the tactics you use will invariably affect the reputation you build. If, for example, you use aggressive tactics you will get a reputation for being confrontational which may be difficult to get rid of.

Misleading your opponent

Some tactics are clearly dishonest and unethical, eg, deliberately misleading your opponent by pretending to have evidence you do not have. They are against the Bar's Code of Conduct and, even if they do not amount to an offence, eg, fraud, using them can result in being debarred. You must never deliberately deceive or mislead your opponent in order to achieve a more favourable offer of compromise (see para 301 of the Code of Conduct).

It is, however, acceptable to use 'bluff', allowing an opponent to form an impression without positively misleading him. However, managing or manipulating information may become sufficiently 'tricky' or misleading to amount to professional misconduct. A barrister's job is to promote the client's case as an advocate. You can quite properly pitch the case at its highest when trying to reach a settlement, even though you may not necessarily succeed in proving the whole case in court. There is not always a clear line between doing the best for your client and misleading or unfair tactics. But you must not pretend that you do know a fact or have particular instructions if this is simply not true. You must also not knowingly conceal something which ought properly to have been disclosed, for example a document, in the hope of securing a more favourable settlement.

Failing to act courteously

While it is absolutely acceptable to be assertive in your manner, aggressive behaviour may become sufficiently insulting or rude to amount to a breach of your professional duty to act courteously. Avoid bickering with your opponent; it does not do your client any good. Nor is it wise to lose your objectivity by taking on the persona of your client in the course of negotiations. For example, 'Your client is totally dishonest, he has already stolen £2,000 from us'. This merely serves to antagonise.

Use of threats

'Threat' is defined as 'a conditional commitment by a negotiator to act in a way that appears detrimental to the other party unless the other party complies with a request', in Donald G. Gifford's book *Legal Negotiation: Theory and Applications* ((1989) (St Paul: Min-West Publishing Co), p 143). Not all threats are unethical. Many negotiation tactics, although not phrased as threats, implicitly involve them, eg, 'the final offer' is basically a threat to end the negotiation if the offer is not accepted.

Difficulties arise in considering actions which a client might take if he or she does not get the desired result from the opponent. Clearly, it would be dishonest and unprofessional to suggest that your client intended to do something he or she did not intend. In addition, your client may be considering action that is not legitimate because it is illegal or impractical, in which case you should be advising your client in strong terms not to take it.

Even where the client has threatened to take particular legitimate action if their demands are not met, eg that they will 'go to the press unless the opponent does X', whatever the facts, counsel must tread a fine line between following the client's instructions and avoiding the aggressive use of threats to secure a favourable outcome. It is unprofessional and unethical to make threats that are tantamount to blackmail. On the other hand it is quite legitimate to point out potential consequences. The dividing line between a legitimate statement and an unethical threat is not clear. This is a difficult area and there is no clear guidance in the Code of Conduct. It frequently comes down to a question of the manner in which the information is imparted to one's opponent.

When in doubt, err on the side of caution, ie do *not* threaten 'My client will go to the press unless your client does XYZ', as this is really simply a threat. However, you may inform the opponent in appropriate language that your client is indicating an intention to go to the newspapers, eg 'I think it is only fair to tell you that my client is so upset by this/feels so strongly about this that she's talking of going to the newspapers'. Although the difference between these two approaches is subtle, it is nevertheless there. The second example is merely a statement of the client's possible intention and *not* linked to any demand in respect of her case.

Going back on your word

Do not go back on your word, or subsequently pretend you did not say something, in order to cover your own mistake or indiscretion. Such behaviour is unacceptable. If you have made an error, admit it.

Acting without authority

Do not make an offer or commit your client to an agreement without instructions or authority to do so. Make it clear to your opponent when your proposal is subject to your lay client's agreement. For example, 'If my client were prepared to do XYZ, would your client do ABC?'

Litigants in person

The above considerations apply whether or not your opponent is a lawyer or a litigant in person. However, where your opponent is a litigant in person you have the additional consideration of ensuring that you do not abuse your professional status and knowledge. This can produce other difficult issues, such as how much and the way in which you explain the law as you understand it, eg to what extent you include in your explanation any points of law which go against you.

7.4.4   The court

The fact that you are seeking to negotiate a settlement may deceive you into thinking of the case as being subject only to your decisions. Never forget the ultimate role of the court and the need for its approval where you are seeking a consent order. The judge may suggest some amendments to your draft order.

If negotiations are taking place at court, keep the court informed of the possibility of a compromise. It may be sufficient to relay this information to the court via the court clerk or usher. At times, it may be necessary to explain this to the judge or tribunal. Provide the court with a realistic estimate of the further time you need to discuss any proposals. Inform the court immediately upon reaching agreement. The Code states:

701   A barrister:

(a) must in all his professional activities be courteous and act promptly conscientiously diligently and with reasonable competence and take all reasonable and practicable steps to avoid unnecessary expense or waste of the Court's time and to ensure that professional engagements are fulfilled; . . .

Paragraph 5.11 of the Written Standards states:

A barrister must take all reasonable and practicable steps to avoid unnecessary expense or waste of the Court's time. He should, when asked, inform the Court of the probable length of his case; and he should also inform the court of any developments which affect information already provided.

If you have time, draw up draft minutes of the agreed terms or order.

When you go into court, either hand up the draft, or, in the absence of a written draft, inform the court of the terms which have been agreed between the parties 'subject to Your Honour/Your Lordship's approval'. It may be necessary even where you have a draft order, to take the judge through its terms. Invite the judge to make the order in the terms proposed.

If agreement is reached between the parties away from the court, for example, in correspondence, remind your professional client to inform the court as soon as possible.

7.4.5 Conclusion

This section has highlighted the various professional conduct issues which arise when a barrister is instructed to negotiate a settlement on behalf of his or her client in a civil case. Acting ethically and professionally in your dealings with your lay and professional client and your opponent in a negotiation is every bit as important as it is when you act as an advocate in court. The way you behave in these circumstances is as open to action by the Bar Council and will have as much, if not more, impact on your reputation.

7.5 Opinion writing and drafting

In written work, you must display the same high standards of integrity and honesty that apply in all other aspects of your practice. The Code of Conduct has a lot to say about the conduct of written work. This section is designed to give you some guidance on matters that arise frequently in opinion writing and drafting in civil and criminal cases.

7.5.1 General provisions relevant to written work

When undertaking any written work on behalf of a client you should have a comprehensive knowledge of:

- the Code of Conduct ('the Code');
- the Written Standards for the Conduct of Professional Work ('the Written Standards');
- Guidance on Preparation of Defence Case Statements;
- Guidance on Preparation of Witness Statements;
- the Funding Code.

The Written Standards in particular provide a guide to the way in which you should carry out your work. They must be read in conjunction with the Code and are to be taken into account in determining whether a disciplinary offence has been committed.

In undertaking any written work, advisory or drafting, or indeed any oral advisory work, you must always bear in mind the fundamental principles of the Code. In particular you:

(a) must not engage in conduct whether in pursuit of your profession or otherwise which is:
  (i)   dishonest or otherwise discreditable;
  (ii) prejudicial to the administration of justice; or
  (iii) likely to diminish public confidence in the legal profession or the administration of justice or otherwise bring the legal profession into disrepute (Code para 301);

(b) have an overriding duty to the court to act with independence in the interests of justice; you must assist the court in the administration of justice and not deceive or knowingly or recklessly mislead the court (Code para 302);

(c) must promote and fearlessly protect the lay client's best interests by all lawful and proper means and without regard to any consequences to yourself or your professional client (Code para 303);

(d) are individually and personally responsible for your conduct and for your professional work; you must exercise personal judgment in all your professional activities (Code para 306);

(e) must not allow your independence integrity or freedom from external pressures to be compromised, or do anything which would lead to an inference that they have been compromised (para 307).

Although these fundamental principles lie at the heart of all written work which you may be asked to undertake on behalf of a lay client, the Code and Written Standards and the Guidance issued by the Bar Council under the Code offer specific guidance in relation to certain types of work which you may be instructed to carry out.

7.5.2 Your duty on receipt of papers

When you obtain instructions to advise or draft a document, you must read them as soon as possible, to ensure that you are competent to deal with the matter, and have adequate time to carry out the task given the pressures of your other work (see para 701(b) and (c) of the Code and para 3.1 of the Written Standards). You must not delay in carrying out this task. You should aim to do this within a few days, or immediately if the instructions are urgent, because if the case is beyond your competence, or you cannot fulfil the task within the required time or a reasonable time, then the professional client must be informed and the instructions passed on to another barrister. Of course, you cannot return instructions without first explaining to your client the reason for doing so, and you obviously cannot pass the papers on to another barrister without the consent of your client (Code para 610).

If you do accept the instructions, then you must ensure that you do the work within the time requested or agreed, or within a reasonable time. If there is a time limit laid down by the Civil Procedure Rules within which the work should be done (for example, filing a Defence, serving Witness Statements, filing a Notice of Appeal) then you must ensure the work is done and returned to your instructing solicitor in good time to enable him or her to comply with the time limit. A failure to comply with time limits laid down by the Civil Procedure Rules may result in your lay client's case being struck out, so drafting work must usually be given priority over advisory work.

Solicitors are frequently heard to complain that a failure to carry out written work within the requested or agreed time, or within a reasonable time, is a very common failing of the Bar. In practice, it sometimes happens that cases run on longer than intended, or urgent and serious matters arise, so that agreed time limits cannot be met or the work requested cannot be undertaken within a reasonable time. If this does happen, it is important to telephone your instructing solicitor immediately. The lay client may be able and prepared to wait, but if he or she is not, then you must return the instructions to the professional client or to another barrister acceptable to your professional and lay client (para 701(e) of the Code and para 5.6 of the Written Standards).

It follows that you must actively manage your practice and keep a close eye on the volume of work that you have. Be realistic and honest about (a) the length of time it will take you to complete each item of work and (b) the work that you are competent to do, having regard to your knowledge and expertise. Do not feel obliged to accept instructions in a complex case involving copyright and passing off if your primary area of expertise is family work and you do not know the first thing about copyright or passing off. Indeed, if you know, or ought to know, that you are not competent to handle the instructions, it would be a clear breach of the Code to accept them.

7.5.3   Opinion writing

7.5.3.1   General principles

Any advice that you give should be 'practical, appropriate to the needs and circumstances of the particular client, and clearly and comprehensively expressed' (para 5.7 of the Written Standards). This is obvious. However, in the remainder of this section, some guidance will be given about your professional obligations when specific types of advice are sought.

7.5.3.2   Advice for the benefit of the Legal Aid Board/Legal Services Commission

If you undertake publicly-funded work you have additional professional responsibilities that you must always follow when it comes to providing written advice about the case. In publicly-funded cases, you will almost always be asked to provide a written opinion before proceedings are issued, and also quite often after service of witness statements, to determine whether it is appropriate for the matter to go to trial. In relation to opinions provided under Legal Aid Certificates granted before April 2000, the Opinion must comply with the *Legal Aid Guidelines* (to be found in the Legal Aid Handbook or on the Bar Council's website). In respect of Legal Services Certificates provided under the Funding Code, the advice must comply with Annex E of the Code of Conduct '*Guidelines on Opinions under the Funding Code*'. Both sets of guidelines are in fairly similar terms and give guidance to barristers on what an Advice or Opinion must contain as to the merits of funding or continuing to fund a case.

Generally, Opinions must be prepared in accordance with *The Funding Code* (see www.legalservices.gov.uk). When you are instructed to advise in writing, you must decide whether a conference is necessary, for example to assess the credibility or reliability of a lay client's evidence.

When you write the Opinion, you must ensure that it states (a) the level of service under which the Opinion is given (or applied for) and (b) the case category into which the proceedings fall. In addition, every Opinion on the merits should comply with the following matters in so far as they are relevant to the issues raised in the particular case:

(a) Where factual issues are involved, set out the factual disputes in sufficient detail to enable the Commission to assess their relative strengths and express a clear opinion on whether the applicant's evidence would be accepted by the court, and give reasons for that opinion.

(b) Where there are issues or disputes of law, these must also be summarised in sufficient detail to enable the Commission to come to a view without having to have recourse to materials outside the Opinion. Express a clear view on whether the applicant's case on the law would be accepted by the court, and give reasons for that opinion.

(c) Draw attention to any lack of evidence, which might have a bearing on the applicant's case or any other factor which might affect the outcome of the case.

(d) State the prospects of success, and in particular specify whether they are:
  (i)   very good (greater than 80%);
  (ii)   good (60%–80%);
  (iii) moderate (50%–60%);
  (iv)   borderline (which means that the prospects of success are not poor, but because there are difficult disputes of fact, law or expert evidence, it is not possible to say that the prospects of success are better than 50%). In this case, the

fact, law or expert evidence, which leads you to put the case in this category must be identified;

(v) poor (less than 50% so the claim is likely to fail);

(vi) unclear (the case cannot be put into any of the above categories because further investigation is needed; in which case, you must also indicate what further investigation is needed).

(e) Cost benefit: the Opinion must set out the benefit to the client, and put a figure on the likely level of damages the client would receive if successful at trial, allowing for any reduction for contributory negligence or otherwise. Likely damages should also be discounted if there is any doubt as to whether the opponent will be able to pay the money award.

(f) Where the application is for investigative help to be granted or continued, the Opinion should indicate what investigations need to be conducted. It should also show that there are reasonable grounds for believing that when the investigative work has been carried out, the claim will be strong enough, in terms of prospects of success and cost benefit, to justify a grant of full representation.

(g) If the case has a wider public benefit, you should set out the nature of the benefit and the parties affected by it.

(h) Finally you should suggest or formulate any appropriate limitation or condition on the certificate, if it is appropriate to do so, in order to safeguard the Fund.

7.5.3.3 What advice do you give if you become aware that your lay client has improperly obtained public funding?

Sometimes your lay client may provide you with information which suggests that public funding has been wrongly obtained by false or misleading information. If this is the case, you cannot simply turn a blind eye to the matter. You should explore the matter, tactfully, with your lay client and/or instructing solicitor. If it becomes apparent that funding has been improperly obtained, your duty, as counsel, is clearly spelt out by paras 303 and 304 and Annex E paras 20 and 22 of the Code of Conduct. In addition to these provisions, Rule C44 of the *Funding Code Procedures* also provides that counsel must inform the Regional Director if, *inter alia*, it appears that the lay client may have given inaccurate, misleading or incomplete information, or new information or a change of circumstances has come to light which may affect the terms or continuation of the Certificate.

Your obligations under the Code of Conduct are therefore clear. You must inform the Commission of any matter which may affect your lay client's entitlement to funding or the terms or continuation of a Certificate. You should discuss the matter with your lay client, explain the nature of the duty imposed on you, and urge him or her personally to make the disclosure required (although personal disclosure by the lay client does not appear to negate the duty imposed on counsel). Note that para 22 of Annex E provides that where you are under a duty to draw matters to the attention of the Commission, you can do so by drawing the matter to the attention of your instructing solicitor, and asking him or her to pass it on to the Commission, or you can contact the Commission directly if that is appropriate in the circumstances of the case. In addition to the reporting obligations set out above, you must cease to act if the lay client refuses to take action to remedy the situation. In these circumstances, you are effectively put in the position of having to make the disclosure to the Commission against your lay client's wishes, and this would obviously make any continuing professional relationship with him or her extremely difficult.

7.5.3.4   Advice on disclosure

In civil cases, it is your duty to advise your client that all relevant documents must be disclosed, even if they are fatal to his or her case (see para 608 of the Code and **7.2.2.4** above). If the lay client fails to follow your advice, you must withdraw from the case.

Applications made 'without notice' impose an even stricter obligation of disclosure on the lay client. In applications of this type, which will usually involve obtaining an urgent injunction or a freezing or search order, you must ensure that full and frank disclosure is made to the court. The duty of disclosure is really that of your lay client, but it is policed by the lawyers. If you fail to ensure that your lay client complies with it, or fail to draw the attention of the court to matters which should be disclosed, then you may be misleading the court, or engaging in conduct which is prejudicial to the administration of justice. You would therefore be in breach of your duties under paras 301 and 302 of the Code. Any failure to make full and frank disclosure may also result in the order being discharged. An order for costs may also be made against your lay client (or perhaps a wasted costs order may be made against you or your instructing solicitors).

Therefore, in advising a client who wishes to obtain urgent 'without notice' interim relief, such an as injunction, a freezing order, or a search order, it is imperative that your lay client understands the nature of the duty of full and frank disclosure. If necessary you must ask questions of the client to ensure that this duty is complied with. If you are asked to draft any document, such as a witness statement, you must also ensure that all relevant matters are fully and properly disclosed in it.

7.5.3.5   Advice following receipt of further information

It is not uncommon for counsel to be asked to advise at an early stage of an action. Subsequently, you may be sent instructions to settle statements of case, or witness statements or advise on a different aspect of the matter. Sometimes the fresh instructions will contain material that will alter the advice which you gave previously.

If you find yourself in this position, you should reassess any previous advice following receipt of further information if you are instructed to do so. Even if you are not instructed to reconsider your previous advice, you should at least warn your instructing solicitor that your previous views have to be reconsidered as a result of the change of circumstances. A failure to do so may lead to a wasted costs order against you: *C v C (Wasted Costs Order)* [1994] 2 FLR 34.

7.5.3.6   Opinions under conditional fee agreements

If you are instructed to act under a conditional fee agreement ('CFA') then you may face a number of ethical problems, not least when you are instructed to carry out written work. The Bar Council CFA Panel has drawn up a lengthy document to offer guidance to those undertaking CFA work. The *Conditional Fee Guidance* does not form part of the Code of Conduct, but you are strongly advised to follow the guidance to ensure compliance with the Code.

If you are acting under a CFA, then during the currency of the CFA agreement, you should use your best endeavours to ensure that:

(a) Any advice you give is communicated and fully explained to the lay client.

(b) Any offer of settlement is communicated to the lay client immediately.

(c) The consequences of particular clauses in the solicitor/lay client agreement and the solicitor/barrister agreement are explained to the lay client as and when they become relevant, particularly after an offer of settlement has been made. This last obligation in particular would require you to give advice on the usual costs consequences of settlement and the success fee that may become payable.

(d) In advising on settlement you must bear in mind only the interests of the lay client (and not your own interests, such as the 'success fee' that may become payable on settlement under the CFA). In order to avoid any allegation by lay clients that they were pressured into an unfavourable settlement, you should give advice in writing, which includes the following matters:

   (i)   the sum offered in settlement;

   (ii) the success fee payable to lawyers on the settlement, assuming it is not recoverable from the other side;

   (iii) whether the settlement is, in your opinion, a good one;

   (iv) an assessment of the prospects of getting more money if the case proceeds, and if so, the likely sum that may be recovered, and an assessment of the prospects of getting less or nothing at all;

   (v)   where you advise that the sum offered in settlement is not adequate, then you must also advise on the likely sum that will be expended in costs, the likely success fee payable in the event that the client succeeds in recovering more at the end of the day, and the net gain to the client taking these matters into account.

(e) The same considerations apply when considering and advising on whether to make a Part 36 offer and on the amount of the offer.

7.5.3.7   Advice in criminal cases

The Code of Conduct and the Written Standards apply equally to criminal cases. However there are a number of other specific duties which you must also bear in mind by virtue of the Written Standards.

In particular, para 10.4(c) of the Written Standards provides that prosecuting counsel should:

   (i)   decide whether any additional evidence is required, and if it is, advise in writing, setting out precisely what additional evidence is required with a view to serving it on the defence as soon as possible;

   (ii) consider whether all the witness statements in the possession of the prosecution have been properly served on the defendant;

   (iii) eliminate all unnecessary material so as to ensure an efficient and fair trial, and also consider the need for particular witnesses and exhibits;

   (iv) draft appropriate admissions and serve them on the defence;

   (v)   in all Class 1 and Class 2 cases and in other cases of complexity, draft a case summary for transmission to the court.

Defence counsel must consider whether:

   (i)   any enquiries or further enquiries are necessary, and if so, should advise in writing as soon as possible;

   (ii) details of an alibi are required and if so, draft an appropriate notice;

   (iii) it is appropriate to call expert evidence for the defence, and advise solicitors to comply with the rules of the Crown Court in relation to notifying the prosecution of the contents of the evidence to be given;

(iv) any admissions can be made with a view to saving time and expense at trial, with the aim of admitting as much evidence as can be admitted in accordance with his or her duty to client;

(v) he or she wishes to examine any exhibits, and if so, should ensure that appropriate arrangements are made to examine them as promptly as possible.

7.5.3.8 Advice on appeal

Frequently barristers are asked to advise on appeal. In criminal cases, defence counsel must always consider whether there are any grounds of appeal against conviction or sentence.

Paragraph 16 of the Written Standards draws counsel's attention to the Guide to Proceedings in the Court of Appeal Criminal Division. In particular, defence counsel is encouraged to follow the procedures set out in paras 1.2 and 1.4 of the Guide. In addition para 16.2 of the Written Standards provides that:

(i) If his client pleads guilty or is convicted, a defence barrister should see his client after sentence in the presence of his professional client or representative. If he is satisfied that there are no reasonable grounds of appeal he should advise orally and confirm this in writing using the form set out in Appendix 1 to the Guide. No further advice is necessary unless a full written advice is required by the lay client, or it is necessary on the particular facts of the case.

(ii) If he is satisfied that there are reasonable grounds for appeal or he needs more time to consider the position then he should give oral advice in these terms, and certify in writing using the form in Appendix 1 of the Guide. Counsel would then provide written advice to the professional client as soon as possible and in any event within 14 days.

Quite often clients may want you to settle appeal documents even if you advise that the appeal is completely hopeless. In these circumstances, you must take care not to settle any grounds of appeal that you do not consider to be properly arguable (para 704 of the Code of Conduct and para 5.11 of the Written Standards). In criminal cases, para 16.3 of the Written Standards states:

Counsel should not settle grounds of appeal unless he considers that such grounds are properly arguable, and in that event, he should provide a reasoned written opinion in support of such grounds.

7.5.3.9 Solicitor asks you to give advice which does not reflect your true opinion

You must not permit your absolute independence, integrity and freedom from external pressures to be compromised or compromise your professional standards in order to please your client, the court or a third party (Code para 307). You therefore must not alter your opinion to suit the needs of any professional client or lay client, and nor should you provide advice, for any purpose, which does not reflect your true opinion.

7.5.3.10 What advice do you give if you consider your solicitor to be negligent

In practice, you may sometimes consider that your lay client may have a claim against your instructing solicitors. For example, the client's case may have been struck out because your instructing solicitors failed to serve witness statements on time. In a property dispute, you may conclude that your client has no legal title to a particular piece of land due to the negligence of your instructing solicitors who acted for the lay client during the purchase of the land. Your instructing solicitor may send you a lot of work, and you know that he or she will not want the lay client to become aware that the firm may have caused the lay client's predicament. What do you do in these circumstances?

Guidance can be obtained from paras 303 and 703 of the Code of Conduct and para 3.3 of the Written Standards. Your duty under these provisions can be broken down into the following parts:

(a) You must promote and protect fearlessly and by all proper and lawful means the lay client's best interests.

(b) You must do so without regard to your own interests or to any consequences to yourself or to any other person, including your instructing solicitors. The fact that you may receive no further instructions from the solicitors must not be allowed to influence your advice. Nor should you permit your instructing solicitor, in any way, to limit your discretion or influence your opinion on how the interests of the lay client would best be served.

(c) As between your lay client and your instructing solicitor, your primary duty is owed to the lay client.

(d) You should always be alert to the possibility of a conflict of interest between the lay client and the professional client, and any such conflict must be resolved in favour of the lay client.

(e) If you form the view that there is a conflict of interest between your lay client and your instructing solicitor (for example, because it appears that the latter may have been negligent) then you must consider whether it would be in the lay client's best interests to instruct another professional adviser or representative. If you consider that it would, you must advise in those terms. You must also take such steps as you consider necessary to ensure that your advice is communicated to the lay client, if necessary by sending a copy of your advice in writing directly to him or her, as well as to the professional client (see para 703 of the Code).

(f) In advising, bear in mind that it may not always be sensible for a lay client to instruct another firm of solicitors to act on his or her behalf immediately, even if it does appear that your instructing solicitors have been negligent. An example of when it might be proper for your instructing solicitors to continue to act for the time being, is where an appeal is pending against an order striking out the claim for failure to follow a procedural step in the action. However even in these circumstances, it may be appropriate to ask the solicitors or the Solicitors Indemnity Fund to fund the appeal. It is equally clear that a firm of solicitors should not continue to act if there is any doubt over whether the litigation should be continued, or if the lay client would clearly be best advised to pursue a remedy against his or her solicitors rather than a third party. The facts of each case must be carefully considered.

(g) Finally, as a matter of common courtesy, always telephone your instructing solicitor and give him or her advance warning of the nature of the advice that it is your professional duty to give to the lay client. This may do much to preserve the relationship between you and your instructing solicitor for the future.

7.5.4 Drafting

7.5.4.1 General principles

Paragraph 704 of the Code offers general advice on drafting any statement of case, witness statement, affidavit, notice of appeal or other document.

704   A barrister must not devise facts which will assist in advancing the lay client's case and must not draft any statement of case, witness statement, affidavit, notice of appeal or other document containing

(a) any statement or fact or contention which is not supported by the lay client or by his instructions;

(b) any contention which he does not consider to be properly arguable.

You must not settle any statement of case or any document which contains abusive or scandalous allegations or any allegation which is intended to insult, vilify or annoy the other party or any other person (para 708(g)).

These general rules must be borne in mind every time you are asked to draft any document. In relation to para 704(b) of the Code, it is impossible to lay down any detailed rules about whether or not something is 'properly arguable'. However, it is clear that a contention will not be 'properly arguable' if it gives rise to no claim or defence at law, or, if properly analysed, there is absolutely no evidence to support it. You must therefore have a firm grasp of the relevant substantive law when drafting any legal document. Furthermore, you must ensure that any contention you put in a document can be properly argued on the facts of the particular case.

7.5.4.2 Pleading fraud

Sometimes a lay client will make allegations of fraudulent or dishonest conduct against the opposing party. Both the lay client and the professional client may ask you to include these allegations in any statement of case that you are instructed to draft. However, you are under a very strict duty not to draft any statement of case, witness statement, affidavit, notice of appeal or other document containing any allegation of fraud unless you have 'clear instructions' to make such an allegation and you have before you 'reasonably credible material which as it stands establishes a *prima facie* case of fraud' (Code para 704(c)). Although this paragraph only refers to fraud, any other dishonourable or dishonest conduct should not be alleged without similar material.

The House of Lords (agreeing with the dissenting judgment of Wilson J in the Court of Appeal) have considered this provision in *Medcalf v Weatherill & Another* [2002] 3 WLR 172. In this case, a wasted costs order was sought by the opposing party from leading and junior counsel ('the barristers') acting for the other party. They had settled a notice of appeal and a skeleton argument containing allegations of fraud, which the court found were not justified by the evidence. The barristers defended the application on the ground that they had not been able to persuade their lay clients to waive privilege, and that being so, it was impossible for the court to know on what material they had acted, and so the application ought to be dismissed.

In the Court of Appeal, Peter Gibson LJ and Schiemann LJJ (Wilson J dissenting), took the view that para 704(c) required a barrister to have reasonably credible material establishing a *prima facie* case of fraud before they could draft an allegation of fraud. That material had to be evidence that could be put before the court to make good the allegation. If there is material before counsel which could not be used in court, the existence of the material could not justify pleading fraud.

Wilson J carefully considered the meaning of the phrase 'reasonably credible material which as it stands establishes a *prima facie* case of fraud'. In his view, the word 'material' in what is now para 704(c) of the Code was wider than evidence in its proper form, and the phrase 'as it stands' means 'at face value'. He took the view (para 80) that, 'To construe the word "establishes" as something that can be achieved only by evidence admissible in court is, in this context, arguably to read too much into it'. In the absence of any evidence as to what the barristers did have before them when pleading the allegations of fraud in the notice of appeal and skeleton argument, he did not feel that he could come to a positive conclusion that the Code of Conduct had been breached.

In the House of Lords, Lord Bingham, agreeing with Wilson J, had this to say:

Paragraph 606(c) [now 704(c)] lays down an important and salutary principle. The parties to contested actions are often at daggers drawn, and the litigious process serves to exacerbate the hostility between them. Such clients are only too ready to make allegations of the most damaging kind against each other. While counsel should never lend his name to such allegations unless instructed to do so, the receipt of instructions is not of itself enough. Counsel is bound to exercise an objective professional judgment whether it is in all the circumstances proper to lend his name to the allegation. As the rule recognises, counsel could not properly judge it proper to make such an allegation unless he had material before him which he judged to be reasonably credible and which appeared to justify the allegation. At the hearing stage, counsel cannot properly make or persist in an allegation which is unsupported by inadmissible evidence, since if there is not admissible evidence to support the allegation the court cannot be invited to find that it has been proved, and if the court cannot be invited to find that the allegation has been proved the allegation should not be made or should be withdrawn. I would however agree with Wilson J that at the preparatory stage the requirement is not that counsel should necessarily have evidence before him in admissible form but that he should have material of such a character that would lead responsible counsel to conclude that serious allegations could properly be based upon it. I could not think, for example, that it would be professionally improper for counsel to plead allegations, however serious, based on the documented conclusions of a DTI inspector or a public inquiry, even though counsel had no access to the documents referred to and the findings in question were inadmissible hearsay. On this point I would accept the judgment of Wilson J.

It is clear from this that:

(a) Allegations of fraud cannot and should not be made simply because the lay client instructs you to make them.

(b) Allegations of fraud should never be made in the absence of 'clear instructions'. You should insist on written instructions from the lay client before you draft any allegation of fraud.

(c) You must scrutinise the papers carefully and decide whether there is enough material to justify pleading an allegation of fraud. The material must be credible and, as it stands, establish a *prima facie* case of fraud.

(d) If the material relied upon includes or consists of the evidence of a witness, it would be prudent to ensure that a signed statement is obtained from the witness before such an allegation is made.

(e) If an allegation of fraud is drafted but it later becomes clear, at any stage of the proceedings, that it cannot be substantiated (for example, because a witness has retracted his or her statement) then you should inform the opposing side immediately that the allegation of fraud is not being pursued.

7.5.4.3   Drafting orders for interim relief

Quite often counsel is instructed to make an application and draft an order for interim relief such as an injunction, search order, or freezing order. If you are instructed to make such an application, you should ensure that you personally undertake the task of drafting the order, and do so as quickly as possible. A copy of the order must be lodged with the court before the oral hearing starts, except in exceptional circumstances.

Mummery LJ had this to say in *Memory Corporation plc v Sidhu (No 2)* [2000] 1 WLR 1443 at 1459(H)–1460(E) about counsel's duty in relation to such hearings:

It is the particular duty of the advocate to see that the correct legal procedures and forms are used; that a written skeleton argument and a properly drafted order are prepared by him personally and lodged with the court before the oral hearing; and that at the hearing, the court's attention is drawn by him to unusual features of the evidence adduced, to the applicable law and to the formalities and procedure to be observed.

It is unsatisfactory for an advocate to hand to the court for the first time during the course of an urgent hearing a long and complex draft order that requires close reading and careful scrutiny by the Court. If the advocate is unable to produce a draft order for the judge to read before the oral hearing starts then the application should not be made, save in the most exceptional circumstances, until the order has been drafted and lodged.

I emphasise the special responsibility of the advocate for the preparation of draft orders for the use of the court. There may be a convenient precedent to hand on the word processor of the instructing solicitor or in their files or in counsel's chambers, but it is the duty of the advocate actually presenting the case on the oral hearing of the application to settle the draft order personally so as to ensure that he is thoroughly familiar with the detail of it and so in the best possible position to respond to the court's concerns and to assist the court on the final form of the order.

If the order differs in any respect from the standard form of order used in such applications, it is also important to draw this to the attention of the court. Failure to do so may render you in breach of your duty not to mislead the court.

7.5.4.4 Witness statements

In relation to witnesses, you may be asked to see a lay client or a witness in conference with a view to discussing their evidence. You may be asked to do this to assess the credibility of the witness or advise on the strength of the case generally, or to take a proof of evidence which can then be used as the basis of a witness statement. You may also be asked to draft a witness statement on behalf of the lay client or some other witness of fact. In civil cases, counsel is increasingly asked to draft and prepare witness statements because the witness statement will usually stand as that witness's evidence-in-chief at the trial of the action. In this section, guidance will be given in relation to:

- the contact which you may have with a witness in both civil and criminal cases;
- the rules you must adhere to when drafting witness statements.

Contact with witnesses

There is no longer any rule which prevents a barrister from having contact with any witness other than the lay client. Under the Code of Conduct (para 705) it is clear what you must not do. You must not:

- rehearse, practise or coach a witness in relation to his evidence;
- encourage a witness to give evidence which is untruthful or which is not the whole truth.

See **7.2** above for further discussion on this point.

In relation to witnesses other than the lay client, you should exercise your discretion and consider very carefully whether and to what extent contact is appropriate for the purpose of interviewing witnesses or discussing with them the substance of their evidence bearing in mind that:

(a) it is not your function, but rather that of your instructing solicitor, to investigate the case and collect the evidence;

(b) even if you do not intend or wish to do so, as a figure in authority, you may subconsciously influence lay witnesses, and discussion of the evidence may unwittingly contaminate the witness's evidence;

(c) you should be alert to the risks that any discussion of the substance of the case with a witness may lead to suspicions of coaching, and thus tend to diminish the value of the witness's evidence in the eyes of the court. It may also place you in a position of professional embarrassment if you yourself became a witness in the case (see para 6.2 of the Written Standards).

In the case of a completely independent witness, you may think it prudent not to discuss the evidence with the witness at all, bearing in mind the matters set out above. If, however, after careful consideration of all matters, you decide to proceed, you should take the following steps to minimise the risk of suspicions of coaching. You should ensure that:

- before any discussion about the evidence takes place, you have been provided with a proof of the witness's evidence;

- any such discussion takes place in the presence of your instructing solicitor or a representative;

- the discussion of one witness's evidence does not take place in the presence of another witness of fact;

- care is taken not to disclose the factual evidence of another witness if it would be inappropriate to do so.

A failure to follow these steps will tend to encourage the rehearsal or coaching of a witness and increase the risk of fabrication or contamination of evidence.

You should also be alert to the distinction between settling a witness statement and the taking of a witness statement. Where you are asked to take a witness statement, as opposed to settling a witness statement from a proof of evidence of the witness which has been taken by your professional client, then it is not appropriate, except in exceptional circumstances, for you to act as counsel in the case because it risks undermining your independence as an advocate (see para 6.2.6 of the Written Standards). It should also be noted that the cab rank rule does not require a barrister to undertake the task of taking a witness statement, as opposed to settling a witness statement. Exceptional circumstances when it may be appropriate for you to take a proof of evidence and continue to act as counsel in the case would be:

- the witness is a minor;

- you have no choice, other than to take a proof, for example, in circumstances where a witness turns up at trial and there is no professional client in attendance;

- you are a junior member in a team and will not be examining the witness.

The 'Guidance on Preparation of Witness Statements' para 9(v) makes it clear that the following distinction should be borne in mind:

(a) Questioning a witness closely in order to:
  (i) enable him or her to present his or her evidence fully and accurately (this must be permissible to ensure that any witness statement that you settle is complete in content); or
  (ii) test the reliability of his or her evidence (which may be necessary to form an informed view of the merits of the case and/or the credibility of the witness)

and

(b) Questioning a witness closely with a view to encouraging him or her to alter, massage or obscure his or her real recollection (which is clearly not permissible).

There is no objection to testing a witness's recollection robustly to ascertain the quality of the evidence or discussing the issues that may arise in cross-examination. What is objectionable is conducting a mock cross-examination of the witness or lay client or rehearsing with the witness particular lines of questioning that you propose to follow or which your opponent is likely to follow.

The rules relating to the settling or taking of witness statements in criminal cases are much more strict than in civil cases. Paragraph 6.3.1 of the Written Standards states that:

As a general principle, with the exception of the lay client, character and expert witnesses, it is wholly inappropriate for a barrister in such a case to interview any potential witness. Interviewing involves discussing with any such witness the substance of his evidence or the evidence of other such witnesses.

Drafting witness statements in a civil case

When asked to draft witness statements in a civil case, you must bear in mind the fact that the statement is likely to stand as the witness's evidence-in-chief. One of the first questions that will be asked of the witness at trial is whether he or she confirms the truth and accuracy of the statement. It is therefore critical that the statement you draft reflects that witness's evidence.

There is often some misunderstanding of the role that counsel can play in drafting a witness statement. Counsel's duty in drafting a witness statement is to:

- understand the evidence that a witness can give;
- help the witness present his or her story *in his or her own words* in a well structured, organised, coherent and persuasive way;
- ensure the witness tells his or her whole story (in other words that the statement is complete in content);
- above all, ensure that the statement reflects the witness's evidence. Paragraph 6(iv) of the Guidance on Preparation of Witness Statements states that:

Save for formal matters and uncontroversial facts, [the witness statement] should be expressed, if practicable in the witness's own words. This is especially important when the statement is dealing with the critical factual issues in the case — eg the accident or the disputed conversation. Thus the statement should reflect the witness's own description of events. It should not be drafted or edited so as to massage or obscure the witness's real evidence.

It is *not* counsel's function to:

- put a gloss on the evidence;
- draft a statement that contains words that the witness would not use, particularly in relation to the central factual issues;
- vet the accuracy of the witness's evidence (see para 5 of Guidance on Preparation of Witness Statements);
- exclude material from the statement where the omission renders untrue or misleading anything that remains in the statement.

Paragraphs 704(a) and (b) of the Code of Conduct apply equally to witness statements as they do to any other document that you may be asked to draft. Therefore, the witness statement must not contain any statement of fact which is not supported by instructions. You should not draft any statement or fact other than the evidence which in substance, according to your instructions, you reasonably believe the witness would give if the evidence contained in the witness statement or affidavit were being given in oral examination (para 704(d) of the Code). However, you can draft a document containing facts or matters which are subject to confirmation of accuracy by the lay client or witness.

Settling defence case statements in criminal cases

It is becoming increasingly common for counsel to be asked to settle defence case statements. The Bar Council has now prepared a document entitled 'Guidance on preparation of Defence Case Statements' to assist counsel undertaking this task. You should not settle the defence case statement until you have seen all relevant documents, particularly all prosecution documents and statements, and obtained full instructions from the lay client from a properly signed proof and also preferably during a conference. In particular, you must ensure that the lay client understands the importance of the defence case statement and the potential adverse effects of an inaccurate or inadequate statement.

Once the statement is drafted, you should ensure that you get proper informed approval for the draft from the lay client. This is particularly important in case the lay client challenges or disowns the statement during the trial. You ought therefore to insist on getting *written* acknowledgment from the lay client that:

- he or she understands the importance and accuracy of the defence case statement; and

- he or she has had the opportunity of considering the contents of the statement carefully and approves it.

If you entrust your solicitor with the task of obtaining this acknowledgement, then you should also prepare a short written advice to enclose with the defence case statement on the importance of obtaining the acknowledgment before the defence case statement is served. The defendant should be asked to sign the statement before it is served.

Due to the absolute necessity for the statement to be accurate, para 6 of the Guidance on Preparation of Defence Case Statements states that counsel ought not to accept any instructions to draft or settle a defence case statement unless he or she has been given adequate time and opportunity to gain proper familiarity with the case and comply with the requirements set out above.

7.5.4.5   Drafting indictments in criminal cases

Prosecution counsel is frequently asked to draft the indictment. If you do obtain instructions to undertake drafting of this type, you must do so promptly and within due time. You should also bear in mind 'the desirability of not overloading an indictment with either too many defendants or too many counts, in order to present the prosecution case as simply and as concisely as possible' (para 10.4 of the Written Standards). See also the Code for Crown Prosecutors, paragraphs 7.1–7.3. Furthermore, even if you are not instructed to settle the indictment, you should ask to see a copy of it and should check it.

7.5.5   Can you refuse to advise and/or draft a document?

You are bound by the cab rank rule (Code para 602). You must therefore accept any instructions at a proper professional fee in the fields in which you profess to practice, irrespective of the party on whose behalf you are instructed, the nature of the case or any belief or opinion that you may have formed as to the character, reputation, cause, conduct or guilt or innocence of that party. This applies whether the case is privately or publicly funded.

There are a number of circumstances in which you can refuse to act when instructed. These are set out in paras 603, 604 and 701 of the Code of Conduct. You may refuse to act if:

(a) you are required to do anything other than during the course of your ordinary working year;

(b) you do not have adequate time to deal with the papers (Code paras 603 and 701);

(c) there is a conflict of interest which would prevent you acting (such as having acted for the other side);

(d) the fee is not a proper professional fee having regard to the complexity and length and difficulty of the case, your expertise and seniority and the expenses you will incur. Note that a publicly-funded matter is deemed to be at a proper professional fee;

(e) if the work is to be done under a conditional fee agreement;

(f) if instructions are received from a solicitor or firm who has had credit facilities withdrawn by the Bar Council on the basis that the firm has been persistently late or has failed to pay counsel's fees. You must then refuse to do any work for the solicitor or firm unless payment of an agreed fee is enclosed with the papers, or you agree in advance to accept no payment for the work (Annex G1, The Terms of Work on which Barristers Offer Their Services to Solicitors and the Withdrawal of Credit Scheme 1988).

Otherwise, you must accept and carry out your instructions to the best of your ability, bearing in mind your duty under the Code and the Written Standards and the other Guidance issued by the Bar Council which has been discussed above.

7.6 Conclusion

This chapter has made it clear that professional conduct and ethical difficulties can arise throughout a case, in a variety of contexts. It has guided you through the problem areas pertinent to the key skills with a discussion of the relevant principles and other sources of guidance you will need as an intending barrister. Furthermore, several situations have been identified which are not expressly covered by the Code, but in applying its spirit with a recognition of the Code's underlying values (see **Chapter 4**), the suggested approaches should now be more easily understood.

Your alertness to these issues will ensure that they are handled appropriately paying due regard if necessary to not only the Code and the application of its spirit, but also to the 'ethical challenge' obligations discussed in **Chapter 1**. Hence, you will continue to develop the skills set out in **Chapter 1**:

- the *identification* of potential professional conduct issues;
- the *sources* of guidance on particular issues;
- the necessity of applying the *spirit* of the Code where there is no letter;
- the need to recognise obligations towards *fair treatment*; and
- how you would deal *practically* with the matter.

Of course, in practice there will be difficult situations in which you find yourself and no matter how disciplined your approach is to handling professional conduct matters, you will struggle to know the best course of action. The point is that you are already half way to dealing with the matter because you have recognised at the earliest opportunity that an issue has arisen. In such a situation do not be afraid to take guidance from fellow barristers or to phone the Bar Council. Remember the need to maintain the highest standards is an ongoing obligation for all members of the Bar — the practical advice and guidance set out in this section and throughout the Manual will only take you so far. You will know if you are cutting corners or deliberately ignoring professional conduct matters. However, it is hoped that you have already decided that the extra time and effort put to solving these areas of practice are the only way to ensure the solid foundation of a continuing and successful practice at the Bar.

The Proceeds of Crime Act 2002

8.1 The problem posed by the Proceeds of Crime Act 2002

Since it came into force, the Proceeds of Crime Act 2002 (POCA 2002) has caused considerable anxiety for lawyers. Following the decision of the Court of Appeal in *Bowman v Fels* [2005] EWCA Civ 226, the main remaining area of concern for lawyers is the reporting obligation under s 330 when working in 'the regulated sector'. However, there is also the need to advise the client when he or she is at risk of liability under s 327 and/or s 329. You should also be aware that the Serious Organised Crime and Police Act 2005 has made amendments to the POCA 2002, which are reflected in this chapter.

This chapter uses the specific example of ancillary relief. Ancillary relief is the process by which divorcing spouses obtain financial resolution of their affairs from the court. However, that should make it no less applicable to other situations. In ancillary relief, the client is in practice obliged to tell his or her adviser about all his or her assets and income because of the obligation to the court of full and frank disclosure. The problem is that this process may disclose that some of those assets are the proceeds of crime.

In order for there to be proceeds of crime, somebody (usually the client or another party in the context of legal proceedings) must have engaged in 'criminal conduct' (s 340(2)). It is not necessary that he or she has actually been convicted of an offence, and your client does not necessarily need to have personally engaged in the criminal conduct, only (for example) to be in possession of criminal property (see **8.2.2**).

It may be that the client has, for example, been involved in mainstream drug dealing. More commonly, there may be issues of tax evasion, eg, the client receives money 'cash in hand'. This is not in itself 'criminal conduct' — anyone can pay their bills in cash or by cheque — but it becomes an offence if he or she fails to disclose these earnings to the Inland Revenue. Tax evasion is a crime, as is benefit fraud.

A number of problems face the lawyer as a result of the POCA 2002. First, there are the 'principal offences' under Part VII of the POCA 2002 (ss 327, 328 and 329) and the secondary offences under s 333 (tipping off) and s 342 (prejudicing an investigation). The lawyer will need to advise the client of potential liability under these sections. There is a *small* residual risk of lawyers being liable under s 328 despite the judgment in *Bowman*. Secondly, since 1 March 2004, lawyers have been subject to the Money Laundering Regulations 2003, and thus may be operating a 'relevant business' in terms of the Regulations, while also being in the 'regulated sector' in terms of the Act (as defined by Sch 9 — definitions of these terms are the same in the Act and the Regulations). Being in the regulated sector exposes lawyers to the risk of criminal liability for breach of s 330 of the POCA 2002 (ie, failure to disclose). The risks are more acute for solicitors owing to the nature of their work (after all, they usually have first, and continuous, contact with the client and handle the client's money) but for certain types of work, the Bar is also under specific obligations and at risk of criminal liability.

8.2 Principal offences

8.2.1 Key differences between the principal and secondary offences

Sections 327, 328 and 329 set out the principal offences in Part VII of the POCA 2002. They differ to the secondary offences (considered below) in a number of key respects:

(a) Disclosure in respect of the principal offences is 'authorised disclosure' under s 338 (not 'protected disclosure' under s 337 which relates to the secondary offences).

(b) The disclosure defence under s 338 requires not only 'authorised disclosure' but also the 'appropriate consent' under s 335. Section 337 does not require a consent because of the fundamental difference in the duties between ss 327–329 and 330: in ss 327–329, disclosure is made in order to exonerate the discloser from criminal responsibility for what he or she would otherwise do; s 330 on the other hand is a general duty (arising from the fact of one's practice in the regulated sector) to disclose the fact that someone is involved in money laundering and in that sense is separate from any activity with which the discloser himself is involved.

8.2.2 Definitions

'Criminal conduct' is defined in s 340(2) (s 340 is in fact the definition section for Part VII of the POCA 2002). It covers conduct which would constitute an offence in any part of the UK — so, for example, tax evasion is a criminal offence in UK law. It also covers conduct which occurs abroad but would be an offence in the UK if it had occurred there, but in those circumstances defendants to offences under ss 327, 328, and 330 may be able to take advantage of the defences in those sections. These provide that if the defendant knew or believed on reasonable grounds that the relevant conduct had occurred in a particular country or territory outside of the UK, *and* that conduct was not criminal according to *local* laws at the time it occurred, *and* it was not conduct of a type prescribed by order of the Secretary of State, the defendant has not committed the offence.

'Criminal property' (s 340(3)) is that which constitutes 'a person's benefit from criminal conduct or … represents such a benefit (in whole or part and whether directly or indirectly', and the alleged offender (ie, the person accused of facilitating money laundering, etc) knows or suspects that it constitutes or represents such a benefit.

If, for example, in an ancillary relief claim, the matrimonial home had been partially paid for by 'criminal property' in the form of unpaid tax monies — say by paying the mortgage instalments partly with these monies — the house could 'represent' the benefit from criminal conduct. The same might be the case for other assets.

8.2.3 Sections 327, 328 and 329

Sections 327, 328 and 329 of the POCA 2002 may affect your client, and the client will need to be advised of this. Section 327 provides that:

(1) A person commits an offence if he —
    (a) conceals criminal property;
    (b) disguises criminal property;
    (c) converts criminal property;
    (d) transfers criminal property;

(e) removes criminal property from England and Wales or from Scotland or from Northern Ireland.

. . .

(3) Concealing or disguising criminal property includes concealing or disguising its nature, source, location, disposition, movement or ownership, or any rights with respect to it.

Section 328 provides that:

(1) A person commits an offence if he enters into or becomes concerned in an arrangement which he knows or suspects facilitates (by whatever means) the acquisition, retention, use or control of criminal property by or on behalf of another person.

As discussed below, 'being concerned in an arrangement' was once thought to include involvement in litigation which resulted in a settlement or an order of the court in relation to proceeds of crime. The Court of Appeal in *Bowman* made it quite clear that s 328 is not intended to affect 'the ordinary conduct of litigation by legal professionals. That includes any step taken by them in litigation from the issue of proceedings and the securing of injunctive relief or a freezing order up to its final disposal by judgment', and that such activities are not to be regarded as 'being concerned in a arrangement'. Subject to the points made at **8.7.2** et seq, s 328 now clearly does not apply to the involvement of a lawyer in litigation or the resolution of litigation by agreement. However, the client may still have committed the offence in relation to an arrangement over property, *independent of the litigation process*, for example, a sham property transaction designed to conceal the proceeds of crime.

Section 329 provides:

(1) A person commits an offence if he —
  (a) acquires criminal property;
  (b) uses criminal property;
  (c) has possession of criminal property.

For example, a wife in an ancillary relief claim who had not personally committed the criminal offence of tax evasion could potentially be accused of the s 329 offence — acquiring, using or possessing criminal property — if the house that she jointly owns with her tax-evading husband was bought with money he had not declared to tax — unless she makes an authorised disclosure under s 338. The husband could conceivably be accused of both s 327 and s 329 offences, as well as tax evasion itself. In order to protect herself, the wife should make an 'authorised disclosure' under s 338.

8.2.4   Defences to the principal offences

The client can obtain a complete defence by making an 'authorised disclosure' under s 338 (in the manner prescribed by s 339), *and* by getting the 'appropriate consent' (s 335).

Generally speaking, disclosure is to the National Criminal Intelligence Service (NCIS). The way that consent works is as follows:

(a) NCIS may consent within seven days of disclosure being made, in which case the client can continue with the act or transaction in question.

(b) If not, the client is required to wait for seven working days from the working day after disclosure. Once that period has passed without a notice of refusal from NCIS, the consent is deemed and the client can continue with the act or transaction.

(c) If NCIS gives notice of refusal within the seven-day period, there is then a moratorium period of 31 calendar days from the day on which refusal is received. Thereafter, the client is free to continue with the act or transaction.

8.2.5   Does s 328 apply to the activities of lawyers?

The judgment in *Bowman* was handed down by the Court of Appeal on 8 March 2005. It is authority of considerable public importance since this was the first full examination by the Court of Appeal of the impact of the POCA 2002 on legal professional privilege between lawyer and client. It effectively overrules *P v P (Ancillary Relief; Proceeds of Crime)* [2003] EWHC Fam 2260.

8.2.5.1   Background

Prior to this decision, it was widely believed that s 328 of the POCA 2002 imposed an obligation on a lawyer to report money laundering by others if that lawyer was entering into or 'becoming concerned in' an arrangement which would facilitate 'the acquisition, retention, use or control of criminal property by or on behalf of another person'. The word 'arrangement' was believed to cover litigation, including settlement of such litigation by agreement. Where a lawyer knew or suspected that money or assets being the subject of litigation were the proceeds of crime, then he or she could only escape criminal liability under s 328 by making an 'authorised disclosure' — in other words, by notifying the National Criminal Intelligence Service (NCIS) of the suspected criminal activity and obtaining the appropriate consent to proceed with the arrangement. For lawyers, it seemed that the fundamental principle of legal professional privilege had been fatally undermined — not only would a lawyer be obliged to report suspected money laundering by the other party, he or she would also be compelled to make disclosure to a third party of suspected money laundering by his or her own client.

8.2.5.2   The central question in *Bowman*

The Court of Appeal identified the following issues (para 24):

(a) Whether s 328 applied to the ordinary conduct of legal proceedings at all.

(b) Whether Parliament could have been taken, without using clear words to that effect, to have intended to override the very important principles of legal professional privilege.

8.2.5.3   The decision in *Bowman*

The Court of Appeal concluded as follows:

(a) (para 83) Section 328 is not intended to affect 'the ordinary conduct of litigation by legal professionals. That includes any step taken by them in litigation from the issue of proceedings and the securing of injunctive relief or a freezing order up to its final disposal by judgment'. In other words, conducting litigation does not involve 'becoming concerned in an arrangement' within the meaning of s 328, and s 328 is therefore inapplicable to such activities.

(b) (para 87) The Court of Appeal further stated that even if the above conclusion was wrong, it was quite clear that on a proper construction s 328 does not override legal professional privilege.

(c) (paras 99 and 100) The Court of Appeal also came to the view that resolution of the whole, or any aspect, of legal proceedings by agreement would equally be outside the scope of s 328.

Clearly, this guidance has brought considerable clarity to an area which caused enormous concern to lawyers involved in litigation when the POCA 2002 was first enacted. A lawyer can advise and represent a client in the vast majority of situations without fear of being obliged to breach legal professional privilege to report suspected money laundering to the authorities. However, some areas of difficulty remain. Section 330 applies in full force to activities in the regulated sector, and it is possible that there remain some situations where s 328 could apply to lawyers. These are discussed below at 8.7.

8.3 Secondary offences

8.3.1 The Money Laundering Regulations 2003

A barrister conducting 'relevant business' as defined in the Regulations will be subject to additional requirements and liability.

8.3.1.1 When is counsel deemed to be involved in 'relevant business'?

The Regulations will affect those members of the Bar who conduct 'relevant business' as defined in reg 2(2), which includes:

> the provision by way of business of legal services by a body corporate or unincorporate or, in the case of a sole practitioner, by an individual and which involves participation in a financial or real property transaction (whether by assisting in the planning or execution of any such transaction or otherwise by acting for, or on behalf of, a client in any such transaction). (reg 2(2)(1))

As the Bar guidance, 'Money Laundering Regulations 2003 — Guidance for the Bar', points out, the Regulations are transaction based. Therefore, in order to decide if he or she is 'conducting relevant business', counsel has to consider for every piece of work undertaken whether it involves his or her participation in a financial or real property transaction.

The guidance gives examples of such transactions:

(a) drafting or structuring of contracts prior to the execution of transactions;

(b) drafting of documents whose purpose is to achieve the execution of a transaction.

The Bar Council has considered the European Directive upon which the POCA 2002 is based and concluded that the following do not constitute participation in a transaction:

(a) ascertaining and advising upon the legal position of a client once a transaction has taken place;

(b) representing a client in legal proceedings which culminate in a settlement or an order of the court, including drafting terms of settlement;

(c) drafting a Will.

It should be noted that this guidance is very important. As yet, it does not have approval from the Treasury (since at the time of preparation there was not as yet a procedure for this in place); however, should your compliance with the Regulations come to be considered by a criminal court, your adherence (or not, as the case may be) to the guidance issued by your professional body would be an important factor in the matter. In addition, the judgment in *Bowman* demonstrates that the Bar Council guidance on this matter is correct as concerns the advising of a client, or representing that client in proceedings.

The Bar Council states that 'barristers must be astute to determine whether any particular piece of work undertaken by them falls within reg 2(2)(1). An error in this regard and consequential failure to implement the requisite systems will result in the commission of a strict liability offence, subject to the provision in reg 3(5) to the effect that 'it is a defence for a person to show that he or she took all relevant steps and exercised all due diligence to avoid committing the offence'.

8.3.1.2   Additional requirements when conducting relevant business

The additional requirements when conducting relevant business include the carrying out of:

(a) identification procedures;

(b) record keeping procedures;

(c) internal reporting procedures;

(d) training of employees.

The latter two are of less significance to the Bar than to other businesses in the regulated sector — as barristers are solely responsible for their own professional practice, there is no need to appoint a nominated Money Laundering Reporting Officer (MLRO) if you have no employees, although as a matter of good practice clerks and chambers staff should report suspect transactions to the individual barrister in the case; and whilst barristers do not have the corporate structures contemplated by the requirement of staff training, again the Bar Council suggests good practice would require training to enable reporting to the individual barrister in the case.

In terms of record keeping and identification procedures, this will have been carried out by the UK solicitor or other regulated professional, and counsel's duty will be discharged by ensuring that in the instructions a letter or certificate is included which confirms the client's identity. Where this is not the case (in particular for Public Access work), much more onerous requirements are imposed on counsel, all of which are detailed in 'Money Laundering Regulations 2003 — Guidance for the Bar' (a link is provided at **8.6**).

8.3.2   Criminal liability under s 330 for barristers operating within the regulated sector in consequence of the Money Laundering Regulations 2003

Perhaps of most significance is that since barristers (from 1 March 2004) are considered to be in the 'regulated sector', they are open to criminal liability under s 330, which is the offence of 'failure to disclose' by a person in the 'regulated sector'. Section 330(1) to (5) (as amended by the Serious Organised Crime and Police Act 2005, s 104) reads as follows:

(1)   A person commits an offence if the conditions in subsections (2) to (4) are satisfied.

(2)   The first condition is that he —

(a) knows or suspects, or

(b) has reasonable grounds for knowing or suspecting, that another person is engaged in money laundering

(3)   The second condition is that the information or other matter —

(a) on which his knowledge or suspicion is based, or

(b) which gives reasonable grounds for such knowledge or suspicion, came to him the course of a business in the regulated sector.

(3A) The third condition is —

(a) that he can identify the other person mentioned in subsection (2) or the whereabouts of any of the laundered property, or

(b) that he believes, or it is reasonable to expect him to believe, that the information or other matter mentioned in subsection (3) will or may assist in identifying that other person or the whereabouts of any laundered property.

(4)   The fourth condition is that he does not make the required disclosure to —
   (a) a nominated officer, or
   (b) a person authorised for the purposes of this Part by the Director General of the Serious Organised Crime Agency,
   as soon as practicable after the information or other matter mentioned in subsection (3) comes to him.
(5)   The required disclosure is a disclosure of —
   (a) the identity of the other person mentioned in subsection (2), if he knows it,
   (b) the whereabouts of the laundered property, so far as he knows it, and
   (c) the information or other matter mentioned in subsection (3).

Note first that, unlike in other parts of Part VII, the standard is objective not subjective. If you have failed to 'know' or 'suspect' personally, you can be liable if there were 'reasonable grounds' on which you should have known or suspected. In other words, the 'moron' defence (that the grounds were there but you simply failed to notice them) is not available to you.

So, for any piece of work you do, you have to consider your obligations under s 330. If the conditions in ss 2 to 4 apply then, subject to the defences described below, you may have an obligation to make a 'protected' disclosure under s 337.

8.3.3 Defences

There are in fact two defences available for a failure to disclose under s 330:

(a) you have a reasonable excuse for not making disclosure;
(b) you are a professional legal adviser and the information (the identity of the other person in subsection (2), or the whereabouts of the laundered property, or the information or matter in subsection (3)) has come to you in privileged circumstances.

In other words, there is a legal professional privilege defence to s 330. Section 330(10) clarifies the circumstances in which it applies. However, it is to some degree limited by s 330(11), which provides that legal professional privilege will not apply where 'information . . . is communicated or given with the intention of furthering a criminal purpose'. The 'intention' which matters is the client's — and it is irrelevant that the client does not realise that the 'purpose' which he or she is trying to further is 'criminal'. Given the wide manner in which criminal behaviour prohibited by ss 327, 328 and 329 is drafted, the lawyer will have to look very closely at what the client is intending to achieve in communicating information to the lawyer. Certainly, in telling you that her husband is taking cash in hand and not declaring it to tax, an ancillary relief client probably is not intending to further a criminal purpose; rather she is telling you this in order to maximise her recovery in the ancillary relief — the sole or dominant purpose of her giving you this information being the conduct of the family proceedings.

If you do make disclosure under s 337 ('protected disclosure'), provided that you comply with the conditions of s 337, you will be protected against litigation by the client for breaching confidentiality by s 337(1). Check that you have (or should have) suspicion based on real grounds, as opposed to mere speculation, or you may be at risk that your disclosure is not in accordance with s 337 and thus leave yourself vulnerable to successful litigation by the client.

8.4   Other secondary offences

There are two other secondary offences which merit consideration. These arise particularly in the context of discussing the issue of disclosure with the client.

8.4.1   Section 333 — 'tipping off'

'Tipping off' relates to a situation where you know or suspect that a disclosure has been made (eg, your solicitor has made a disclosure already). The offence cannot be committed in relation to a disclosure that is yet to be made (as to which see s 342 below). Where you 'make a disclosure which is likely to prejudice any investigation which might be conducted' as a result of the primary disclosure, you may be guilty of an offence. The 'disclosure' you make could be to your client, or to the other side, the point being that by revealing what you know or intend to do, you could enable a criminal or money launderer to cover his or her tracks, conceal the evidence, etc. Defences are available — see s 333(2) — and include legal professional privilege as defined in ss 3. However, as for s 330, legal professional privilege is limited where the disclosure is made with the intention of furthering a criminal purpose. The essential difference with s 330(11) is that, for s 333, the relevant intention is that of the *lawyer*, not the client. You may therefore be able to take advantage of the legal professional privilege defence provided that your intentions are not to further a criminal purpose, including a criminal purpose of the client.

8.4.2   Section 342 — prejudicing an investigation

Unlike s 333, this offence *can* be committed in advance of a disclosure being made, and relates to conduct, including making disclosures, which could prejudice an investigation which is being made or is contemplated. (Other conduct could include, for example, concealing or falsifying or destroying relevant documents.)

A variety of defences are available, including legal professional privilege. Again, legal professional privilege is limited where there is an intention to further a criminal purpose, and again the relevant intention is that of the lawyer.

In the circumstances, it may be hard to see how a lawyer could be considered to be furthering a criminal intention of his own (in relation to 'tipping off' and the prejudicing an investigation offences) in simply advising a client of the state of the law with regard to his or her position, for example the risk of the client committing an offence under s 329.

8.5   Penalties

8.5.1   Section 334

Sections 327, 328 and 329	on summary conviction, imprisonment of up to six months or a fine or both; on indictment, a fine or imprisonment of up to 14 years.
Sections 330 and 333	on summary conviction, imprisonment of up to six months or a fine or both; on indictment, a fine or imprisonment of up to five years.

8.5.2 Section 342

Section 342   on summary conviction, imprisonment of up to six months or a fine or both; on indictment, a fine or imprisonment of up to five years.

Clearly, it pays to get it right. And note that the mere fact that you advise the solicitor that he has a reporting obligation under the POCA 2002 does not discharge your own obligations. However, it is perfectly possible to make joint disclosure to NCIS on the part of the solicitor, counsel and possibly the client. In addition, NCIS indicates in its guidance that if a solicitor has made a report in advance of instructing counsel and counsel's report would be based on the exact same facts, there is no obligation on counsel to report further.

8.6 Sources of useful information

(a) The Law Society (www.lawsoc.org.uk) — there is much helpful guidance on this site, and you can download a document containing the main parts of the Act.

(b) NCIS (www.ncis.co.uk) — for information such as how to go about making a report, and for NCIS guidance.

(c) The Bar Council (www.barcouncil.org.uk) — under the section on professional rules and guidance you can obtain two documents which are the Bar Council's current 'last word' on these areas, and are referred to above: first, 'Proceeds of Crime Act: Note to the Bar'; secondly, 'Money Laundering Regulations 2003 — Guidance for the Bar'. The main guidance is in fact contained in a Word document at the end of the shorter version on the website, and it is the Word document you need.

(d) *Bowman v Fels* [2005] EWCA Civ 226 can be accessed through the Court Service website (www.hmcourt-service.gov.uk) — search under the 'Legal/Professional' section — or at www.bailii.org.

8.7 Areas in which counsel remains at risk of liability under the POCA 2002

The decision in *Bowman v Fels* [2005] EWCA Civ 226 has provided considerable clarity on an issue of acute concern to litigators. However, lawyers still need to tread carefully in certain areas — and in others, confusion remains. References to paragraph numbers below are to paragraphs in *Bowman*.

8.7.1 Section 330 and the regulated sector

Bowman has little impact in this area. It is quite clear from the judgment of the Court of Appeal that the decision relates to s 328. In particular, it seems that in any event the Court of Appeal had little difficulty with the drafting of s 330 since it preserves the entitlement to legal professional privilege (see s 330(6), (10) and (11)). Therefore, lawyers will have to continue to keep possible liability under s 330 in mind when operating in the regulated sector (principally in relation to financial and real estate transactions). This will be of particular concern to certain sectors of the Bar, such as tax specialists and Chancery practitioners who are routinely involved in such work — although every lawyer needs to be aware of potential application of s 330 since it is transaction based; in other words, its applicability depends on the subject matter of every individual transaction rather than the lawyer's general area of work. It may well be that specialist Bar associations issue future guidance specific to their areas in relation to s 330 obligations. Of course, availability of the legal professional privelege defence is likely to mean that you are very rarely obliged to report money laundering by the client.

8.7.2   Negotiation and agreement in the absence of issued proceedings

At paras 99 to 102, the Court of Appeal considered resolution of the whole, or part, of legal proceedings by agreement. The obvious point was made that if the ordinary conduct of litigation was to be treated as outside the scope of s 328, as the Court had already concluded, then it would be inconsistent and illogical to nevertheless treat any step in such proceedings taken by *agreement*, or a settlement of the litigation obtained by agreement, as subject to s 328. Given the considerable emphasis on resolution of litigation by agreement not only in domestic law (the 'Woolf reforms') but also in international law, the Court concluded that consensual steps — including final resolution by agreement — were not subject to s 328.

However, the Court indicated (para 101) that the situation might be different where the agreed settlement was *independent* of litigation. The Court was careful to use the phrase 'in a litigious context' when discussing consensual agreement. This appears to extend to situations of *existing or contemplated legal proceedings* only. As the Court pointed out (para 101), this is in line with the language of the relevant European directives, as well as relevant sections of the POCA 2002. It does, however, leave something of a grey area. Surely a lawyer with his or her client's interests foremost in his mind will attempt to negotiate a settlement without recourse to legal proceedings. At what point would a court regard him or her as negotiating in the context of 'contemplated' legal proceedings (and thus beyond the reach of s 328)? Will lawyers have to threaten legal proceedings as a first step to attempting negotiation in all cases in order to escape the confines of s 328?

There is considerable emphasis on the use and observance of pre-action protocols since the Woolf reforms. It is suggested that observance of such protocols (the purpose of which is to avoid litigation where possible by agreed settlement) could, and would, be considered by a court as negotiation in the context of contemplated legal proceedings. Clearly, legal proceedings are the likely result if negotiation under the protocol fails, and protocols additionally have as their aim the efficient preparation of the case for litigation in the event of failed negotiation. It may be that this aspect of the applicability, or not, of s 328 will serve to emphasise and increase use of the protocols.

8.7.3   Sham litigation

While not expressing a concluded view on the point, the Court of Appeal referred to the possibility that s 328 could potentially apply to lawyers in the situation in which:

one were concerned with a settlement which did not reflect the legal and practical merits of the parties' respective positions in the proceedings, and was known or suspected to be no more than a pretext for agreeing on the acquisition, retention, use or control of criminal property. (para 102)

This would be an entirely logical position on the basis of the Court's interpretation of the legislation. Firstly, s 330, used by the Court to illuminate the intentions of the legislator in respect of s 328, clearly provides for a situation where legal professional privilege does not apply (s 330(11)), whereby if the client intends to further a criminal purpose (such as concealing proceeds of crime) in communicating the relevant information to his lawyer, privilege does not attach and the lawyer working in the regulated sector must report. Secondly, recital 17 of the 2001 Directive (Directive 2001/97/EC amending Council Directive 91/308/EEC on prevention of the use of the financial system for the purpose of money laundering), on which the Court placed so much reliance in interpreting the applicability of s 328 to litigation, states:

... legal advice remains subject to the obligation of professional secrecy unless the legal counsellor is taking part in money laundering activities, the legal advice is provided for money laundering purposes, or the lawyer knows that the client is seeking legal advice for money laundering purposes.

The consequences are that a lawyer conducting litigation must be astute to the possibility that the litigation is a sham in order to pursue money laundering. A good indication might be that the settlement did not substantially reflect the merits of each side's case. The Court of Appeal further made the point that this still leaves the question of at what point the s 328 offence could be said to have been committed by the lawyer. In paras 67 and 68 of the judgment, the Court took the view that an offence under s 328 could not have been committed until the 'arrangement' was actually made.

8.7.4   Transactions resulting from the judgment

The Court of Appeal stated at para 59 that:

while legal advice may be given in any area, one would not often expect legal professionals assisting in the planning or execution of or acting for a client in respect of a financial or real estate transaction of a kind specified in Article 2a(5) to have received from, or obtained on, their client relevant information 'in the course of performing their task of defending or representing that client in, or concerning judicial proceedings'.

This viewpoint is doubtless entirely accurate in relation to many situations. However, the question arises, what is the position in relation to the 'fruits' of litigation? More often than not, the implementation of an order, or an agreed resolution to litigation, will involve lawyers in transactions — financial, commercial, real property. An example could be an ancillary relief case, involving the transfer of a house, or a shareholding, to one of the parties. This is clearly within the meaning of 'transaction' in Art 2a(5) of the 2001 Directive, and therefore subject to s 330. Quite often (if not always), the law firms involved in the litigation will be those dealing with the transactions required to finally resolve the dispute. To what degree could the knowledge of a client's wrongdoing gained by the litigation team be imputed to the team dealing with the transactions flowing from resolution of the litigation? Or perhaps even more acutely, what about the situation of a sole practitioner dealing with the litigation and the transactions flowing from it?

One answer to this dilemma seems to depend on how one interprets the reference to 'ordinary course of litigation' in the judgment. If it includes those transactions required to give effect to the order or agreement, then the difficulty is removed. Support for such an interpretation comes from para 62 of the judgment. Reference is made to the function of litigation — 'resolving the rights and duties of two parties according to law'. Such 'resolution' would be threatened if parties were deterred from litigating due a fear of a report of their activities at the stage of actually effecting the remedy obtained. More importantly, the Court's reference to assets, being proceeds of money laundering, being 'retained *or used to satisfy any liability according to the outcome of proceedings*' seems to suggest that execution of the order or agreement would not be 'carrying out' a 'transaction' relating to money laundering.

Of course, such transactions, subject as they are to s 330, will benefit from the defence in s 330(6) and (10) — that the information has come to the lawyer in privileged circumstances and so disclosure will not be required. However, under s 330(11), privilege will afford no defence to the obligation to disclose if the client's purpose in communicating the information is a criminal purpose, and it may well be here that the problem arises.

8.7.5 Conclusion

Clearly, *Bowman* has provided considerable clarity to lawyers in terms of their obligations under s 328 of the POCA 2002, and to their clients in terms of legal professional privilege. However, some caution may still be required with regard to the situations suggested above. As ever, it is crucial that you are familiar with, and remain up to date with, guidance issued by the Bar Council, and specialist Bar associations in practice areas likely to be exposed to s 330.

9

Professional conduct problems

Question 1

Objectives

(a) To consider the meaning and importance of the 'Cab-rank' rule in all aspects of a practising barrister's work.

(b) To consider the meaning of 'professional embarrassment'.

A solicitor seeks to instruct you to act for notoriously bad landlords in an action for possession of premises occupied by a highly regarded charitable organisation. The case is likely to draw adverse publicity. You hold yourself out to act in landlord and tenant cases, you have no connection with either party or with the premises, you have no conflicting professional commitment and the fee offered is a proper fee for you and for the case. Your clerk tells you that he wishes you to refuse the instructions because:

(a) it is chambers' policy not to act for landlords; and

(b) he fears that your normal professional clients will be reluctant to instruct you in future cases as their clients (tenants, consumers, etc) would refuse to have as counsel one who had acted for these particular claimants.

What do you do?

Question 2

Objectives

(a) To illustrate the possibility of different interpretations of the Bar Code.

(b) To consider the relationship between the 'Cab-rank' rule and the practising barrister's duty not to discriminate nor to victimise on prohibited grounds.

You act for a father whose former wife is now cohabiting with a black boyfriend. Your client instructs you to resist her application for contact with the parties' son on thinly veiled racist grounds. Can you refuse to put forward instructions even if wrapped up as seeking to avoid 'exposing his son to a cultural environment totally alien to him . . .'.

Question 3

Objectives

(a) To emphasise the continuing duty of confidentiality.

(b) To illustrate its relationship with the cause(s) of professional embarrassment.

You have successfully appeared for the claimants in an action where the unsuccessful defendants now wish to seek a Part 20 indemnity or contribution from a third party who was not a party to the original action. The defendants' solicitors were impressed with your performance and want you to be able to use your knowledge of the case against the third party. Do you accept the instructions?

Question 4

Objectives

To introduce the general rules governing the receipt of instructions.

A solicitor, who regularly instructs you and your chambers, telephones you and instructs you to attend at a particular police station where a lay client is about to be interviewed and to advise the client as necessary. The solicitor undertakes to pay you a proper fee. If the matter leads to a charge or charges being preferred, the brief is likely to come into chambers for someone of your experience.

(a) Can you act?

(b) Would it make any difference if the brief would certainly be beyond your competence?

Question 5

Objective

To show the importance of the Written Standards for the Conduct of Professional Work.

You are prosecuting a plea of guilty where the defendant is unrepresented. It is a type of case in which the Court of Criminal Appeal has given sentencing guidelines. The judge does not appear to be familiar with criminal work. You are aware from discussion with the officer in the case of a number of facts favourable to the defendant which he does not bring out when mitigating on his own behalf. What are your duties?

Question 6

Objectives

(a) To underline that, under paras. 306 and 403 of the Bar Code, the barrister is responsible for the organisation of his or her own work.

(b) To underline that, under para 701(a) of the Bar Code, advocates must in all their activities be courteous and act promptly, conscientiously, diligently and with reasonable competence and take all reasonable and practicable steps to avoid unnecessary expense or waste of the court's time and to ensure that professional engagements are fulfilled. Under para 610(d) of the Bar Code, if a case is to be returned it must be returned in good and sufficient time for the client and the court to be properly serviced when it is called on.

You have received and accepted instructions to appear in case 'A' (a civil case fixed to be heard on 20 April). You have done a lot of preparatory work upon it and have seen the professional and lay clients in conference on a number of occasions. You have also accepted instructions to defend in a serious criminal case (case 'B') expected to be tried in the week beginning 1 April and to last for five days, but which may well go on longer. Before you have conferred with the client in case 'B' you learn that it will not be heard until the week beginning 15 April. Both solicitors assert priority and both clients are anxious to have your services. Which case do you do? Why?

Question 7

Objective

To illustrate some of the 'fundamental principles' applicable to all barristers.

You have represented your client successfully in court. After the hearing, the client stuffs a £20 note in your pocket and tells you to enjoy a drink on him.

(a) Do you keep the money?

(b) Would it make any difference if your client instead sent you a bottle of whiskey?

Question 8

Objective

To consider scenarios where your client's instructions may render you professionally embarrassed, and the action you must take as a consequence.

(a) The defendant in a rape case instructs you that intercourse took place between him and the victim with her consent. At trial he tells you that he did not have intercourse with her and gives you names of alibi witnesses.

(b) Your client is mentally disturbed. His instructions differ each time you speak to him.

What should you do in these circumstances?

Question 9

Objective

To explore the relationship between the duty of disclosure and the grounds on which a practising barrister must cease to act and withdraw from a case.

You act for the claimant in civil proceedings. In the course of his evidence-in-chief, he produces several documents from his pocket which he alleges support his claim. You have never seen them before nor have they been disclosed to the defence. What do you do?

Question 10

Objective

To explore counsels' duties where conflicts of interest exist between their professional and lay clients.

You receive a set of instructions to advise and settle civil proceedings for a claimant from X and Co, a firm of solicitors who have instructed you on a number of occasions and are among your best clients. It is apparent that they have been negligent in handling the claimant's affairs. It appears to you that the claimant's chances have not been badly affected and he is likely to succeed in the litigation, but he has at least been prejudiced in the sense that, if the relevant matter 'surfaces' in the litigation, the defendants will be able to make use of it to reduce the damages or to obtain a better settlement than would otherwise have been open to them. (For example, there has been a failure to secure evidence relevant to proving the amount of the claimant's loss and damage.) What, if anything, should you do?

Question 11

Objectives

(a) To highlight the practising barrister's overriding duty to the Court.
(b) To highlight the concomitant duties to the lay client.

You are defending a trial at the Crown Court. In the course of giving his evidence the defendant makes an allegation which, although it is in your instructions, you had not put to the victim. It is apparent that it should have been, and the victim has gone on holiday and cannot be recalled. The judge is furious. What do you do?

Question 12

Objectives

(a) To introduce the rules regarding media comment.
(b) To introduce the rules regarding advertising.

You are appearing for a well-known businessman in his local magistrates' court on a charge of drink driving. After a preliminary hearing, you are approached by a reporter from the local newspaper who asks you for information about the client and the case. What should you do?

Question 13

Objective

To illustrate the relationship between a practising barrister's duty of confidentiality to the lay client and the overriding duty to the Court.

You are asked to advise, in conference, upon the acceptability of an offer of £3,000 in settlement of your client's claim for damages in a personal injury case. The medical report, which has been disclosed to the defence, is now ten months old. In the course of the conference, your client informs you that the doctor's prognosis was unduly pessimistic as his condition has improved since the report was prepared. In the circumstances, the offer is generous and more than your client is likely to receive from the court.

- (a) What advice do you give?
- (b) Would it make any difference if the client's information was contained in a more recent, but undisclosed medical report?

Question 14

Objective

To illustrate the relationship between the overriding duty to the Court and the rules under the Civil Procedure Rules 1998 regarding witnesses at trial.

You are instructed to represent the defendant in proceedings for damages for breach of contract. Upon your arrival at court, your instructing solicitor informs you that one of your witnesses has just telephoned his office to say that she is ill and cannot attend court to give evidence. Her testimony is vital to the defendant's case. You have no option but to seek an adjournment. At that moment, your opponent approaches you and asks if he can have a word with you. He indicates that he has witness difficulties and invites you to agree to an adjournment of the hearing for two weeks. In so doing:

- *(a) Do you inform your opponent and the court of your own witness difficulties?*
- *(b) If not, do you make an application for the claimant to pay defendant's costs thrown away by the adjournment?*

APPENDICES

APPENDIX 1
CODE OF CONDUCT OF THE BAR OF ENGLAND AND WALES

CODE OF CONDUCT

OF

THE BAR OF ENGLAND AND WALES

AND

WRITTEN STANDARDS FOR THE CONDUCT
OF PROFESSIONAL WORK

8th Edition

Adopted by the Bar Council on 18 September 2004

Effective from 31 October 2004

The General Council of the Bar of England and Wales
289–293 High Holborn
London WC1V 7HZ

SECTION 1   THE CODE OF CONDUCT OF THE BAR OF ENGLAND AND WALES

Arrangement of Sections

Code of Conduct of the Bar of England and Wales

The Bar's Code of Conduct sets out the duties which all barristers must obey.

It is divided into the following sections:

Part I — Preliminary

The Preliminary section sets out the details about the commencement of the Code, the rules governing amendments to the Code, the general purpose of the Code, to whom it applies and the Bar Council's powers to waive its provisions.

Part II — Practising Requirements

The Practising Requirements section sets out the rules governing the circumstances in which individuals may practise as a barrister, exercise rights of audience and supply legal services to the public. Part II also contains the requirement to be insured and the prohibition on barristers practising in partnership.

Part III — Fundamental Principles

The Fundamental Principles section includes the duty to not act dishonestly or bring the profession into disrepute, the duties to the court and to act in the best interest of the client. It also contains the duties to the Legal Services Commission, the duty to not discriminate on grounds of race, sex etc and the duty to maintain independence.

306   *Barrister's individual and personal responsibility, exercise of personal judgement*

307   *A barrister must not:*

  (a) *Compromise his independence and integrity*

  (b)

  (c) *Compromise professional standards*

  (d) *Must not give commission, a present or money for any professional purpose*

  (e) *Make payment for purposes of procuring instructions*

  (f) *Receive or handle client money, securities or other assets*

Part IV — Self-employed Barristers

This section concerns self-employed barristers only. It provides that they can only accept instructions from solicitors or other professional clients and sets out the work that they may not undertake. This section also contains further rules governing insurance, the duties of barristers and heads of chambers to administer their practice efficiently and the rules about fees.

401   Instructions

  (a) *Supply legal services when property instructed*

  (b) (i) *Management/administration/general conduct of lay client's affairs*

    (ii) *Conduct litigation, inter-partes work*

    (iii) *Investigate/collect evidence for use in Court*

    (iv) *Take proof of evidence in criminal cases*

    (v) *Attend at police stations*

    (vi) *Act as supervisor — s 84(2) of the Immigration and Asylum Act 1999*

  (c) *Enter into contract for the supply of legal services*

  (d) *Compliance with Licensed Access Rules*

402   Insurance

403   Administration and conduct of self-employed practice

403.1   *Sharing the administration of a barrister's practice*

403.2   (a) (i) Efficient and proper administration of practice

    (ii) *Keeping proper records*

    (iii) *Compliance with Terms of Work/Withdrawal of Credit Scheme 1998*

  (b) *Access to library facilities*

  (c) *Have regard to Bar Council guidance*

  (d) (i) *Handle complaints promptly/courteously*

    (ii) *Have and comply with an appropriate written complaints procedure — provide copies when requested*

404   Heads of Chambers

404.1   *To whom the obligations in this section apply.*

404.2   *The Head of Chambers must ensure that:*

  (a) *Chambers are property staffed and efficiently and competently administered*

  (b) *Affairs of chambers are conducted fairly and equitably*

  (c) *Proper arrangements are made for dealing with pupils and pupillage, including:*

    (i) *pupillage vacancies*

    (ii) *arrangements for funding of pupils*

    (iii) *pupillage guidelines and the Equality Code are considered*

  (d) *All members have insurance with BMIF*

  (e) *All members comply with 403.2(a)(iii)*

(f) *All employees and staff are:*
   (i) *competent to carry out duties*
   (ii) *carry out duties efficiently*
   (iii) *are made aware of the provisions of the Code*
   (iv) *complaints against them are dealt with in accordance with 403(e).*

(g) *Registered foreign lawyers/foreign lawyers comply with the Code*

(h) *Fee notes are sent promptly and pursued efficiently*

(i) *Every member has a Practising Certificate*

404.3   Regard to Bar Council guidance when carrying out 404.2.

Fees and Remuneration

405   *Basis on which self-employed barristers can charge for work.*

406.1   *Payment of fees to other barristers.*

406.2   *Duty to pay proper financial remuneration to another barrister and to be paid within a reasonable time.*

Part V — Employed Barristers

This section sets out the rules governing Employed Barristers.

501   *To whom an employed barrister can supply legal services when employed:*

   (a) *by a company*

   (b) *by a public authority*

   (c) *as a justices clerk*

   (d) *by a trade association*

502   *When employed barristers may offer services to the public:*

   (a) *when employed by a solicitor or authorised litigator*

   (b) *by the Legal Services Commission*

   (c) *by a Legal Advice Centre*

   (d) *when supplying legal services free of charge*

503   *Requirements for supplying legal services under a contract for services.*

504   *Right to conduct litigation*

Part VI — Acceptance and Return of Instructions

This section deals with the occasion on which barristers are required to accept instructions (the 'Cab Rank rule'), when they are required to refuse or withdraw from a case and when they may choose to refuse or withdraw from a case.

601   *A barrister cannot withhold advocacy services:*

   (a) *if nature of case is objectionable*

   (b) *opinion/belief of prospective client unacceptable to the barrister*

   (c) *on the basis of any financial support given to the prospective client*

602   *The Cab Rank Rule and when it applies.*

603   *When a barrister must not accept instruction:*

   (a) *lacks sufficient experience/competence*

   (b) *does not have adequate time to properly prepare*

   (c) *instructions seek to limit barrister's discretion as to how to conduct the proceedings*

   (d) *the barrister is likely to be a witness/has difficulty maintaining professional independence/cause the administration of justice to be, or appears to be, prejudiced*

   (e) *conflict of interest*

(f) *risk of a breach of confidentiality*

(g) *non-compliance with the Terms of Work on which Barristers offer their Services to the Solicitor/Withdrawal of Credit Scheme 1988*

604   *When (subject to Paragraph 601) a barrister is not obliged to accept instructions:*

(a) *work outside of his ordinary working year*

(b) *other than at a proper fee*

(c) *work under a conditional fee agreement*

(d) *save when funded by the Legal Services Commission /Community Legal Service/ Criminal Defence Service*
  (i)   *unless and until fee is agreed*
  (ii) *if required fee to be paid before accepting instruction — fee is not then paid*

(e) *in a licensed access matter where lay client is also the professional client*

(f) *to do any work under contractual terms*

605   *When a self-employed Queen's Counsel is not obliged to accept instructions*

606.1   *Duty to consider whether it is in the best interests of the client for him to be instructed or remain instructed.*

606.2   *Duty to consider whether it is in the best interests of the client to have more than one advocate.*

606.3   *Duty to consider whether it is in the best interests of the lay client for a barrister to be instructed directly or by an intermediary who is not a solicitor or an authorised litigator.*

606.4   *Duty to consider in cases involving several parties, whether it is in the best interests of the client to be separately or jointly represented.*

607   *Obligation to advise client if barrister considers that it is in the best interests of the client to have different representation.*

608   *When a barrister must cease to act and return instructions.*

(a) *witness on a material question of fact*

(b) *if acting for more than one client and they do not consent to him continuing to act*
  (i)   *conflict or risk of conflict*
  (ii) *risk of a breach of confidence*

(c) *funding wrongly obtained*

(d) *refusal of client to permit disclosure of barrister to the court*

(e) *where a barrister becomes aware of documents which should have been disclosed on discovery and the client fails to the disclose it*

(f) *disclosure of documents*

609   *(Subject to Paragraph 610) When a barrister may withdraw from a case:*

(a) *instructions withdrawn*

(b) *professional conduct impugned*

(c) *advice given in accordance with Paragraph 607 or 703 has not been heeded*

(d) *some other substantial reason*

610   (a) *must explain to client why ceasing to act/returning instructions*

(b) *return instructions to another barrister without client's consent*

(c) *return of brief for social engagement*

(d) *except as provided at Paragraph 608, return of instructions/withdrawal which prevents the client from finding other legal assistance in time to prevent prejudice to their case*

Part VII — Conduct of Work by Practising Barristers

This section contains the duties of barristers when conducting work, including the general duties to act courteously and promptly, the duty of confidentiality, duties where there is a conflict between clients, duties when drafting documents and appearing in court, the rules concerning contact with witnesses and media comment and advertising.

701   *Duty of a barrister:*

    (a) *to act courteously and promptly*

    (b) *not to undertake a task which:*

       (i)   *not competent to handle*

       (ii) *does not have adequate time to prepare for*

       (iii) *cannot be discharged within time requested*

    (c) *duty to read instructions promptly*

    (d) *duty to have regard to Written Standards for the Conduct of Professional Work produced by the Bar Council*

    (e) *subject to Paragraph 610, duties to return instructions or to another barrister if:*

       (i)   *unable to complete work within the time requested*

       (ii) *if there is a risk that they may unable to undertake the brief or fulfil a professional engagement*

    (f) *a duty to keep adequate records supporting the fees charged or claimed in a case*

702   Confidentiality

703   Conflicts between lay clients and intermediaries

704   *Drafting documents, duty not to include*

    (a) *unsupported statements of facts/contention*

    (b) *contentions not properly arguable*

    (c) *allegations of fraud*

    (d) *statements other than those that the witness/client would give.*

705   *Duties governing contact with witnesses*

706   *Dispensing with the attendance of the professional client*

707   *When a barrister may interview witnesses and take proofs of evidence.*

708   *Duties when conducting proceedings in court.*

    (a) *personal responsibility for conduct of his case*

    (b) *assertion of a personal opinion of the facts or the law*

    (c) *inform the Court of all relevant authorities*

    (d) *inform the Court of any procedural irregularity*

    (e) *must not adduce evidence other than from the client or devise facts*

    (f) *property arguable submission*

    (g) *scandalous statements / vilifying witnesses*

    (h) *impugning third parties by naming in Court*

    (i) *impugning a witness*

    (j) *suggestion that a victim/witness or other person is guilty of crime, fraud or misconduct or making defamatory aspersions*

709   Media comment

710   Advertising and publicity

710.1   *What advertising or promotion may include.*

710.2   *Advertising or promotion must not:*

    (a) *be inaccurate/misleading*

    (b) *diminish public confidence in the legal profession or the administration of justice*

    (c) *be comparative*

(d) *contain success rates*

(e) *indicate willingness to accept instructions / restrict instructions*

(f) *be frequent/obtrusive*

Part VIII — Miscellaneous

This section sets out miscellaneous provisions concerning pupillage, working at a Legal Advice Centre, dual qualification and relationships with foreign lawyers.

801   *Responsibilities of a barrister who is a pupil.*

802   *When a barrister who is a pupil can supply legal services, exercise a right of audience and accept a noting brief.*

803.1   *Pupil barristers as members of chambers.*

803.2   *Barrister who is a pupil of an employed barrister.*

804   *Duties of a pupil supervisor.*

805   *Payment by a barrister to a pupil for work done by him.*

806   *Supplying legal services at a Legal Advice Centre*

807   *Barristers employed by a Legal Advice Centre — prohibitions.*

808.1

808.2   Dual qualification

808.3

808   Foreign lawyers

Part IX — Compliance

This section sets out the duty to inform the Bar Council in the event of criminal convictions, bankruptcy etc and the duties concerning the complaints procedure.

901   *Non-compliance with the Code — professional misconduct.*

902   *False declaration by a barrister on Call to the Bar/discreditable or dishonest conduct before Call.*

903   *Annexes of the Code dealing with the complaints and disciplinary system.*

904   *Redress to the client for inadequate professional service.*

905   *Duties of a practising barrister to:*

  (a) (i) *respond promptly to the Bar Council*
      (ii) *permit the Bar Council to inspect premises from which they practise*

  (b) *duty to report being charged or convicted of a serious criminal offence or convicted of a disciplinary offence*

  (c) *duties regarding bankruptcy and directors disqualification proceedings*

  (d) *duty to respond promptly to correspondence from the Bar Council relating to a complaint or to circumstances relating to Paragraph 905(b)–(c)*

  (e) *duty to respond to letter of notification or request to attend before any tribunal panel body or person*

  (f) *duty to comply with any decision of a tribunal body or person*

Part X — Definitions

This section contains the definition of terms used in the Code.

Part XI — Transitional Provisions

This section contains the transitional arrangements affecting people who were barristers before this edition of the Code came into force.

The Code also contains various annexes, which set out the rules for particular situations.

PART I — PRELIMINARY

101   The Eighth Edition of the Code was adopted by the Bar Council on 18 September 2004 and came into force on 31 October 2004.

102   This Code includes the Annexes.

103   Amendments and additions to this Code may be made by Resolution of the Bar Council which shall be operative upon such date as the Resolution shall appoint or if no such date is appointed on the later of:

(a)   the date of the Resolution; and

(b)   the date when approval of the amendment or addition, if required, is given under Schedule 4 of the Act.

Amendments and additions will be published from time to time in such manner as the Bar Council may determine.

General purpose of the Code

104   The general purpose of this Code is to provide the requirements for practice as a barrister and the rules and standards of conduct applicable to barristers which are appropriate in the interests of justice and in particular:

(a)   in relation to self-employed barristers to provide common and enforceable rules and standards which require them:

(i)   to be completely independent in conduct and in professional standing as sole practitioners;

(ii)   to act only as consultants instructed by solicitors and other approved persons (save where instructions can properly be dispensed with);

(iii)   to acknowledge a public obligation based on the paramount need for access to justice to act for any client in cases within their field of practice;

(b)   to make appropriate provision for employed barristers taking into account the fact that such barristers are employed to provide legal services to or on behalf of their employer.

Application of the Code

105   A barrister must comply with this Code which (save as otherwise provided) applies to all barristers whenever called to the Bar.

106   Subject to the International Practice Rules (reproduced in Annex A) this Code applies to International work and whether a barrister is practising in England and Wales or elsewhere.

107   A registered European lawyer must comply with this Code in the manner provided for by the Registered European Lawyers Rules (reproduced in Annex B).

Waiver of the Code

108   The Bar Council shall have the power to waive the duty imposed on a barrister to comply with the provisions of this Code in such circumstances and to such extent as the Bar Council may think fit and either conditionally or unconditionally.

PART II — PRACTISING REQUIREMENTS

General

201   For the purposes of this Code:

(a) a barrister practises as a barrister if he supplies legal services and in connection with the supply of such services:

(i)   he holds himself out or allows himself to be held out as a barrister; or

(ii)   he exercises a right which he has by reason of being a barrister;

(b) any reference to the supply of legal services includes an offer to supply such services.

202   Subject to the provisions of this Code a barrister may practise as a barrister provided that:

(a) he has complied with any applicable training requirements imposed by the Consolidated Regulations which were in force at the date of his Call to the Bar;

(b) he has complied with any applicable requirements of the Continuing Professional Development Regulations (reproduced in Annex C);

(c) he has a current practising certificate issued by the Bar Council in accordance with the Practising Certificate Regulations (reproduced in Annex D);

(d) he has provided in writing to the Bar Council details of the current address(es) with telephone number(s) of the chambers or office from which he supplies legal services and (if he is an employed barrister) the name address telephone number and nature of the business of his employer;

(e) a barrister who practises as a self-employed barrister or as an employed barrister may not also supply legal services for reward other than in the course of his practice except as permitted by paragraph 806.

Rights of audience

203.1   A barrister may exercise any right of audience which he has by reason of being a barrister provided that:

(a) he is entitled to practise as a barrister in accordance with paragraph 202; and

(b) if he is of less than three years' standing his principal place of practice is either:

(i)   a chambers or annexe of chambers which is also the principal place of practice of a qualified person who is readily available to provide guidance to the barrister; or

(ii)   an office of an organisation of which an employee, partner or director is a qualified person who is readily available to provide guidance to the barrister.

203.2   For the purpose of paragraph 203.1(b) and 204(c)(i) a barrister shall be treated as being of a particular number of years' standing if he:

(a) has been entitled to practise and has practised as a barrister (other than as a pupil who has not completed pupillage in accordance with the Consolidated Regulations) or as a member of another authorised body;

(b) has made such practice his primary occupation; and

(c) has been entitled to exercise a right of audience before every Court in relation to all proceedings

for a period (which need not be continuous and need not have been as a member of the same authorised body) of at least that number of years.

203.3   A person shall be a qualified person for the purpose of paragraph 203.1(b) if he:

(a) has been entitled to practise and has practised as a barrister (other than as a pupil who has not completed pupillage in accordance with the Consolidated Regulations) or as a member of another authorised body for a period (which need not have been as a member of the same authorised body) of at least six years in the previous eight years;

(b) for the previous two years

(i)   has made such practice his primary occupation, and

(ii)   has been entitled to exercise a right of audience before every Court in relation to all proceedings;

(c) is not acting as a qualified person in relation to more than two other people; and

(d) has not been designated by the Bar Council as unsuitable to be a qualified person.

203.4   This paragraph 203 is subject to the transitional provisions at paragraphs 1102 to 1105.

Supply of legal services to the public

204   A practising barrister may supply legal services to the public provided that:

(a) he complies with the requirements of paragraph 203.1; and

(b) he is covered (and in the case of an employed barrister his employer is covered) by insurance against claims for professional negligence arising out of the supply of his services in such amount and upon such terms as are currently required by the Bar Council; and

(c) In the case of legal services supplied pursuant to paragraph 401(a)(iii):

(i)   he is more than three years' standing;

(ii)   he has complied with such training requirements as may be imposed by the Bar Council; and

(iii) he has notified the Bar Council that he holds himself out as willing to accept instructions from lay clients.

205   A practising barrister must not supply legal services to the public through or on behalf of any other person (including a partnership company or other corporate body) except as permitted by paragraph 502.

PART III — FUNDAMENTAL PRINCIPLES

Applicable to all barristers

301   A barrister must have regard to paragraph 104 and must not:

(a) engage in conduct whether in pursuit of his profession or otherwise which is:

(i)   dishonest or otherwise discreditable to a barrister;

(ii) prejudicial to the administration of justice; or

(iii) likely to diminish public confidence in the legal profession or the administration of justice or otherwise bring the legal profession into disrepute;

(b) engage directly or indirectly in any occupation if his association with that occupation may adversely affect the reputation of the Bar or in the case of a practising barrister prejudice his ability to attend properly to his practice.

Applicable to practising barristers

302   A barrister has an overriding duty to the Court to act with independence in the interests of justice: he must assist the Court in the administration of justice and must not deceive or knowingly or recklessly mislead the Court.

303   A barrister:

(a) must promote and protect fearlessly and by all proper and lawful means the lay client's best interests and do so without regard to his own interests or to any consequences to himself or to any other person (including any professional client or other intermediary or another barrister);

(b) owes his primary duty as between the lay client and any professional client or other intermediary to the lay client and must not permit the intermediary to limit his discretion as to how the interests of the lay client can best be served;

(c) when supplying legal services funded by the Legal Services Commission as part of the Community Legal Service or the Criminal Defence Service owes his primary duty to the lay client subject only to compliance with paragraph 304.

304   A barrister who supplies legal services funded by the Legal Services Commission as part of the Community Legal Service or the Criminal Defence Service must in connection with the supply of such services comply with any duty imposed on him by or under the Access to Justice Act 1999 or any regulations or code in effect under that Act and in particular with the duties set out in Annex E.

305.1   A barrister must not in relation to any other person (including a client or another barrister or a pupil or a student member of an Inn of Court) discriminate directly or indirectly or victimise because of race, colour, ethnic or national origin, nationality, citizenship, sex, sexual orientation, marital status, disability, religion or political persuasion.

305.2   A barrister must not in relation to any offer of a pupillage or tenancy discriminate directly or indirectly against a person on grounds of age, save where such discrimination can be shown to be objectively and reasonably justifiable.

305.3   In respect of indirect discrimination, there is no breach of paragraph 305.1 and 305.2 if the barrister against whom the complaint is brought proves that the act of indirect discrimination was committed without any intention of treating the claimant unfavourably on any ground in that paragraph to which the complaint relates.

306   A barrister is individually and personally responsible for his own conduct and for his professional work: he must exercise his own personal judgment in all his professional activities.

307   A barrister must not:

(a) permit his absolute independence integrity and freedom from external pressures to be compromised;

(b) do anything (for example accept a present) in such circumstances as may lead to any inference that his independence may be compromised;

(c) compromise his professional standards in order to please his client the Court or a third party;

(d) give a commission or present or lend any money for any professional purpose to or (save as a remuneration in accordance with the provisions of this Code) accept any money by way of loan or otherwise from any client or any person entitled to instruct him as an intermediary;

(e) make any payment (other than a payment for advertising or publicity permitted by this Code or in the case of a self-employed barrister remuneration paid to any clerk or other employee or staff of his chambers) to any person for the purpose of procuring professional instructions;

(f) receive or handle client money securities or other assets other than by receiving payment of remuneration or (in the case of an employed barrister) where the money or other asset belongs to his employer.

PART IV — SELF-EMPLOYED BARRISTERS

Instructions

401   A self-employed barrister whether or not he is acting for a fee:

(a) may supply legal services only if appointed by the Court or is instructed:

(i) by a professional client; or

(ii) by a licensed access client, in which case he must comply with the Licensed Access Rules (reproduced in Annex F1); or

(iii) subject to paragraph 204(c), by or on behalf of any other lay client, in which case he must comply with the Public Access Rules (reproduced in Annex F2); or

(b) must not in the course of his practice:

(i) undertake the management administration or general conduct of a lay client's affairs;

(ii) conduct litigation or inter-partes work (for example the conduct of correspondence with an opposite party, instructing any expert witness or other person on behalf of his lay client or accepting liability for the payment of any such person);

(iii) investigate or collect evidence for use in any Court;

(iv) except as permitted by paragraph 707, or by the Public Access Rules, take any proof of evidence in any criminal case;

(v) attend at a police station without the presence of a solicitor to advise a suspect or interviewee as to the handling and conduct of police interviews;

(vi) act as a supervisor for the purposes of section 84(2) of the Immigration and Asylum Act 1999.

Insurance

402.1   Every self-employed barrister (other than a pupil who is covered under his pupil-master's insurance) must be entered as a member with BMIF.

402.2   Every barrister entered as a member with BMIF shall:

(a) pay immediately when due the appropriate insurance premium required by BMIF for the purpose of insurance against claims for professional negligence for such amount and upon such terms as may be approved by the Bar Council from time to time;

(b) supply immediately upon being requested to do so such information as BMIF may from time to time require pursuant to its Rules.

Administration and conduct of independent practice

403.1   A self-employed barrister must not practise from the office of or in any unincorporated association (including any arrangement which involves sharing the administration of his practice) with any person other than a self-employed barrister or any of the following:

(a) a registered European lawyer;

(b) subject to compliance with the Foreign Lawyers (Chambers) Rules (reproduced in Annex H) and with the consent of the Bar Council a foreign lawyer;

(c) a non-practising barrister or retired judge who is practising as an arbitrator or mediator.

403.2   A self-employed barrister:

(a) must take all reasonable steps to ensure that:

(i) his practice is efficiently and properly administered having regard to the nature of his practice;

(ii) proper records are kept;

(iii) he complies with the Terms of Work on which Barristers Offer their Services to Solicitors and the Withdrawal of Credit Scheme 1988 as amended and in force from time to time (reproduced in Annex G1) and with any Withdrawal of Credit Direction issued by the Chairman of the Bar pursuant thereto.

(b) must have ready access to library facilities which are adequate having regard to the nature of his practice;

(c) must have regard to any relevant guidance issued by the Bar Council including guidance as to:

(i) the administration of chambers;

(ii) pupillage and further training; and

(iii) good equal opportunities practice in chambers in the form of the Equality Code for the Bar;

(d) (i) must deal with all complaints made to him promptly, courteously and in a manner which addresses the issues raised; and

(ii) must have and comply with an appropriate written complaints procedure and make copies of the procedure available to a client on request.

Heads of chambers

404.1   The obligations in this paragraph apply to the following members of chambers:

(a) any barrister who is head of chambers;

(b) any barrister who is responsible in whole or in part for the administration of chambers;

(c) if there is no one within (a) and (b) above, all the members of the chambers.

404.2   Any person referred to in paragraph 404.1 must take all reasonable steps to ensure that:

(a) his chambers are administered competently and efficiently and are properly staffed;

(b) the affairs of his chambers are conducted in a manner which is fair and equitable for all barristers and pupils;

(c) proper arrangements are made in his chambers for dealing with pupils and pupillage and, in particular,

(i)   that all pupillage vacancies are advertised in the manner prescribed by the Bar Council;

(ii)   that such arrangements are made for the funding of pupils by chambers as the Bar Council may by resolution from time to time require;

(iii) that in making arrangements for pupillage, regard is had to the pupillage guidelines issued from time to time by the Bar Council and to the Equality Code for the Bar;

(d) all barristers practising from his chambers whether they are members of the chambers or not are entered as members with BMIF and have effected insurance in accordance with paragraph 402 (other than any pupil who is covered under his pupil- master's insurance);

(e) all barristers practising from his chambers comply with paragraph 403.2(a)(iii);

(f) all employees and staff in his chambers (i) are competent to carry out their duties, (ii) carry out their duties in a correct and efficient manner, (iii) are made clearly aware of such provisions of this Code as may affect or be relevant to the performance of their duties and (iv) all complaints against them are dealt with in the manner set out in paragraph 403(e) above;

(g) all registered European lawyers and all foreign lawyers in his chambers comply with this Code to the extent required by the Registered European Lawyers Rules (reproduced in Annex B) and the Foreign Lawyers (Chambers) Rules (reproduced in Annex H);

(h) fee notes in respect of all work undertaken by all members of chambers and pupils and (unless expressly agreed with the individual) former members and pupils of chambers are sent expeditiously to clients and in the event of non-payment within a reasonable time, pursued efficiently;

(i) every barrister practising from his chambers has a current practising certificate in accordance with paragraph 202(c) of the Code of Conduct and the Practising Certificate Regulations (reproduced in Annex D).

404.3   In carrying out the obligations referred to in paragraph 404.2 any person referred to in paragraph 404.1 must have regard to any relevant guidance issued by the Bar Council including guidance as to:

(a) the administration of chambers;

(b) pupillage and further training; and

(c) good equal opportunities practice in chambers in the form of the Equality Code for the Bar.

Fees and remuneration

405   Subject to paragraph 307 a self-employed barrister may charge for any work undertaken by him (whether or not it involves an appearance in Court) on any basis or by any method he thinks fit provided that such basis or method:

(a) is permitted by law;

(b) does not involve the payment of a wage or salary.

406.1   A self-employed barrister who receives fees in respect of work done by another barrister must himself and without delegating the responsibility to anyone else pay forthwith the whole of the fee in respect of that work to that other barrister.

406.2   Subject to paragraph 805 a self-employed barrister who arranges for another barrister to undertake work for him (other than a pupil or a person who has asked to do the work in order to increase his own skill or experience) must himself and without delegating the responsibility to anyone else:

(a) pay proper financial remuneration for the work done;

(b) make payment within a reasonable time and in any event within three months after the work has been done unless otherwise agreed in advance with the other barrister.

PART V — EMPLOYED BARRISTERS

501   An employed barrister whilst acting in the course of his employment may supply legal services to his employer and to any of the following persons:

(a) any employee, director or company secretary of the employer in a matter arising out of or relating to that person's employment;

(b) where the employer is a public authority (including the Crown or a Government department or agency or a local authority):

(i)   another public authority on behalf of which the employer has made arrangements under statute or otherwise to supply any legal services or to perform any of that other public authority's functions as agent or otherwise;

(ii) in the case of a barrister employed by or in a Government department or agency, any Minister or Officer of the Crown;

(c) where the barrister is or is performing the functions of a justices' clerk, the justices whom he serves;

(d) where the barrister is employed by a trade association, any individual member of the association.

502   An employed barrister may supply legal services only to the persons referred to in paragraph 501 and must not supply legal services to any other person save that whilst acting in the course of his employment:

(a) a barrister employed by a solicitor or other authorised litigator or by an incorporated solicitors' practice may supply legal services to any client of his employer;

(b) a barrister employed by the Legal Services Commission may supply legal services to members of the public;

(c) a barrister employed by or at a Legal Advice Centre may supply legal services to clients of the Legal Advice Centre;

(d) any employed barrister may supply legal services to members of the public free of charge (to any person).

503   A barrister employed to supply legal services under a contract for services may be treated as an employed barrister for the purpose of this Code provided that the contract is:

(a) in writing;

(b) (subject to any provision for earlier termination on notice) for a determinate period; and

(c) the only contract under which the barrister is supplying legal services during that period (unless the Bar Council grants a specific waiver of this requirement).

504   An employed barrister shall have a right to conduct litigation in relation to every Court and all proceedings before any Court and may exercise that right provided that he complies with the Employed Barristers (Conduct of Litigation) Rules (reproduced in Annex I).

PART VI — ACCEPTANCE AND RETURN OF INSTRUCTIONS

Acceptance of instructions and the 'Cab-rank rule'

601   A barrister who supplies advocacy services must not withhold those services:

(a) on the ground that the nature of the case is objectionable to him or to any section of the public;

(b) on the ground that the conduct opinions or beliefs of the prospective client are unacceptable to him or to any section of the public;

(c) on any ground relating to the source of any financial support which may properly be given to the prospective client for the proceedings in question (for example, on the ground that such support will be available as part of the Community Legal Service or Criminal Defence Service).

602   A barrister in independent practice must comply with the 'Cab-rank rule' and accordingly except only as otherwise provided in paragraphs 603 604 605 and 606 he must in any field in which he professes to practise in relation to work appropriate to his experience and seniority and irrespective of whether his client is paying privately or is publicly funded:

(a) accept any brief to appear before a Court in which he professes to practise;

(b) accept any instructions;

(c) act for any person on whose behalf he is instructed;

and do so irrespective of (i) the party on whose behalf he is instructed (ii) the nature of the case and (iii) any belief or opinion which he may have formed as to the character reputation cause conduct guilt or innocence of that person.

603   A barrister must not accept any instructions if to do so would cause him to be professionally embarrassed and for this purpose a barrister will be professionally embarrassed:

(a) if he lacks sufficient experience or competence to handle the matter;

(b) if having regard to his other professional commitments he will be unable to do or will not have adequate time and opportunity to prepare that which he is required to do;

(c) if the instructions seek to limit the ordinary authority or discretion of a bar-rister in the conduct of proceedings in Court or to require a barrister to act otherwise than in conformity with law or with the provisions of this Code;

(d) if the matter is one in which he has reason to believe that he is likely to be a witness or in which whether by reason of any connection with the client or with the Court or a member of it or otherwise it will be difficult for him to maintain professional independence or the administration of justice might be or appear to be prejudiced;

(e) if there is or appears to be a conflict or risk of conflict either between the inter-ests of the barrister and some other person or between the interests of any one or more clients (unless all relevant persons consent to the barrister accepting the instructions);

(f) if there is a significant risk that information confidential to another client or former client might be communicated to or used for the benefit of anyone other than that client or former client without their consent;

(g) if he is a self-employed barrister where the instructions are delivered by a solicitor or firm of solicitors in respect of whom a Withdrawal of Credit Direction has been issued by the Chairman of the Bar pursuant to the Terms of Work on which Barristers Offer their Services to Solicitors and the Withdrawal of Credit Scheme 1988 as amended and in force from time to time (reproduced in Annex G1) unless his fees are to be paid directly by the Legal Services Commission or the instructions are accompanied by payment of an agreed fee or the barrister agrees in advance to accept no fee for such work or has obtained the consent of the Chairman of the Bar.

(h) If the barrister is instructed by or on behalf of a lay client who has not also instructed a solicitor or other professional client, and if the barrister is satisfied that it is in the interests of the client or in the interests of justice for the lay client to instruct a solicitor or other professional client.

604   Subject to paragraph 601 a self-employed barrister is not obliged to accept instructions:

(a) requiring him to do anything other than during the course of his ordinary working year;

(b) other than at a fee which is proper having regard to:

(i)   the complexity length and difficulty of the case;

(ii)   his ability experience and seniority; and

(iii) the expenses which he will incur;

and any instructions in a matter funded by the Legal Services Commission as part of the Community Legal Service or the Criminal Defence Service for which the amount or rate of the barrister's remuneration is prescribed by regulation or subject to assessment shall for this purpose unless the Bar Council or the Bar in general meeting otherwise determines (either in a particular case or in any class or classes of case or generally) be deemed to be at a proper professional fee;[1,2]

---

[1] On 30 April 2001 the Bar Council decided that, with effect from 1 May 2001, all cases subject to family graduated fees are no longer deemed to be at a proper professional fee for the purposes of paragraph 604(b).

[2] On 15 November 2003 the Bar Council decided that, effective immediately, all cases subject to criminal graduated fees are no longer deemed to be at a proper professional fee for the purposes of paragraph 604(b).

    (c) to do any work under a conditional fee agreement;

    (d) save in a matter funded by the Legal Services Commission as part of the Community Legal Service or the Criminal Defence Service:

        (i)   unless and until his fees are agreed;

        (ii) if having required his fees to be paid before he accepts the instructions those fees are not paid;

    (e) from anyone other than a professional client who accepts liability for the barrister's fees

    (f) to do any work under the Contractual Terms on which Barristers offer their Services to Solicitors 2001 as amended and in force from time to time (reproduced in Appendix G2) or on any other contractual terms.

605   A self-employed Queen's Counsel is not obliged to accept instructions:

    (a) to settle alone any document of a kind generally settled only by or in conjunction with a junior;

    (b) to act without a junior if he considers that the interests of the lay client require that a junior should also be instructed.

606.1   A barrister (whether he is instructed on his own or with another advocate) must in the case of all instructions consider whether consistently with the proper and efficient administration of justice and having regard to:

    (a) the circumstances (including in particular the gravity complexity and likely cost) of the case;

    (b) the nature of his practice;

    (c) his ability experience and seniority; and

    (d) his relationship with the client;

the best interests of the client would be served by instructing or continuing to instruct him in that matter.

606.2   Where a barrister is instructed in any matter with another advocate or advocates the barrister must in particular consider whether it would be in the best interests of the client to instruct only one advocate or fewer advocates.

606.3   A barrister who in any matter is instructed either directly by the lay client or by an intermediary who is not a solicitor or other authorised litigator should consider whether it would be in the interests of the lay client or the interests of justice to instruct a solicitor or other authorised litigator or other appropriate intermediary either together with or in place of the barrister.

606.4   In cases involving several parties, a barrister must on receipt of instructions and further in the event of any change of circumstances consider whether, having regard to all the circumstances including any actual or potential conflict of interest, any client ought to be separately represented or advised or whether it would be in the best interests of any client to be jointly represented or advised with another party.

607   If at any time in any matter a barrister considers that it would be in the best interests of any client to have different representation, he must immediately so advise the client.

Withdrawal from a case and return of instructions

608   A barrister must cease to act and if he is a self-employed barrister must return any instructions:

(a) if continuing to act would cause him to be professionally embarrassed within the meaning of paragraph 603 provided that if he would be professionally embarrassed only because it appears to him that he is likely to be a witness on a material question of fact he may retire or withdraw only if he can do so without jeopardising the client's interests;

(b) if having accepted instructions on behalf of more than one client there is or appears to be:

(i) a conflict or risk of conflict between the interests of any one or more of such clients; or

(ii) risk of a breach of confidence;

and the clients do not all consent to him continuing to act;

(c) if in any case funded by the Legal Services Commission as part of the Community Legal Service or Criminal Defence Service it has become apparent to him that such funding has been wrongly obtained by false or inaccurate information and action to remedy the situation is not immediately taken by the client;

(d) if the client refuses to authorise him to make some disclosure to the Court which his duty to the Court requires him to make;

(e) if having become aware during the course of a case of the existence of a document which should have been but has not been disclosed on discovery the client fails forthwith to disclose it;

(f) if having come into possession of a document belonging to another party by some means other than the normal and proper channels and having read it before he realises that it ought to have been returned unread to the person entitled to possession of it he would thereby be embarrassed in the discharge of his duties by his knowledge of the contents of the document provided that he may retire or withdraw only if he can do so without jeopardising the client's interests.

609   Subject to paragraph 610 a barrister may withdraw from a case where he is satisfied that:

(a) his instructions have been withdrawn;

(b) his professional conduct is being impugned;

(c) advice which he has given in accordance with paragraph 607 or 703 has not been heeded; or

(d) there is some other substantial reason for so doing.

610   A barrister must not:

(a) cease to act or return instructions without having first explained to the client his reasons for doing so;

(b) return instructions to another barrister without the consent of the client;

(c) return a brief which he has accepted and for which a fixed date has been obtained or (except with the consent of the lay client and where appropriate the Court) break any other engagement to supply legal services in the course of his practice so as to enable him to attend or fulfil an engagement (including a social or non-professional engagement) of any other kind;

(d) except as provided in paragraph 608 return any instructions or withdraw from a case in such a way or in such circumstances that the client may be unable to find other legal assistance in time to prevent prejudice being suffered by the client.

PART VII — CONDUCT OF WORK BY PRACTISING BARRISTERS

General

701   A barrister:

(a) must in all his professional activities be courteous and act promptly conscientiously diligently and with reasonable competence and take all reasonable and practicable steps to avoid unnecessary expense or waste of the Court's time and to ensure that professional engagements are fulfilled;

(b) must not undertake any task which:

(i)   he knows or ought to know he is not competent to handle;

(ii) he does not have adequate time and opportunity to prepare for or perform; or

(iii) he cannot discharge within the time requested or otherwise within a reasonable time having regard to the pressure of other work;

(c) must read all instructions delivered to him expeditiously;

(d) must have regard to any relevant Written Standards for the conduct of Professional Work issued by the Bar Council;

(e) must inform his client forthwith and subject to paragraph 610 return the instructions to the client or to another barrister acceptable to the client:

(i)   if it becomes apparent to him that he will not be able to do the work within the time requested or within a reasonable time after receipt of instructions;

(ii) if there is an appreciable risk that he may not be able to undertake a brief or fulfil any other professional engagement which he has accepted.

(f) must ensure that adequate records supporting the fees charged or claimed in a case are kept at least until the last of the following: his fees have been paid, any taxation or determination or assessment of costs in the case has been completed, or the time for lodging an appeal against assessment or the determination of that appeal, has expired, and must provide his professional or licensed access client or other intermediary or lay client with such records or details of the work done as may reasonably be required.

Confidentiality

702   Whether or not the relation of counsel and client continues a barrister must preserve the confidentiality of the lay client's affairs and must not without the prior consent of the lay client or as permitted by law lend or reveal the contents of the papers in any instructions to or communicate to any third person (other than another barrister, a pupil, in the case of a Registered European Lawyer, the person with whom he is acting in conjunction for the purposes of paragraph 5(3) of the Registered European Lawyers Rules or any other person who needs to know it for

the performance of their duties) information which has been entrusted to him in confidence or use such information to the lay client's detriment or to his own or another client's advantage.

Conflicts between lay clients and intermediaries

703   If a self-employed barrister forms the view that there is a conflict of interest between his lay client and a professional client or other intermediary (for example because he considers that the intermediary may have been negligent) he must consider whether it would be in the lay client's interest to instruct another professional adviser or representative and, if he considers that it would be, the barrister must so advise and take such steps as he considers necessary to ensure that his advice is communicated to the lay client (if necessary by sending a copy, of his advice in writing directly to the lay client as well as to the intermediary).

Drafting documents

704   A barrister must not devise facts which will assist in advancing the lay client's case and must not draft any statement of case, witness statement, affidavit, notice of appeal or other document containing:

(a) any statement of fact or contention which is not supported by the lay client or by his instructions;

(b) any contention which he does not consider to be properly arguable;

(c) any allegation of fraud unless he has clear instructions to make such allegation and has before him reasonably credible material which as it stands establishes a prima facie case of fraud;

(d) in the case of a witness statement or affidavit any statement of fact other than the evidence which in substance according to his instructions the barrister reasonably believes the witness would give if the evidence contained in the witness statement or affidavit were being given in oral examination;

provided that nothing in this paragraph shall prevent a barrister drafting a document containing specific factual statements or contentions included by the barrister subject to confirmation of their accuracy by the lay client or witness.

Contact with witnesses

705   A barrister must not:

(a) rehearse practise or coach a witness in relation to his evidence;

(b) encourage a witness to give evidence which is untruthful or which is not the whole truth;

(c) except with the consent of the representative for the opposing side or of the Court, communicate directly or indirectly about a case with any witness, whether or not the witness is his lay client, once that witness has begun to give evidence until the evidence of that witness has been concluded.

Attendance of professional client

706   A self-employed barrister who is instructed by a professional client should not conduct a case in Court in the absence of his professional client or a representative of his professional client unless the Court rules that it is appropriate or he is

satisfied that the interests of the lay client and the interests of justice will not be prejudiced.

707   A self-employed barrister who attends Court in order to conduct a case in circumstances where no professional client or representative of a professional client is present may if necessary interview witnesses and take proofs of evidence.

Conduct in Court

708   A barrister when conducting proceedings in Court:

(a) is personally responsible for the conduct and presentation of his case and must exercise personal judgement upon the substance and purpose of statements made and questions asked;

(b) must not unless invited to do so by the Court or when appearing before a tribunal where it is his duty to do so assert a personal opinion of the facts or the law;

(c) must ensure that the Court is informed of all relevant decisions and legislative provisions of which he is aware whether the effect is favourable or unfavourable towards the contention for which he argues;

(d) must bring any procedural irregularity to the attention of the Court during the hearing and not reserve such matter to be raised on appeal;

(e) must not adduce evidence obtained otherwise than from or through the client or devise facts which will assist in advancing the lay client's case;

(f) must not make a submission which he does not consider to be properly arguable;

(g) must not make statements or ask questions which are merely scandalous or intended or calculated only to vilify insult or annoy either a witness or some other person;

(h) must if possible avoid the naming in open Court of third parties whose character would thereby be impugned;

(i) must not by assertion in a speech impugn a witness whom he has had an opportunity to cross-examine unless in cross-examination he has given the witness an opportunity to answer the allegation;

(j) must not suggest that a victim, witness or other person is guilty of crime, fraud or misconduct or make any defamatory aspersion on the conduct of any other person or attribute to another person the crime or conduct of which his lay client is accused

unless such allegations go to a matter in issue (including the credibility of the witness) which is material to the lay client's case and appear to him to be supported by reasonable grounds.

Media comment

709.1   barrister must not in relation to any anticipated or current proceedings in which he is briefed or expects to appear or has appeared as an advocate express a personal opinion to the press or other media or in any other public statement upon the facts or issues arising in the proceedings.

709.2   Paragraph 709.1 shall not prevent the expression of such an opinion on an issue in an educational or academic context.

Advertising and publicity

710.1   Subject to paragraph 710.2 a barrister may engage in any advertising or promotion in connection with his practice which conforms to the British Codes of Advertising and Sales Promotion and such advertising or promotion may include:

(a)   photographs or other illustrations of the barrister;

(b)   statements of rates and methods of charging;

(c)   statements about the nature and extent of the barrister's services;

(d)   information about any case in which the barrister has appeared (including the name of any client for whom the barrister acted) where such information has already become publicly available or, where it has not already become publicly available, with the express prior written consent of the lay client.

710.2   Advertising or promotion must not:

(a)   be inaccurate or likely to mislead;

(b)   be likely to diminish public confidence in the legal profession or the administration of justice or otherwise bring the legal profession into disrepute;

(c)   make direct comparisons in terms of quality with or criticisms of other identifiable persons (whether they be barristers or members of any other profession);

(d)   include statements about the barrister's success rate;

(e)   indicate or imply any willingness to accept instructions or any intention to restrict the persons from whom instructions may be accepted otherwise than in accordance with this Code;

(f)   be so frequent or obtrusive as to cause annoyance to those to whom it is directed.

PART VIII — MISCELLANEOUS

Pupils

801   A barrister who is a pupil must:

(a)   comply with Part V of the Consolidated Regulations;

(b)   apply himself full time to his pupillage save that a pupil may with the permission of his pupil-supervisor or head of chambers take part time work which does not in their opinion materially interfere with his pupillage;

(c)   preserve the confidentiality of every client's affairs and accordingly paragraph 702 applies to him in the same way as it does to his pupil-master and to every person whom he accompanies to Court or whose papers he sees.

802   A barrister who is a pupil may supply legal services as a barrister and exercise a right of audience which he has by reason of being a barrister provided that:

(a)   he has completed or been exempted from the non-practising six months of pupillage; and

(b)   he has the permission of his pupil-supervisor or head of chambers;

provided that such a barrister may during the non-practising six months of pupillage with the permission of his pupil-supervisor or head of chambers accept a
noting brief.

803.1   So long as he is a pupil a self-employed barrister may not become or hold himself
out as a member of chambers or permit his name to appear anywhere as such a
member.

803.2   A barrister who is a pupil of an employed barrister or who pursuant to Regulation
46 of the Consolidated Regulations spends any period of external training with
an employed barrister or with a solicitor shall be treated for the purpose of the
Code as if he were during that period employed by the employed barrister's
employer or by the solicitor's firm as the case may be.

Pupil-Supervisors

804   A barrister who is a pupil-supervisor must:

(a) comply with Part V of the Consolidated Regulations;

(b) take all reasonable steps to provide his pupil with adequate tuition supervision and experience;

(c) have regard to the pupillage guidelines issued from time to time by the Bar
Council and to the Equality Code for the Bar.

805   Except where a pupil is in receipt of an award or remuneration which is paid on
terms that it is in lieu of payment for any individual item of work, a barrister
must pay any pupil (or in the case of an employed barrister ensure that a pupil
is paid) for any work done for him which because of its value to him warrants
payment.

Legal Advice Centres

806   A self-employed barrister may supply legal services at a Legal Advice Centre on a
voluntary or part time basis and, if he does so, shall in connection with the supply
of those services be treated for the purpose of this Code as if he were employed by
the Legal Advice Centre.

807   A barrister who is employed by a Legal Advice Centre:

(a) must not in any circumstances receive either directly or indirectly any fee
or reward for the supply of any legal services to any client of the Legal
Advice Centre other than a salary paid by the Legal Advice Centre;

(b) must ensure that any fees in respect of legal services supplied by him to any
client of the Legal Advice Centre accrue and are paid to the Legal Advice
Centre;

(c) must not have any financial interest in the Legal Advice Centre.

Dual qualification

808.1   A barrister who is a member of another authorised body and currently entitled to
practise as such shall not practise as a barrister.

808.2   A barrister who becomes entitled to practise as a member of another authorised
body shall forthwith inform the Bar Council and the Inn(s) of Court of which he
is a member in writing of that fact.

808.3   A barrister who:

(a) has had his name struck off the roll of solicitors or been excluded from membership of an authorised body; or

(b) has at any time been found guilty of any professional misconduct or is the subject of any continuing disciplinary proceedings in relation to his professional conduct as a member of an authorised body; or

(c) has at any time been refused a practising certificate as a solicitor or had his practising certificate suspended or made subject to a condition

shall not practise as a barrister until the PCC has considered his case and, if it decides to refer the case to a Disciplinary Tribunal, until the case is finally determined.

Foreign lawyers

809   A barrister called to the Bar under Part IV of the Consolidated Regulations (temporary membership of the Bar) may not practise as a barrister other than to conduct the case or cases specified in the certificate referred to in Regulation 39.

PART IX — COMPLIANCE

901   Any failure by a barrister to comply with this Code shall constitute professional misconduct.

902   If the declaration made by a barrister on Call to the Bar is found to have been false in any material respect or if the barrister is found to have engaged before Call in conduct which is dishonest or otherwise discreditable to a barrister and which was not, before Call, fairly disclosed in writing to the Benchers of the Inn calling him or if any undertaking given by a barrister on Call to the Bar is breached in any material respect that shall constitute professional misconduct.

903   A barrister is subject to:

(a) the Complaints Rules (reproduced in Annex J);

(b) the Disciplinary Tribunals Regulations (reproduced in Annex K);

(c) the Summary Procedure Rules (reproduced in Annex L);

(d) the Hearings before the Visitors Rules (reproduced in Annex M);

(e) the Interim Suspension Rules (reproduced at Annex N);

(f) the Fitness to Practise Rules (reproduced at Annex O);

(g) the Adjudication Panel and Appeals Rules (reproduced at Annex P) which are concerned with inadequate professional service.

904   Pursuant to the Rules referred to in paragraph 903 a barrister may be directed to provide redress to a lay client for inadequate professional service whether or not such inadequate professional service also constitutes professional misconduct.

905   A barrister must:

(a) if he is practising, or the Bar Council has reason to believe may be practising, as a barrister:

(i) respond promptly to any requirement from the Bar Council for comments on or documents relating to the arrangements made for administering his practice and chambers or office whether or not any complaint has been received or raised arising out of those arrangements;

(ii) permit the Bar Council or any agent appointed by it to inspect forthwith and on request and at any time which is reasonable having regard to the circumstances and the urgency of the matter any premises from which he practises or is believed to practise as a barrister, the arrangements made for administering his practice and chambers or office, and any records relating to such practice and to the administration of his chambers or office.

(b) report promptly to the Bar Council if:

(i) he is charged with a serious criminal offence;

(ii) he is convicted of any relevant criminal offence; or

(iii) he is convicted of a disciplinary offence by another professional body;

(c) report promptly to the Bar Council if;

(i) bankruptcy proceedings are initiated in respect of or against him;

(ii) directors disqualification proceedings are initiated against him;

(iii) a bankruptcy order or directors disqualification order is made against him; or

(iv) if he enters into a individual voluntary arrangement with his creditors;

(d) where a complaint about a barrister has been made to or by the Bar Council, or where the Bar Council has reasonable grounds for believing that a breach of this Code may have occurred or is about to occur, or where circumstance referred to in sub-paragraph (b) or (c) above has been reported to the Bar Council, respond promptly to any request from the Bar Council for comments or information on the matter whether it relates to him or to another barrister;

(e) respond promptly to any letter of notification sent to him or attend before any tribunal panel body or person when so required pursuant to the rules referred to in paragraph 903;

(f) comply in due time with any sentence or suspension imposed or direction made or undertaking accepted by a tribunal panel body or person pursuant to the rules referred to in paragraph 903.

provided for the avoidance of doubt that nothing in this paragraph shall require a barrister to disclose or produce any document or information protected by law or in circumstances to which paragraph 702 applies.

PART X — DEFINITIONS

1001   In this Code except where otherwise indicated:

'the Act' means the Courts and Legal Services Act 1990 and where the context permits includes any orders or regulations made pursuant to powers conferred thereby;

'the Act of 1985' means the Administration of Justice Act 1985;

'advocacy services' means advocacy services as defined in Section 119 of the Act;

'authorised body' means any body other than the Bar Council authorised under the Act to grant rights of audience or rights to conduct litigation;

'authorised litigator' means an authorised litigator as defined in Section 119 of the Act;

'bankruptcy order' includes a bankruptcy order made pursuant to the Insolvency Act 1986 and any similar order made in any jurisdiction in the world;

'Bar' means the Bar of England and Wales;

'Bar Council' means The General Council of the Bar as constituted from time to time or a Committee thereof;

'barrister' means an individual who has been called to the Bar by one of the Inns of Court and who has not ceased to be a member of the Bar; and in Parts III (other than paragraph 301), VI, VII and VIII of this Code means a practising barrister;

'BMIF' means Bar Mutual Indemnity Fund Limited;

'brief' means instructions to a barrister to appear as an advocate before a Court;

'Call' means Call to the Bar in accordance with the Consolidated Regulations;

'chambers' means a place at or from which one or more self-employed barristers carry on their practices and also refers where the context so requires to all the barristers (excluding pupils) who for the time being carry on their practices at or from that place;

'client' means lay client or intermediary;

'complaint' means an allegation by any person or by the Bar Council of its own motion of professional misconduct or of inadequate professional service and includes a legal aid complaint;

'conditional fee agreement' means a conditional fee agreement as defined in Section 58 of the Act;

'Consolidated Regulations' means the Consolidated Regulations of the Inns of Court;

'Court' includes any court or tribunal or any other person or body whether sitting in public or in private before whom a barrister appears or may appear as an advocate;

'Disciplinary Tribunal' means a disciplinary tribunal constituted under the Disciplinary Tribunals Regulations (reproduced in Annex K);

'employed barrister' means a practising barrister who is employed either under a contract of employment or by virtue of an office under the Crown or in the institutions of the European Communities and who supplies legal services as a barrister in the course of his employment;

'employer' means a person by whom an employed barrister is employed as such and any holding subsidiary or associated company corporate body or firm of that person;

'English law' includes international law and the law of the European Communities;

'Establishment Directive' means Directive 98/5/EC of the European Parliament and of the Council of February 1998 to facilitate practice of the profession of lawyer on a permanent basis in a Member State other than that in which the qualification was obtained;

'European lawyer' means a person who is a national of a Member State and who is authorised in any Member State to pursue professional activities under any of the professional titles appearing in article 2(2) of the European Communities (Lawyer's Practice) Order 1999, but who is not any of the following:

(a) a solicitor or barrister of England and Wales or Northern Ireland; or

(b) a solicitor or advocate under the law of Scotland.

'foreign lawyer' means a person (other than a registered European lawyer or a practising barrister of the bar of England and Wales) who is authorised by a competent professional body to practise in a system of law other than English law;

'home professional body' means the body in a Member State which authorises a European lawyer to pursue professional activities under any of the professional titles appearing in article 2(2) of the European Communities (Lawyer's Practice) Order 1999 and, if he is authorised in more than one Member States, it shall mean any such body;

'home professional title' means, in relation to a European lawyer, the professional title or any of the professional titles specified in relation to his home State in article 2(2) of the European Communities (Lawyer's Practice) Order 1999 under which he is authorised in his home State to pursue professional activities;

'home State' means the Member State in which a European lawyer acquired the authorisation to pursue professional activities under his home professional title and, if he is authorised in more than one Member State, it shall mean any such Member State;

'inadequate professional service' means such conduct towards a lay client or performance of professional services for that client which falls significantly short of that which is to be reasonably expected of a barrister in all the circumstances;

'incorporated solicitors' practice' means a body recognised under section 9 of the Act of 1985;

'instructions' means instructions or directions in whatever form (including a brief) given to a practising barrister to supply legal services whether in a contentious or in a non-contentious matter and 'instructed' shall have a corresponding meaning;

'intermediary' means any person by whom a barrister in independent practice is instructed on behalf of a lay client and includes a professional client who is not also the lay client;

'International work' shall have the meaning set out in the International Practice Rules (re- produced in Annex A);

'lay client' means the person on whose behalf a practising barrister (or where appropriate in the case of an employed barrister his employer) is instructed;

'lay representative' means a lay person appointed by the Bar Council to serve on Disciplinary Tribunals;

'legal aid complaint' shall mean a complaint so described in section 40 of the Act of 1985 as amended by the Access to Justice Act 1999;

'Legal Advice Centre' means a centre operated by a charitable or similar non-commercial organisation at which legal services are habitually provided to members of the public without charge (or for a nominal charge) to the client and:

(a) which employs or has the services of one or more solicitors pursuant to paragraph 7(a) of the Employed Solicitors' Code 1990 or for whom the Law Society has granted a waiver, or

(b) which has been and remains designated by the Bar Council as suitable for the employment or attendance of barristers subject to such conditions as may be imposed by the Bar Council in relation to insurance or any other matter whatsoever;

'legal services' includes legal advice representation and drafting or settling any statement of case witness statement affidavit or other legal document but does not include:

(a) sitting as a judge or arbitrator or acting as a mediator;

(b) lecturing in or teaching law or writing or editing law books articles or reports;

(c) examining newspapers, periodicals, books, scripts and other publications for libel, breach of copyright, contempt of court and the like;

(d) communicating to or in the press or other media;

(e) exercising the powers of a commissioner for oaths;

(f) giving advice on legal matters free to a friend or relative or acting as unpaid or honorary legal adviser to any charitable benevolent or philanthropic institution;

(g) in relation to a barrister who is a non-executive director of a company or a trustee or governor of a charitable benevolent or philanthropic institution or a trustee of any private trust, giving to the other directors trustees or governors the benefit of his learning and experience on matters of general legal principle applicable to the affairs of the company institution or trust;

'Legal Services Commission' means a body established by or under Section 1 or Section 2 of the Access to Justice Act 1999 and includes any body established and maintained by such a body;

'Licensed Access client' means a person or organisation approved as such by the Bar Council in accordance with the Licensed Access Recognition Regulations (reproduced in Annex F);

'litigation services' means litigation services as defined in section 119 of the Act;

'Member State' means a state which is a member of the European Communities;

'non-practising barrister' means a barrister who is not a practising barrister;

'the PCC' means the Professional Conduct and Complaints Committee of the Bar Council;

'practising barrister' means a barrister who is practising as such within the meaning of paragraph 201;

'professional client' means a solicitor or other professional person by whom a self-employed barrister is instructed that is to say:

(a) a solicitor, authorised litigator, Parliamentary agent, patent agent, trade mark agent, Notary or a European lawyer registered with the Law Society of England and Wales;

(b) a licensed conveyancer in a matter in which the licensed conveyancer is providing conveyancing services;

(c) an employed barrister or registered European lawyer;

(d) any practising barrister or registered European lawyer acting on his own behalf;

(e) a foreign lawyer in a matter which does not involve the barrister supplying advocacy services;

(f) a Scottish or Northern Irish Solictor;

(g) the representative of any body (such as a Legal Advice Centre or Pro Bono or Free Representation Unit) which arranges for the supply of legal services to the public without a fee, and which has been and remains designated by the Bar Council (subject to such conditions as may be imposed by the Bar Council in relation to insurance or any other matter whatsoever) as suitable for the instruction of barristers, and which instructs a barrister to supply legal services without a fee;

'professional misconduct' shall bear the meaning given in paragraphs 901 and 902;

'the PSC' means the Professional Standards Committee of the Bar Council;

'the public' includes any lay client of a practising barrister (or in the case of an employed barrister of the barrister's employer) other than any of the persons referred to in paragraph 501;

'public access instructions' means instructions given to a barrister by or on behalf of a lay client pursuant to paragraph 401(a)(iii);

'registered European lawyer' means a European lawyer registered as such by the Bar Council and by an Inn pursuant to a direction of the JRC under Regulation 30 of the Consolidated Regulations;

'relevant criminal offence' means any criminal offence committed in any part of the world except:

(a) an offence committed in the United Kingdom which is a fixed penalty offence for the purposes of the Road Traffic Offenders Act 1988 or any statutory modification or replacement thereof for the time being in force;

(b) an offence committed in the United Kingdom or abroad which is dealt with by a procedure substantially similar to that applicable to such a fixed penalty offence; and

(c) an offence whose main ingredient is the unlawful parking of a motor vehicle;

'right of audience' means a right of audience as defined in Section 119 of the Act;

'right to conduct litigation' means a right to conduct litigation as defined in Section 119 of the Act;

'self-employed barrister' means a practising barrister other than an employed barrister acting in the course of his employment;

'serious criminal offence' means an offence involving dishonesty or deception or a serious arrestable offence (as defined by section 116 of the Police and Criminal Evidence Act 1984);

'solicitor' means a solicitor of the Supreme Court of England and Wales;

'Summary Procedure Panel' means a panel constituted under the Summary Procedure Rules (reproduced in Annex L);

'trade association' means a body of persons (whether incorporated or not) which is formed for the purpose of furthering the trade interests of its members or of persons represented by its members, and does not include any association formed primarily for the purpose of securing legal assistance for its members;

any reference to the masculine shall be deemed to include the feminine and any reference to the singular shall include the plural.

PART XI — TRANSITIONAL PROVISIONS

1101   In respect of anything done or omitted to be done or otherwise arising before 31 October 2004:

    (a) this Code shall not apply;

    (b) the Code of Conduct in force at the relevant time shall notwithstanding paragraph 101 apply as if this Code had not been adopted by the Bar Council.

1102   Any barrister called to the Bar before 1 January 2002 but who has not completed or been exempted from 12 months' pupillage in accordance with the Consolidated Regulations in force at the relevant time may practise as a barrister notwithstanding paragraph 202(a) of this Code provided that such a barrister shall not be entitled to exercise a right of audience under paragraph 203.1 unless he:

    (a) has notified the Bar Council in writing of his wish to do so; and

    (b) either (i) has complied with any conditions as to further training which the Bar Council may require or (ii) has been informed by the Bar Council that he is not required to comply with any such conditions.

1103   Any barrister who on 31 July 2000 was entitled to exercise any right of audience which he had by reason of being a barrister shall notwithstanding paragraph 203 of this Code remain entitled to exercise that right of audience.

1104   Any barrister who during any period before 31 July 2000 was entitled to exercise a right of audience as an employed barrister may for the purpose of paragraph 203.2(c) of this Code count that period as if he had been entitled during that period to exercise a right of audience before every Court in relation to all proceedings provided that he:

    (a) has notified the Bar Council in writing of his wish to do so; and

    (b) either (i) has complied with any conditions (including any conditions as to further training) which the Bar Council may require or (ii) has been informed by the Bar Council that he is not required to comply with any such conditions.

1105   Any person who was entitled on 31 July 2000 or becomes entitled before 31 July 2002 to exercise a right of audience before every Court in relation to all proceedings shall be a qualified person without having satisfied paragraph 203.3(b)(ii) of this Code if he:

    (a) has satisfied the other requirements of paragraph 203.3;

    (b) has notified the Bar Council in writing of his wish to act as a qualified person; and

    (c) has been designated by the Bar Council as suitable so to act.

1106   Any barrister who before 31 July 2000 had delivered to the Bar Council the notification and information referred to in paragraph 212(b)(ii) of the Sixth Edition of the Code of Conduct or was exempted by waiver from that requirement shall until 31 July 2005 remain entitled to supply legal services to the public on condition that he complies with those requirements of paragraph 212(b)–(e) of the Sixth Edition of the Code of Conduct which on 31 July 2000 applied to him and provided that he shall not thereby be entitled to exercise any right of audience which he has by reason of being a barrister.

SECTION 2

Table of Annexes

ANNEXE A

THE INTERNATIONAL PRACTICE RULES

1. 'International work' means practice as a barrister:

    (a) where the work (i) relates to matters or proceedings essentially arising taking place or contemplated outside England and Wales and (ii) is to be substantially performed outside England and Wales; or

    (b) where the lay client carries on business or usually resides outside England and Wales provided that:

        (i) the instructions emanate for outside England and Wales; and

        (ii) the work does not involve the barrister in providing advocacy services.

2. In connection with any International work, a barrister must comply with any applicable rule of conduct prescribed by the law or by any national or local Bar of (a) the place where the work is or is to be performed (b) the place where any proceedings or matters to which the work relates are taking place or contemplated, unless such rule is inconsistent with any requirement of Part III of this Code ('Fundamental Principles').

3. Paragraphs 401(a) and (c) and 602 of the Code shall not apply to International work.

4. In relation to International work substantially performed outside England and Wales:

    (a) a practising barrister may enter into any association (including partnership) with any lawyer other than a member of another authorised body for the purpose of sharing any office, services or fees;

    (b) paragraphs 401(b) and 402.1 of the Code shall not apply;

    (c) paragraph 405 of the Code shall apply on the basis that the applicable law is that of the place where the work is performed; and

    (d) a practising barrister employed by a foreign lawyer or foreign legal practice may supply legal services to any client of his employer.

    (e) Notwithstanding paragraph 201, a barrister who is practising as a foreign lawyer and who does not:

        (i) give advice on English law; or

        (ii) supply legal services in connection with any proceedings or contemplated proceedings in England and Wales (other than as an expert witness on foreign law),

Shall not be treated as a practising barrister for the purposes of the Code.

5. In respect of a barrister who is exercising a right to practise in a Member State other than the United Kingdom pursuant to the Establishment Directive, or in Scotland, or Northern Ireland pursuant to the European Communities (Lawyer's Practice) Regulations 2000, a person shall be a qualified person for the purpose of paragraph 203.1(b) of the Code if he:

    (a) has been designated by the Bar Council as possessing qualifications and experience in that State or country which are equivalent to the qualifications and experience required by sub-paragraphs (a) and (b) of paragraph 203.3 of the Code;

    (b) is not acting as a qualified person in relation to more than two other people; and

    (c) has not been designated by the Bar Council as unsuitable to be a qualified person.

6. A practising barrister who supplies legal services as a barrister (other than to his employer) outside England and Wales must be covered (and in the case of an employed barrister his employer must be covered) by insurance against claims for professional negligence arising out of the supply of his services in an amount not less

than the minimum level of insurance cover required by law or by the rules of the Bar in the place where the services are sup- plied or, if there is no such minimum, the current minimum sum insured for barristers practising in England and Wales.

7. A barrister who solicits work in any jurisdiction outside England and Wales must not do so in a manner which would be prohibited if the barrister were a member of the local Bar.

ANNEXE B

THE REGISTERED EUROPEAN LAWYERS RULES

1. The Bar Council shall maintain a register of European lawyers.

2. The Bar Council shall:

    (1) enter a European lawyer on the register pursuant to a direction of the Joint Regulations Committee under Regulation 30 of the Consolidated Regulations;

    (2) remove a European lawyer from the register:

        (i) pursuant to a sentence of a Disciplinary Tribunal; or

        (ii) if the registered European lawyer ceases to be a European lawyer;

    (3) suspend a European lawyer from the register:

        (i) pursuant to a sentence of either a Disciplinary Tribunal or a Summary Procedure Panel; or

        (ii) if the European lawyer's authorisation in his home state to pursue professional activities under his home professional title is suspended; and

    (4) notify the European lawyer's home professional body:

        (i) of his entry on or removal or suspension from the register; and

        (ii) of any criminal conviction or bankruptcy order of which it becomes aware against a registered European lawyer.

3. A registered European lawyer must not hold himself out to be a barrister.

4. A registered European lawyer must in connection with all professional work undertaken in England and Wales:

    (1) use his home professional title as determined by the Joint Regulations Committee pursuant to the Consolidated Regulations;

    (2) indicate the name of his home professional body or the Court before which he is entitled to practise in that Member State; and

    (3) indicate that he is registered with the Bar Council as a European lawyer.

5. A registered European lawyer may supply legal services, including the exercise of rights of audience, under these Rules provided that:

    (1) he has a current practising certificate issued by the Bar Council in accordance with the Practising Certificate Regulations;

    (2) in the case of a registered European lawyer who supplies legal services to the public, unless exempted by the Joint Regulations Committee he is covered by insurance against claims for professional negligence arising out of the supply of his services in England and Wales in such amount and upon such terms as are currently required by the Bar Council, and has delivered to the Bar Council a copy of the current insurance policy or the current certificate of insurance issued by the insurer;

    (3) where the professional activities in question may (but for the European Communities (Lawyer's Practice) Order 1999) be lawfully provided only by a solicitor or barrister, he must act in conjunction with a solicitor or barrister who is entitled to practise before the Court, tribunal or public authority concerned and who could lawfully provide those professional activities.

6. A registered European lawyer in connection with all professional work undertaken in England and Wales must comply with all of the provisions of the Code (except

paragraphs 201 to 204, 401, 402 and 801 to 804) as if he were a self-employed barrister or an employed barrister as the case may be and as if references in the Code to barristers included reference to registered European lawyers.

7. A registered European lawyer must inform the Bar Council of:

    (1) any investigation into his conduct by his home professional body;

    (2) any findings of professional misconduct made by his professional body; and

    (3) the withdrawal or suspension of his authorisation in his home state to pursue professional activities under his home professional title.

ANNEXE C

THE CONTINUING PROFESSIONAL DEVELOPMENT REGULATIONS

Application

1. These Rules apply;

    (a) to all barristers who have commenced practice on or after 1 October 1997;

    (b) from 1 January 2003, to all barristers who were called to the Bar in or after 1990;

    (c) from 1 January 2004, to all barristers who were called to the Bar between 1980 and 1989; and

    (d) from 1 January 2005, to all barristers who were called to the Bar before 1980.

The Mandatory Continuing Professional Development Requirements

2. For the purpose of these Regulations:

    (a) 'calendar year' means a period of one year commencing on 1 January in the year in question;

    (b) the 'mandatory requirements' are those set out in paragraphs 3 to 7 below.

3. Any barrister to whom these Regulations apply and who as at 1 October 2001 had commenced but not completed the period of three years referred to in the Continuing Education Scheme Rules at Annex Q to the Sixth Edition of the Code of Conduct must complete a minimum of 42 hours of continuing professional development during that period.

4. Any barrister to whom these Regulations apply who commences practice on or after 1 October 2001 must during the first three calendar years (running from 1 January) in which the barrister holds a practising certificate complete a minimum of 42 hours of continuing professional development.

5. Any barrister to whom these Regulations apply:

    (a) must, if he holds a practising certificate or certicates throughout the whole of any calendar year, complete a minimum of 12 hours of continuing professional development during that period; and

    (b) must, if he holds a practising certifcate or certificate for part only of a calendar year, complete one hour of continuing professional development during that calendar year for each month for which he holds a practising certificate.

6. Regulation 5 does not apply:

    (a) in the case of a barrister to whom regulation 3 applies, to any calendar year forming or containing part of the period of 3 years referred to in regulation 3; or

    (b) in the case of a barrister to whom regulation 4 applies, during the first three calendar years in which the barrister holds a practising certificate.

7. Any barrister to whom these Regulations apply must submit details of the continuing professional development he has undertaken to the Bar Council in the form prescribed, and at the time specified, by the Bar Council.

8. The Bar Council may, by resolution, specify the nature, content and format of courses and other activities which may be undertaken by barristers (or any category of barristers) in order to satisfy the mandatory requirements.

9. The Bar Council may, by resolution and following consultation with the Inns, Circuits and other providers as appropriate, increase the minimum number of hours of continuing professional development which must be completed in order to satisfy any of the mandatory requirements.

Waivers

10. The Bar Council shall have the power in relation to any barrister to waive any or all of the mandatory requirements in whole or in part or to extend the time within which the barrister must complete any of the mandatory requirements.

11. Any application by a barrister to the Bar Council for a waiver of any of the mandatory requirements or to extend the time within which to complete any of the mandatory requirements must be made in writing, setting out all mitigating circumstances relied on and supported by all relevant documentary evidence.

ANNEXE D

THE PRACTISING CERTIFICATE REGULATIONS

The Authority to Issue Practising Certificates

1. The Access to Justice Act 1999 (s. 46) included provision for the Bar Council to make rules prohibiting barristers from practising unless authorised by a certificate issued by the Bar Council (a 'practising certificate'). The rules may include provision for the payment of different fees by different descriptions of barristers, but the Council may not set fees with a view to raising a total amount in excess of that applied by the Council for the purposes of the regulation, education and training of barristers, and those wishing to become barristers and for any other purpose approved by the Lord Chancellor under subsection (3)(a) of s. 46 of the Access to Justice Act 1999.

2. No provision included in the rules shall have effect unless approved by the Lord Chancellor.

3. Section 46 of the Access to Justice Act 1999, as amended by Order by statutory instrument with effect from 31 January 2001, is at Appendix 1 to these rules.

Application

4. These rules shall apply to all barristers and registered European lawyers holding themselves out as offering legal services as barristers to the public or to their employer. They shall not apply to non-practising barristers.

The Calculation of Income from Practising Certificates

5. The income to be raised by the Bar Council from Practising Certificate Fees shall not exceed the forecast expenditure for the year ahead starting 1 January each year to be applied to the activities and purposes set out below, less any subventions for those purposes received from the Inns of Court.

6. The activities, including education and training, to which practising certificate fees shall be applied shall be as follows:

    (a) The formulation and implementation of rules and regulations;

    (b) The development and dissemination to the profession of guidance, recommendations and other standards (whether binding or advisory) contributing to the control, government and direction of the profession and the way in which it practises: those activities shall include the definition, review and supervision of the standards of professional conduct and work expected of members of the profession;

    (c) Participation in the legislative process in relation to proposals relevant to the organisation or conduct of the profession;

    (d) Law reform work: that is, participation in the legislative process in relation to proposals falling outside paragraph 5(c);

    (e) Support for the administration of provision of legal services to the public *pro bono*;

    (f) the furtherance of human rights;

    (g) the development of international relations.

7. The maximum sum to be raised from Practising Certificate Fees shall include, as agreed by the Lord Chancellor, the annual forecast full cost of work in the following areas:

    (a) Activities which are entirely regulatory:
        (i) Professional Standards

        (ii) Professional Conduct and Complaints

        (iii) Equal Opportunities

        (iv) Records

    (b) Education and Training

    (c) Activities qualifying under the Statutory Instrument laid under s. 46 subsection (3)(a) of the Access to Justice Act 1999:

        (i) Human Rights and Pro Bono administration

        (ii) Law Reform

8.   The maximum sum to be raised from Practising Certificate Fees shall include, as agreed by the Lord Chancellor, the proportion as shown of the annual forecast full cost of work in the following areas qualifying as regulatory activity or for purposes agreed under the Statutory Instrument laid under s. 46 sub-section (3)(a) of the Access to Justice Act 1999:

(a)	Legal Services	80%
(b)	International Relations	90%
(c)	Policy	75%
(d)	Remuneration	80%
(e)	Public Affairs	30%
(f)	Employed Bar	70%
(g)	Young Bar	60%
(h)	Information Technology	60%

9.   For the purpose of calculating the maximum sum to be raised from Practising Certificate Fees, Administration costs shall be added in proportion to the cost of activities set out in paragraphs 8 and 9, to include the following:

Chairman's Office

Executive Office

Council and General Management Committee work Finance

Library/Registry

Print and Distribution

Reception and Meeting Rooms

Publications

Website

Contingency funds up to 3% of total expenditure

Provision for capital expenditure not covered by depreciation

The Issue of Practising Certificates

10.   Subject to paragraphs 14 and 15 of these Rules, the Bar Council shall issue Full Practising Certificates to all barristers and registered European lawyers notifying the Bar Council that they wish to commence or re-commence practice and annually thereafter on each renewal date.

11.   A Practising Certificate shall be valid until the due date for renewal of the Certificate unless:

    (a) the barrister's status changes; or

    (b) the barrister is disbarred or suspended from practice as a barrister by a Disciplinary Tribunal, Summary Procedure Panel, Fitness to Practice Panel or Interim Suspension Panel.

12. The Bar Council shall amend a Practising Certificate if a barrister changes his category from independent practice to employed practice or vice versa provided that the barrister has paid any additional amount to cover the difference in fee applicable to each category.

13. The Bar Council shall endorse a Practising Certificate to reflect any qualification restriction or condition imposed on the barrister by the Bar Council or by a Disciplinary Tribunal, Summary Procedure Panel, Informal Panel, Interim Suspension Panel or Fitness to Practise Panel.

14. The Bar Council shall not issue a Practising Certificate to any barrister who has been disbarred or is subject to an order suspending him from practice.

15. The Bar Council may refuse to issue a Practising Certificate to a barrister if it is satisfied that the barrister:

    (a) has failed to comply with the training requirements applicable to him at the date of his Call to the Bar;

    (b) has failed to comply with any applicable requirements of the Continuing Professional Development Regulations;

    (c) has not provided in writing to the Bar Council details of the current address(es) with telephone number(s) of the chambers or office from which he supplies legal services and (if he is an employed barrister) the name, address, telephone number and nature of the business of his employer;

    (d) has not paid to the Bar Council the Practising Certificate Fee currently prescribed by the Bar Council for barristers of his/her description.

    (e) has failed to pay the appropriate insurance premium so as to be insured with the Bar Mutual Indemnity Fund against claims for professional negligence, as required by the Code of Conduct;

    (f) would be practising in breach of the provisions of paragraphs 203, 204, 205, 401, 501, 502 or 503 of the Code of Conduct.

The Renewal of Practising Certificates

16. The due date for the payment of the Practising Certificate Fee for barristers in independent practice and registered European lawyers in independent practice shall be 1 January each year. The due date for the payment of the Practising Certificate fee for employed barristers and registered European lawyers in employment shall be 6 April each year.

Practising Certificate Fees

17. Each year, the Bar Council shall decide the appropriate Practising Certificate Fees for the following year so that the projected income from these fees shall not exceed the total amount calculated under paragraphs 8 to 10 of these rules

18. The Bar Council may set different fees for different categories of barristers reflecting, for example, the barrister's seniority and whether he is in independent or employed practice.

19. The Practising Certificate Fee following Call to the Bar or registration as a Registered European Lawyer shall become due on the relevant renewal date of the year following the year of Call or registration, as appropriate to each category of barrister or Registered European Lawyer.

20. The Bar Council shall provide four weeks' notice of the date by which payment of the Practising Certificate Fee is due and shall confirm in writing the validity of the Practising Certificate following payment of the Practising Certificate Fee. Notification to practising barristers of the Practising Certificate Fee shall include a statement of any separate voluntary subscription to the Bar Council, other than for a Practising Certificate.

21. On application of individual barristers, the Bar Council may reduce the Practising Certificate Fee in recognition of certified periods of continuous absence from practice exceeding three months in the previous year. The Bar Council may reduce the full Practising Certificate Fee payable by those whose certified gross fee income or salary for the previous year is less than such annual amount as the Council may decide from time to time. Applications for such reduction must be received no later than the end of the practising certificate year following the year in which the absence occurred or low fee income received.

Non-Payment of the Practising Certificate Fee

22. A practising barrister who fails to pay the Practising Certificate Fee within one month of the due date shall be liable to a penalty to cover the administrative costs of the Bar Council in dealing with the delay in payment. If the fee is paid later than one month and earlier than two months following the due date, the penalty shall amount to 15% of the full fee applicable to his seniority and status. If the fee is paid later than two months after the due date, the penalty shall be 30% of that fee. The full penalty applies even if the barrister has been granted or is eligible for any reduction of the full Fee under these rules.

23. The Bar Council shall notify any practising barrister who has not paid the Practising Certificate Fee by the due date that if the Fee is not paid within one month of the due date, he shall become liable for the surcharge under paragraph 22 and may be reported to the Professional Conduct and Complaints Committee for that Committee to investigate and consider whether there has been a breach of paragraph 202 of the Code of Conduct.

24. The Bar Council shall report all barristers who it has reason to believe are practising and who have not paid the Practising Certificate Fee and, where applicable, the penalty to the Professional Conduct and Complaints Committee unless the Fee and, where applicable, the penalty are both paid in within 3 months of the due date provided that the barrister has not incurred the penalty for more than two years out of the last five in which case his default may be reported to the Professional Conduct and Complaints Committee within such shorter time as may appear appropriate in all the circumstances.

25. The Bar Council may, with the consent of the Chairman of the Professional Conduct and Complaints Committee, withdraw any complaint made under paragraph 24 where it is satisfied that:

    (a) the Fee and surcharged have been paid within 3 months of the due date;

    (b) the barrister was not in fact practising during the relevant period; or

    (c) there is some other reason why it would be unjust to continue the complaint.

Appendix To ANNEX D

ACCESS TO JUSTICE ACT

s. 46 Bar Practising Certificates

(1)   If the General Council of the Bar makes rules prohibiting barristers from practising as specified in the rules unless authorised by a certificate issued by the Council (a 'practising certificate'), the rules may include provisions requiring the payment of fees to the Council by applicants for practising certificates.

(2)   Rules made by virtue of subsection (1)—

    (a) may provide for the payment of different fees by different descriptions of applicants, but

    (b) may not set fees with a view to raising a total amount in excess of that applied by the Council for the purposes of:

        (i)   the regulation, education and training of barristers and those wishing to become barristers;

        (ii)   the participation by the Council in law reform and the legislative process;

        (iii) the provision by barristers and those wishing to become barristers of free legal services to the public;

        (iv)   the promotion of the protection by law of human rights and fundamental freedoms; and

        (v)   the promotion of relations between the Council and bodies representing the members of legal professions in jurisdictions other than England and Wales.

(3)   The Lord Chancellor may by order made by statutory instrument—

    (a) amend subsection (2)(b) by adding to the purposes referred to in it such other purposes as the Lord Chancellor considers appropriate, or

    (b) vary or revoke an order under paragraph (a).

(4)   No order shall be made under subsection (3) unless—

    (a) the Lord Chancellor has consulted the Council, and

    (b) a draft of the order has been laid before, and approved by a resolution of, each House of Parliament.

(5)   No provision included in rules by virtue of subsection (1), and no other provision of rules made by the Council about practising certificates, shall have effect unless approved by the Lord Chancellor.

(6)   The Council shall provide the Lord Chancellor with such information as he may reasonably require for deciding whether to approve any provision of rules made by the Council about practising certificates.

ANNEXE E

GUIDELINES ON OPINIONS UNDER THE FUNDING CODE

Status of these Guidelines

1. These Guidelines are prepared by the Legal Services Commission. They are intended as statements of good practice to be followed when opinions are prepared on the merits of applications or certificates issued under the Funding Code. As statements of good practice these Guidelines should not be too rigidly applied. An opinion will, however, be rejected if it does not contain the information necessary for the Commission to make its decision under the Code.

2. These Guidelines have been agreed by the Bar Council for incorporation in the Code of Conduct of the Bar of England and Wales.

Scope

3. These Guidelines apply to legal opinions sent to the Legal Services Commission for the purpose of decisions made in individual cases under the Funding Code. The Guidelines are most relevant to decisions made under certificates or contracts covering Legal Representation or Support Funding, but also may be relevant to other levels of service.

   The Guidelines apply to counsel and to solicitors with higher rights of audience who are instructed to give an independent opinion on the merits of a case. The term 'counsel' in the Guidelines therefore includes a solicitor with higher rights of audience.

4. The Guidelines do not apply directly to solicitors giving a report to the regional office in a case which they are conducting or proposing to conduct. Such a report may be shorter and more informal than an opinion on the merits, but these Guidelines should still be borne in mind by solicitors when such reports are prepared.

Preliminary Considerations

5. All opinions must be prepared in accordance with the Funding Code and having regard to the Funding Code guidance prepared by the Commission. This guidance is set out in the Commission's Manual, and on the Commission's website at www.legalservices.gov.uk. Every person preparing an opinion must have access to and consult the guidance as necessary.

6. When counsel is instructed to provide an opinion in writing, counsel should first consider whether it is necessary to have a conference, for example to enable counsel to assess the reliability of the client's evidence in a case where that evidence is likely to be contested. Where counsel considers that a conference is necessary and would be cost effective, the costs of such a conference may be covered by the certificate provided it is within any overall cost limitation on the certificate and is justified as reasonable on assessment at the end of the case. In the case of a high cost case contract, any conference must be justified within the agreed case plan for the action.

Contents of Opinions
Issues to be Covered

7. The primary purpose of an opinion is to provide the Commission with the information and legal opinion necessary to apply all relevant Funding Code criteria, rather than to provide a personal opinion on what the funding decision should be.

8.   Each opinion should state at the outset:

(a) the level of service under which the opinion is given and if appropriate, the level of service being applied for;

(b) the case category into which the proceedings fall, giving reasons if there is likely to be an issue as to which case category is appropriate.

9.   In every opinion counsel should identify any potentially excluded work in the case, i.e. aspects of the case which may fall within the excluded categories in paragraph 1 of Schedule 2 of the Access to Justice Act 1999. Where excluded work arises counsel should specify any of the Lord Chancellor's directions which may bring the case back into scope.

10. It is not necessary for an opinion to discuss separately every criterion relevant to the decision. For example, it is not usually necessary for counsel to refer to the standard criteria in section 4 of the Code unless, in the particular circumstances of the case, one or more of these criteria is likely to be material to the Commission's decision. Unless otherwise instructed an opinion should always cover the following:

(a) Prospects of success (except for special Children Act proceedings or other proceedings which do not have a prospect of success criterion). The opinion should specify what constitutes a successful outcome for the client, having regard to guidance, and must specify with reasons the prospects in one of the six categories provided for in the Code. Where prospects are 'borderline', the issues of fact, law or expert evidence which give rise to that assessment must be identified. Where prospects of success are 'unclear' the necessary work to clarify prospects of success must be identified.

(b) Cost benefit (save for those cases which do not have a cost benefit criterion). The opinion must identify the benefit to the client from the proceedings and, for quantifiable claims, provide a figure for 'likely damages' as defined in the Code. See paragraph 14 below as to estimates of 'likely costs'.

(c) Where the application is for Investigative Help to be granted or continued, the opinion must deal with matters relevant to criteria 5.6.2 (the need for investigation) and 5.6.4 (prospects after investigation). The opinion should explain why there are reasonable grounds for believing that when the investigative work has been carried out the claim will be strong enough, in terms of prospects of success and cost benefit, to satisfy the relevant criteria for full representation.

(d) Where the issue is whether funding should be withdrawn on the merits, the opinion should cover matters relevant to applying criteria 14.2 to 14.4, taking into account the interests of the client, the interests of the Community Legal Service Fund and relevant guidance.

11. An opinion on merits should:

(a) where factual issues are involved (a) set out in sufficient detail, (although not necessarily at great length), the rival factual versions to enable the Commission to assess their relative strengths, and (b) express a clear opinion as to the likelihood of the applicant's version being accepted by a court and why;

(b) where legal issues or difficulties of law are involved (a) summarise those issues or difficulties in sufficient detail to enable the Commission to come to a view about them without looking outside the opinion, and (b) express a clear view as to the likelihood of the applicant's case on the law being accepted by a court and why;

(c) draw attention to (a) any lack or incompleteness of material which might bear on the reliability or otherwise of the applicant's version, and (b) any other factor which could — whether now or in the future — materially affect the assessment of the out-come of the case.

12. Where appropriate an opinion should suggest or formulate for the Commission any limitation or condition, whether as to the scope of work that should be covered, or as to costs, which ought to be imposed on the grant of funding in order to safeguard the Fund. In complex cases, including cases proceeding on the multi-track, the opinion should, specify any future point in the proceedings at which it is likely to be sensible to re-assess the merits.

Information From Other Sources

13. There will often be information relevant to a merits decision which is not readily available to counsel. Where such information is not included in counsel's instructions, the opinion should specify the information which should be provided by the instructing solicitors, usually in the form of a covering letter to accompany counsel's opinion.

14. The following issues should usually be dealt with by instructing solicitors:

    (a) estimates of likely costs. This includes estimates of whether costs incurred to date, likely future costs to disposal, or future costs to trial. Assessments of likely costs may be relevant not just to any cost benefit criteria, but also to other criteria such as the thresholds for support funding, or the affordability of a high cost case. Such estimates will sometimes best be made in the light of counsel's opinion as to prospects of success and the future conduct of the case. Alternatively instructing solicitors may provide relevant estimates of costs to counsel with counsel's instructions so that such figures may be incorporated in the body of the opinion;

    (b) assessments of whether a case is suitable for a Conditional Fee Agreement and whether affordable insurance is available, in cases which are being considered under the General Funding Code.

Specific Issues

15. Where it is suggested that a case has a significant wider public interest counsel's opinion should:

    (a) identify the nature of the benefits which the case might bring to persons other than the client;

    (b) identify the group or section of the public who might benefit from the case, if possible giving at least a rough estimate of likely numbers;

    (c) where people may benefit indirectly from a test case, explain the individual issues which other clients would need to establish in order to succeed with their claims;

    (d) where the public interest of the case derives from establishing an important point of law, set out that legal issue clearly and explain the likelihood of the court resolving the issue one way or another for the benefit of other cases.

16. Where it is suggested that a judicial review or claim against a public authority raises significant human rights issues, the opinion should identify the specific articles of the Convention which may have been breached by the public body and the importance of those issues to the client and the general public.

17.   Where it is suggested that a case has overwhelming importance to the client as this is defined in the Code, the nature of the importance to the client must be identified in the opinion having regard to the Commission's guidance on this issue.

18.   In cases involving more than two parties, counsel should consider carefully whether separate representation for each client is justified (criterion 5.4.5). This is particularly important in many family cases and in appeals where the points at issue in the appeal may not require separate representation from every party to the proceedings at first instance. Counsel should consider whether the arguments on which his or her client relies will be put forward on behalf of another party whose interests in the proceedings are substantially the same. Counsel should report to the Commission with proposals for minimising representation by solicitors and counsel.

19.   In high cost cases in which the Commission will be considering whether the action is affordable in the light of available resources (criterion 6.4) counsel's opinion should address those aspects of the case which, in accordance with the Commission's guidance, are relevant to the affordability decision. It will not be possible or appropriate for counsel to consider the question of the resources available to the Commission, or the reasonableness of funding the individual case as against other cases, as these are matters solely for the Commission.

Continuing Duties to the Fund

20.   A barrister is under a specific duty to comply with the provisions of the Access to Justice Act 1999 and any regulations or code in effect under that Act (paragraph 304 of the Bar Code of Conduct). Since these duties are directed at ensuring that public funding is granted and continued only in justifiable cases, it follows that counsel acting under a funding certificate is under a duty to bring to the attention of the Commission any matter which might affect the client's entitlement to funding, or the terms of his or her certificate, at whatever stage of the proceedings that might occur.

21.   Counsel and any other legal representative acting under a certificate or contract are also subject to the specific obligations set out in Rule C44 of the Code Procedures. This includes a general obligation to inform the Regional Director of new information or a change of circumstances which has come to light which may affect the terms or continuation of a certificate.

22.   Where counsel is under an obligation to draw matters to the attention of the Commission, he or she may do so by drawing matters to the attention of his or her instructing solicitors and asking that they be passed on to the Commission, or counsel may contact the Commission directly if that is appropriate in the particular circumstances of the case.

ANNEXE F1

THE LICENSED ACCESS RULES

1. Subject to these rules and to compliance with the Code of Conduct (and in particular to paragraphs 401 and 403) a self-employed barrister may accept instructions from a licensed access client in circumstances authorised in relation to that client by the Licensed Access Recognition Regulations (reproduced in Annex C1) whether that client is acting for himself or another.

2. These rules apply to every matter in which a self-employed barrister is instructed by a licensed access client save that paragraphs 4(b), 6, 7 and 9 of these rules do not apply to any matter in which a licensed access client is deemed to be a licensed access client by reason only of paragraph 7 or paragraph 8 of the Licensed Access Recognition Regulations.

3. A barrister is only entitled to accept instructions from a licensed access client if at the time of giving instructions the licensed access client

    (a) is identified; and

    (b) sends the barrister a copy of the Licence issued by the Access to the Bar Committee.

4. A barrister must not accept any instructions from a licensed access client

    (a) unless the barrister and his Chambers are able to provide the services required of them by that licensed access client;

    (b) if the barrister considers it in the interests of the lay client or the interests of justice that a solicitor or other authorised litigator or some other appropriate intermediary (as the case may be) be instructed either together with or in place of the barrister.

5. A barrister who accepts instructions from a licensed access client otherwise than on the terms of the Licensed Access Terms of Work as approved from time to time by the Access to the Bar Committee

    (a) must first agree in writing the terms upon which he has agreed to do the work and the basis upon which he is to be paid;

    (b) must keep a copy of the agreement in writing with the licensed access client setting out the terms upon which he has agreed to do the work and the basis upon which he is to be paid.

6. A barrister who accepts instructions from a licensed access client

    (a) must promptly send the licensed access client

        (i) a statement in writing that the instructions have been accepted (as the case may be) (1) on the standard terms previously agreed in writing with that licensed access client or (2) on the terms of the Licensed Access Terms of Work (and thereafter if requested a copy of the Licensed Access Terms of Work); or

        (ii) if he has accepted instructions otherwise than on such standard terms or on the terms of the Licensed Access Terms of Work, a copy of the agreement in writing with the licensed access client setting out the terms upon which he has agreed to do the work and the basis upon which he is to be paid;

(b) unless he has accepted instructions on the terms of the Licensed Access Terms of Work or on terms which incorporate the following particulars must at the same time advise the licensed access client in writing of:

    (i) the effect of paragraph 401 of the Code of Conduct as it relevantly applies in the circumstances;

    (ii) the fact that the barrister cannot be expected to perform the functions of a solicitor or other authorised litigator and in particular to fulfil limitation obligations disclosure obligations and other obligations arising out of or related to the conduct of litigation;

    (iii) the fact that circumstances may require the client to retain a solicitor or other authorised litigator at short notice and possibly during the case.

7. If at any stage a barrister who is instructed by a licensed access client considers it in the interests of the lay client or the interests of justice that a solicitor or other authorised litigator or some other appropriate intermediary (as the case may be) be instructed either together with or in place of the barrister:

    (a) the barrister must forthwith advise the licensed access client in writing to instruct a solicitor or other authorised litigator or other appropriate intermediary (as the case may be); and

    (b) unless a solicitor or other authorised litigator or other appropriate intermediary (as the case may be) is instructed as soon as reasonably practicable thereafter the barrister must cease to act and must return any instructions.

8. If at any stage a barrister who is instructed by a licensed access client considers that there are substantial grounds for believing that the licensed access client has in some significant respect failed to comply either with the terms of the Licence granted by the Access to the Bar Committee or (where applicable) with the terms of the Licensed Access Terms of Work the barrister must forthwith report the facts to the Access to the Bar Committee.

9. A barrister who accepts instructions from a licensed access client must keep a case record (whether on card or computer) which sets out:

    (a) the date of receipt of the instructions, the name of the licensed access client, the name of the case, and any requirements of the licensed access client as to time limits;

    (b) the date on which the instructions were accepted;

    (c) the dates of subsequent instructions, of the despatch of advices and other written work, of conferences and of telephone conversations;

    (d) when agreed, the fee.

10. A barrister who accepts instructions from a licensed access client must either himself retain or take reasonable steps to ensure that the licensed access client will retain for six years after the date of the last item of work done:

    (a) copies of instructions (including supplemental instructions);

    (b) copies of all advices given and documents drafted or approved;

    (c) a list of all documents enclosed with any instructions;

    (d) notes of all conferences and of all advice given on the telephone.

LICENSED ACCESS

THE LICENSED ACCESS RECOGNITION REGULATIONS

1. Authorised licensed access clients are those persons and organisations and/or their members and/or their or their members' employees (as the case may be) who have from time to time been approved as such by the Access to the Bar Committee.

2. Any person or organisation wishing to be approved as an authorised licensed access client shall apply in writing to the Access to the Bar Committee by completing an application form in such form and supplying such other information as the Access to the Bar Committee may from time to time or in any particular case require.

3. In approving any person or organisation as an authorised licensed access client the Access to the Bar Committee may grant such approval in each case as the Access to the Bar Committee may think appropriate:

   (a) (i) on a provisional basis or (ii) on a full basis;

   (b) (i) for a fixed period or (ii) for a fixed period subject to extension or (iii) indefinitely;

   (c) (i) to the person or organisation and/or (ii) to some or all of the members of the organisation and/or (iii) to some or all of the employees of the person or organisation or its members;

   (d) in relation to matters concerning (i) the person or organisation and/or its members (as the case may be) and/or (ii) his or its or its members' employees and/or (iii) his or its or its members' clients or customers;

   (e) subject to such limitations or conditions as the Access to the Bar Committee may think appropriate relating to:

      (i) the matters in relation to which the authorised licensed access client may instruct a barrister and/or

      (ii) the courts or tribunals before which a barrister so instructed may exercise a right of audience and/or

      (iii) such other matters (including the means by which the authorised licensed access client shall instruct a barrister) as seem relevant in the circumstances.

4. The Access to the Bar Committee shall issue to every person or organisation approved as an authorised licensed access client a Licence in such form as the Access to the Bar Committee may from time to time or in the particular case think appropriate. Such Licence (which may be a provisional Licence or a full Licence):

   (a) shall specify (i) the name of the person or organisation who has been approved as an authorised licensed access client (ii) the period (if any) for which the Licence has been granted or (as the case may be) that the Licence has been granted indefinitely and (iii) the limitations or conditions (if any) subject to which the Licence has been granted;

   (b) may if the Access to the Bar Committee think appropriate provide that unless otherwise first agreed in writing with an individual barrister or chambers all instructions accepted by any barrister from the authorised licensed access client will be deemed to be given and accepted on the terms of the Licensed Access Terms of Work as approved from time to time by the Access to the Bar Committee;

   (c) may if the Access to the Bar Committee think appropriate provide that a copy of the Licence shall be sent with every set of instructions to any barrister instructed by the authorised licensed access client;

(d) shall remain at all times the property of the General Council of The Bar to whom (or to whose duly appointed officer) it shall be surrendered on demand.

5. The Access to the Bar Committee may from time to time:

   (a) approve additional persons or organisations as authorised licensed access clients;

   (b) withdraw approval (either wholly or in part) from any person or organisation as an authorised licensed access client;

   (c) increase reduce or otherwise alter the period for which a person or organisation is approved as an authorised licensed access client;

   (d) alter or revoke the limitations or conditions (if any) attached to any approval of a person or organisation as an authorised licensed access client or impose new or additional limitations or conditions;

   (e) cancel and demand the surrender of any Licence issued under paragraph 4 of these regulations.

6. In exercising their functions under paragraphs 1, 2, 3, 4 and 5 of these regulations the Access to the Bar Committee shall comply with the statutory objectives referred to in section 17(1) of the Courts and Legal Services Act 1990 and section 1(2) of the Access to Justice Act 1999 may consult with such persons organisations or bodies as they think appropriate and shall to such extent as they may think appropriate in the particular case have regard to the following matters:

   (a) the fact that barristers in independent practice operate as a referral profession of specialist consultants;

   (b) the extent to which the person or organisation or its members (as the case may be) are likely to have a significant requirement to retain the services of a barrister for their own benefit or for the benefit of their employers employees members clients or customers (as the case may be);

   (c) the extent to which whether as a result of professional or other relevant training or by reason of practice and experience the person or organisation or its employees or members (as the case may be) are or may reasonably be expected to be
      (i)   providers of skilled and specialist services
      (ii) competent in some identifiable area of expertise or experience
      (iii) familiar with any relevant area of law
      (iv) possessed of the necessary skills to obtain and prepare information and to organise papers and information sufficiently to enable the barrister to fulfill his duties in a non-contentious matter to the client and in a contentious matter both to the client and to the court
      (v)   possessed of the necessary skills to take charge and have the general conduct of the matters in respect of which they wish to retain the services of a barrister;

   (d) the extent to which the affairs and conduct of the person or organisation or its members (as the case may be) are subject to some appropriate professional disciplinary regulatory or other organisational rules;

   (e) the extent to which the person or organisation or its members (as the case may be)
      (i)   are insured against claims for negligence in relation to their handling of matters in respect of which they wish to retain the services of a barrister
      (ii) have made and continue to comply with satisfactory arrangements for holding in separate accounts and maintaining as trust monies any monies received from third parties

(iii) have made and continue to comply with satisfactory arrangements for ensuring that barristers' fees are promptly paid;

(f) such other facts and matters (if any) as seem to them to be relevant in the circumstances.

7.   Notwithstanding paragraphs 2, 3 and 4 of these regulations any member of any of the bodies referred to in the First Schedule to these regulations shall be deemed to be an authorised licensed access client (including in relation to matters concerning that member's clients or customers) but

(a) only in a matter of a kind which falls generally within the professional expertise of the members of the relevant body; and

(b) not for the purpose of briefing counsel to appear in or exercise any right of audience before the Judicial Committee of the House of Lords the Privy Council the Supreme Court the Crown Court a County Court or the Employment Appeals Tribunal.

8.   Notwithstanding paragraphs 2, 3 and 4 of these regulations any of the following shall be deemed to be an authorised licensed access client:

(a) an arbitrator (including for these purposes an adjudicator under the Housing Grants Construction and Regeneration Act 1996) but only when instructing counsel for the purpose of advising on any point of law practice or procedure arising in or connected with an arbitration in which he has been or may be appointed;

(b) any person who has been appointed to one of the offices of Ombudsman referred to in the Second Schedule to these regulations but only when instructing counsel for the purpose of advising on any point of law practice or procedure arising in the course of the performance of his duties.

9.   Nothing in paragraphs 7 and 8 of these regulations shall prevent

(a) any person to whom paragraph 7 or paragraph 8 applies making an application in accordance with paragraph 2 of these regulations (in which event paragraphs 3, 4, 5 and 6 of these regulations shall apply to such application and to any Licence issued pursuant to such application);

(b) the Access to the Bar Committee exercising in relation to any person to whom paragraph 7 or paragraph 8 applies the powers conferred by paragraphs 5(b) 5(c) and 5(d) of these regulations (in which event paragraph 6 of these regulations shall apply).

THE FIRST SCHEDULE

Part I — Accountants and taxation advisers

(1)   The Association of Authorised Public Accountants
(2)   Association of Taxation Technicians
(3)   The Chartered Association of Certified Accountants
(4)   The Chartered Institute of Management Accountants
(5)   Institute of Chartered Accountants
(6)   The Institute of Chartered Accountants in Ireland
(7)   Institute of Chartered Accountants in Scotland
(8)   The Chartered Institute of Taxation
(9)   The Institute of Financial Accountants

Part II — Insolvency practitioners

(1)   Insolvency Practitioners Association

Part III — Architects surveyors and town planners

(1)   The Architects Registration Council of the UK
(2)   The Architects and Surveyors Institute
(3)   Association of Consultant Architects
(4)   The Royal Institute of British Architects
(5)   The Royal Institution of Chartered Surveyors
(6)   The Royal Town Planning Institute

Part IV — Engineers

(1)   The Institution of Chemical Engineers
(2)   The Institution of Civil Engineering Surveyors
(3)   The Institution of Civil Engineers
(4)   The Institution of Electrical Engineers
(5)   Institution of Mechanical Engineers
(6)   The Institution of Structural Engineers

Part V — Valuers

(1)   The Incorporated Society of Valuers & Auctioneers

Part VI — Actuaries

(1)   The Faculty of Actuaries
(2)   Institute of Actuaries

Part VII — Chartered secretaries and administrators

(1)   The Institute of Chartered Secretaries and Administrators

Part VIII — Insurers

(1)   The Association of Average Adjusters
(2)   The Chartered Institute of Loss Adjusters
(3)   The Chartered Insurance Institute

THE SECOND SCHEDULE

(1)   Parliamentary Commissioner for Administration
(2)   Commissioner for Local Administration (England)
(3)   Commissioner for Local Administration (Wales)
(4)   Health Service Commissioner
(5)   Banking Ombudsman
(6)   Building Society Ombudsman
(7)   Insurance Ombudsman Bureau
(8)   The Personal Investment Authority Ombudsman Bureau Ltd
(9)   The Legal Services Ombudsman

ANNEXE F2

THE PUBLIC ACCESS RULES

1.   These rules apply to barristers instructed by or on behalf of lay clients (other than licensed access clients) pursuant to paragraph 401(a)(iii) of the Code of Conduct.

2.   Before accepting any public access instructions from or on behalf of a lay client who has not also instructed a solicitor or other professional client, a barrister must take such steps as are reasonably necessary to ascertain whether it would be in the best interests of the client or in the interests of justice for the lay client to instruct a solicitor or other professional client.

3.   A barrister may not accept direct instructions from or on behalf of a lay client:

   (1)   in, or in connection with, any matter or proceedings concerning immigration or asylum;

   (2)   in, or in connection with:

      (a)   any family business or family proceedings (as those terms are defined in section 65 of the Magistrates' Courts Act 1980 or in section 32 of the Matrimonial and Family Proceedings Act 1984 or in section 8 of the Children Act 1989); or

      (b)   any criminal cause or matter;

      unless:

      (i)   the barrister is instructed by the lay client and not by or through an intermediary on behalf of the lay client; and

      (ii)   the barrister is instructed solely:

         (A)   to provide advice or draft documents (but not to attend interviews conducted by prosecuting or investigating authorities), other than in connection with proceedings which have been commenced (and, for the avoidance of doubt, proceedings are commenced, inter alia, when the Defendant is charged or a summons is issued); or

         (B)   in, or in connection with, proceedings:

            (1)   before the European Court of Human Rights or the Courts of the European Communities;

            (2)   on appeal to the House of Lords or the Privy Council;

            (3)   on appeal to the Court of Appeal, provided that there is no reason to believe that any party to the proceedings will seek to adduce new evidence;

            (4)   on appeal to the High Court by way of case stated by a Magistrates' Court or the Crown Court;

            (5)   on appeal to the Crown Court from a sentence imposed by a Magistrates' Court, provided that there is no reason to believe that the appeal will involve a Newton hearing; or

            (6)   on appeal to the Child Support Appeal Tribunal or the Child Support Commissioners

4.   In any case where a barrister is not prohibited by rule 3 from accepting instructions, it is a matter for consideration in the circumstances of the case whether it is in the best interests of the client or in the interests of justice for the lay client to instruct a solicitor or other professional client.

5.   A barrister must have regard to guidance published from time to time by the Bar Council in considering whether to accept and in carrying out any public access instructions.

6.   A barrister who accepts public access instructions must forthwith notify his lay client in writing, and in clear and readily understandable terms, of:

   (a) the work which the barrister has agreed to perform;

   (b) the fact that in performing his work the barrister will be subject to the require-ments of the Code of Conduct and, in particular, paragraphs 401(b) and 608;

   (c) the fact that the barrister cannot be expected to perform the functions of a solicitor or other authorised litigator and in particular to fulfil limitation obligations, disclosure obligations and other obligations arising out of or related to the conduct of litigation;

   (d) the fact that the barrister is a sole practitioner, is not a member of a firm and does not take on any arranging role;

   (e) in any case where the barrister has been instructed by an intermediary:
      (i) the fact that the barrister is independent of and has no liability for the intermediary; and
      (ii) the fact that the intermediary is the agent of the lay client and not the agent of the barrister;

   (f) the fact that the barrister may be prevented from completing the work by reason of his professional duties or conflicting professional obligations, and what the client can expect of the barrister in such a situation;

   (g) the fees which the barrister proposes to charge for that work, or the basis on which his fee will be calculated;

   (h) the barrister's contact arrangements; and

   (i) the barristers' complaints procedure and that of the General Council of the Bar.

7.   Save in exceptional circumstances, a barrister will have complied with rule 6 above if he has written promptly to the lay client in the terms of the draft letter annexed hereto.

8.   In any case where a barrister has been instructed by an intermediary, he must give the notice required by rule 6 above both:

   (a) directly to the lay client; and

   (b) to the intermediary.

9.   A barrister who accepts public access instructions must keep a case record which sets out:

   (a) the date of receipt of the instructions, the name of the lay client, the name of the case, and any requirements of the client as to time limits;

   (b) the date on which the instructions were accepted;

   (c) the dates of subsequent instructions, of the despatch of advices and other written work, of conferences and of telephone conversations;

   (d) when agreed, the fee.

10. A barrister who accepts public access instructions must either himself retain or take reasonable steps to ensure that the lay client will retain for at least seven years after the date of the last item of work done:

(a) copies of all instructions (including supplemental instructions);

(b) copies of all advices given and documents drafted or approved;

(c) the originals, copies or a list of all documents enclosed with any instructions;

(d) notes of all conferences and of all advice given on the telephone.

11. Save where otherwise agreed:

(a) A barrister shall be entitled to copy all documents received from his lay client, and to retain such copies permanently.

(b) A barrister shall return all documents received from his lay client on demand, whether or not the barrister has been paid for any work done for the lay client.

(c) A barrister shall not be required to deliver to his lay client any documents drafted by the barrister in advance of receiving payment from the lay client for all work done for that client.

A barrister who has accepted public access instructions in any matter may take a proof of evidence from his client in that matter.

CONTRACTS WITH SOLICITORS

To: All Heads of Chambers
         All Clerks and Practice Managers

From: Geoffrey Vos QC, Chairman of the Fees Collection Committee

This memorandum and its attachments is important. Please circulate it to all members of your chambers

Introduction

1. On 24th March 2001, the Bar Council approved the following (copies of which are attached hereto):—

    (1)   Amendments to the 'Terms of Work on which barristers offer their services to solicitors and the Withdrawal of Credit Scheme 1988' ('Terms of Work'), to be appended to the Code of Conduct at Annexe G1.

    (2)   The 'Contractual Terms of Work on which barristers offer their services to solicitors 2001' ('Contractual Terms') to be appended to the Code of Conduct at Annexe G2.

    (3)   Certain minor consequential changes to paragraphs 403, 603 and 604 of the Code of Conduct.

2. The object of the changes is to allow barristers to act on the instructions of solicitors pursuant to contractual terms, should both parties wish to do so.

3. The Code of Conduct has been altered so as to provide that the Cab-Rank rule does not apply to contractual work. In other words, a barrister is not required to accept work on the Contractual Terms or on any other contractual basis (see paragraph 604(f) of the Code of Conduct).

4. The new Contractual Terms themselves are not mandatory. Barristers may enter into contracts with solicitors for the provision of services on other terms should they so wish. The new Contractual Terms are, however, recommended.

5. If no agreement is made between a barrister and solicitor, the Terms of Work (as amended) will continue to apply (see paragraph 27 of the Terms of Work).

6. Both the Terms of Work and the Contractual Terms now provide for the payment of interest on barristers' fees from one month after the dispatch of letter 'A' (as appended to each of the Terms of Work and the Contractual Terms) until payment at 2% above Bank of England Base Rate.

7. **Clerks and practice managers should note that:—**

    (1)   **the recommended terms of letter A have changed, and**

    (2)   **para. 28 of the revised Terms of Work provide that the new terms only apply to briefs and instructions accepted on or after 24th March 2001 (the date on which the new terms were adopted). As a result, interest is only payable on fees in respect of such work.**

How can barristers contract with solicitors?

8. A barrister wishing to accept a brief or instructions on the Contractual Terms must agree in writing to that effect (see paragraph 1 of the Contractual Terms).

9. The terms of sections 5(2), (3) and (4) of the Arbitration Act 1996 are applied so as to define how an agreement in writing can be made (see paragraph 15(v) of the Contractual Terms).

10. In short:

    (1)   An agreement can be made in writing whether or not it is signed by the parties.

    (2)   An agreement can be made by exchange of written communications (in any form).

    (3)   An agreement will be an agreement in writing if it is evidenced in writing, for example if it is recorded in writing by one of the parties or by a third party (e.g. a clerk) with the authority of the parties to the agreement.

11. In practice, if a clerk or practice manager agrees orally with a solicitor that the Contractual Terms shall apply (with the authority of the barrister concerned), and if he then confirms that oral agreement in writing to the Solicitor, the provisions will be satisfied. It would, however, be better practice to ask the solicitor to confirm that the Contractual Terms apply by a response in writing.

What kind of work is covered by the Contractual Terms?

12. The Contractual Terms apply to all kinds of privately funded work, except work undertaken on a conditional fee basis (see paragraph 1(4) of the Contractual Terms).

13. The Contractual Terms do not apply to any publicly funded work (see paragraph 1(3) of the Contractual Terms).

What is the effect of using the Contractual Terms?

14. The Contractual Terms have the following significant effects:—

    (1)   The complaints system operated under the Terms of Work can still be used under the Contractual Terms. Accordingly, solicitors will still be subject to directions (better known as 'black-listing') if they fail to pay fees, which are contractually due, and complaints are made.

    (2)   The Joint Tribunal system will also still be applicable to resolve any dispute as to the payment of Contractual Fees. The decision of a Joint Tribunal will be final binding and conclusive (see paragraph 12(3)(a) of the Contractual Terms).

    (3)   If a dispute arises from the solicitor challenging the barrister's fees, and the solicitor fails to agree to a Joint Tribunal, it will be open to a barrister to sue for his fees. It is hoped that this will be a course of last resort.

15. A term has been included (see paragraph 12(4) of the Contractual Terms), which is intended to prevent a solicitor from refusing to pay a barrister's fees or setting off any cross-claim against the barrister (for example arising from a contention that the barrister's work was unsatisfactory or negligent), unless the solicitor has challenged the fees in due time and has agreed to submit the dispute to a Joint Tribunal. This term will help to protect a barrister against non-payment pending resolution of a negligence claim.

How do the new interest provisions work?

16. Under the revised Terms of Work (see paragraphs 12(5) and 13(2) of the Terms of Work) and under the Contractual Terms (see paragraphs 9(3) and 11(5) of the Contractual Terms), privately paid fees will carry simple interest at the rate of 2% above Bank of England base rate from one month after the date of letter 'A'.

17. This date has been chosen to assist administration. Letter A marks the beginning of the process of the enforcement of payment of fees. The new draft letter A (under both the Terms of Work and the Contractual Fees) warns solicitors that interest will be charged if payment is not made within one month. Letter A may be sent one month after the first fee note. So, in practice, interest will be payable from not less than 2 months after the delivery of the fee note, if the administration is efficiently undertaken.

Geoffrey Vos QC
Chairman, Fees Collection Committee

26 March 2001

ANNEXE G1

THE TERMS OF WORK ON WHICH BARRISTERS OFFER THEIR SERVICES TO SOLICITORS AND THE WITHDRAWAL OF CREDIT SCHEME 1988

(As authorised by the General Council of the Bar on 16 July 1988 and amended by authority of the General Council of the Bar on 10 November 1990, 17 July 1999, and 24 March 2001)

WHEREAS:

(1) These Terms have been authorised by the General Council of the Bar and are intended to apply (save as hereinafter provided) in any case where a barrister is instructed by a solicitor;

(2) Any solicitor who sends a brief or instructions to a barrister will be deemed to instruct that barrister on these Terms unless and to the extent that the barrister and the solicitor have agreed in writing in relation to the particular matter or generally (a) that the Contractual Terms on which Barristers Offer their Services to Solicitors 2000 shall apply, or (b) to exclude or vary these Terms;

AND WHEREAS:

(3) By the established custom of the profession a barrister looks for payment of his fees to the solicitor who instructs him and not to his lay client;

(4) Except in publicly funded cases a solicitor is personally liable as a matter of professional conduct for the payment of a barrister's proper fees whether or not he has been placed in funds by his lay client;

(5) Where instructions have been given in the name of a firm all partners at that date incur personal liability and remain liable for the payment of counsel's fees incurred on behalf of the firm by a deceased bankrupt or otherwise defaulting former partner of the firm; and

(6) The liability of a sole practitioner and of partners for the liabilities of their co-partners is a continuing one and is not cancelled or superseded by any transfer of the practice or dissolution of the partnership;

WITH EFFECT from 24 March 2001 the following will take effect:

General

1. A solicitor may in his capacity as a director partner member employee consultant associate or other agent of a company firm or other body brief or instruct a barrister.

2. In any case where a barrister accepts a brief or instructions from a solicitor in his capacity as a director partner member employee consultant associate or agent of a company firm or other body:

   (1) the solicitor warrants that he is authorised by his company firm or other body to instruct the barrister;

   (2) the obligations of the solicitor under these Terms (including in particular his responsibility for the payment of the barrister's fees) shall be the joint and several obligations of him and that company firm or other body.

Instructions

3. A barrister has the duty or the right in certain circumstances set out in the Bar Code of Conduct to refuse to accept a brief or instructions and these Terms will apply only where the barrister has accepted the brief or instructions.

4. Notwithstanding that a brief or instructions have been delivered to a barrister the barrister shall not be deemed to have accepted that brief or those instructions until he has had a reasonable opportunity:

    (1) to peruse them;

    (2) in the case of a brief to agree a fee with the solicitor.

5. A barrister accepts a brief or instructions upon the understanding:

    (1) that he must and will comply with the Bar Code of Conduct;

    (2) that he will deal with instructions as soon as he reasonably can in the ordinary course of his work;

    (3) that he may return the brief or instructions in accordance with the Bar Code of Con- duct, and that, if he does so, he will incur no liability to the solicitor under these terms as a result of so doing.

6. (1) Where for any reason time is of the essence the solicitor must at the time when he delivers the brief or instructions but separately from the brief or instructions themselves inform the barrister of that fact and of the particular reason for urgency in order that the barrister may decide whether in those circumstances he can accept the brief or instructions. In addition the brief or instructions must be clearly marked 'Urgent'.

    (2) In the case of publicly funded work, the solicitor must at the time when he delivers the brief or instructions (or if any relevant certificate is not then available to him as soon as reasonably practicable thereafter) supply the barrister with copies of any relevant public funding certificates.

Copies of Briefs and Instructions and Records of Advice

7. A barrister shall be entitled for the purposes of his records (but not otherwise) to retain his brief or instructions or any papers delivered therewith or (if the solicitor requires the return of such brief or instructions and papers) to take and retain a copy of such brief or instructions and papers and of any written advice PROVIDED that nothing shall entitle a barrister to exercise any lien over any brief instructions or papers.

Fees

8. Save in the case of publicly funded work or in the case of a Notified Solicitor a barrister and solicitor may (subject to any rules regarding contingent fees) make such agreement or arrangement between them as to the time or times whether at the time of delivery of the brief or instructions or subsequently thereto or otherwise at which the barrister's fees shall be paid as they may think fit and the barrister's fees shall be paid by the solicitor accordingly PROVIDED that every such agreement or arrangement shall be recorded in writing.

9. Save in the case of publicly funded work or in the case of work the fees for which are to be paid out of a fund but cannot be so paid without an order of the court a barrister may and in the case of fees payable by a Notified Solicitor a barrister (unless and except as

otherwise previously authorised in writing by the Chairman) must require his fees to be agreed and paid before he accepts the brief or instructions to which the fees relate.

10. (1) Fees and/or charging rates shall be (i) as agreed between the barrister and the solicitor before the barrister commences work under the brief or instructions; or, in default of such agreement, (ii) a reasonable professional rate for the barrister instructed.

    (2) The barrister shall submit an itemised fee note not later than three months after the work to which the fee note relates has been done or at the conclusion of the matter in which the barrister is briefed or instructed whichever is the sooner.

    (3) The barrister shall as soon as reasonably practicable comply with a request by the solicitor for a fee note.

    (4) Every fee note shall include the solicitor's reference and (where appropriate) the barrister's case reference number, the barrister's relevant account number for the purpose of receiving payment in publicly funded cases and (if known to the barrister) any relevant public funding certificate number and date of issue.

    (5) If any fees remain outstanding at the conclusion of a case the solicitor shall as soon as reasonably practicable inform the barrister that the case has concluded.

11. In the case of publicly funded work:

    (1) The solicitor and barrister shall respectively take such steps as may be open to each of them to take under the applicable Regulations for the time being in force for the purpose of obtaining payment of the barrister's fees as soon as reasonably practicable;

    (2) The solicitor shall as soon as reasonably practicable comply with a request by the barrister for information by (i) notifying the barrister of the date of issue and number and supplying the barrister with copies of any relevant public funding certificates (ii) notifying the barrister of the date of any order for assessment of costs under the relevant certificate or other event giving rise to a right to such assessment (iii) informing the barrister of the steps taken by him pursuant to paragraph 11(1) hereof;

    (3) The barrister unless such information and an explanation for non-payment satisfactory to him is thereupon received from the solicitor shall then report the facts to the Chairman.

12. In the case of work the fees for which are to be paid out of a fund but cannot be so paid without an order of the court:

    (1) The solicitor shall use his best endeavours to obtain such order or orders as may be requisite to enable payment of the fees to be made as soon as reasonably practicable;

    (2) The solicitor shall as soon as reasonably practicable comply with a request by the barrister for information by informing the barrister of the steps taken by him pursuant to paragraph 12(1) hereof;

    (3) The barrister unless such information and an explanation for non-payment satisfactory to him is thereupon received from the solicitor shall then report the facts to the Chairman;

    (4) Subject to paragraph 12(5) below, the barrister's fees shall be payable one month after the making of the order of the court required for the payment of such fees out of the fund;

(5) In the event of any breach by the solicitor of his obligations under paragraph 12(1) and/or 12(2) above, the fees will be payable forthwith and the amount outstanding from time to time will carry simple interest at the stipulated rate from one month after the date of the letter referred to in paragraph 15(1) hereof until payment.

13. (1) Subject to any such agreement or arrangement as is referred to in paragraph 8 hereof the barrister's fees if and to the extent that such fees have not been previously paid shall unless challenged by the solicitor as hereinafter provided be paid by the solicitor within one month after the fee note relating thereto has been sent to the solicitor whether or not the solicitor has been placed in funds by his client and whether or not the case is still continuing.

    (2) In the event that the barrister's fees are not paid in full in accordance with sub-paragraph (1) above, the fees outstanding from time to time will carry simple interest at the stipulated rate from one month after the date of the letter referred to in paragraph 15(1) hereof until payment if that letter includes a statement to that effect.

14. (1) Any challenge by a solicitor to a barrister's fee (whether giving rise to an issue of competence or a dispute on quantum or otherwise) must be made by the solicitor in writing within three months after the first fee note relating to that fee has been sent to him or within one month after such letter relating to that fee as is referred to in paragraph 15(1) hereof has been sent to him whichever is the later.

    (2) No challenge to a barrister's fees will be accepted either by the barrister or in the case of a complaint by the barrister to the Bar Council of failure to pay those fees by the Bar Council unless:

    (a) the challenge was made in accordance with paragraph 14(1) hereof; and

    (b) the solicitor has within 14 days of being requested to do so either by the barrister or by the Bar Council agreed in writing (i) to submit the issue or dispute giving rise to the challenge to the decision of a Tribunal (ii) to abide by and forthwith give effect to the decision of the Tribunal.

    (3) If a dispute is referred to a Tribunal in accordance with paragraph 14(2) above:

    (i) The Tribunal shall act as experts and not as arbitrators and its decision shall be conclusive, final and binding for all purposes upon the solicitor and the barrister.

    (ii) No payment need be made in respect of the fees (unless the Tribunal orders an interim payment) until the Tribunal has made its decision and communicated it to the parties.

    (iii) If the Tribunal determines that any sum is payable in respect of the fees, paragraph 13(2) above shall apply to that sum as if it had become payable when it would have become payable if no challenge had been made, and the Tribunal shall also determine the amount payable in respect of interest thereon under that paragraph.

    (4) Unless the solicitor has challenged the barrister's fees and agreed to submit the issue or dispute in accordance with paragraphs 14(1) and (2), the fees will be payable in full, without any set-off whatsoever, in the amount set out in the relevant fee note and at the time specified in paragraph 13(1) above.

15. Save as aforesaid and subject to any such agreement or arrangement as is referred to in paragraph 8 hereof the barrister if and to the extent that his fees have not been previously paid:

    (1) may at any time after the expiration of one month after the first fee note relating thereto has been sent send a reminder substantially in the form of the letter annexed hereto and marked 'A' or some reasonable adaptation thereof; and

    (2) unless an explanation for non-payment satisfactory to the barrister has been received shall at the expiration of three months after the first fee note relating thereto has been sent send a further reminder substantially in the form of the letter annexed hereto and marked 'B' or some reasonable adaptation thereof; and

    (3) unless an explanation for non-payment satisfactory to the barrister is thereupon received shall then report the facts to the Chairman.

Withdrawal of Credit

16. In any case where a barrister has made a report to the Chairman in accordance with paragraphs 11(3), 12(3) or 15(3) hereof or under the equivalent terms of any contract and in any other case in which he is satisfied that it is appropriate to do so, the Chairman may write a letter in the form of one of the letters annexed hereto and marked 'C' or some reasonable adaptation thereof.

17. (1) This paragraph applies where the following conditions are satisfied namely where:

    (a) such a letter as is referred to in paragraph 16 hereof has been sent and no explanation for non-payment satisfactory to the Chairman has been received; and

    (b) either (i) any fees referred to in such letter which are in the opinion of the Chairman properly payable remain unpaid or (ii) in the event that all such fees have been paid not more than twelve months have elapsed since payment; and

    (c) circumstances have arisen in which the Chairman would otherwise have occasion to send to any person liable for the fees or to any connected person a further letter such as is referred to in paragraph 16 hereof.

    (2) In any case in which paragraph 17(1) hereof applies the Chairman shall write to such person or persons (as the case may be) to the effect that unless written representations received by him within 14 days after the date of such letter or within such extended period as he may allow justify an exceptional departure from the following course he will and unless persuaded by such representations not to do so the Chairman whether or not any fees remain unpaid shall:

    (a) issue a direction that no barrister may without the written consent of the Chairman (which consent may be sought urgently in exceptional cases) knowingly accept instructions from any person or firm named in such direction or from any person who or firm which is or has at any time since the direction was issued been a connected person unless his fees are to be paid directly by the Legal Services Commission or such instructions are accompanied by payment of an agreed fee for such work or unless he agrees in advance to accept no fee for such work; and

      (b)   cause the names of the persons or firms named in such direction to be included in a list of persons and firms named in such directions to be circulated by pre- paid first-class post to all such persons and firms to all the Clerks and Heads of Chambers in England and Wales to the Master of the Rolls and to the President of the Law Society notifying them of such direction.

18.   Notwithstanding anything to the contrary herein if in any case the Chairman is satisfied that it is appropriate to issue a direction such as is referred to in paragraph 17(2)(a) hereof in respect of any person or firm named in such direction and to cir-culate a list such as is referred to in paragraph 17(2)(b) hereof including the names of the persons or firms named in such direction he may after giving such persons and firms due notice of why he considers it appropriate to take such course and after con-sidering any written representations and after consultation with the Law Society issue a direction in respect of and cause the list to include the names of such persons and firms as may be appropriate.

18A. Upon issuing a direction pursuant to either paragraph 17(2)(a) or paragraph 18 hereof, the Chairman shall report the facts to the OSS and shall request the OSS to commence proceedings before the Solicitors' Disciplinary Tribunal against the per-sons, the firms, or the partners in the firms named in such direction.

19.   The list referred to in paragraphs 17 and 18 hereof shall be circulated monthly unless there have been in the meantime no additions to or deletions from the list.

20.   Any Notified Solicitor and any barrister may at any time after the expiration of six months after the name of any person or firm was first included in such a list seek the revocation of any relevant direction and the amendment of the list and the Chairman after considering any written representations and after consultation with the Law Society shall be empowered (but shall not be obliged) to accede to such application upon such terms as he considers appropriate.

Definitions and consequential provisions

21.   For the purpose hereof:

    (1) 'Bar Code of Conduct' shall mean the Code of Conduct of the Bar of England and Wales for the time being in force;

    (2) 'brief' 'instructions' and 'lay client' shall have the meanings assigned to them respectively in the Bar Code of Conduct;

    (3) 'solicitor' shall where the context admits include any solicitor liable for the fees;

    (4) 'person liable for the fees' shall mean any solicitor liable for the fees and any person company firm or other body responsible by virtue of paragraph 2(2) hereof for the payment of the fees;

    (5) section 5(2), (3) and (4) of the Arbitration Act 1996 apply to the interpretation of all references in these Terms to parties having agreed, or made an agree-ment, in writing;

    (6) 'connected person' shall mean any person who from time to time is either

       (a)   a partner employee consultant or associate of any firm of which any per-son liable for the fees or any Notified Solicitor is a partner employee con-sultant or associate;

       (b)   the employer of any person liable for the fees or of any Notified Solicitor;

(c) an employee of any person liable for the fees or of any Notified Solicitor;

(d) a firm of which any person liable for the fees or any Notified Solicitor is a partner employee consultant or associate;

(7) 'Notified Solicitor' shall mean any person or firm whose name is for the time being included in the list referred to in paragraphs 17 and 18 hereof and any person who or firm which is or has at any time since the direction was issued been a connected person;

(8) 'Tribunal' shall mean a Tribunal consisting of a barrister nominated by the Chairman and a solicitor nominated by the President of the Law Society;

(9) 'the Chairman' shall mean the Chairman of the Bar Council and shall include any person including in particular the Vice Chairman of the Bar and the Chairman of the Remuneration and Terms of Work Committee and the Chairman of the Fees Collection Committee to whom the Chairman may have delegated either the whole or any part of his responsibilities hereunder;

(10) 'the OSS' shall mean the Office for the Supervision of Solicitors;

(11) 'publicly funded work' shall mean cases funded and paid directly to the barrister by the Legal Services Commission, as part of the Community Legal Service or the Criminal Defence Service;

(12) where the context admits, references to fees include any interest accrued in respect of them under paragraph 13(2) hereof;

(13) the 'stipulated rate' shall mean 2% above the Bank of England base rate from time to time;

(14) any letter written by the Chairman to any person pursuant to or which would otherwise have been effective for the purposes of either the Withdrawal of Credit Scheme which came into effect on 2 March 1987 or the Withdrawal of Credit Scheme 1988 as originally enacted or in force from time to time shall in relation to such person be deemed to be such a letter as is referred to in paragraph 16 hereof.

22.   (1) Subject to sub-paragraph (2) below, any fee note and any such letter as is referred to in paragraphs 15(1), 15(2), 16, 17(2) or 18 hereof may be sent and shall be treated as having been properly and sufficiently sent to each and every person liable for the fees and to each and every connected person (as the case may be) if posted by prepaid first-class post or sent through any Document Exchange or by facsimile transmission addressed to:

(a) any person liable for the fees; or

(b) if any person liable for the fees is either a partner of or consultant to or associate of or employed by another or others to the person liable for the fees or to his employer or to his senior partner (as the case may be); or

(c) if any such person practises (whether on his own or in partnership with others or otherwise) under a name other than his own to the firm under whose name he practises;

and addressed to any place at which such person or his employer or any partner of his carries on practice.

(2) Where a firm or a sole proprietor is liable for the fees, if any letter under paragraphs 15(2), 16, 17(2) or 18 hereof is addressed to some person other than

the senior partner of the firm or the sole proprietor, a copy must also be sent to the senior partner or sole proprietor at the same time.

23. Any such letter as is referred to in paragraphs 17(2) or 18 hereof shall:

(1) identify any relevant earlier matters of complaint;

(2) state the Chairman's proposed course of action; and

(3) enclose a copy of this document provided that any accidental omission or failure to enclose such a copy may be remedied by the sending of a separate copy as soon as the Chairman is made aware of such omission or failure.

24. Any such direction as is referred to in paragraphs 17 or 18 hereof may contain or be amended so as to add or include any or all of the names and addresses:

(1) of any person liable for the fees;

(2) of any connected person; and

(3) if any such person practises (whether on his own or in partnership with others or otherwise) under a name other than his own, of the firm under whose name he practises.

Status of these Terms

25. Neither the General Council of the Bar in authorising these Terms nor a barrister in offering his services to a solicitor on these Terms has any intention to create legal relations or to enter into any contract or other obligation binding in law.

26. Neither the sending by a solicitor of a brief or instructions to a barrister nor the acceptance by a barrister of a brief or instructions nor anything done in connection therewith nor the arrangements relating thereto (whether mentioned in these Terms or in the Bar Code of Conduct or to be implied) nor these Terms or any agreement or transaction entered into or payment made by or under them shall be attended by or give rise to any contractual relationship rights duties or consequences whatsoever or be legally enforceable by or against or be the subject of litigation with either the barrister or the General Council of the Bar.

Exclusion or variation

27. A solicitor who sends a brief or instructions to a barrister will be deemed to instruct that barrister on these Terms unless and to the extent that the barrister and the solicitor have agreed in writing in relation to the particular matter or generally (a) that the Contractual Terms on which Barristers Offer their Services to Solicitors 2000 shall apply, or (b) to exclude or vary these Terms.

Transitional

28. Unless otherwise agreed in writing:

(1) any amendment to these Terms has effect only with regard to briefs and instructions accepted on or after the date the amendment is expressed to take effect; and

(2) as regards briefs and instructions accepted before that date, these Terms continue to have effect in the form in which they stood before the amendment.

LETTER 'A'

(To be sent 1 month after fee note)

Privately funded cases

Dear Sir,

Re:_____

I refer to the fee note of [name of barrister] in respect of the above case which was sent to you on the [date].

My records indicate that this is a privately funded case in which your relationship with [Name of Barrister] is governed by the Terms of Work on which Barristers offer their Services to Solicitors and the Withdrawal of Credit Scheme 1988 (as amended; 'the Terms'). Under paragraph 13(1) of the Terms, the fees were due and payable within 1 month of the fee note.

I would be grateful if you could make arrangements for these fees to be paid or let me know when payment may be expected.

[Please note that under paragraph 13(2) of the Terms, any such fees remaining outstanding one month after the date of this letter will carry interest at 2% above the Bank of England base rate from time to time from one month after the date of this letter until payment.]*

Yours faithfully,

Clerk to [name of barrister]

* Words substantially in the form of those shown in square brackets must be included if (but only if) it is wished to charge interest on the fees which are the subject of this letter A.

Publicly funded cases

Dear Sir,   [Relevant Public Funding Certificate Number]
                                                                    [Date of issue]

Re:_____

I refer to the fee note of [name of barrister] in respect of the above case which was sent to you on [date].

My records indicate that this is a publicly funded case and I would be grateful if you could let me know when payment may be expected.

Yours faithfully,

Clerk to [name of barrister]

LETTER 'B'

(To be sent 3 months after fee note)

Privately funded cases

Dear Sir,

Re:

I have referred to [name of barrister] the letter I wrote to you concerning the fees in this matter. To date payment has not been made and no explanation for the non-payment has been forthcoming.

As you know Counsel is required as a matter of professional conduct to report to the Chairman of the General Council of the Bar the fact that these fees have been outstanding for more than three months without satisfactory explanation. Unless, therefore, I hear from you within the next 14 days I regret that Counsel will have no alternative other than to make such a report.

I sincerely trust that this will not be necessary and look forward to hearing from you in early course.

Yours faithfully,

Clerk to [name of barrister]

Publicly funded cases

Dear Sir,   [Relevant Public Funding Certificate Number]
                                                [Date of issue]

Re:

I have referred to [name of barrister] the letter I wrote to you concerning the fees in this matter. To date payment has not been received.

My records indicate that this is a publicly funded case. I must therefore ask you to notify me of:

(a) the date of issue and number of the relevant public funding certificate(s);

(b) the date of any order for assessment of costs under the relevant certificate or other event giving rise to a right to such assessment; and

(c) the steps you have taken under the relevant Regulations for the purpose of obtaining payment of [name of barrister]'s fees.

Would you also supply me with copies of the relevant Public Funding Certificate(s).

As you know Counsel is required as a matter of professional conduct to report the matter to the Chairman of the General Council of the Bar unless he receives in response to this letter the information requested above and a satisfactory explanation for the fact that he has not yet been paid. Unless, therefore, I hear from you within the next 14 days I regret that Counsel will have no alternative other than to make such a report.

I sincerely trust that this will not be necessary and look forward to hearing from you in early course.

Yours faithfully,

Clerk to [name of barrister]

LETTER 'C'

First Chairman's Letter: Private

PRIVATE AND CONFIDENTIAL

RECORDED DELIVERY

The Senior Partner

Dear Sir,

I refer to Counsel's fees particulars of which are set out in the Schedule to this letter. Copies of the relevant fee notes are attached. Letters have been written regarding payment of these fees. Payment has not been received. As a result the matter has been referred to the General Council of the Bar in accordance with Counsel's professional obligations.

I would remind you of your professional obligation to pay Counsel's fees in non publicly funded matters irrespective of whether you have been placed in funds by your client.

Unless you challenged Counsel's fees in writing within 3 months after the first fee note was sent to you, or you are able to provide a satisfactory explanation for non-payment, I would ask you to pay Counsel within 14 days of the date of this letter. In addition, please provide an explanation for the delay in payment, again within 14 days of the date of this letter.

I am also enclosing for your attention a copy of the Terms of Work on which Barristers offer their services to Solicitors and the Withdrawal of Credit Scheme 1988 (as amended). You will appreciate from reading the text of the Scheme that its effect is such that, unless there is a satisfactory explanation for non-payment or you challenged the fees in time, and the Chairman has occasion to write again in respect of other outstanding fees within the period referred to in paragraph 17(1)(b) of the Scheme, then the consequences spelt out in paragraph 17(2) of the Scheme will, save in the most exceptional circumstances, follow. In other words, credit will be withdrawn. Furthermore, the Chairman will report the facts to the Office for the Supervision of Solicitors with a request that it should commence proceedings against you before the Solicitors Disciplinary Tribunal.

If, therefore, you consider that a satisfactory explanation for non-payment exists, it is in your interests to provide it *now*.

I hope that it will not prove necessary to implement the Scheme in your case and that Counsel's fees will be paid promptly when due. I am, however, concerned that you should be fully informed in advance of the problems which would arise should you fail to pay Counsel's fees on time.

Yours faithfully,

[Name]
CHAIRMAN OF THE BAR

encls:

THE SCHEDULE

Name and address of Counsel   Fees in the matter of

[Here list name(s) and address(es) of Counsel and name(s) of case(s)]

First Chairman's Letter: Publicly funded

<u>PRIVATE AND CONFIDENTIAL</u>

<u>RECORDED DELIVERY</u>

<u>The Senior Partner</u>

Dear Sir,

I refer to Counsel's fees, particulars of which are set out in the Schedule to this letter. Copies of the relevant fee notes are attached. Letters have been written regarding payment of these fees. Payment has not been received. As a result, the matter has been referred to the General Council of the Bar in accordance with Counsel's professional obligations.

Since this complaint relates to a publicly funded matter, I would be grateful if you would supply the following information within 14 days of the date of this letter:—

(a) notify me of the date of issue and number and supply me with copies of any relevant publicly funded certificates;

(b) notify me of the date of any order for assessment of costs under the relevant certificate or other event giving rise to a right to such assessment; and

(c) inform me of what steps you have taken under the relevant Regulations for the purpose of obtaining payment of Counsel's fees.

I am also enclosing for your attention a copy of the Terms of Work on which Barristers offer their services to Solicitors and the Withdrawal of Credit Scheme 1988 (as amended). You will appreciate from reading the text of the Scheme that its effect is such that if (1) no satisfactory explanation for non-payment of the fees referred to in the Schedule to this letter has been provided and (2) the Chairman has occasion to write again in respect of other outstanding fees within the period referred to in paragraph 17(1)(b) of the Scheme, then the consequences spelt out in paragraph 17(2) of the Scheme will, save in the most exceptional circumstances, follow. In other words, credit will be withdrawn. Furthermore, the Chairman will report the facts to the Office for the Supervision of Solicitors with a request that it should commence proceedings against you before the Solicitors Disciplinary Tribunal.

If, therefore, you consider that a satisfactory explanation for non-payment exists, it is in your interests to provide it *now*.

I hope that it will not prove to be necessary to implement the Scheme in your case, and that Counsel's fees will be paid promptly when due. I am, however, concerned that you should be fully informed in advance of the problems which would arise should you fail to pay Counsel's fees on time.

Yours faithfully,

[Name]
CHAIRMAN OF THE BAR

encls:

THE SCHEDULE

Name and address of Counsel   Fees in the matter of

[Here list name(s) and address(es) of Counsel and name(s) of case(s)]

First Chairman's Letter: Private and Publicly funded

PRIVATE AND CONFIDENTIAL

RECORDED DELIVERY

The Senior Partner

Dear Sir,

I refer to Counsel's fees, particulars of which are set out in the Schedule to this letter. Copies of the relevant fee notes are attached. Letters have been written regarding payment of these fees. Payment has not been received. As a result, the matter has been referred to the General Council of the Bar in accordance with Counsel's professional obligations.

I would remind you of your professional obligation to pay Counsel's fees in privately funded matters irrespective of whether you have been placed in funds by your client.

Unless you challenged Counsel's fees in writing within 3 months after the first fee note was sent to you, or you are able to provide a satisfactory explanation for non-payment, I would ask you to pay Counsel within 14 days of the date of this letter. In addition, please provide an explanation for the delay in payment, again within 14 days of the date of this letter.

Insofar as this complaint relates to a publicly funded matter, I would be grateful if you would supply the following information within 14 days of the date of this letter:—

(a) notify me of the date of issue and number and supply me with copies of any relevant publicly funded certificates;

(b) notify me of the date of any order for assessment of costs under the relevant certificate or other event giving rise to a right to such assessment; and

(c) inform me of what steps you have taken under the relevant Regulations for the purpose of obtaining payment of Counsel's fees.

I am also enclosing for your attention a copy of the Terms of Work on which Barristers offer their services to Solicitors and the Withdrawal of Credit Scheme 1988 (as amended). You will appreciate from reading the text of the Scheme that its effect is such that, unless there is a satisfactory explanation for non-payment or you challenged the fees in time, and the Chairman has occasion to write again in respect of other outstanding fees within the period referred to in paragraph 17(1)(b) of the Scheme, then the consequences spelt out in paragraph 17(2) of the Scheme will, save in the most exceptional circumstances, follow. In other words, credit will be withdrawn. Furthermore, the Chairman will report the facts to the Office for the Supervision of Solicitors with a request that it should commence proceedings against you before the Solicitors Disciplinary Tribunal.

If, therefore, you consider that a satisfactory explanation for non-payment exists, it is in your interests to provide it now.

I hope that it will not prove to be necessary to implement the Scheme in your case, and that Counsel's fees will be paid promptly when due. I am, however, concerned that you should be fully informed in advance of the problems which would arise should you fail to pay Counsel's fees on time.

Yours faithfully,

[Name]
CHAIRMAN OF THE BAR

encls:

THE SCHEDULE

Name and address of Counsel   Fees in the matter of

[Here list name(s) and address(es) of Counsel and name(s) of case(s)]

ANNEXE G2

THE CONTRACTUAL TERMS OF WORK ON WHICH BARRISTERS OFFER THEIR SERVICES TO SOLICITORS 2001

(As Authorised by The General Council of the Bar on 24 March 2001)

WHEREAS:

(1) These terms have been authorised by the General Council of the Bar;

(2) These terms are intended to apply in any case where a barrister is instructed by a solicitor, and both the barrister and the solicitor have agreed in writing that the barrister's retainer shall be contractually binding;

(3) Any such agreement shall operate in accordance with paragraph 27 of the Terms of Work to exclude paragraphs 1–15 and 25–26 thereof as regards the instructions to which it relates;

AND WHEREAS:

(4) By the established custom of the profession a barrister looks for payment of his fees to the solicitor who instructs him and not to his lay client;

(5) Except in cases funded by the Legal Services Commission, Community Legal Service or Criminal Defence Service a solicitor is personally liable as a matter of professional conduct for the payment of a barrister's proper fees whether or not he has been placed in funds by his lay client;

(6) Where instructions have been given in the name of a firm all partners at that date incur personal liability and remain liable for the payment of counsel's fees incurred on behalf of the firm by a deceased bankrupt or otherwise defaulting former partner of the firm; and

(7) The liability of a sole practitioner and of partners for the liabilities of their co-partners is a continuing one and is not cancelled or superseded by any transfer of the practice or dissolution of the partnership;

Application of these terms

1. These terms apply in any case where a barrister is instructed by a solicitor and where both the barrister and the solicitor have agreed in writing that the barrister's retainer shall be contractually binding subject to the following:—

    (1) these terms apply to any particular contract only insofar as they have not been expressly varied or excluded by written agreement between the barrister and the solicitor;

    (2) these terms will apply to briefs and instructions only where they have been accepted by the barrister;

    (3) these terms do not apply to publicly funded work; and

    (4) these terms do not apply to any work undertaken by a barrister on a conditional fee basis.

General

2. The solicitor may in his capacity as a director partner member employee consultant associate or other agent of a company firm or other body brief or instruct the barrister.

3. In any case where the barrister accepts a brief or instructions from the solicitor in his capacity as a director partner member employee consultant associate or agent of a company firm or other body:

(1) the solicitor warrants that he is authorised by his company firm or other body to instruct the barrister;

(2) the obligations of the solicitor under these terms (including in particular his responsibility for the payment of the barrister's fees) shall be the joint and several obligations of him and that company firm or other body.

Instructions

4. The barrister has the duty or the right in certain circumstances set out in the Bar Code of Conduct to refuse to accept a brief or instructions and these terms will apply only where the barrister has accepted the brief or instructions.

5. Notwithstanding that a brief or instructions have been delivered to the barrister he shall not be deemed to have accepted that brief or those instructions until he has had a reasonable opportunity:

(1) to peruse them;

(2) in the case of a brief, to agree a fee with the solicitor.

6. The barrister accepts a brief or instructions upon the understanding:

(1) that he must and will comply with the Bar Code of Conduct;

(2) that he will deal with instructions as soon as he reasonably can in the ordinary course of his work;

(3) that he may return the brief or instructions in accordance with the Bar Code of Conduct, and that, if he does so, he will incur no liability to the solicitor under these terms as a result of so doing.

7. Where for any reason time is of the essence the solicitor must at the time when he delivers the brief or instructions but separately from the brief or instructions themselves inform the barrister of that fact and of the particular reason for urgency in order that the barrister may decide whether in those circumstances he can accept the brief or instructions. In addition the brief or instructions must be clearly marked 'Urgent'.

Copies of briefs and instructions and records of advice

8. The barrister shall be entitled for the purposes of his records (but not otherwise) to retain his brief or instructions or any papers delivered therewith or (if the solicitor requires the return of such brief or instructions and papers) to take and retain a copy of such brief or instructions and papers and of any written advice PROVIDED that nothing shall entitle the barrister to exercise any lien over any brief instructions or papers.

Fees and interest

9. Subject to the Bar Code of Conduct, the following provisions shall apply:

(1) Fees and/or charging rates shall be (a) as agreed between the barrister and the solicitor before the barrister commences work under the brief or instructions; or, in default of such agreement, (b) a reasonable professional rate for the barrister instructed.

(2) Subject to paragraphs 11 and 12 below, the solicitor shall pay the barrister's fees in respect of work to which these terms apply within one month after receipt by the solicitor of the barrister's fee note in respect of such fees.

(3) In the event that the barrister's fees are not paid in full in accordance with sub-paragraph (2) above, the fees outstanding from time to time will carry simple interest at the stipulated rate from one month after the date of the letter referred to in paragraph 13(1) hereof until payment.

10. (1) The barrister shall submit an itemised fee note not later than three months after the work to which the fee note relates has been done or at the conclusion of the matter in which the barrister is briefed or instructed whichever is the sooner.

(2) The barrister shall as soon as reasonably practicable comply with a request by the solicitor for a fee note.

(3) Every fee note shall include the solicitor's reference and (where appropriate) the barrister's case reference number.

(4) If any fees remain outstanding at the conclusion of a case the solicitor shall as soon as reasonably practicable inform the barrister that the case has concluded.

11. In the case of work the fees for which are to be paid out of a fund but cannot be so paid without an order of the court:

(1) The solicitor shall use his best endeavours to obtain such order or orders as may be requisite to enable payment of the fees to be made as soon as reasonably practicable;

(2) The solicitor shall as soon as reasonably practicable comply with a request by the barrister for information by informing the barrister of the steps taken by him pursuant to paragraph 11(1) hereof;

(3) The barrister unless such information and an explanation for non-payment satisfactory to him is thereupon received from the solicitor shall then report the facts to the Chairman.

(4) Subject to paragraph 11(5) below, the barrister's fees shall be payable one month after the making of the order of the court required for the payment of such fees out of the fund.

(5) In the event of any breach by the solicitor of his obligations under paragraph 11(1) and/or (2) above, the fees will be payable forthwith and the amount outstanding from time to time will carry simple interest at the stipulated rate from one month after the date of the letter referred to in paragraph 13(1) hereof until payment if that letter includes a statement to that effect.

12. (1) Any challenge by the solicitor to the barrister's fee (whether giving rise to an issue of competence or a dispute on quantum or otherwise) must be made by the solicitor in writing within three months after the first fee note relating to that fee has been sent to him or within one month after such letter relating to that fee as is referred to in paragraph 13(1) hereof has been sent to him whichever is the later.

(2) No challenge to a barrister's fees will be accepted either by the barrister or in the case of a complaint by the barrister to the Bar Council of failure to pay those fees by the Bar Council unless:

(a) the challenge was made in accordance with paragraph 12(1) hereof; and

(b) the solicitor has within 14 days of being requested to do so either by the barrister or by the Bar Council agreed in *writing* (i) to submit the issue or dispute giving rise to the challenge to the decision of a Tribunal (ii) to abide by and forthwith give effect to the decision of the Tribunal.

(3) If a dispute is referred to a Tribunal in accordance with paragraph 12(2) above:

  (a) The Tribunal shall act as experts and not as arbitrators and its decision shall be conclusive, final and binding for all purposes upon the solicitor and the barrister.

  (b) No payment need be made in respect of the fees (unless the Tribunal orders an interim payment) until the Tribunal has made its decision and communicated it to the parties.

  (c) If the Tribunal determines that any sum is payable in respect of the fees, paragraph 9(3) above shall apply to that sum as if it had become payable when it would have been payable if no challenge had been made, and the Tribunal shall also determine the amount payable in respect of interest thereon under that paragraph.

(4) Unless the solicitor has challenged the barrister's fees and agreed to submit the issue or dispute in accordance with paragraphs 12(1) and (2);

  (a) the fees will be payable in full, without any deductions or set-off whatsoever, in the amount set out in the relevant fee note and at the time specified in paragraph 9(2) above

  (b) for the avoidance of doubt, it shall not be open to the solicitor to withhold or delay such payment or any part thereof on the grounds that a claim or complaint has been made or maybe made against the barrister arising out of the brief or instruction to which the fees relate or any other ground.

13. Save as aforesaid and if and to the extent that his fees have not been previously paid, and without prejudice to any other remedy open to him in order to recover them, the barrister:

  (1) may at any time after the expiration of one month after the first fee note relating thereto has been sent send a reminder substantially in the form of the letter annexed hereto and marked 'A' or some reasonable adaptation thereof; and

  (2) unless an explanation for non-payment satisfactory to the barrister has been received, shall at the expiration of three months after the first fee note relating thereto has been sent send a further reminder substantially in the form of the letter annexed hereto and marked 'B' or some reasonable adaptation thereof; and

  (3) unless an explanation for non-payment satisfactory to the barrister is thereupon received shall then report the facts to the Chairman.

Withdrawal of credit

14.   (1) In any case where a barrister has made a report to the Chairman in accordance with paragraphs 11(3) or 13(3) hereof, paragraphs 16 to 24 (inclusive) of the Terms of Work shall, so far as applicable, apply to the relationship created between the barrister and the solicitor under these terms.

       (2) Paragraph 22 of the Terms of Work shall also apply to any fee note or letter referred to in paragraphs 9, 10 and 13 above as it does to those referred to in paragraphs 15–18 of the Terms of Work.

Definitions and consequential provisions

15. For the purpose hereof:

  (i)   'Bar Code of Conduct' shall mean the Code of Conduct of the Bar of England and Wales for the time being in force;

(ii)   'brief' 'instructions' and 'lay client' shall have the meanings assigned to them respectively in the Bar Code of Conduct;

(iii)   'solicitor' shall where the context admits include any solicitor liable for the fees;

(iv)   'person liable for the fees' shall mean any solicitor liable for the fees and any person company firm or other body responsible by virtue of paragraph 3(2) hereof for the payment of the fees;

(v)   Section 5(2), (3) and (4) of the Arbitration Act 1996 apply to the interpretation of all references in these Terms to parties having agreed, or made an agreement, in writing;

(vi)   'Terms of Work' shall mean the Terms of Work on which Barristers offer their Services to Solicitors and the Withdrawal of Credit Scheme 1988 (as amended and in force from time to time);

(vii)   'Tribunal' shall mean a Tribunal consisting of a barrister nominated by the Chairman and a solicitor nominated by the President of the Law Society;

(viii)   'the Chairman' shall mean the Chairman of the General Council of the Bar (also referred to as the 'Bar Council') and shall include any person including in particular the Vice Chairman of the General Council of the Bar and the Chairman of the Remuneration and Terms of Work Committee and the Chairman of the Fees Collection Committee to whom the Chairman may have delegated either the whole or any part of his responsibilities hereunder;

(ix)   'publicly funded work' shall mean cases funded and paid directly to the barrister by the Legal Services Commission, as part of the Community Legal Service or the Criminal Defence Service.

(x)   Where the context admits, references to fees include any interest accrued in respect of them under paragraph 9(3) hereof.

(xi)   The 'stipulated rate' shall mean 2% above the Bank of England base rate from time to time.

The General Council of the Bar

16. Neither the sending by the solicitor of a brief or instructions to the barrister nor the acceptance by the barrister of a brief or instructions nor anything done in connection therewith nor the arrangements relating thereto (whether mentioned in these Terms or in the Bar Code of Conduct or to be implied) nor these Terms or any agreement or transaction entered into or payment made by or under them shall be attended by or give rise to any contractual relationship rights duties or consequences whatsoever (except between the solicitor and barrister) or be legally enforceable by or against or be the subject of litigation with the General Council of the Bar.

LETTER 'A'

(To be sent 1 month after fee note)

Dear Sir

Re:

I refer to the Fee Note of [*Name of Barrister*] in respect of the above case which was sent to you on the [*Date*].

My records indicate that this is a privately funded case in which your relationship with [Name of Barrister] is governed by the Contractual Terms on which Barristers Offer their

Services to Solicitors 2000 (the 'Contractual Terms'). Under paragraph 9(2) of those terms, the fees were due and payable within 30 days of the Fee Note.

[Please note that under paragraph 9(3) of the Contractual Terms, any such fees remaining outstanding within one month after the date of this letter will carry interest at 2% above the Bank of England base rate from time to time from 1 month after the date of this letter until payment.]*

I would be grateful if you could now make arrangements for these fees to be paid.

Yours faithfully

Clerk to [*Name of Barrister*]

* Words substantially in the form of those shown in square brackets must be included if (but only if) it is wished to charge interest on the fees which are the subject of this letter A.

LETTER 'B'

(To be sent 3 months after fee note)

Dear Sir

Re:

I have referred to [*Name of Barrister*] the letter I wrote to you concerning the fees in this matter. To date payment has not been made and no explanation for the non-payment has been forthcoming.

As you know Counsel is required as a matter of professional conduct to report to the Chairman of the General Council of the Bar the fact that these fees have been outstanding for more than three months without satisfactory explanation. Unless, therefore, I hear from you within the next 14 days I regret that Counsel will have no alternative other than to make such a report.

I sincerely trust that this will not be necessary and look forward to hearing from you in early course.

Yours faithfully

Clerk to [Name of Barrister]

ANNEXE H

THE FOREIGN LAWYERS (CHAMBERS) RULES

1. Before permitting a foreign lawyer to practise from chambers the head of chambers or if there is no head of chambers every member of chambers must:

    (a) obtain the written undertaking of the foreign lawyer to comply with the Code as if he were a self-employed barrister except in so far as any requirement of the Code conflicts with the rules of his own profession;

    (b) ensure that the foreign lawyer is covered by insurance against claims for professional negligence in such amount and upon such terms as are currently required by the Bar Council;

    (c) provide the Bar Council in writing with the name and details of the foreign lawyer and with a copy of the undertaking referred to in (a) above and a copy of the current insurance policy or certificate of insurance covering the foreign lawyer; and

    (d) obtain the consent in writing of the Bar Council to the foreign lawyer so practising.

2. Thereafter for so long as the foreign lawyer is permitted to practise from chambers the head of chambers or if there is no head of chambers every member of chambers must:

    (a) satisfy himself that the foreign lawyer complies with and continues to comply with the undertaking referred to in paragraph 1(a) above;

    (b) ensure that the foreign lawyer remains covered by insurance in accordance with paragraph 1(b) above and that the Bar Council has a copy of the current insurance policy or certificate of insurance covering the foreign lawyer; and

    (c) inform the Bar Council of any failure by the foreign lawyer to comply with the undertaking referred to in paragraph 1(a) above which may be known to him.

3. No barrister shall permit a foreign lawyer to practise or continue to practise from chambers of which the barrister is a member if the consent of the Bar Council to the foreign lawyer so practising has not been given or is at any time withdrawn.

4. A European lawyer registered with the Law Society of England and Wales may not practise from or be a member of chambers.

ANNEXE I

THE EMPLOYED BARRISTERS (CONDUCT OF LITIGATION) RULES

1. An employed barrister may exercise any right that he has to conduct litigation provided that:

   (a) he is entitled to practise as a barrister in accordance with paragraph 202 of the Code;

   (b) he has spent a period of at least twelve weeks working under the supervision of a qualified person or has been exempted from this requirement by the Bar Council on the grounds of his relevant experience;

   (c) if he is of less than one year's standing (or three years' standing in the case of a barrister who is supplying litigation services to any person other than a person referred to in paragraph 501 of the Code) his principal place of practice is an office which is also the principal place of practice of a qualified person who is able to provide guidance to the barrister; and

   (d) if he is of less than three years' standing, he completes at least six hours of continuing professional development on an approved litigation course during any year in which he is required to undertake continuing professional development by the Continuing Professional Development Regulations (reproduced in Annex C).

2. For the purpose of paragraph 1(c) above an employed barrister shall be treated as being of a particular number of years' standing if he:

   (a) has been entitled to practise and has practised as a barrister (other than as a pupil who has not completed pupillage in accordance with the Consolidated Regulations) or as a member of another authorised body;

   (b) has made such practice his primary occupation; and

   (c) has been entitled to exercise a right to conduct litigation in relation to every Court and all proceedings

   for a period (which need not be continuous and need not have been as a member of the same authorised body) of at least that number of years.

3. A person shall be a qualified person for the purpose of paragraph 1(c) above if he:

   (a) has been entitled to practise and has practised as a barrister (other than as a pupil who has not completed pupillage in accordance with the Consolidated Regulations) or as a member of another authorised body for a period (which need not have been as a member of the same authorised body) of at least six years in the previous eight years;

   (b) for the previous two years

      (i) has made such practice his primary occupation, and

      (ii) has been entitled to exercise a right to conduct litigation in relation to every Court and all proceedings;

   (c) is not acting as a qualified person in relation to more than two other people; and

   (d) has not been designated by the Bar Council as unsuitable to be a qualified person.

4. If an employed barrister in the conduct of litigation gives an undertaking, any breach of that undertaking shall constitute professional misconduct.

ANNEXE J

THE COMPLAINTS RULES

Introduction

1. These Rules prescribe the manner in which all complaints about the conduct of or services provided by barristers shall be processed.

2. The membership of the Professional Conduct and Complaints Committee ('the Committee') shall be as prescribed by the Standing Orders of the Bar Council as amended from time to time.

3. Anything required by these Rules to be done or any discretion required to be exercised by, and any notice required to be given to, the Complaints Commissioner ('the Commissioner') or the Secretary of the Committee ('the Secretary'), may be done or exercised by, or given to, any person authorised by the Complaints Commissioner to act in his stead or by the Chief Executive of the Bar Council to act instead of the Secretary of the Committee (either prospectively or retrospectively and either generally or for a particular purpose).

Procedure for dealing with complaints

4. The Secretary shall take such steps as are reasonably practicable to inform the complainant of the progress and result of his complaint.

5. Any complaint other than a complaint raised by the Bar Council of its own motion shall be referred to and considered by the Commissioner before any further step is taken in accordance with these rules. The Commissioner's powers in relation to a complaint so considered by him shall be those set out in paragraph 8 *et seq.* below.

6.   (a) If a complaint is not dismissed by the Commissioner following consideration as aforesaid, or is a complaint raised by the Bar Council, it shall be investigated by the Secretary of the Committee in the manner set out in paragraph 16 *et seq.* below.

      (b) Following such investigation, the Secretary shall refer the complaint back to the Commissioner together with the results of such investigation and the Commissioner shall reconsider the complaint and the results and shall exercise the powers given to him by paragraph 21 *et seq.* below in respect of the complaint.

7. If the Commissioner does not dismiss the complaint following reconsideration under paragraph 6(b) above, he shall refer the complaint to the Committee for consideration with his observations on it, if any. The Committee's powers in relation to such a complaint shall be those set out in paragraph 26 *et seq.* below.

Commissioner's powers under paragraph 5

8. The powers of the Commissioner shall be to consider complaints made by outside persons and to determine whether in his view such a complaint discloses a *prima facie* case of professional misconduct or inadequate professional service and is apt for consideration by the Committee. In the exercise of that power he shall observe the following provisions.

9. If it appears to him that the complaint relates to a matter within the domestic jurisdiction of an Inn or a Circuit, he may refer the complaint without further consideration to the Treasurer of the Inn or the Leader of the Circuit concerned and notify the complainant of his decision.

10. (a) If it appears to the Commissioner that the complaint arises out of a barrister's actions in a part-time or temporary judicial or quasi-judicial capacity, he shall act as follows:

   (i)   If it appears to him that the complaint would otherwise fall to be dismissed under these provisions, he shall so dismiss it.

   (ii) If it appears to him that the complaint would otherwise not fall to be dismissed, the Commissioner shall refer the complaint without further consideration to the person responsible for the appointment of the barrister to the judicial or quasi-judicial office concerned (whether the Lord Chancellor, a Minister of the Crown or other person as appropriate), requesting him to notify the Commissioner when the complaint has been dealt with and of any action taken, and the Commissioner shall notify the complainant of his decision so to refer it. Where the Commissioner considers it inappropriate to refer the complaint to a person other than the Lord Chancellor or a Minister of the Crown or where that other person refuses to deal with a complaint, he shall consider the complaint and, subject to (iv) below, direct it to be proceeded with in accordance with paragraph 16 *et seq.* below.

   (iii) If the Lord Chancellor, Minister of the Crown, or other person responsible for the appointment, having dealt with a complaint, believes that it may be appropriate for further consideration by the Bar Council, he may, subject to (iv) below, refer the matter to the Commissioner who may reconsider the complaint and may, if he sees fit, direct it to be proceeded with in accordance with paragraph 16 *et seq.* below.

   (iv) No such reference to the Commissioner as is mentioned in (iii) above by the Lord Chancellor, Minister of the Crown, or other person responsible for the appointment shall be acted upon by the Commissioner, nor shall the Commissioner exercise the powers under the last sentence of paragraph (ii) above in respect of any part of the complaint relating to anything said or done by the barrister in the exercise of his judicial functions or affecting the independence of the barrister in his judicial or quasi-judicial capacity.

   (b) If it appears to the Commissioner that the complaint relates to the conduct of or professional services provided by a barrister who, since the events giving rise to the complaint took place, has been appointed to and continues to hold full-time judicial office and has ceased practice, the Commissioner shall not consider the complaint further and shall inform the complainant that his complaint should be directed to the Lord Chancellor.

11. If he has not disposed of any complaint under paragraph 9 or 10 above, he shall consider whether:

   (a) the complaint fails to disclose a *prima facie* case of professional misconduct or inadequate professional service;

   (b) the complaint has been made more than six months after the act or omission complained of and the complaint is not of sufficient seriousness nor are there any exceptional circumstances which justify further consideration of the complaint despite the lapse of time since the matters complained of;

   (c) the complaint is trivial;

   (d) the complaint obviously lacks validity; or

   (e) for any other reason the complaint ought to be dismissed summarily.

In order to decide this question, he may seek information or assistance, orally or in writing, as he thinks fit, from the complainant, any potential witness, any member of the Committee, the Secretary or the Equal Opportunities Officers of the Bar Council.

12. If he considers that it should be dismissed on any of the grounds set out in paragraph 11 above, he shall so dismiss it, and shall notify the complainant of his decision and of his reasons for it.

13. If in considering whether a complaint should be dismissed summarily the Commissioner decides that the complaint does not disclose any evidence of professional misconduct, and it appears to him that the complaint might be capable of resolution by agreement, he may invite the complainant and the barrister concerned to attempt to conciliate their differences.

14. The Commissioner may at any time adjourn consideration of a complaint for such period as he thinks fit, whether while the complainant and the barrister attempt conciliation, during the currency of related legal proceedings or for any other reason.

15. The Commissioner may reopen or reconsider a complaint which has been disposed of under paragraphs 9, 10 or 12 above:

    (a) following a recommendation of the Legal Services Ombudsman that he do so, or

    (b) where new evidence becomes available to him which leads him to conclude that he should do so, or

    (c) for some other good reason.

    Following such reconsideration he may take such further or different action as he thinks fit, as if the former decision had not been made.

Investigation of complaints by the Secretary

16. The investigation of complaints shall be carried out by the Secretary under the direction of the Commissioner or the Committee in such manner as they or either of them think fit. In directing the carrying out of such investigation, the Committee and the Commissioner shall have regard to the following provisions.

17. The complaint shall be sent to the barrister concerned together with a letter requiring him to comment in writing on the complaint and to make any written representations he sees fit as to his conduct or the services he has provided to the complainant. That letter shall be sent to the address notified by the barrister pursuant to paragraphs 202(d) of the Code of Conduct.

    If no response is received within 28 days of the date of posting of such letter, the Secretary may proceed as if the barrister's response had been to deny the allegations made in the complaint in their entirety.

18. The complaint should normally also be sent to any solicitor or solicitor's agent named on the form of complaint as having instructed the barrister, and if the Commissioner directs to any other person whose name and address is provided by the complainant as a person able to assist the Committee together with a letter seeking their comments upon the complaint.

19. Any comments received by the Secretary from the barrister concerned in answer to the complaint should normally be sent to the complainant, under cover of a letter seeking his response to the barrister's comments, but the Commissioner may at his discretion direct that this step be omitted if, for example, issues of privilege or confidentiality make it inappropriate.

20. The Secretary may enter into further correspondence with any of the parties whose comments have been sought, or any other party who the Secretary, the Commissioner or the Committee think capable of affording further assistance.

Commissioners powers under paragraph 6(b)

21. When a complaint is referred to the Commissioner following investigation, as set out in paragraph 6(b) above, the Commissioner shall consider whether, on the information now available to him, it discloses a *prima facie* case of professional misconduct or inadequate professional service.

22. In order to decide this question, he may direct any further investigations to be made that he sees fit, and may seek further information or assistance from any other person whom he considers may be capable of affording it.

23. The Commissioner may at any time adjourn consideration of a complaint for such period as he thinks fit, whether during the currency of related legal proceedings or for any other reason.

24. If the Commissioner decides that a *prima facie* case of professional misconduct or inadequate professional service is not shown, he shall dismiss the complaint, and shall notify the complainant and the barrister complained against of his decision and of his reasons for it.

25. The Commissioner may reopen or reconsider a complaint which has been disposed of under paragraph 24 above:

    (a) following a recommendation of the Legal Services Ombudsman that he do so, or

    (b) where new evidence becomes available to him which leads him to conclude that he should do so, or

    (c) for some other good reason.

Following such reconsideration he may take such further or different action as he thinks fit, as if the former decision had not been made.

Powers and functions of the Committee

26. The powers of the Committee shall be as follows:

    (a) to determine whether any complaint discloses a *prima facie* case of professional misconduct, and if so to deal with it in accordance with these Rules.

    (b) to determine whether the complaint discloses a *prima facie* case of inadequate professional service by the barrister concerned and if so to deal with it in accordance with these Rules.

    (c) to prefer charges of professional misconduct before Disciplinary Tribunals (as provided by the Disciplinary Tribunals Regulations at Annex K to the Code of Conduct), to refer to such tribunals any legal aid complaint relating to the conduct of a barrister and to be responsible for prosecuting any such charges or legal aid complaints before such Tribunals.

    (d) to prefer and deal summarily with charges of professional misconduct in accordance with the Summary Procedure Rules forming Annex L to the Code of Conduct.

    (e) to take such other actions in relation to complaints as are permitted by these Rules.

(f) to make recommendations on matters of professional conduct to the Professional Standards Committee, as the Committee may think appropriate.

(g) to make rulings on matters of professional conduct when the Committee considers it appropriate to do so.

(h) to exercise the power of the Bar Council under paragraph 108 of the Code of Conduct to grant waivers of the provisions of that Code either generally or in particular cases.

(i) to exercise the power of the Bar Council to designate Legal Advice Centres.

27. The Committee shall consider complaints and the results of investigations thereof referred to it by the Commissioner pursuant to paragraph 7 above, together with the Commissioner's comments thereon, in such manner as it shall see fit.

28. Upon considering any complaint and subject to the provisions of paragraph 30 below, the Committee may:

(a) dismiss the complaint provided that each of the Lay Members present at the meeting consents to such dismissal, whereupon the Secretary shall notify the complainant and the barrister complained against of the dismissal and the reasons for it.

(b) determine that no further action shall be taken on the complaint.

(c) at any time postpone consideration of the complaint, whether to permit further investigation of the complaint to be made, or during the currency of related legal proceedings or for any other reason it sees fit,

(d) if the complaint does not disclose a *prima facie* case of professional misconduct but the barrister's conduct is nevertheless such as to give cause for concern, draw it to his attention in writing. The Committee may in those circumstances advise him as to his future conduct either in writing or by directing him to attend on the Chairman of the Committee or some other person nominated by the Committee to receive such advice, and may thereafter exercise the powers given to it by paragraph (e) below, or dismiss the complaint. If the Committee considers that the circumstances of the complaint are relevant to the barrister's position as a pupilmaster, it may notify the barrister's Inn of its concern in such manner as it sees fit.

If the complaint is dismissed the Secretary shall notify the complainant of the dismissal and the reasons for it.

(e) if a *prima facie* case of inadequate professional service is disclosed and the following conditions are satisfied:

(i) the complainant is the barrister's lay client or his duly authorised representative or in the case of an employed barrister the person to whom he has supplied the professional service in question, and

(ii) if a prima facie case of professional misconduct is also disclosed by the complaint, the matter is in the opinion of the Committee not serious enough to warrant treatment under sub-paragraphs (g) or (h) below,

the Committee may direct that the complaint be referred to an Adjudication Panel to be dealt with in accordance with the Adjudication Panel Rules (Annex P to the Code of Conduct).

(f) if a *prima facie* case of professional misconduct (whether with or without inadequate professional service) is disclosed but in the opinion of the Committee the matter is not serious enough to warrant treatment under sub-paragraphs (g) or (h) below, direct that the complaint be dealt with by informal attendance by the barrister to explain his conduct following the procedure set out in paragraphs 43 *et seq.* below

(g) if a *prima facie* case of professional misconduct (whether with or without inadequate professional service) is disclosed but in the opinion of the Committee there are no disputes of fact which cannot fairly be resolved by a summary procedure, provided it is satisfied that the powers of a summary procedure are adequate to deal with the gravity of the issues, deal with the matter summarily in accordance with the Summary Procedure Rules (Annex L to the Code of Conduct)

(h) if a *prima facie* case of professional misconduct (whether with or without inadequate professional service) is disclosed in circumstances where in the opinion of the Committee paragraph (g) above does not apply, direct that the complaint should form the subject-matter of a charge before a Disciplinary Tribunal.

29. If the Committee considers that the Complaint discloses a *prima facie* case of inadequate professional service or of professional misconduct against a registered European lawyer, the secretary shall

   (i)   inform the professional body of which the registered European lawyer is a Member in his home Member State;

   (ii) offer that professional body the opportunity to make representations to the Adjudication Panel, Informal Hearing, Summary Procedure or Disciplinary Tribunal to which the Complaint has been referred; and

   (iii) notwithstanding paragraph 53 of these rules, inform that professional body of findings made by any panel under these rules or under Annexes K, L, M or N of this Code.

30. If the subject matter of the complaint involves a conviction for an offence of dishonesty or deception or some other serious arrestable offence (as defined by section 116 of the Police and Criminal Evidence Act 1984) the Committee shall direct that the complaint should form the subject-matter of a charge before a Disciplinary Tribunal.

31. The Committee may reopen or reconsider a complaint which has been disposed of (except where it has been disposed of following a hearing before a Disciplinary Tribunal or the Visitors):

   (i)   following a recommendation of the Legal Services Ombudsman that they do so, or

   (j)   where new evidence becomes available to the Committee which leads them to conclude that they should do so, or

   (k)   for some other good reason.

32. Following such reopening or reconsideration, the Committee may take any further or different action it thinks fit, as if the former decision had not been made, provided that if a direction under paragraph 28(h) or 30 above has been given, and charges have been forwarded to the Clerk and served on the Defendant, the Committee's actions shall be confined to instructing counsel for the Committee to

   (l)   offer no evidence on a charge, or

   (m) apply to the Directions Judge for the making of additions to or amendments of a charge.

33. The Bar Council shall respect the confidentiality of complaints. The Bar Council shall not disclose the fact that a complaint has been made or details of the complaint or its disposal save in the following circumstances:

    (a) for the purpose of investigating the complaint;

    (b) for the purpose of keeping the complainant and the barrister informed of the progress of the complaint;

    (c) where the complainant and the barrister consent;

    (d) where the publication of a finding is required by the provisions of the Disciplinary Tribunals Regulations 2000 or the Summary Procedure Rules or paragraphs 52 and 53 of these rules;

    (e) in response to a request from the Lord Chancellor or officials of his Department in respect of an application by a barrister for silk or judicial appointment or a request from some other body or a Certificate of Good Standing in respect of a barrister, in which case

        (i) if any complaint has been made against the barrister concerned which has not been dismissed by the Commissioner, disposed of by the Committee under paragraph 28(a), (d) or (e) of these rules or by any other panel to which it may have been referred by the Committee, the Bar Council shall simply indicate that a complaint has been received which has not been dismissed; and

        (ii) if a finding of professional misconduct has been recorded against the barrister concerned, the Bar Council shall disclose the finding and the penalty;

    (f) for any other good reason.

Disciplinary Charges

34. If the Committee directs under paragraph 28(h) or 30 above that a complaint shall form the subject matter of a charge before a Disciplinary Tribunal, the following paragraphs shall have effect.

35. If the Committee considers that

    (a) the facts of the complaint are unlikely to be disputed (for example because it involves a criminal conviction),

    (b) witnesses are unlikely to be called for the hearing, or

    (c) the case needs to be resolved urgently,

    the Committee may direct that the prosecution of the charges be expedited.

36. The Committee shall nominate one of its members ('the PCC Representative') to be responsible for the conduct of the proceedings on its behalf. If for any reason he is unable to act at any time, the Chairman of the Committee may nominate another member to act in his place. Where no further investigation is required, the PCC representative shall settle the charge having regard to the provisions of paragraph 38 below.

37. Save in cases where the charges have been settled by the PCC Representative, the Secretary or investigations officer shall arrange for the appointment of counsel to settle the charge and to present the case before the Tribunal, and may arrange for the appointment of a solicitor or such other person as may be necessary to assist counsel and prepare the case.

38. Save in cases where the charges have been settled by the PCC Representative, counsel shall settle such charges as he considers appropriate founded upon the facts or evidence from which the complaint arose and any further or other matters which have been revealed by investigations directed by either counsel, the PCC Representative or the Committee. Such charges may be of professional misconduct and, where appropriate, of inadequate professional service, save that no charges of inadequate professional service shall be settled unless:

    (i) the complainant is the barrister's lay client or his duly authorised representative or in the case of an employed barrister the person to whom he has supplied the professional service in question, and

    (ii) the subject-matter of the complaint is something in respect of which the barrister would not be entitled to immunity from suit as an advocate in civil law.

39. It shall be the responsibility of the investigations officer at the Bar Council, subject to the supervision of the PCC Representative and/or the Committee:

    (a) to forward the charge to the Clerk to the Tribunal, as required by Regulation 5 of the Disciplinary Tribunal Regulations, together with the other documents specified therein, and

    (b) to make any necessary administrative arrangements for the summoning of witnesses, the production of documents, and generally for the proper presentation of the case on behalf of the PCC Representative before the Tribunal.

40. Enquiries shall be made of the Under- or Sub-Treasurer of the barrister's Inn and of the Bar Council concerning any previous findings of misconduct against him, so that this information may be available to be placed before the Tribunal if any charge against him is found to have been proved.

41. If a barrister is a member of more than one Inn, references in these Rules to his Inn shall mean the Inn by which he was called, unless he is a Bencher in which case his Inn shall mean the Inn of which he is a Bencher.

42. The Committee may, with the approval of the Finance and the Professional Standards Committees, authorise the Secretary or investigations officer in an appropriate case to arrange that Counsel, or any other person appointed pursuant to paragraph 37 above, be paid reasonable remuneration for work done on the Committee's behalf. The cost of such remuneration shall be borne by the Bar Council.

Informal Hearings

43. Where the Committee decides under paragraph 28(f) above that a complaint should be dealt with informally it shall direct that the barrister attend upon a panel consisting of two barrister members of the Committee and two lay members, one of whom may be the Commissioner. When the Committee directs such attendance it shall specify:

    (a) what, in summary form, are the matters upon which the Committee has found a *prima facie* case of misconduct to be disclosed and on which the barrister's explanation of his conduct is required, and

    (b) whether, on the information available to them, the Committee also regard a *prima facie* case of inadequate professional service as having been disclosed, and if so what, in summary form, are the matters arising in that regard which the barrister will also be asked to explain.

44. The Secretary shall notify both the barrister and the complainant of the matters specified in paragraph 43. As soon as practicable thereafter he shall send them a bundle of the papers to be considered by the panel and shall invite them within 14 days (which period may be extended with the permission of the Chairman of the PCC or the Complaints Commissioner) to comment in writing on any of those matters or to send other document to which they wish the panel to have regard.

45. The Secretary shall make such further enquiries as he sees fit, or as are directed by the Commissioner or the Committee to assist the deliberation of the panel, such as whether the complainant claims to have suffered financial loss as a result of the conduct complained of, and if so the exact nature and amount of that claimed loss and the evidence available to support the claim, and from the barrister the nature of the work he carried out for the complainant out of which the complaint arose, the fee rendered for such work, and whether or not such fee has been paid.

46. Subject to the direction of the Chairman of the panel:

    (a) the Secretary shall keep the complainant informed of the progress of the complaint and of any further documents and other information to be considered by the panel;

    (b) the Secretary shall, so far as practicable, require the barrister and afford the complainant an opportunity to comment in advance of the hearing on any such information or documents.

47. The barrister shall attend on the panel at the day and time arranged, and shall provide to the panel orally such information as he wishes to put before them in connection with his conduct in relation to the matters specified, and shall answer so far as he is able such further questions as the panel may put to him which may relate to any aspects of the conduct complained of. The panel shall consider whether to adjourn the hearing in order to enable the complainant to comment on any information provided by the barrister at the hearing which had not previously been disclosed by him.

48. Following such hearing, the panel may reach the following decisions and shall provide reasons for reaching the decision

    (a) It may conclude that the barrister's explanation of his professional conduct has been satisfactory, whereupon it shall dismiss the complaint.

    (b) It may conclude that no further action shall be taken on the complaint.

    (c) It may conclude that the barrister's explanation of his professional conduct has not been satisfactory, whereupon it may either orally or in writing

        (i)   give him advice as to his future conduct, or
        (ii) reprimand him.

    (d) Regardless of the conclusion reached in relation to the barrister's professional conduct, the panel may conclude that a barrister has provided inadequate professional service in respect of the subject-matter of the complaint, provided the following conditions are satisfied:

        (i)   the complainant is the barrister's lay client or his duly authorised representative or in the case of an employed barrister the person to whom he has supplied the professional service in question, and

        (ii) the subject-matter of the complaint is not something in respect of which the barrister would be entitled to immunity from suit as an advocate in civil law.

(e) Whatever conclusion it may reach, the panel may refer any issue of policy which arises to the relevant Committee of the Bar Council.

(f) The panel may refer a matter back to the Committee for reconsideration if it considers that its powers are not sufficient to deal with the gravity of the complaint revealed at the hearing or that other issues are raised which require further consideration by the Committee.

49. If the panel is not unanimous on any issue, the finding made shall be that of the majority of them. If the panel is equally divided, the burden of proof being on the complainant the finding made shall be that most favourable to the barrister.

50. If a finding of inadequate professional service is made under paragraph 48(d), the panel shall consider what remedy should be granted to the complainant in respect of such inadequate service. The panel may:

(a) determine that it is not appropriate to take any action in respect of the complaint,

(b) adjourn consideration of the remedy to permit investigation or further investigation of the consequences of the inadequate professional service for the complainant and reconvene the panel when the results of such investigations are known,

(c) direct the barrister to make a formal apology to the complainant for the conduct complained of,

(d) direct the barrister to repay or remit all or part of any fee rendered in respect of the inadequate service,

(e) direct the barrister to pay compensation to the complainant in such sum as the panel shall direct not exceeding £5,000,

(f) direct the barrister to complete continuing professional development of such nature and duration as the Tribunal shall direct and to provide satisfactory proof of compliance with this requirement to the Committee.

In determining whether any sum is to be paid under paragraph (e) hereof, or in fixing the amount of such sum, the panel shall in particular have regard to any loss suffered by the applicant as a result of the inadequate professional service, the availability to the complainant of other forms of redress, to the gravity of the conduct complained of, and to the fee claimed by the barrister for the inadequate service.

51. An appeal shall lie at the instance of the barrister from any decision of a panel that a barrister has provided inadequate professional service, and against any decision as to the remedy to be granted to the complainant for such service in the same manner as an appeal lies from a decision of an Adjudication Panel in respect of the same matters.

52. The Secretary shall notify both the complainant and the barrister of the decision and, if the complaint is dismissed, of the reasons for it.

53. If the panel considers that the circumstances of the complaint are relevant to the barrister's position as a pupilmaster, it may notify the barrister's Inn of its concerns in such manner as it sees fit.

Definitions

54. In these Rules unless the context otherwise requires

(a) Any term defined in the Code of Conduct shall carry the same meaning as it does in the Code of Conduct.

(b) Any reference to a person includes any natural person, legal person and/or firm. Any reference to the masculine gender includes the feminine and the neuter, and any reference to the singular includes the plural, and in each case *vice versa*.

Commencement and Transitional Provisions

55. If a complaint has been raised in the Bar Council's complaints records before 31 October 2004, these Rules shall not apply but the Complaints Rules in force immediately before that date shall apply to that complaint, save that where the PCC has referred a complaint to an informal hearing after 31 October 2004, these rules shall apply. In relation to complaints raised after the Commencement Date, the procedure set out in these Rules shall apply, save that no finding of inadequate professional service may be made against a barrister in respect of any conduct of his which took place before 13 July 1996.

ANNEXE K

THE DISCIPLINARY TRIBUNALS REGULATIONS 2004

Arrangement of Regulations

1. Definitions

    In these regulations:

    (a) 'The relevant procedure' shall mean the procedure adopted by the PCC from time to time for preferring such charges.

    (b) Any reference to the Inns' Council or to the members thereof shall be a reference to the Inns' Council or the members thereof other than the Officers and the Chairman of the Council of Legal Education.

    (c) Other expressions shall have the meanings respectively assigned to them by Paragraph 1 of the Introduction to the Constitutions of the General Council of the Bar, the Council of the Inns of Court and the Council of Legal Education, or by Part X of the Code of Conduct.

2. Composition of Disciplinary Tribunals

(1)   A Disciplinary Tribunal shall consist of the following five persons nominated by the President:

(a) a Judge (who may be a retired Circuit Judge or retired judge of the High Court provided that he

(i)   continues to be permitted to sit as an Additional Judge

(ii) has done so in the last 12 months

(iii) has, within the last 12 months and following consultation with the Chairman of the Bar, being appointed to a panel of such judges by the President)

(b) two Lay Representatives

(c) two practising Barristers of not less than five years standing and not more than 70 years of age.

Provided that:

(i)   if the Barrister charged is an Employed or Non-Practising Barrister, at least one of the barristers nominated should normally be Employed or Non-Practising;

(ii) no Barrister or Lay Representative shall be nominated to serve on a Tribunal which is to consider a charge arising in respect of any matter considered at any meeting of the PCC which he attended;

(iii) in the case of a registered European lawyer, one of the members of the Tribunal shall be a registered European lawyer rather than a barrister.

(2)   The President shall select another member of the relevant class to fill any vacancy in the Disciplinary Tribunal membership that has arisen prior to the substantive hearing of the charge.

(3)   At any time before the commencement of the substantive hearing of the charge, the President may cancel any or all of the nominations made pursuant to this regulation, and make such alternative nominations as in the exercise of his discretion he deems to be expedient.

(4)   The proceedings of a Disciplinary Tribunal shall be valid notwithstanding that after the convening order has been issued one or more of the members other than the Chairman or one of the Lay Representatives becomes unable to continue to act or disqualified from continuing to act, so long as the number of members present throughout the substantive hearing of the charge is not reduced below three and continues to include the Chairman and a Lay Representative.

(5)   A member of a Disciplinary Tribunal who has been absent for any time during a sitting shall take no further part in the proceedings.

3. Sittings of Disciplinary Tribunals

The President shall appoint Disciplinary Tribunals to sit at such times as are necessary for the prompt and expeditious determination of charges preferred against barristers in accordance with the provisions of these Regulations.

4. Clerks

The President shall appoint a person or persons to act as Clerk or Clerks to the Disciplinary Tribunals to perform the functions specified in these Regulations and such other functions as the President or the Chairman of any Tribunal may direct. No person who has been engaged in the investigation of a complaint against a barrister in accordance with the relevant procedure or otherwise shall act as Clerk in relation to disciplinary proceedings arising out of that complaint.

5. Service of Charges

(1) Following the formulation of the charge or charges by counsel appointed by the PCC Representative in accordance with the relevant procedure, the PCC Representative shall cause a copy thereof to be served on the barrister concerned ('the defendant'), together with a copy of these Regulations and details of any Directions sought not later than 10 weeks (or 5 weeks if the PCC has directed that the prosecution of the charges be expedited) after the date on which the complaint was referred to a Disciplinary Tribunal by the PCC.

(2) The PCC Representative shall at the same time cause copies of the charge or charges to be supplied to the President.

6. Representation of complainant's interests

(a) the PCC representative shall keep the complainant informed of the progress of the complaint and of any further documents and other information to be considered by the panel and shall, so far as practicable, afford the complainant an opportunity to comment in advance of the hearing on any such information of documents.

(b) It shall be the responsibility of the PCC Representative and counsel appointed by the PCC Representative to represent the interests of the complainant in relation to any charge of inadequate professional service.

7. Convening Orders

(1) After receipt of the copy charge or charges supplied pursuant to Regulation 5, and in any case not less than 14 days before the substantive hearing, the President shall issue an Order ('the Convening Order') specifying

(a) the date of the sitting of the Disciplinary Tribunal at which it is proposed the charge or charges should be heard

(b) the identities of those persons who it is proposed should constitute the Disciplinary Tribunal to hear his case

(c) the identity of the Clerk.

(2) The President shall arrange for the service of the Convening Order on the defendant, and for copies thereof to be supplied to the nominated members of the Disciplinary Tribunal and the Clerk. In the order the defendant's attention will be drawn to:

(a) his right to represent himself or be represented by counsel, with or without instructing a solicitor, as he shall think fit

(b) his right to inspect and be given copies of documents referred to in the List served pursuant to Regulation 7 below

(c) his right (without prejudice to his right to appear and take part in the proceedings) to deliver a written answer to the charge or charges if he thinks fit.

(3) The defendant shall have the right upon receipt of the Convening Order to give notice to the President objecting to any one or more of the proposed members of the Disciplinary Tribunal. Such notice shall specify the ground of objection.

(4) Upon receipt of such objection, the President shall, if satisfied that it is properly made (but subject to Paragraph (5) of this Regulation) exercise the power conferred on

him by Paragraph (3) of Regulation 2 to nominate a substitute Member or Members of the Tribunal, and notify the defendant accordingly. Upon receipt of such notification, the defendant shall have *mutatis mutandis* in relation to such substitute Member or Members the like right of objection as is conferred by Paragraph (3) of this Regulation.

(5)   No objection to any Member of the Tribunal shall be valid on the ground that he has or may have had knowledge of a previous charge of professional misconduct or breach of proper professional standards or a charge consisting of a legal aid complaint against the defendant or any finding on any such charge, or of any sentence imposed on the defendant in connection therewith.

(6)   The Convening Order shall contain words drawing the attention of the defendant to the rights conferred by Paragraphs (2)–(5) of this Regulation.

8.   Documents to be Served

(1)   A barrister who is to be charged before a Disciplinary Tribunal shall, as soon as practicable, be supplied with:

   (a) a copy of the statement of the evidence of each witness intended to be called in support of the charge or charges

   (b) a list of the documents intended to be relied on by the PCC Representative.

(2)   If the documents referred to in paragraph (1) of this Regulation are not supplied to the barrister at least 10 days before the date of the Preliminary Hearing then the PCC representative shall provide to the barrister and the Directions Judge at least 10 days before the date of the Preliminary Hearing:

   (a) details of the statements of evidence that are still being sought and

   (b) a statement of when it is believed that it will be practicable to supply those statements to the barrister.

(3)   Nothing in this Regulation shall preclude the reception by a Disciplinary Tribunal of the evidence of a witness a copy of whose statement has not been served on the defendant (within the time specified aforesaid, or at all), or of a document not included in the List of Documents, provided the Tribunal is of opinion that the defendant is not materially prejudiced thereby, or on such terms as are necessary to ensure that no such prejudice arises.

9.   Preliminary Hearings; Directions Judge; Powers of Chairman etc.

(1)   The President shall designate a judge or judges ('the Directions Judge(s)') to exercise the powers and functions specified in this Regulation.

(2)   The Directions Judge shall (subject to Paragraph (9) of this Regulation) hold a Preliminary Hearing for the purpose of giving directions and of taking such other steps as he considers suitable for the clarification of the issues before the tribunal and generally for the just and expeditious handling of the proceedings.

(3)   The Preliminary Hearing shall be held not less than 10 days and not more than 4 weeks (or 3 weeks if the PCC has directed that prosecution of charges be expedited) after service of the charge or charges on the barrister. For the purpose of calculating these periods, no account shall be taken of any period outside the law terms.

(4)   The directions to be given and steps taken by the Directions Judge may concern, but shall not be limited to, the following matters:

   (a) whether the hearing should not be held in public

   (b) applications for separate hearings

   (c) applications to sever charges

(d) applications to strike out charges

(e) attendance of witnesses

(f) a requirement that the parties provide each other with the names of all witnesses to be called at the hearing within a specified time limit

(g) admission of documents, including any documents intended to be relied upon by the PCC Representative in relation to charges of inadequate professional service

(h) admission of facts, in accordance with the procedure set out at Paragraph (6) of this Regulation

(i) the estimated duration of the substantive hearing

(j) such other matters as he deems expedient for the efficient conduct of the hearing

(k) consideration of any application under Regulation 21(12)(ii)

(l) a requirement that such action as appears to him to be necessary for a fair hearing of the matter be undertaken within such period as he may decide

(m) where he is satisfied that the matter is ready for hearing by a Tribunal setting a date for the Tribunal hearing.

(5) The defendant may plead guilty to any charge or charges at the Directions Hearing, in which case the Tribunal shall find the defendant guilty of that charge at the Tribunal Hearing.

(6) (a) The Directions Judge may, if he thinks fit, request the defendant or his representative to state (either forthwith or in writing within such time as may be specified) whether any and if so which of such of the facts relied on in support of the charges as may be specified is disputed, and/or the grounds on which such fact is disputed.

(b) The Clerk shall cause a record to be made of the making of such a request as aforesaid, and of the defendant's response thereto, and the same shall be drawn to the attention of the Disciplinary Tribunal at the conclusion of the substantive hearing, if relevant, on the question of costs.

(7) The powers and functions specified in this Regulation may be exercised by a Judge nominated by the President other than the Directions Judge, including the Judge designated in the Convening Order as Chairman of the Tribunal appointed to hear and determine the charge or charges against the defendant.

(8) The Clerk shall take a note of the proceedings at a Preliminary Hearing and shall cause a record to be drawn up and served on the parties setting out the directions given or admissions made at the Preliminary Hearing, including, without prejudice to the generality of the directions given, a record of any directions which relate to any of the matters specifically set out under Paragraph (4) of this Regulation.

(9) A defendant aggrieved by a direction given or other step taken pursuant to this Regulation may, provided that he acts promptly following the service on him of the record of any directions, give notice to the Clerk of his intention to apply for a review of such direction or step; such review will be conducted by the Chairman of the Tribunal sitting with a Lay Representative, who shall, on such application being made, give such directions or take such other steps as they see fit.

(10) The PCC Representative and the defendant or his representative may, in advance of the date fixed for the Preliminary Hearing, agree upon the directions to be made and/or steps to be taken thereat, or that no such directions or steps are required and shall notify the Clerk in writing of such agreement; following such notification

the Directions Judge may, if he thinks fit, make directions in the terms agreed and/or direct that no Preliminary Hearing is required.

(11)   For the avoidance of doubt the Directions Judge, or the Chairman of the Disciplinary Tribunal designated in the Convening Order (or failing the Directions Judge or the Chairman, any other Judge nominated by the President) may

(a)   upon the application of either party at any time extend or abridge any time limit governing the disciplinary procedures on such terms as he thinks just

(b)   upon the application of either party, or of his own motion, hold further preliminary hearings for the purpose of giving any further directions or taking any other steps which he considers necessary for the proper conduct of the proceedings

(c)   adjourn the preliminary hearing from time to time and for such periods of time as he considers appropriate and set such time limits as he may decide for action to be taken during such adjournments

(d)   consider applications for adjournment of the Tribunal Hearing prior to that Hearing and grant such adjournments as they consider appropriate.

10. Provision of Documents

There shall be provided to each member of the Disciplinary Tribunal prior to the commencement of the substantive hearing copies of the following documents:

(a)   the Order of the President constituting the Tribunal

(b)   the Charges and any particulars thereof

(c)   any documents proposed to be relied on by the PCC Representative or by the defendant, unless a direction has been made at the Preliminary Hearing or otherwise, that copies of such documents be withheld

(d)   any written answer to the charges submitted by or on behalf of the defendant

(e)   such other documents (which may include copies of witness statements) as at the Preliminary Hearing or otherwise have been directed to be or the PCC Representative and the defendant or his representative have agreed, should be laid before the Tribunal prior to the start of the hearing

(f)   the record of directions given at each preliminary hearing which has been drawn up and served on the parties pursuant to Regulation 9(8).

11. Procedure At The Hearing

The Proceedings of a Disciplinary Tribunal shall be governed by the rules of natural justice, subject to which the tribunal may

(a)   admit any evidence, whether oral or written, whether direct or hearsay, and whether or not the same would be admissible in a court of law

(b)   give such directions with regard to the conduct of and procedure at the hearing, and with regard to the admission of evidence thereat, as it considers appropriate for securing that the defendant has a proper opportunity of answering the charge or otherwise as shall be just

(c)   exclude any hearsay evidence if it is not satisfied that reasonable steps have been taken to obtain direct evidence of the facts sought to be proved by the hearsay evidence.

The tribunal shall apply the criminal standard of proof when adjudicating upon charges of professional misconduct, and the civil standard of proof when adjudicating upon charges of inadequate professional service, if any.

12. Hearing in Private

    The hearing before a Disciplinary Tribunal shall be in public unless at a Preliminary Hearing or otherwise it has been directed that it shall not be held in public, and this direction has not been over-ruled by the Tribunal.

13. Decision of a Court or Tribunal

    (1)   In proceedings before a Disciplinary Tribunal which involve the decision of a court or tribunal, the following rules of evidence shall apply provided that it is proved in each case that the decision relates to the defendant:

    (a)   the fact that the defendant has been convicted of a criminal offence may be proved by producing a certified copy of the certificate of conviction relating to the offence; proof of a conviction in this matter shall constitute prima facie evidence that the defendant was guilty of the offence the subject thereof.

    (b)   the finding and sentence of any tribunal in or outside England and Wales exercising a professional disciplinary jurisdiction may be proved by producing a certified copy of the finding and sentence.

    (c)   the judgment of any civil court may be proved by producing a certified copy of the judgment.

    (2)   In any case set out in Paragraph (1) of this Regulation, the findings of fact by the court or tribunal upon which the conviction, finding, sentence or judgment is based shall be admissible as *prima facie* proof of those facts.

14. Absence of Defendant

    (1)   If a Disciplinary Tribunal is satisfied that the relevant procedure has been complied with and the defendant has been duly served (in accordance with Regulation 29 of these Regulations) with the documents required by Regulations 5, 7 and 8 and the defendant has not attended at the time and place appointed for the hearing, the tribunal may nevertheless proceed to hear and determine the charge or charges, subject to compliance with Paragraph (12)(i) of Regulation 21 in the event of any charge being found proved.

    (2)   If a Disciplinary Tribunal is satisfied that it has not been practicable to comply with the relevant procedure, the Tribunal shall hear and determine the charge or charges in the absence of the defendant subject to compliance with Paragraph (12)(ii) of Regulation 21 in the event of any charge being found proved.

15. Recording of Proceedings

    The Clerk shall arrange for a record of the proceedings before a Disciplinary Tribunal to be made by the employment of a shorthand writer or the use of a recording machine.

16. Amendment of Charges

    A Disciplinary Tribunal may at any time before or during the hearing direct that the charge or charges shall be amended provided always:

    (a)   that the Tribunal is satisfied that the defendant will not by reason of such an amendment suffer any substantial prejudice in the conduct of his defence,

(b)   that the Tribunal shall, if so requested by the defendant, adjourn for such time as is reasonably necessary to enable him to meet the charge or charges as so amended,

(c)   that the Tribunal shall make such Order as to the costs of or occasioned by the amendment, or of any consequential adjournment of the proceedings, as it considers appropriate.

17. Adjournment

(1)   Subject to the provisions of the following Paragraph, the Disciplinary Tribunal shall sit from day to day until it has arrived at a finding and if any charge has been found proved until sentence is pronounced.

(2)   Notwithstanding the provisions of Paragraph (1) of this Regulation, a Disciplinary Tribunal may, if the Tribunal decides an adjournment is necessary for any reason, adjourn the hearing for such period as it may decide. In particular, if a finding of inadequate professional service is made and the Tribunal considers that an award of compensation to the complainant may be appropriate, it may adjourn to enable further investigation of that question to take place, if it does not already have the necessary material before it.

18. The Finding

At the conclusion of the hearing, the finding of the Disciplinary Tribunal on each charge, together with its reasons, shall be set down in writing and signed by the chairman and all members of the Tribunal. If the members of the Tribunal are not unanimous as to the finding on any charge, the finding to be recorded on that charge shall be that of the majority. If the members of the Tribunal are equally divided as to the finding on any charge, then, the burden of proof being on the PCC Representative, the finding to be recorded on that charge shall be that which is the most favourable to the defendant. The chairman of the Tribunal shall then announce the Tribunal's finding on the charge or charges.

19. The Sentence

(1)   If the Disciplinary Tribunal shall have found the charge or any of the charges proved, evidence may be given of any previous finding of professional misconduct or of breach of proper professional standards or of inadequate professional service or any finding on a charge consisting of a legal aid complaint against the defendant. After hearing any representations by or on behalf of the defendant the Tribunal shall set down in writing its decision as to the sentence. If the members of the Tribunal are not unanimous as to the sentence, the sentence to be recorded shall be that decided by the majority. If the members of the Tribunal are equally divided as to the sentence, the sentence to be recorded shall be that which is the most favourable to the defendant. The chairman of the Tribunal shall then announce the Tribunal's decision as to sentence.

(2)(a) A barrister against whom a charge of professional misconduct has been found proved may be sentenced by the Disciplinary Tribunal to be:
   (i)   disbarred (or in the case of a registered European lawyer, removed from the register of European lawyers);
   (ii)   suspended (or in the case of a registered European lawyer suspended from the register of European lawyers) for a prescribed period (either unconditionally or subject to conditions);
   (iii) prohibited, either indefinitely or for a prescribed period and either unconditionally or subject to conditions, from accepting or carrying out any public access instructions;

(iv)   ordered to pay a fine of up to £5,000 to the Bar Council;

(v)   ordered to repay or forego fees;

(vi)   ordered to complete continuing professional development of such nature and duration as the Tribunal shall direct and to provide satisfactory proof of compliance with this order to the PCC;

(vii)   reprimanded by the Treasurer of his Inn;

(viii)   reprimanded by the Tribunal; or

(ix)   given advice by the Tribunal as to his future conduct; or

(x)   ordered by the Tribunal to attend on a nominated person to be reprimanded; or

(xi)   ordered by the Tribunal to attend on a nominated person to be given advice as to his future conduct.

(b)   A barrister against whom a charge of inadequate professional service has been found proved may be

(i)   directed to make a formal apology to the complainant for the conduct in relation to which the finding was made;

(ii)   directed to repay or remit all or part of any fee rendered in respect of the inadequate service;

(iii)   directed to pay compensation to the complainant in such sum as the Tribunal shall direct not exceeding £5,000; or

(iv)   directed to complete continuing professional development of such nature and duration as the Tribunal shall direct and to provide satisfactory proof of compliance with this requirement to the PCC;

(v)   prohibited, either indefinitely or for a prescribed period and either unconditionally or subject to conditions, from accepting or carrying out any public access instructions.

In determining whether any sum is to be paid under paragraph (iii) hereof, or in fixing the amount of such sum, the Tribunal shall in particular have regard to any loss suffered by the applicant as a result of the inadequate professional service, the availability to the complainant of other forms of redress, to the gravity of the conduct complained of and to the fee claimed by the barrister for the inadequate service.

(c)   In any case where a charge of professional misconduct or inadequate professional service has been found proved, the Tribunal may decide that no action should be taken against the defendant.

(3)   Sections 41 and 42 of the Administration of Justice Act 1985 (as substituted by Section 33 of the Legal Aid Act 1988 and amended by Schedule 4 to the Access to Justice Act 1999) confer certain powers (relating to the reduction or cancellation of fees otherwise payable by the Legal Services Commission in connection with services provided as part of the Community Legal Service or Criminal Defence Service and to exclusion from providing representation funded by the Legal Services Commission as part of the Community Legal Service or Criminal Defence Service) on a Disciplinary Tribunal in the cases to which those Sections apply. Accordingly:

(a)   Any Disciplinary Tribunal which hears a charge consisting of a legal aid complaint relating to the conduct of a barrister may if it thinks fit (and whether or not it sentences the barrister in accordance with paragraph (2) of this Regulation in respect of any conduct arising out of the same legal aid complaint) order that any such fees as are referred to in Section 41(2) of the Act of 1985 shall be reduced or cancelled.

(b) Where a Disciplinary Tribunal hears a charge of professional misconduct against a barrister it may (in addition to or instead of sentencing that barrister in accordance with Paragraph (2) of this Regulation) order that he shall be excluded from providing representation funded by the Legal Services Commission as part of the Community Legal Service or Criminal Defence Service either temporarily or for a specified period if it determines that there is good reason for the exclusion arising out of (i) his conduct in connection with any such services as are mentioned in Section 40(1) of the Act of 1985; or (ii) his professional conduct generally.

(4)   Whether or not a Disciplinary Tribunal shall have found any charge proved, if the Disciplinary Tribunal considers that the circumstances of the complaint are relevant to the barrister in his capacity as a pupilmaster, it may notify the barrister's Inn of its concerns in such manner as it sees fit.

20. Sentence of Suspension

(1)   Any sentence of suspension may apply to the whole of a barrister's practice or to such part only as the Disciplinary Tribunal may determine.

(2)   The conditions to which a sentence of suspension may be made subject include a requirement that the barrister shall undergo such further pupillage or training or attain such standard of competence as the Tribunal may determine.

21. Wording of the Sentence

The sentence determined by a Disciplinary Tribunal if a charge of professional misconduct has been found proved shall be recorded as follows:

(1) <u>Disbarment</u>
'That . . . . . be disbarred and expelled from the Honourable Society of . . . . .'

(2) <u>Suspension</u>
'That . . . . . be suspended from practice as a barrister and from enjoyment of all rights and privileges as a member of the Honourable Society of . . . . . and be prohibited from holding himself out as being a barrister without disclosing his suspension for (stating the length of the prescribed period)'. (Note: If the Tribunal decides that the sentence of suspension shall apply to part only of the barrister's practice or shall be subject to conditions, such part or such conditions (as the case may be) shall be specified in the wording of the sentence.)

(3) <u>Proibition on Accepting or Carrying out Public Access Instructions</u>
'That . . . . . . be prohibited from accepting or carrying out any public access instructions (as defined in the Code of Conduct of the Bar of England and Wales)' (Note: If the Tribunal decides that the sentence shall apply for a prescribed period or shall be subject to conditions, such periods or such conditions or both (as the case may be) shall be specified in the wording of the sentence).

(4) <u>Payment of Fine</u>
'That . . . . . pay a fine of £ . . . . . to the Bar Council.'

(5) <u>Repayment or Foregoing of Fees</u>
'That . . . . . shall repay all fees (fees amounting to £ . . . . .) received by him (shall forego all fees (fees amounting to £ . . . . .) due to be paid to him) in connection with . . . . .'

(6) <u>Continuing Professional Development</u>
'That . . . . . shall by [date] complete a minimum of . . . hours of continuing professional development (in addition to the mandatory requirements set out in the Continuing Professional Development Regulations at Annex C to the Code of Conduct) [in the

subject of . . .] and provide satisfactory proof of compliance with this order to the Professional Conduct and Complaints Committee of the Bar Council.'

(7)   Reprimand

'That . . . . . be reprimanded by the Treasurer of the Honourable Society of . . . . .', or 'That . . . . . is hereby ordered to attend . . . . . to be reprimanded'.

(8)   Advice as to Future Conduct

'That . . . . . has been advised by the Tribunal as to his future conduct in regard to . . . . .' or ' That . . . . . is hereby ordered to attend on . . . . . to be given advice as to his future conduct in regard to . . . . .'.

(9)   Order for Reduction of Legal Aid Fees

'That the fees otherwise payable to . . . . . by the Legal Services Commission in connection with his services provided by him as part of the Community Legal Service or Criminal Defence Service or otherwise in relation to the items or matters specified in the first column of the Schedule hereto be reduced to the sum or sums specified in the second column of that Schedule'.

The record of the sentence shall then contain a Schedule setting out the matters referred to above.

(10)   Order for Cancellation of Legal Aid Fees

'That the fees otherwise payable to . . . . . by the Legal Services Commission in connection with services provided by him as part of the Community Legal Service or Criminal Defence Service in relation to the items or matters specified in the Schedule hereto be cancelled'.

The record of the sentence shall then contain a Schedule identifying the items or matters referred to above.

(11)   Exclusion from Legal Aid Work

'That . . . . . be excluded from providing representation funded by the Legal Services Commission as part of the Community Legal Service or Criminal Defence Service (as explained in Section 42(4)(b) of the Administration of Justice Act 1985 as substituted by Section 33 of the Legal Aid Act 1988 and amended by Schedule 4 to the Access to Justice Act 1999 (until . . . . .) (for a period of . . . . . beginning on . . . . .)'.

(12)   Membership of More than One Inn

If the barrister is a member of more than one Inn, each Inn of which he is a member shall be mentioned in the sentence.

(13)   Absence of the Barrister Charged

If the barrister charged has not been present throughout the proceedings, the sentence shall include one of the following two statements:

(i) If the relevant procedure under Regulation 14(1) has been complied with, that the finding and sentence were made in the absence of the barrister in accordance with Regulation 14(1).

(ii) If the procedure under Regulation 14(2) has been complied with, that the finding and the sentence were made in the absence of the barrister and that he has the right to apply to the Directions Judge for an order that there should be a new hearing before a fresh Disciplinary Tribunal.

(14)   Removal from the Register of European Lawyers

'That . . . be removed from the register of European lawyers maintained by the Bar Council.'

(15) Suspension from the Register of European Lawyers

'That . . . be suspended from the register of European lawyers maintained by the Bar Council and be prohibited from holding himself out as registered with the Bar Council or an Inn of Court without disclosing his suspension for (state length of prescribed period).' (Note: If the Tribunal decides that the sentence of suspension shall apply to part only of the registered European lawyer's practice or shall be subject to conditions, such part or such conditions (as the case may be) shall be specified in the wording of the sentence).

22. Report of Finding and Sentence

(1)   As soon as practicable after the conclusion of the proceedings of a Disciplinary Tribunal, the chairman of the Tribunal shall prepare a report in writing of the finding on the charges of professional misconduct and the reasons for that finding and, where applicable, the sentence. At the discretion of the chairman of the Tribunal, the report may also refer to matters which, in the light of the evidence given to the Tribunal, appear to require investigation or comment. He shall send copies of the report to the following:

(2)   In all cases

    (i)   The Lord Chancellor

    (ii)   The Lord Chief Justice

    (iii)   The Attorney General

    (iv)   The President

    (v)   The Chairman of the Bar Council

    (vi)   The Chairman of the Professional Conduct and Complaints Committee

    (vii)   The barrister charged

    (viii) The Treasurer of the barrister's Inn of Call

    (xi)   The Treasurer of any other Inn of which the barrister is a member.

(3)   In cases where one or more charges of professional misconduct have been found proved and any such charge constitutes or arises out of a legal aid complaint, and/or the sentence includes an order under Regulation 20(8), (9) or (10), the Legal Services Commission.

23. Appeal to the Visitors

(1)   In cases where one or more charges of professional misconduct have been proved, an appeal may be lodged with the Visitors in accordance with the Hearings Before the Visitors Rules:

    (a)   against conviction by the defendant; and/or

    (b)   against sentence, by the defendant or (with the Consent of the Chairman of the Bar or the Chairman of the PCC) the Bar Council.

(2)   In cases where no professional misconduct has been proved, but one or more charges of inadequate professional service have been proved, an appeal shall lie at the instance of the barrister from any such finding, and against any decision as to the remedy to be granted to the complainant for such service in the same manner as an appeal lies from a decision of an Adjudication Panel in respect of the same matters.

(3)   Where a defendant lodges an appeal against a sentence of disbarment, he may at the same time lodge with the Visitors an appeal against any requirement imposed pursuant to Regulation 28.

24. Appeal: Sum Payable

Where an appeal is lodged with the Visitors by the Defendant, the Notice of Appeal must be accompanied by the sum of £250 payable to the General Council of the Bar to defray expenses, such sum to be refunded in the discretion of the Visitors in the event of an appeal which is successful wholly or in part.

25. Action by the Barrister's Inn

(1)   On receipt of the report prepared in accordance with Regulation 22, the Treasurer of the barrister's Inn of Call shall not less than 21 days after the conclusion of the Tribunal's proceedings pronounce the sentence decided on by the Tribunal, and take such further action as may be required to carry the sentence into effect. The Treasurer shall inform the persons specified in Paragraph (2) of Regulation 22 of the date on which the sentence is to take effect.

(2)   Similar action shall be taken by the Treasurer of any other Inn of which the barrister is a member in conjunction with the Treasurer of the barrister's Inn of Call.

(3)   In any case in which the barrister has given notice of appeal to the visitors against the finding and/or sentence of the Tribunal on the charges of professional misconduct, the action set out in paragraphs (1) and (2) of this Regulation shall be deferred until the appeal has been heard by the Visitors or otherwise disposed of without a hearing.

26. Action by the Bar Council

(1)   In the case of a registered European lawyer, on receipt of the report prepared in accordance with Regulation 22, the Bar Council shall not less than 21 days after the conclusion of the Tribunal's proceedings pronounce the sentence decided on by the Tribunal and take such further action as may be required to carry the sentence into effect. The Bar Council shall inform the persons specified in paragraph (2) of Regulation 22 of the date on which the sentence is to take effect.

(2)   In any case in which a registered European lawyer has given notice of appeal to the Visitors against the finding and/or sentence of the Tribunal on the charges of professional misconduct, the actions set out in paragraph (1) of this Regulation shall be deferred until the appeal has been heard by the Visitors or otherwise disposed of without a hearing.

(3)   The Bar Council shall take all such steps as may be necessary or expedient in order to give effect to any requirement made by the Tribunal pursuant to Regulation 27 below.

27. Publication of Finding and Sentence

(1)   The following procedures are to be observed in regard to publication of the finding and sentence of a Disciplinary Tribunal:

(i)   When the Tribunal has found one or more charges of professional misconduct have been proved the President shall publish the charges found proved and the sentence as soon as he has been informed by the Treasurer(s) of the barrister's Inn(s) of the date from which the sentence is to take effect.

(ii)   When the Tribunal has found that one or more charges of inadequate professional service have been proved, the President shall not publish the charges found proved and the finding unless the barrister charged so requests.

(iii) When the Tribunal has found that any charge whether of professional misconduct or of inadequate professional service has not been proved the President shall not publish that charge and the finding unless the barrister charged so requests.

(2)   When publishing any finding, sentence or decision in accordance with sub-paragraph (1) of this Regulation, the President shall communicate the same in writing to:—

  (i)   the Lord Chancellor;

  (ii)   the Lord Chief Justice;

  (iii)   the Attorney General;

  (iv)   the Director of Public Prosecutions;

  (v)   the Treasurer of each Inn for screening in the Hall, Benchers' Room and Treasurer's Office of the Inn;

  (vi)   the Leaders of the six circuits;

  (vii)   the barrister concerned;

  (viii) such one or more press agencies or other publications as the President may decide;

  (xi)   in the case of a registered European lawyer, his home professional body.

(3)   Nothing in this Regulation shall prevent the Bar Council publishing the finding and sentence of the Tribunal in such manner and in such a time as it sees fit unless:

  (a) the hearing was held in private; and

  (b) the Chairman of the Tribunal directs that publication shall be delayed until the President has published the finding under sub-paragraph (1) of this Regulation.

28. Suspension Pending Appeal

(1)   This regulation applies in relation to any barrister who has been sentenced to be disbarred or to be suspended or prohibited from accepting or carrying out public access instructions for a period of more than one year.

(2)   Where this regulation applies the Tribunal shall seek representations from the defendant and the PCC Representative as to whether it would be inappropriate to take action under paragraphs (3) or (4) below;

(3)   Having heard any representations under paragraph (2) above, the Tribunal shall:

  (a) unless in the particular circumstances of the case it appears to the Tribunal to be inappropriate to do so, either:

    (i)   require the Bar Council to suspend immediately the practising certificate of the barrister in question;

    (ii)   determine that its sentence prohibiting the barrister from accepting or carrying out any public access instructions shall take effect immediately; or

  (b) where the barrister has been sentenced to be disbarred or to be suspended and where that barrister does not currently hold a practising certificate, require the Bar Council not to issue any practising certificate to him.

(4)   If pursuant to paragraph (3)(a) above the Tribunal concludes that it would be inappropriate to require immediate suspension it may nonetheless require the Bar Council to suspend the practising certificate of the barrister in question from such date as the Tribunal may specify.

(5)   Where this regulation applies but the barrister in question is permitted to continue to practise for any period the Tribunal may require the Bar Council to impose such terms in respect of the barrister's practice as the Tribunal deems necessary for the protection of the public.

(6)   If a barrister in relation to whom a requirement has been made pursuant to paragraphs (3) to (5) considers that, due to a change in the circumstances, it would be appropriate for that requirement to be varied, he may apply to the President in writing for a variation to be made.

(7)   On receiving an application made pursuant to paragraph (6) above the President shall refer it to the Chairman and one of the lay representatives of the Tribunal which originally imposed the requirement.

(8)   Any application made pursuant to paragraph (6) above shall be sent by the applicant, on the day that it is made, to the PCC and the PCC may make such representations as they think fit on that application to those to whom the application has been referred by the President.

(9)   The persons to whom an application made pursuant to paragraph (6) above is referred may vary or confirm the requirement in relation to which the application has been made.

29. Costs

(1)   A Disciplinary Tribunal shall have power to make such Orders for costs, whether against or in favour of a defendant, as it shall think fit.

(2)   Upon making such an Order a Disciplinary Tribunal shall either itself determine the amount of such costs or appoint a suitably qualified person to do so on its behalf.

(3)   Any costs ordered to be paid by or to a defendant shall be paid to or by the Bar Council.

(4)   Subject as aforesaid, all costs and expenses incurred by a Disciplinary Tribunal or by the PCC in connection with or preparatory to the hearing before the Tribunal shall be borne by the Bar Council.

30. Service of Documents

Any documents required to be served on a barrister arising out of or in connection with disciplinary proceedings shall be deemed to have been validly served:

(1)   If sent by registered post, or recorded delivery post, or receipted hand delivery to:

(a) the address notified by such barrister pursuant to Paragraph 202(d) of the Code of Conduct of the Bar of England and Wales (or any provisions amending or replacing the same); or

(b) an address to which the barrister may request in writing that such documents be sent; or

(c) in the absence of any such request, to his last known address;

and such service shall be deemed to have been made on the fifth working day after the date of posting or on the next working day after receipted hand delivery;

(2)   If actually served;

(3)   If served in any way which may be directed by the Directions Judge or the Chairman of the Disciplinary Tribunal.

For the purpose of this regulation 'receipted hand delivery' means by a delivery by hand which is acknowledged by a receipt signed by the barrister or his clerk.

31. Miscellaneous Provisions

(1)   Any duty or function or step which, pursuant to the provisions of these regulations, is to be discharged or carried out by the President may, if he is unable to act due

to absence or any other reason, be discharged or carried out by any other member of the Inns Council, the Treasurer of any Inn or by any other person nominated in writing by the President for any specific purpose.

(2)   When the Treasurer of an Inn is a Royal Bencher, references in these Regulations to such Treasurer shall be read as references to his deputy.

32. Exclusion from Providing Representation Funded by the Legal Services Commission — Application for Termination

(1)   A barrister who has been excluded from legal aid work under Section 42 of the Act of 1985 may apply for an order terminating his exclusion from providing representation funded by the Legal Services Commission as part of the Community Legal Service or Criminal Defence Service in accordance with this Regulation.

(2)   Any such application shall be in writing and shall be addressed to the President.

(3)   On considering any such application the President may dismiss the application or may determine that the barrister's exclusion from providing representation funded by the Legal Services Commission as part of the Community Legal Service or Criminal Defence Service be terminated forthwith or on a specified future date.

(4)   The President shall give notification of his decision in writing to the same persons as received copies of the report of the Disciplinary Tribunal which ordered that the barrister be excluded from providing such representation legal aid work.

(5)   Upon the receipt of any such report the Treasurer of the applicant's Inn of Call and of any other Inn of which he is a member shall take action equivalent to that which it took in respect of the report of the Disciplinary Tribunal which sentenced the barrister to be excluded from providing representation funded by the Legal Services Commission as part of the Community Legal Service or Criminal Defence Service.

(6)   The procedures to be observed in regard to the publication of the decision of the President on any such application as is referred to in this Regulation shall be those which were applicable to the publication of the finding and sentence whereby the applicant was excluded from providing representation funded by the Legal Services Commission as part of the Community Legal Service or Criminal Defence Service.

(7)   The President shall have power to make such order for costs as he thinks fit and Regulation 28 shall apply with all necessary modifications.

33. Citation, Commencement, Revocations and Transitional Provisions

(1)   These Regulations may be cited as 'The Disciplinary Tribunals Regulations 2004' and shall come into operation on 31 October 2004 save that no finding of inadequate professional service may be made against a barrister in respect of any conduct of his which took place before 13 July 1996.

(2)   Subject to Paragraph (3) below, the Disciplinary Tribunals Regulations of the Council of the Inns of Court and any other rules or regulations relating to Disciplinary Tribunals made prior to the commencement of these Regulations shall cease to have effect on 30 October 2004.

(3)   In relation to any case in which a barrister was served with the charge or charges before 31 October 2004 these Regulations shall not apply and the matter shall continue to be dealt with pursuant to the Disciplinary Tribunals Regulations 1996, save that Regulation 23 shall apply to any decision made by a Disciplinary Tribunal on or after 31 October 2004.

ANNEXE L

THE SUMMARY PROCEDURE RULES

1. Definitions

   In these Rules:

   (a) 'The Act of 1985' shall mean the Administration of Justice Act 1985 as amended by the Legal Aid Act 1988 and the Access to Justice Act 1999.

   (b) 'Disciplinary Tribunal Regulations' shall mean those Regulations as amended from time to time in Annex K to the Code of Conduct of the Bar of England and Wales.

   (c) 'The defendant' shall mean the barrister against whom complaint has been made.

   (d) 'Sponsor member' shall mean the member of the PCC to whom the file was originally or subsequently assigned and who reported to the PCC on the complaint.

   (e) 'Summary case' shall mean a complaint referred by the PCC for summary determination under these Rules.

   (f) 'Summary hearing' shall mean the hearing of a summary case by a panel appointed under these Rules.

2. Composition of Summary Hearing Panels

   A panel shall consist of not more than five, and not less than three people nominated by the Chairman of the PCC which number shall include at least:

   (a) One Queen's Counsel as chairman of the panel

   (b) One Junior over five years call

   (c) When the number of barristers on the panel exceeds two, two lay representatives

   Provided that:

   (i) No barrister shall be nominated to serve on a panel who has acted as sponsor member in relation to the summary case to be dealt with.

   (ii) The proceedings of a summary hearing shall be valid notwithstanding that one or more of the members other than the chairman or lay representative becomes unable to continue to act or disqualified from continuing to act, so long as the number of members present throughout the substantive hearing of the charge(s) is not reduced below three and continues to include the chairman and at least one of the lay representatives.

3. Timetable

   (a) As soon as possible after referral of a case to summary procedure, the Secretary of the PCC shall write to the defendant notifying him of the PCC's decision and enclosing a copy of the Summary Procedure Rules.

   (b) The defendant shall receive as soon as possible thereafter, the documents to be served upon him together with a letter laying down a fixed time and date (normally 5 pm on a working day within 60 calendar days or less from the date of the letter) for the hearing to take place. One alternative shall be given.

   (c) The defendant shall be invited to accept one or other of the dates proposed or to provide a written representation to the Chairman of the PCC, objecting to both dates with reasons and providing two further alternative dates. The Chairman of the PCC shall consider this representation and either confirm one of the original dates or re-fix the hearing. His decision shall be final.

(d) Once fixed, a hearing date shall be vacated only in exceptional circumstances and with the agreement of the Chairman of the PCC.

4. Documents to be Served

On referral of a complaint to summary procedure, the PCC shall prepare and serve the following documents on the defendant and the complainant who shall be invited within 14 days (which period may be extended with the permission of the Chairman of the PCC or the Complaints Commissioner) to comment in writing on any of those matters or to send other document to which they wish the panel to have regard:

(a) Notification of the PCC's decision to refer the matter to summary procedure.

(b) Statement of the charges made against the barrister which may include charges of inadequate professional service provided that:

(i)   the complainant is the barrister's lay client or his duly authorised representative or in the case of an employed barrister the person to whom he has supplied the professional service in question, and

(ii) the subject-matter of the complaint is something in respect of which the barrister would not be entitled to immunity from suit as an advocate in civil law.

(c) Statement of facts upon which the charge(s) is or are founded and upon which the PCC proposes to rely.

(d) Copies of any documents which will be available to the summary hearing and which have not previously been served on the defendant. Any document shall be deemed to have been validly served in the circumstances laid down in Paragraph 29 of Disciplinary Tribunal Regulations 2000.

5. Acceptance of the Statement of Facts and of Summary Procedure

(a) In the letter of notification:

(i)   The defendant shall be required to state in writing whether or not he admits the charge(s) and, if he does not, whether or not he challenges any of the facts detailed in the statement of facts.

(ii) If he admits the charge(s) or if he does not challenge any of the facts detailed in the statement of facts, he shall also be asked to say whether he is prepared to agree that the charge(s) should be dealt with by summary procedure.

(iii) If:

(1) the only charges(s) allege(s) breach of paragraph 402 of the Code of Conduct of the Bar of England and Wales;

(2) the PCC has so directed when referring the case to summary procedure: and

(3) the defendant admits the charge(s) and agrees that the charges(s) should be dealt with by summary procedure.

he shall also be asked to say whether he wishes to attend the summary hearing.

(b) If the defendant admits the charge(s) or does not challenge any significant facts and, in either case, if he agrees that his case should be dealt with by summary procedure, the case shall proceed to a summary hearing, failing which it shall proceed to a Disciplinary Tribunal.

(c) Failure of the defendant to respond to these questions within 30 days of the date of the Secretary's letter shall be construed as refusal to admit the charge(s), to agree the statement of facts and to accept summary procedure.

6. Submission of Further Documents

    (a) If, following service of and agreement to the statement of facts and of documents relevant to summary procedure, the defendant seeks to submit further proofs of evidence, representations or other material for consideration at the summary hearing, he must do so not later than 21 days before the date fixed for the hearing.

    (b) If either before or at the summary hearing, it becomes apparent that the material submitted amounts to a denial of any significant fact in the statement of facts, the Chairman of the PCC or the panel shall refer the matter to a Disciplinary Tribunal.

7. Procedure

    (a) Procedure at summary hearings shall be informal, the details being at the discretion of the chairman of the panel.

    (b) Subject to the direction of the Chairman of the panel, the Bar Council shall keep the complainant informed of the progress of the complaint and of any further documents and other information to be considered by the panel; and shall so far as practicable, require the barrister and afford the complainant an opportunity to comment in advance of the hearing on any such information or documents.

    (c) Subject to sub-paragraph (e), the defendant shall be entitled to be represented by counsel of his choice, by a solicitor or by any other representative he may wish. The PCC should be represented by counsel (normally the sponsor member) only in particularly complex cases and subject to the prior agreement of the chairman of the panel in each case.

    (d) A summary hearing shall take place in public unless:

        (i)   the panel considers that there are special reasons why the hearing ought to be held in private; and

        (ii)   the defendant consents to the hearing taking place in private.

    (e) No witnesses may be called at a summary hearing without the prior consent of the chairman of the panel and without the submission of a proof of evidence.

    (f) Subject to sub-paragraph (e), the attendance of the defendant shall be required. Should he nevertheless fail to attend, the summary hearing may proceed in his absence, subject to the panel being satisfied that this course is appropriate, that all relevant procedures requiring the defendant's attendance have been complied with and that no acceptable explanation for the defendant's absence has been provided. Should the panel not be so satisfied, they shall have the power to adjourn the matter, to a specific date or sine die, or to refer the matter back to the PCC, as they may think fit.

    (g) If the defendant has stated in response to a request under paragraph 5(a)(iii) of these Rules that he does not wish to attend the hearing, then:

        (i)   the defendant shall not be required to attend and if he does not attend, shall not be entitled to be represented at the hearing: but

        (ii)   the panel shall require the defendant to attend an adjourned hearing (and sub- paragraphs (b) and (d) shall apply to the adjourned hearing) if the panel consider that a sentence of suspension may be appropriate.

(h) A record of each summary hearing shall be taken electronically and the tape retained under the arrangements of the Secretary of the PCC for two years, until the expiry of the period allowed for notification of intention to appeal or until the conclusion of any appeal, whichever period is longest.

8. Finding

At the conclusion of a summary hearing, the finding on each charge shall be set down in writing and signed by the chairman of the panel together with the reasons for that finding. If the members of the panel are not unanimous as to the finding on any charge, the finding to be recorded on that charge shall be of the majority. If the members of the panel are equally divided as to the finding on any charge, then, the burden of proof being on the complainant, the finding to be recorded on that charge shall be that which is most favourable to the defendant. The chairman of the panel shall then announce the panel's decisions as to finding.

9. Sentence

(a) If the panel shall have found any charge proved, the Secretary of the PCC shall lay before the panel details of any previous finding of professional misconduct, or of breach of proper professional standards or of inadequate professional service or any finding of guilt on a charge consisting of a legal aid complaint against the defendant. After hearing any representations or considering any written submissions by or on behalf of the defendant, the panel's decision as to sentence shall be set down in writing and signed by the chairman. If the members of the panel are not unanimous as to the sentence, the sentence to be recorded shall be of the majority. If the members of the panel are equally divided as to the sentence, the sentence to be recorded shall be that which is most favourable to the defendant. The chairman of the panel shall then announce the panel's decision as to sentence.

(b) A barrister against whom a charge of professional misconduct has been found proved may be sentenced by the summary hearing to be:

(i)   Suspended from practice for up to three months, either unconditionally or subject to conditions;

(ia) prohibited, either indefinitely or for a prescribed period and either unconditionally or subject to conditions, from accepting or carrying out public access instructions.

(ii) Ordered to pay a fine of up to £500 to the Bar Council;

(iii) Ordered to forego or repay all or part of his fees;

(iv) Ordered to complete continuing professional development of such nature and duration as the Tribunal shall direct and to provide satisfactory proof of compliance with this order to the PCC;

(v)   Reprimanded;

(vi) Advised as to his future conduct.

(c) A barrister against whom a charge of inadequate professional service has been found proved may be

(i)   directed to make a formal apology to the complainant for the conduct in relation to which the finding was made;

(ii) directed to repay or remit all or part of any fee rendered in respect of the inadequate service; or

(iii) directed to pay compensation to the complainant in such sum as the Tribunal shall direct not exceeding £5,000; or

(iv) directed to complete continuing professional development of such nature and duration as the Tribunal shall direct and to provide satisfactory proof of compliance with this requirement to the PCC; or

(v) prohibited, either indefinitely or for a prescribed period and either unconditionally or subject to conditions, from accepting or carrying out public access instructions.

In determining whether any sum is to be paid under paragraph (iii) hereof, or in fixing the amount of such sum, the summary hearing shall have regard in particular to any loss suffered by the applicant as a result of the inadequate professional service the availability to the complainant of other forms of redress, to the gravity of the conduct complained of and to the fee claimed by the barrister for the inadequate service.

(d) In any case where a charge of professional misconduct or inadequate professional service has been found proved, the summary hearing may decide that no action should be taken against the barrister.

(e) Under the powers conferred by Sections 41 and 42 of the Act of 1985, any summary hearing which hears a charge consisting of a legal aid complaint relating to the conduct of a barrister may if it thinks fit (and whether or not it sentences the barrister in accordance with paragraph 9(b) or (c) of these Rules in respect of any conduct arising out of the same legal aid complaint) order that any such fees as are referred to in Sections 41(2) of the Act of 1985 shall be reduced or cancelled.

(f) Where a summary hearing deals with a charge of professional misconduct against a barrister it may (in addition to or instead of sentencing that barrister in accordance with paragraph 9(b) of these Rules), if it determines that there is good reason for the exclusion arising out of:

(i) His conduct in connection with any such services as are maintained in Section 40(c) of the Act of 1985, or:

(ii) His professional conduct generally:

order that he shall be excluded from providing representation funded by the Legal Services Commission as part of the Community Legal Service or Criminal Defence Service for a period of up to six months.

(g) The sentence determined by a summary hearing if a charge of professional misconduct has been proved shall be recorded as follows:

(i) Suspension

'That . . . . be suspended from practice as a barrister and from enjoyment of all rights and privileges as a member of the Honourable Society of . . . and be prohibited from holding himself out as being a barrister without disclosing his suspension for (stating the length of the prescribed period)'.

(Note: If the panel decides that the sentence of suspension shall apply to part only of the barrister's practice or shall be subject to conditions, such part or such conditions (as the case may be) shall be specified in the wording of the sentence.)

(ia) Prohibition on Accepting or Carrying out Public Access Instructions

'That . . . be prohibited from accepting or carrying out any public access instructions (as defined in the Code of Conduct of the Bar of England and Wales)' (Note: If the Tribunal decides that the sentence shall apply for a prescribed period or shall be subject to conditions, such periods or such conditions or both (as the case may be) shall be specified in the wording of the sentence).

(ii)   Payment of Fine

'That . . . pay a fine of £ . . . to the Bar Council.'

(iii) Repayment or Foregoing of Fees

'That . . . shall repay all fees (fees amounting to £ . . .) received by him (shall forego all fees (fees amounting to £ . . .) due to be paid to him) in connection with . . .'

(iv)   Continuing Professional Development

'That . . . . . . shall by [date] complete a minimum of . . . hours of continuing professional development (in addition to the mandatory requirements set out in the Continuing Professional Development Regulations at Annex C to the Code of Conduct) [in the subject of . . .] and provide satisfactory proof of compliance with this order to the Professional Conduct and Complaints Committee of the Bar Council.'

(v)   Reprimand

'That . . . is hereby reprimanded' or 'That . . . is hereby ordered to attend on . . . to be reprimanded'.

(vi)   Advice as to Future Conduct

'That . . . has been advised by the panel as to his future conduct in regard to . . .' or 'That . . . is hereby ordered to attend on . . . to be given advice as to his future conduct in regard to . . .'.

(vii) Order for Reduction of Fees Payable by the Legal Services Commission

'That the fees otherwise payable by the Legal Services Commission in connection with Services provided by him as part of the Community Legal Service or Criminal Defence Service to . . . in relation to the items or matters specified in the first column of the Schedule hereto be reduced to the sum or sums specified in the second column of that Schedule.'

The record of the sentence shall then contain a Schedule setting out the matters referred to above.

(viii) Order for Cancellation of Fees Payable by the Legal Services Commission

'That the fees otherwise payable by the Legal Services Commission in connection with Services provided by him as part of the Community Legal Service or Criminal Defence Service to . . . in relation to the items or matters specified in the Schedule hereto be cancelled'.

The record of the sentence shall then contain a Schedule identifying the items or matters referred to above.

(ix)   Exclusion from Providing Representation Funded by the Legal Services Commission

'That . . . be excluded from providing representation funded by the Legal Services Commission as part of the Community Legal Service or Criminal Defence Service (as explained in Section 42(4)(b) of the Administration of Justice Act 1985 as substituted by Section 33 of the Legal Aid Act 1988 and amended by Schedule 4 to the Access to Justice Act 1999 (until . . .) (for a period of . . . beginning on . . .)'.

(x)   Absence of the Defendant

If the defendant has not been present throughout the proceedings, the sentence shall include the statement that the finding and sentence were made in the absence of the barrister in accordance with paragraph 7(d) of these Rules.

(xi) Suspension from the Register of European Lawyers

'That . . . be suspended from the register of European lawyers maintained by the Bar Council and be prohibited from holding himself out as registered with the Bar Council or an Inn of Court without disclosing his suspension for (state length of prescribed period).' (Note: If the Tribunal decides that the sentence of suspension shall apply to part only of the registered European lawyer's practice or shall be subject to conditions, such part or such conditions (as the case may be) shall be specified in the wording of the sentence.)

(h) Sentences under paragraphs 9(b)(i), (ii) and (iii), 9(d) and 9(e) shall not be put into effect until expiry of the period allowed for service of Notice of Appeal under Hearings before the Visitors Rules or until the conclusion of any appeal, whichever period is the longer.

(i) Sentences under paragraphs 9(b)(iv), (v) and (vi) may be put into effect at and by the summary hearing or by directing the defendant to attend on a person or persons to be nominated by the panel, as the panel may think fit. Any sentence of suspension may apply to the whole of the defendant's practice or to such part only as may be determined. The conditions to which a sentence of suspension may be made subject include a requirement that the barrister shall undergo such further pupillage or training or attain such standard of competence as the panel may determine.

(j) Whether or not the panel shall have found any charge proved, if it considers that the circumstances of the complaint are relevant to the barrister's capacity as a pupil- master, it may notify the barrister's Inn of its concerns in such manner as it sees fit.

(k) Whether or not the panel shall have found any charge proved, it may refer any matter of policy which arises to the relevant Committee of the Bar Council.

10. Costs

A summary hearing shall have no power to award costs.

11. Report of Finding and Sentence

(a) As soon as practicable after the conclusion of a summary hearing, the Secretary of the PCC shall confirm the finding and sentence to the defendant in writing.

(b) In cases where one or more charges of professional misconduct have been found proved and on expiry of the period allowed for service of Notice of Appeal under Hearings Before the Visitors Rules or on the conclusion of any appeal, whichever period is the longer, the Secretary of the PCC shall communicate the finding and sentence (as varied on appeal) and, where the latter includes orders under paragraphs 9(b)(i), (ia), (ii), (iii), 9(c) or 9(d), the date on which these were carried into effect, in writing to the following:

(i) The Lord Chancellor

(ii) The Lord Chief Justice

(iii) The Attorney General

(iv) The President of the Council of the Inns of Court

(v) The Chairman of the Bar Council

(vi) The Chairman of the PCC

(vii) The defendant

(viii) The Treasurers of the defendant's Inn of Call and of any other Inns of which he is a member.

Provided that the Lord Chancellor, the Lord Chief Justice, the Attorney General and the President shall be informed only when a charge constituting or arising out of a legal aid complaint has been found proved or the sentence includes an order of suspension or prohibition from accepting or carrying out any public access instructions for any period.

12. Appeals

(1)   In cases where one or more charges of professional misconduct have been proved, an Appeal may be lodged with the Visitors against finding and/or sentence (including any finding of inadequate professional service) in accordance with the Hearings Before the Visitors Rules in force. Notice of appeal must be accompanied by the sum of £250 payable to the Bar Council to defray expenses, a sum to be refunded in the discretion of the Visitors in the event of an appeal which is successful wholly or in part.

(2)   In cases where no professional misconduct has been proved, but one or more charges of inadequate professional service have been proved, an appeal shall lie at the instance of the barrister from any such finding, and against any decision as to the remedy to be granted to the complainant for such service in the same manner as an appeal lies from a decision of an Adjudication Panel in respect of the same matters.

13. Action by the Defendant's Inn

In a case where the sentence, where applicable as confirmed on appeal, includes an order under paragraph 9(b)(i) or (ia) and on expiry of the period allowed for service of Notice of Appeal under Hearings before the Visitors Rules or on the conclusion of any appeal, whichever period is the longer, the Secretary of the PCC shall invite the Treasurers of the defendant's Inn of Call and of any other Inns of which he is a member to pronounce the sentence of suspension as at paragraph 9(g)(i) or the sentence of prohibition as at paragraph 9(g)(ia) and to take such further action as may be required to carry it into effect. As seems to them fit, the Treasurer(s) will then pronounce the sentence and inform the Secretary of the PCC of the date on which it is to take effect.

14. Publication of Finding and Sentence

(a) The finding and sentence of a summary hearing on any charge or charges of professional misconduct shall be published.

(b) When publishing any finding and sentence in accordance with sub-paragraph (a) above, the Secretary of the PCC shall communicate the same in writing to those listed in paragraph 11(b) of these Rules, together with the following:

(i)   The Director of Public Prosecutions.

(ii)   The Treasurers of all four Inns for screening.

(iii)   The Leaders of the six circuits.

(iv)   One or more press agencies or other publications, as the Chairman of the PCC may direct.

(v)   In the case of a registered European lawyer, his home professional body.

(c) When the summary hearing has found that one or more charges of inadequate professional service have been proved, the charge and finding shall not be published unless the barrister charged so requests.

(d) When the Tribunal has found that any charge whether of professional misconduct or of inadequate professional service has not been proved the President shall not publish that charge and the finding unless the barrister charged so requests.

Commencement and Transitional Provisions

15.   (a) In relation to any summary hearing arising out of a complaint which had been referred to be Summary Procedure by the Professional Conduct Committee before 31 October 2004, these Rules shall not apply but the Summary Procedure Rules in force immediately before that date shall apply to that summary hearing save that paragraphs 5(a)(iii) and 7(e) of those rules shall apply only to cases referred to summary procedure on or after 17 July 1999.

(b) No finding of inadequate professional service may be made against a barrister in respect of any conduct of his which took place before 13 July 1996.

ANNEXE M

THE HEARINGS BEFORE THE VISITORS RULES 2002

We, the Judges of Her Majesty's High Court of Justice, in the exercise of our powers as Visitors to the Inns of Court, hereby make the following rules for the purpose of appeals to the Visitors from Disciplinary Tribunals of the Council of the Inns of Court and certain other appeals to the Visitors:

Citation and Commencement

1. These rules may be cited as the Hearings before the Visitors Rules 2002 and shall come into effect on 4 February 2002.

Interpretation

2. (1) The Interpretation Act 1978 shall apply in relation to the interpretation of these Rules as it applies for the interpretation of an Act of Parliament.

   (2) In these Rules, unless the context otherwise requires

   'answer' means the answer served pursuant to rule 11;

   'appellant' means an appellant from an order of a tribunal;

   'appellant student' means a student disciplined by or expelled from an Inn of Court, or a person refused admission to an Inn of Court as a student, who is appealing to the Visitors;

   'appellant legal practitioner' means a legal practitioner wishing to appeal to the Visitors from a decision, on review, by the JRC under Part IV of the Consolidated Regulations of the Inns of Court;

   'JRC' means the Joint Consolidated Regulations and Transfer Committee of the Inns' Council and the Bar Council;

   'Bar Council' means The General Council of the Bar;

   'defendant' means the barrister against whom an order of a tribunal was made;

   'Directions Judge' means a Judge nominated pursuant to rule 5;

   'directions function' means any of the functions and powers conferred on a Directions Judge by rule 5;

   'the Inns' Council' means the Council of the Inns of Court;

   'lay representative' means one of the lay persons appointed by the Bar Council to serve on Disciplinary Tribunals;

   'petition' means the petition of appeal served pursuant to rule 7;

   'the tribunal' means a Disciplinary Tribunal of the Council of the Inns of Court and includes a panel appointed to hear a summary case under the Summary Procedure Rules to be found at Annex L to the Code of Conduct of the Bar of England and Wales; and

   'the Visitors' means the panel nominated to hear the appeal pursuant to rule 10 or, in the case of an appeal within rule 10(4) or (5), the single judge nominated to hear the appeal.

Service of Documents

3. (1)   Where pursuant to these Rules any document is to be served on any of the persons specified in the first column of the table in the Schedule to these Rules, that document shall be served on that person by sending it to the person specified and the address specified in the second column of that table against the person to be served.

(2)   Such documents shall be served

(a) by recorded delivery post,

(b) by hand delivery, if a written confirmation of receipt is obtained, or

(c) by facsimile transmission, if a return facsimile confirming receipt is obtained.

Notice of Appeal

4. (1)   Written notice of intention to appeal against the finding or sentence of the tribunal must be served by the appellant on the persons specified in paragraph (2) below within the period of 21 days beginning with the date on which the order of the tribunal was made or within such further time as may be allowed by the Lord Chief Justice or the Directions Judge.

(2)   The persons to be served are

(a) the Lord Chief Justice;

(b) the Chairman of the Bar Council (unless the Bar Council is the appellant);

(c) the President of the Inns' Council;

(d) the Treasurer of the Inn of which the appellant or defendant (as the case may be) is a member; and

(e) if the Bar Council is the appellant, the defendant.

(3)   The notice of intention to appeal shall specify the Inn of which the appellant or defendant (as the case may be) is a member.

(4)   When serving a notice of intention to appeal, an appellant other than the Bar Council shall also give notice of an address at which service is to be made on the appellant.

Directions Judge

5. (1)   Upon service on him of a notice of appeal under rule 4 above (whether or not served in time) the Lord Chief Justice shall nominate a single judge of the High Court or the Court of Appeal ('the Directions Judge') who is not a Bencher of the appellant's or defendant's (as the case may be) Inn to exercise the powers and functions conferred by this rule.

(2)   The Directions Judge may hold a hearing in order to determine how (if at all) he should exercise the directions functions.

(3)   The Directions Judge shall consider the course of any appeal in relation to which he is appointed and may at any time give such directions and take such steps as appear to him to be necessary or desirable for the purpose of securing the just, expeditious and economical disposal of the appeal.

(4)   The directions that may be given and the steps that may be taken by the Directions Judge may relate to (but shall not be limited to) the following matters

(a) the anticipated duration of the hearing;

(b) the variation of any timetable specified in these Rules;

(c) further procedural steps that should be taken before the hearing;

(d) the failure by either party to comply with any timetable specified in these Rules or directed by him; and

(e) the adjournment of the hearing.

(5) The Directions Judge may, on application made by the appellant (which must be served on the Bar Council at the time of making the application) and after giving the Bar Council the opportunity to respond to the application, vary or set aside an order made against the appellant under regulation 27(2) or (3) of the Disciplinary Tribunal Rules on such terms and subject to such conditions (if any) as he considers appropriate.

(6) If, at any time, the Directions Judge concludes that a party has failed to comply with any obligation imposed by, or timetable specified in, these Rules or directed by him in exercise of his directions functions (as the case may be), he may also

(a) make a final order for compliance by the party in default;

(b) direct that that party may not serve a petition or answer;

(c) dismiss or strike out the petition or answer of that party;

(d) order that any further step that appears to him to be necessary or desirable in order to provide for a fair and expeditious hearing of the matter be undertaken within a specified period;

(e) direct an expedited hearing where the party in default has been prohibited from serving an answer or the answer has been struck out.

(7) If, on an application made by the appellant, the Directions Judge concludes that payment of the sum required by the Disciplinary Tribunal Rules or by the Summary Procedure Rules to defray the expenses of the appeal would cause undue hardship to the appellant, the Directions Judge shall direct that such sum shall not be payable and that the petition of appeal may be served notwithstanding rule 7(5) below, and may grant any extension of time necessary for serving the petition of appeal.

No appeal from Directions Judge

6. There shall be no appeal against an order of the Directions Judge.

Service of Petition

7. (1) A written petition of appeal containing the information required by rule 8 below must be served by the appellant on the persons specified in paragraph (2) below within the period of 42 days beginning with the date on which the order of the tribunal was made or within such further time as may be allowed by the Lord Chief Justice or the Directions Judge.

(2) The persons to be served are

(a) the Lord Chief Justice;

(b) the Chairman of the Bar Council (unless the Bar Council is the appellant);

(c) the President of the Inns' Council;

(d) the Treasurer of the Inn of which the appellant or defendant (as the case may be) is a member; and

(e) if the Bar Council is the appellant, the defendant.

(3) If an application for an extension of the period of 42 days specified in paragraph (1) above is made to the Lord Chief Justice or the Directions Judge before the expiry of that period, the Lord Chief Justice or the Directions Judge may, if he sees fit, extend the period within which the petition must be served.

(4)   Where no petition is served within the period specified in paragraph (1) above or (where that period has been extended pursuant to paragraph (3)) the extended period, no further action may be taken in relation to the appeal unless the Lord Chief Justice directs otherwise.

(5)   A petition of appeal may not be served, subject to any direction of the Directions Judge to the contrary under rule 5(7) above, unless any sum payable under the Disciplinary Tribunals Regulations or under the Summary Procedure Rules to defray the expenses of the appeal has been paid to the Bar Council.

Petition of Appeal

8. (1)   The petition shall state whether the appeal is against the findings or sentence of the tribunal, or both.

   (2)   The petition shall contain the following particulars
   - (a) the charges;
   - (b) a summary of the facts on which the charges were based;
   - (c) the findings of the tribunal;
   - (d) the sentence;
   - (e) any finding against which the appellant appeals (if any);
   - (f) the grounds for appeal, including for each matter appealed against the specific evidence on which the appellant will place reliance;
   - (g) the relief sought.
   - (h) if the hearing is estimated to last longer than one day, an estimate of the time required for the hearing.

   (3)   In the case of an appeal against sentence the petition may also refer to
   - (a) any factors which it is contended make the sentence unduly severe (or lenient) in relation to the appellant's (or the defendant's) record; and
   - (b) to sentences in other similar cases.

Service of other documents

9. (1)   Subject to paragraph (2) below, the appellant shall, at the same time as serving the petition, serve on the Lord Chief Justice the number of copies specified in paragraph (4) below of the transcript of the proceedings before the tribunal whose decision is being appealed or, where the tribunal in question was a panel appointed to hear a summary matter, the statement of findings and sentence of the tribunal.

   (2)   If any transcript to be served pursuant to paragraph (1) above is not available when the petition is served, the copies of that transcript shall be served on the Lord Chief Justice as soon as practicable thereafter.

   (3)   Not less than 14 days before the date set for the hearing of an appeal
   - (a) a copy of every document intended to be produced at the hearing by any party shall be served by that party on every other party; and
   - (b) the number of copies of any such document specified in paragraph (4) below shall be served on the Lord Chief Justice.

   (4)   The number of copies required to be served on the Lord Chief Justice is
   - (a) if the appeal is of a type falling within rule 10(2) below, five copies; and
   - (b) in any other case, three copies.

Appointment of panel to hear appeal

10. (1)   When a petition is served upon him (whether or not served in time), the Lord Chief Justice shall nominate the persons who are to hear the appeal.

(2)   An appeal against an order for disbarment or a decision of a tribunal presided over by a Judge of the High Court shall be heard by a panel comprised of

    (a) three judges of the High Court or the Court of Appeal (one of whom may be a retired judge of the High Court or Court of Appeal, provided that he has not attained the age of 75 on the date set for the hearing of the appeal);

    (b) a Queen's Counsel; and

    (c) a lay representative.

(3)   Subject to paragraph (4) below, an appeal that is not of a type mentioned in paragraph (2) and is an appeal against a decision of a Disciplinary Tribunal shall be heard by panel comprised of

    (a) a Judge of the High Court or the Court of Appeal;

    (b) a barrister; and

    (c) a lay representative.

(4)   An appeal that is not of a type mentioned in paragraph (2) and that is an appeal against a decision of a Disciplinary Tribunal may be heard by a Judge of the High Court or of the Court of Appeal sitting alone, if the Lord Chief Justice or the Directions Judge directs that the appeal relates solely to a point of law and is appropriate to be heard by a judge sitting alone.

(5)   Any other appeal shall be heard by a Judge of the High Court or the Court of Appeal.

(6)   No judge or barrister member of the panel shall be a Bencher of the appellant's or defendant's (as the case may be) Inn.

Answer

11. (1)   The Bar Council or, if the Bar Council is the appellant, the defendant may (or, if so directed by the Directions Judge, shall) serve on the Lord Chief Justice an answer to the petition within the period of 28 days starting with the date on which the petition is served or such further time as may be allowed by the Directions Judge.

(2)   Where an answer is served pursuant to paragraph (1) the person serving it shall also serve forthwith a copy of that answer on the appellant.

(3)   The answer shall follow the form of the petition and shall state which points in the petition are accepted and which are rejected.

(4)   The Bar Council may, in any answer it serves, refer to any factors which it is contended make the sentence unduly lenient in relation to the appellant's record or to sentences in other cases.

(5)   If, in the view of the person serving an answer, the hearing is likely to last longer than one day, the answer shall include an estimation of the time required for the hearing and the reasons for that estimation.

Date of Hearing

12. (1)   Unless it has been indicated either in the petition or answer that the time required for the hearing is likely to exceed one day, the time allocated for the hearing of an appeal shall be one day.

(2)   The appeal shall be listed by the clerk to the Visitors for a hearing on the first available date after the expiry of a period of four weeks beginning with the date of service on the Lord Chief Justice of the answer (or, where no answer is served, beginning with the last date for service of the answer under rule 11 above).

(3)   A notice of the hearing of the appeal shall be served on the Bar Council and on the appellant or defendant (as the case may be) at least 14 days before the date fixed for hearing of the appeal.

Procedure at hearing

13. (1)   Subject to the following paragraphs of this Rule, the Visitors may give any directions with regard to the conduct of, and procedure at, a hearing of an appeal they consider appropriate.

(2)   The Visitors may give such directions before or during the hearing.

(3)   The hearing shall be held in public unless either party has made an application that the hearing shall not be in public and the public interest does not require that it shall be held in public.

(4)   A hearing may proceed in the absence of an appellant (or defendant), but not in the absence of a representative of the Bar Council.

(5)   No witness may be called at the hearing without the consent of the Visitors.

(6)   Evidence that was not before the tribunal whose decision is being appealed may be given at the hearing only in exceptional circumstances and with the consent of the Visitors.

(7)   An appellant or defendant (as the case may be) may only challenge before the Visitors a decision of a court of law on which the tribunal's decision was based in exceptional circumstances and with the consent of the Visitors.

(8)   The proceedings of the Visitors shall continue to be valid notwithstanding that one or more of the members of the panel becomes unable to continue or is or becomes disqualified from continuing to act, if the remaining members of the panel include a judge (other than a retired judge) and a lay representative.

(9)   A full shorthand record shall be made of the hearing.

(10)   A transcription of the shorthand record shall be provided upon request to either party to the hearing but at his own expense.

Findings of the Visitors

14. (1)   The findings of the Visitors shall be pronounced in a single decision.

(2)   The findings may be pronounced in public or in private but should normally be pronounced in public unless a party to the hearing requests otherwise and the public interest does not require that the findings be pronounced in public.

(3)   The Visitors may
   (a) allow an appeal in whole or in part;
   (b) confirm or vary an order of the tribunal whose decision is being appealed;
   (c) order a re-hearing on such terms as they may deem appropriate in the circumstances.

(4)   The Visitors shall give reasons for their decision.

(5)   The Visitors may order, in the event of an appeal which is successful wholly or in part, a refund to the appellant of any sum paid to the General Council of the Bar in accordance with the Disciplinary Tribunal Regulations of the Inns' Council.

Barrister's Exclusion from providing representation funded by the Legal Services Commission as part of the Community Legal Service or Criminal Defence Service

15. (1)   These Rules shall apply in relation to an appeal against an order of the tribunal that a barrister's exclusion from providing representation funded by the Legal Services Commission as part of the Community Legal Service or Criminal Defence Service pursuant to section 42(3) of the Administration of Justice Act 1985 (as substituted by Section 33 of the Legal Aid Act 1988 and amended by section 24, Schedule 4, paragraphs 32 and 35 of the Access to Justice Act 1999) is not to be terminated, subject to the following modifications set out in the following paragraphs of this rule.

(2)   The petition shall contain the following particulars

(a) the date of the order of the tribunal that excluded the appellant from providing representation funded by the Legal Services Commission as part of the Community Legal Service or Criminal Defence Service;

(b) the charges in respect of which that order was made;

(c) a summary of the facts on which those charges were based;

(d) the findings of the tribunal;

(e) the findings against which the appeal is brought; and

(f) the grounds for appeal.

(3)   An order of the tribunal to terminate a barrister's exclusion from providing representation funded by the Legal Services Commission as part of the Community Legal Service or Criminal Defence Service only from a date that is subsequent to that order shall, for the purposes of any appeal, be treated as an order that the barrister's exclusion from such work is not to be terminated.

Appeals by an appellant student against a decision of an Inn

16. (1)   These Rules shall apply in relation to an appeal by an appellant student against a decision of an Inn subject to the modifications set out in the following paragraphs of this rule.

(2)   In rules 4 and 7 references to the order, finding or sentence of the tribunal shall be construed as references to the decision of the Inn.

(3)   Any documents required by rules 4 or 7 to be served shall, in place of the persons specified in those rules, be served on

(a) the Lord Chief Justice;

(b) the Chairman of the Bar Council;

(c) the President of the Inns' Council;

(d) and the Treasurer of the Inn of which the appellant student is a member or the Treasurer of the Inn that has refused to admit the appellant student.

(4)   There shall be substituted for rule 8

'8. The petition shall contain the following particulars:

(a)   the decision of the Inn against which the appeal is brought;

(b)   a summary of the facts giving rise to the decision of the Inn;

(c)   the grounds for appeal; and

(d)   the relief sought.'

(5) Paragraphs (1) and (2) of rule 9 shall not apply.

(6) The appellant student shall serve on the Lord Chief Justice, with the petition, copies of all relevant documents including any complaint in respect of the appellant and the decision of the Inn.

(7) In paragraph (3) of rule 9, for the persons specified as the persons to be served there shall be substituted the persons specified in paragraph (3) of this rule.

(8) In paragraph (1) of rule 11 and paragraph (4) of rule 13 references to the Bar Council shall be construed as references to the Inn in question.

(9) There shall be substituted for paragraph (4) of rule 11

'(4) The Inn may, in any answer it serves, refer to any factors that it took into account when making its decision, including the appellant student's record and the Inn's practice in similar cases.'

(10) Paragraphs (3) and (5) of rule 14 shall not apply.

(11) The panel appointed to hear the appeal may

(a) allow an appeal in whole or in part;

(b) confirm or vary the decision of the Inn; or

(c) order the Inn to reconsider its decision on such terms as the Visitors may determine to be appropriate in the circumstances.

(12) Rules 15 and 18 shall not apply.

Appeals not permitted under these Rules

17. (1) No appeal shall lie under these Rules from a decision of an educational institution (other than an Inn) or any officer or committee of such an institution in respect of any matter relating to a course recognised by the Bar Council as satisfying

(a) the requirements of the Academic Stage of Training for the Bar (including Common Professional Examination requirements),

(b) the Vocational Stage of Training for the Bar, or

(c) the Stage of Continuing Education and Training at the Bar,

or any examination or assessment in connection with any such course.

(2) An appeal from a decision of a type mentioned in paragraph (1) above shall be made through the appropriate appeal procedures of the institution concerned.

Appeals by an appellant legal practitioner

18. (1) In an appeal by an appellant legal practitioner, these Rules shall apply subject to the modifications set out in the following paragraphs of this rule.

(2) In rules 4 and 7 any reference to the order, finding or sentence of the tribunal shall be construed as a reference to the decision, on review, of the JRC.

(3) Any documents required by rules 4 and 7 to be served shall, in place of the persons specified in those rules, be served on

(a) the JRC;

(b) the Lord Chief Justice;

(c) the Chairman of the Bar Council; and

(d) the President of the Inns' Council.

(4) There shall be substituted for rule 8

'8. The petition shall contain the following particulars

(a) the decision, on review, of the JRC against which the appeal is being made;

(b) a summary of the facts giving rise to that decision;

(c) the grounds for appeal; and

(d) the relief sought.'

(5)   Paragraphs (1) and (2) of rule 9 shall not apply but the appellant legal practitioner shall serve on the Lord Chief Justice with the petition copies of any relevant documents, which shall include the decision of the JRC against which the appeal is brought.

(6)   In paragraph (3) of rule 9, for the persons specified as the persons to be served there shall be substituted the persons specified in paragraph (1) of this rule.

(7)   In paragraph (1) of rule 11 and paragraph (4) of rule 13 the references to the Bar Council shall be construed as references to the JRC.

(8)   There shall be substituted for paragraph (4) of rule 11

'(4)   The JRC may, in any answer it serves, refer to any factors that it took into account when making its decision, including the appellant legal practitioner's record and the JRC's practice in similar cases.'

(9)   Paragraphs (3) and (5) of rule 14 shall not apply.

(10)   The panel appointed to hear the appeal may

(a) allow an appeal in whole or in part;

(b) confirm or vary the decision of the JRC; or

(c) order the JRC to reconsider its decision on such terms as the panel appointed to hear the appeal may determine to be appropriate in the circumstances.

(11)   Rules 15 and 16 shall not apply.

Costs

19. (1)   The Visitors may make such order for costs of the appeal as they consider appropriate.

(2)   Any order for costs made may include an order for payment of the cost of any transcript required for the purposes of the appeal.

Transition

20. (1)   Subject to paragraph (2) below, where any appeal has been commenced before 4th February 2002 but has not been completed by that date, these Rules shall apply to that appeal from that date but any steps that have been taken in relation to that appeal pursuant to any provision of the Hearings Before the Visitors Rules 2000 shall be regarded as having been taken pursuant to the equivalent provision of these Rules.

(2)   In relation to appeals brought by students registered at the Inns of Court School of Law before 1 September 1997, the procedure provided by Rule 13 of the Hearings before the Visitors Rules 1991 shall continue to apply in place of that provided by these Rules.

Revocation

22. The Hearings before the Visitors Rules 2000 are hereby revoked.

On behalf of the Judges of Her Majesty's
High Court of Justice

Lord Chancellor
Lord Chief Justice
President
Vice-Chancellor

SCHEDULE Rule 3(1)

ADDRESSEE AND PLACE FOR SERVICE OF DOCUMENTS

Person to be served	Addressee and place of service
The Lord Chief Justice.	Addressed to the Clerk to the Visitors at the Royal Courts of Justice, Strand, London WC2A 2LL.
The President of the Inns' Council.	Addressed to the Secretary to the Council of the Inns of Court at Treasury Office, 8 South Square, Gray's Inn, London WCIR 5EU.
The Chairman of the Bar Council.	Addressed to the Chief Executive of the General Council of the Bar at 289–293 High Holborn, London WCIV 7 HZ.
The JRC.	Addressed to the Chief Executive of the General Council of the Bar at 289–293 High Holborn, London WCIV 7 HZ.
The Treasurer of an Inn.	Addressed to the Sub-Treasurer or Under-Treasurer (as the case may be) of that Inn at the treasury office of that Inn.
An appellant, appellant student or appellant legal practitioner.	Addressed to him at the address specified by him pursuant to rule 6(3).
A defendant.	Addressed to him at— (a) the address notified by him pursuant to Paragraphs 304(a)(i) or 402(a) of the Code of Conduct of the Bar of England and Wales (or any provisions amending or replacing those paragraphs); (b) if he has specified in writing an address to which documents may be sent, that address; or (c) where no address has been notified pursuant to the provisions mentioned in paragraph (a) above or specified as mentioned in paragraph (b) above, to his last known address.

ANNEXE N

INTERIM SUSPENSION RULES

Introduction

1.   These Rules are supplemental to:

(a) the Complaints Rules;

(b) the Disciplinary Tribunals Regulations; and

(c) the Summary Procedure Rules;

as approved from time to time and annexed to the Code of Conduct of the Bar of England and Wales.

Definitions

2.   In these Rules:

(a) 'the Commissioner' means the Complaints Commissioner;

(b) 'Suspension Panel' means a Suspension Panel as provided for in rule 3 of these Rules;

(c) 'Appeal Panel' means an Appeal Panel as provided for in rule 4 of these Rules;

(d) 'Lay Representative' means a lay person appointed by the Bar Council to serve on Disciplinary Tribunals;

(e) 'the Defendant' means the barrister who is the subject of a referral to a Suspension Panel pursuant to the procedure prescribed by these Rules.

Composition of Panels

3.   A Suspension Panel shall consist of five members nominated by the Chairman of the PCC being:

(a) the Chairman of the PCC or, if unable to attend, a Vice-Chairman of the PCC, who shall be Chairman of the Panel;

(b) three other barristers of at least ten years Call one of whom shall be a Queen's Counsel and who are current members of the PCC or the PSC;

(c) a Lay Representative

Provided that:

(1) no barrister (save for the Chairman or a Vice Chairman of the PCC) or Lay Representative shall be nominated to serve on a Panel which is to consider any matter which has been considered at any meeting of the PCC which he attended; and

(2) the proceedings of a Suspension Panel shall be valid notwithstanding that one or more of the members other than the Chairman or Lay Representative becomes unable to continue to act or disqualified from continuing to act, so long as the number of members present throughout the substantive hearing is not reduced below three and continues to include the Chairman and the Lay Representative.

4.   An Appeal Panel shall consist of:

(a) The Chairman of the Bar or, if unable to attend, the Vice-Chairman, who shall be Chairman of the Panel;

(b) a representative nominated by the Treasurer of the Defendant's Inn;

(c) a Lay Representative

Provided that no individual shall sit on both the Suspension Panel and the Appeal Panel considering the same matter.

Referral to a Suspension Panel

5. Upon the Bar Council receiving notification from a barrister that he has been convicted of or charged with a Serious Criminal Offence, the Commissioner and/or the PCC shall consider whether to refer the matter to a Suspension Panel.

6. Either the Commissioner or the PCC may refer a matter to a Suspension Panel if:

(a) the matter has been referred to the Commissioner or the PCC under rule 5 above; or

(b) a complaint has been referred to the Commissioner or the PCC during the investigation of which it is disclosed that a barrister has been convicted of or charged with a Serious Criminal Offence; or

(c) in any other circumstances it is disclosed to the Commissioner or the PCC that a barrister has been convicted of or charged with a Serious Criminal Offence.

No matter shall be referred to a Suspension Panel unless the Commissioner or the PCC considers that the conviction(s) or criminal charge(s) (if such charge(s) were subsequently to lead to conviction(s)) would warrant a charge of professional misconduct and referral to a Disciplinary Tribunal.

7. As soon as practicable after the decision has been made to refer a matter to a Suspension Panel, the Secretary of the PCC shall write to the Defendant notifying him of the decision, together with a copy of these Rules, giving brief details of the conviction(s) or criminal charge(s) that have caused the referral to the Panel. The letter of notification:

(a) shall lay down a fixed time and date (normally not less than fourteen and not more than twenty-one days from the date of the letter) for the hearing to take place. One alternative shall be given;

(b) shall invite the Defendant to accept one or other of the dates proposed or to provide a written representation to the Chairman of the PCC, objecting to both dates with reasons and providing two further alternative dates not more than twenty-one days from the date of the letter of notification. Any such representation must be received by the Chairman of the PCC not more than fourteen days from the date of the letter of notification. The Chairman of the PCC shall consider any such representation and either confirm one of the original dates or re-fix the hearing. If no such representation is received within fourteen days of the date of the letter of notification the hearing shall take place at the time and date first fixed pursuant to rule 7(a) above. The Chairman's decision, which shall be notified in writing to the Defendant by the Secretary of the PCC, shall be final. Once fixed, a hearing date shall be vacated only in exceptional circumstances and with the agreement of the Chairman of the PCC;

(c) shall inform the Defendant that he may by letter to the Chairman of the PCC undertake immediately either (i) to be suspended from practice or (ii) not to accept or carry out any public access instructions pending the disposal of any charges of professional misconduct by a Disciplinary Tribunal based on the conviction(s) or criminal charge(s) that have caused the referral to the Panel;

      (d) shall inform the Defendant that he is entitled to make representations in writing or orally, by himself or by another member of the Bar on his behalf:

          (1) where a conviction or convictions have caused the referral to the Panel, as to whether a period of interim suspension or an interim prohibition from accepting or carrying out any public access instructions should be imposed; or

          (2) where a criminal charge or charges have caused the referral to the Panel, as to whether and if so in what terms any notification should be given to professional clients and lay clients and the conditions subject to which the Defendant should be permitted to continue to practice;

      pending the disposal of any charges of professional misconduct by a Disciplinary Tribunal;

      (e) shall inform the Defendant that he is entitled to request an expedited hearing of any charges of professional misconduct by a Disciplinary Tribunal.

8.   If a Defendant sends a letter in accordance with rule 7(c) above which is satisfactory to the Chairman of the PCC the Chairman shall accept the undertaking contained in the letter in lieu of imposing a period of interim suspension or an interim prohibition from accepting or carrying out any public access instructions and so inform the Defendant in writing, whereupon the Defendant shall (as the case may be) either:

      (i) immediately be suspended from practice, or

      (ii) immediately be prohibited from accepting or carrying out any public access instructions,

    until after the disposal by a Disciplinary Tribunal of any charges of professional misconduct based on the conviction(s) or criminal charges(s) that have caused the referral to the Panel.

Powers of Suspension Panels

9.   If, prior to the date fixed for a hearing under rules 7(a) or (b) above, a Defendant shall not have produced a letter in accordance with rule 7(c) above satisfactory to the Chairman of the PCC, a Suspension Panel nominated in accordance with rule 3 above shall, at the time and place notified to the Defendant in accordance with rules 7(a) or (b) above, consider:

      (a) where a conviction or convictions have caused the referral to the Panel, whether a period of interim suspension or an interim prohibition from accepting or carrying out any public access instructions should be imposed on the Defendant;

      (b) where a criminal charge or charges have caused the referral to the Panel, whether the Defendant should be directed to notify his professional clients and lay clients of the criminal offence(s) with which he has been charged before undertaking any work or (as the case may be) further work for any such client.

10.   At any hearing of a Suspension Panel the proceedings shall be governed by the rules of natural justice, subject to which:

      (a) the procedure shall be informal, the details being at the discretion of the Chairman of the Panel;

(b) the Defendant shall be entitled to make representations in writing or orally, by himself or by another member of the Bar or a solicitor on his behalf, as to;

(1) where a conviction or convictions have caused the referral to the Panel, why a period of interim suspension or an interim prohibition from accepting or carrying out any public access instructions should not be imposed; or

(2) where a criminal charge or charges have caused the referral to the Panel, why the Panel should not direct that the Defendant should notify his professional clients and lay clients of the criminal offence(s) with which he has been charged before undertaking any work or (as the case may be) further work for any such client;

pending the disposal of any charges of professional misconduct by a Disciplinary Tribunal;

(c) no witnesses may be called without the prior consent of the Chairman of the Panel and without the submission of a proof of evidence;

(d) the attendance of the Defendant shall be required. Should he nevertheless fail to attend, the hearing may proceed in his absence, subject to the Panel being satisfied that this course is appropriate, that all relevant procedures requiring the Defendant's attendance have been complied with and that no acceptable explanation for the Defendant's absence has been provided. Should the Panel not be so satisfied, it shall have the power to adjourn the hearing;

(e) the hearing shall not be in public unless so requested by the Defendant and a record shall be taken electronically. The tape of the hearing shall be retained under the arrangements of the Secretary of the PCC for two years or until any charges of professional misconduct against the Defendant based on the convictions or criminal charges which caused the referral to the Panel have been finally disposed of by a Disciplinary Tribunal and any appeal procedure has been exhausted whichever period is the longer;

(f) if it decides an adjournment is necessary for any reason, the Panel may adjourn the hearing for such period and to such time and place, and upon such terms, as it may think fit.

11. If the members of a Suspension Panel are not unanimous as to any decision the decision made shall be that of the majority of them. If the members of the Panel are equally divided the decision shall be that which is the most favourable to the Defendant.

12. Where a conviction or convictions have caused the referral to a Suspension Panel, at the conclusion of the hearing the Panel:

(a) may decide not to impose any period of interim suspension or interim prohibition from accepting or carrying out any public access instructions;

(b) may impose a period of interim suspension or interim prohibition from accepting or carrying out any public access instructions (either unconditionally or subject to conditions) of up to six months pending the hearing before a Disciplinary Tribunal, provided that:

(i) no period of interim suspension should be imposed unless the Panel considers that it is likely that a Disciplinary Tribunal would impose a sentence of disbarment or suspension for more than twelve months for a charge or charges of professional misconduct based on the conviction or convictions that have caused the referral to the Panel and it considers that it is in the public interest that the Defendant should be suspended pending the hearing before a Disciplinary Tribunal; and

(ii) no period of interim prohibition from accepting or carrying out any public access instructions should be imposed unless the Panel considers that it is likely that a Disciplinary Tribunal would impose a sentence of disbarment or suspension for more than twelve months or prohibition from accepting or carrying out any public access instructions for a charge or charges of professional misconduct based on the conviction or convictions that have caused the referral to the Panel and it considers that it is in the public interest that the Defendant should be prohibited from accepting or carrying out any public access instructions pending the hearing before a Disciplinary Tribunal.

(c) in lieu of imposing a period of suspension or prohibition from accepting or carrying out any public access instructions may accept from the Defendant an undertaking in writing in terms satisfactory to the Panel (and subject to such conditions and for such period as the Panel may agree) either:

(i) immediately to be suspended from practice; or

(ii) not to accept or carry out any public access instructions

pending the disposal of any charges of professional misconduct by a Disciplinary Tribunal based on the conviction or convictions that have caused the referral to the Panel;

(d) shall set down in writing signed by the Chairman of the Panel the decision of the Panel and the terms of any period of interim suspension or prohibition imposed under rule 12(b) above or undertaking accepted under rule 12(c) above.

(i) The imposition of any period of suspension shall be recorded as follows:

'That...........be suspended from practice as a barrister and from enjoyment of all rights and privileges as a member of the Honourable Society of......and be prohibited from holding himself out as being a barrister without disclosing his interim suspension for a period expiring on the day of....................or such earlier date as a Disciplinary Tribunal shall have disposed of any charges based on the conviction or convictions that have caused the interim suspension or such Disciplinary Tribunal may otherwise direct.' (Note: If the Panel decides that the suspension should apply to part only of the Defendant's practice or shall be subject to conditions, such part or such conditions (as the case may be) shall be recorded.)

(ii) The imposition of any period of prohibition from accepting or carrying out any public access instructions shall be recorded as follows:

'That....be prohibited from accepting or carrying out any public access instructions (as defined in the Code of Conduct of the Bar Of England and Wales) for a period expiring on the day of..................or such earlier date as a Disciplinary Tribunal shall have disposed of any charges based on the conviction or convictions that have caused this interim prohibition or such Disciplinary Tribunal may otherwise direct.' (Note: If the Panel decides that the sentence shall be subject to conditions, such conditions shall be specified in the wording of the sentence.)

(e) shall, if a period of interim suspension or interim prohibition is imposed under rule 12(b) above or a written undertaking is accepted under rule 12(c) above:

   (1) fix a time and date within the period of suspension or prohibition imposed, alternatively inform the Defendant that such a time and date will be fixed by the Secretary of the PCC and notified to the Defendant not less than fourteen days prior to such date, when, unless a Disciplinary Tribunal shall in the meantime have disposed of any charges of professional misconduct based on the conviction or convictions that have caused the referral to the Panel, a Panel shall be convened for the purpose of reviewing the matter;

   (2) inform the Defendant of his right to request a Panel to review the matter prior to the date fixed in (1) above as provided in rule 14 below;

   (3) inform the Defendant of his right of appeal as provided in rule 16 below;

   (4) inform the Defendant that he is entitled to request an expedited hearing of any charges of professional misconduct by a Disciplinary Tribunal and, if so requested, the Chairman of the Panel may so direct;

(f) may, if it has not already been referred to a Disciplinary Tribunal, refer the matter to a disciplinary Tribunal.

13. Where a criminal charge or charges have caused the referral to a Suspension Panel, at the conclusion of the hearing the Panel:

(a) may decide to make no direction as to the conduct of the Defendant's practice;

(b) may decide to direct the Defendant to notify his professional clients and lay clients of the criminal offence(s) with which he has been charged, in which case the Panel shall set out the terms of the written notification to be given (for such period as the Panel may think fit) to such clients and may include such comments as the Defendant may wish to make and the Panel may approve concerning the criminal charge(s). In addition to directing the notification of professional clients and lay clients, the Panel may direct that the conduct of Defendant's practice shall be subject to such conditions as the Panel may think fit;

(c) in lieu of making any direction under rule 13(b) above the Panel may accept one or more undertakings in writing in such terms and upon such conditions as the Panel may think fit as to the form of written notification to be given to any professional client or lay client and as to the conduct of the Defendant's practice;

(d) shall set down in writing signed by the Chairman of the Panel the terms of any direction or undertaking accepted under rules 13(b) or (c) above together with a copy or copies of the letter or letters approved as the form of notification to professional clients and lay clients;

(e) shall, if any direction is given or undertaking accepted under rules 12(a) or (b) above limited to any specified period:

   (1) fix a time and date within that period, alternatively inform the Defendant that such a time and date will be fixed by the Secretary of the PCC and notified to the Defendant not less than fourteen days prior to the expiration of such period when, unless a Disciplinary Tribunal shall in the meantime have disposed of any charges of professional misconduct based

on the criminal charge or charges that have caused the referral to the Panel, a Panel shall be convened for the purpose of reviewing the matter;

(2) inform the Defendant of his right to request a Panel to review the matter prior to the date fixed in (1) above as provided in rule 14 below;

(3) inform the Defendant of his right of appeal as provided in rule 16 below;

(4) inform the Defendant that he is entitled to request an expedited hearing of any charges of professional misconduct by a Disciplinary Tribunal and, if so requested, the Chairman of the Panel may so direct;

(f) may, if not already referred to a Disciplinary Tribunal, refer the matter to a Disciplinary Tribunal.

14. In the event of a significant change in circumstances or other good reason the Defendant may at any time while suspended pursuant to a decision of a Suspension Panel or an undertaking under rules 13(b) or (c) above or subject to a direction or undertaking under rules 12(b) or (c) make a request in writing to the Chairman of the PCC for a Panel to be convened to review the matter. The letter must set out the details of any alleged change in circumstances or good reason. On receipt of such a letter the Chairman may in his discretion convene a Panel or refuse the request. In either case the Secretary of the PCC shall notify the Defendant in writing of the Chairman's decision. The Chairman shall not be obliged to give reasons and his decision shall be final. If the Chairman decides to convene a Panel the procedure to be followed for fixing the time and date of the hearing shall be as set out in rules 7(a) and (b) above.

15. Unless in the meantime the hearing before a Disciplinary Tribunal of any charges based on the conviction(s) or criminal charge(s) which had caused the referral to a Suspension Panel has commenced, a hearing by a Suspension Panel convened pursuant to rules 12(e)(1), 13(e)(1) or 14 above shall take place at the time and date fixed. Such hearing shall be a rehearing of the matter by the Panel which may reconsider the matter as if there had been no previous hearing. The provisions of rules 10, 11, 12 and 13 above shall apply at the first and any subsequent reconsideration of the matter save that in imposing any further period of interim suspension or interim prohibition from accepting or carrying out any public access instructions the Panel shall have regard to the length of any period of suspension already served by the Defendant. If the hearing before a Disciplinary Tribunal of any charges based on the conviction(s) or criminal charge(s) which had caused the referral to a Suspension Panel has commenced before the date fixed for a rehearing by a Suspension Panel, such date shall be vacated and any interim suspension or prohibition or the terms of any direction made or undertaking accepted by a Suspension Panel shall continue until such charges have been disposed of by the Disciplinary Tribunal.

16. A Defendant may by letter served on the Secretary of the PCC not more than fourteen days after the date of the relevant decision of a Suspension Panel give notice of his wish to appeal against the decision.

17. Unless a Disciplinary Tribunal shall otherwise direct, any period of interim suspension or prohibition shall cease or the Defendant shall cease to be bound by the terms of any direction made or undertaking accepted by a Suspension Panel or an Appeal Panel immediately upon:

(a) all charges of professional misconduct based on the conviction(s) or criminal charge(s) which had caused the referral to a Suspension Panel being disposed of by a Disciplinary Tribunal;

(b) any appeal by the Defendant against the conviction or all the conviction(s) which had caused the referral to a Suspension Panel being successful;

(c) the acquittal of the Defendant of the criminal charge or all the criminal charges which had caused the referral to a Suspension Panel;

(d) the criminal charge or all the criminal charges which had caused the referral to a Suspension Panel being withdrawn.

Appeals

18. As soon as practicable after receipt of a letter in accordance with rule 16 above the Secretary of the PCC shall convene an Appeal Panel and write to the Defendant notifying him of a fixed time and date (normally not less than fourteen and not more than twenty-one days from the date of receipt of the letter) for the hearing to take place. The Defendant may make a written representation, addressed to the Chairman of the proposed Appeal Panel, objecting to the date with reasons and providing two further alternative dates. Any such representation must be received by the Chairman of the Appeal Panel not more than fourteen days from the date of the letter of notification. The Chairman shall consider any such representation and either confirm the original date or re-fix the hearing. If no such representation is received within ten days of the date of the letter of notification the hearing shall take place at the time and date originally notified to the Defendant. The Chairman's decision, which shall be notified in writing to the Defendant by the Secretary of the PCC, shall be final. Once fixed, a hearing date shall be vacated only in exceptional circumstances and with the agreement of the Chairman of the Appeal Panel.

19. The proceedings before an Appeal Panel shall be by way of a rehearing and the provisions of rule 10 above shall apply as if for references therein to the Suspension Panel and the Chairman of the Suspension Panel there were substituted references respectively to the Appeal Panel and the Chairman of the Appeal Panel.

20. Where the appeal concerns a period of interim suspension or interim prohibition from accepting or carrying out any public access instructions, at the conclusion of the hearing the Appeal Panel:

(a) may remove the period of interim suspension or interim prohibition and/or any conditions attached thereto;

(b) may confirm the period of interim suspension or interim prohibition (subject to any conditions), impose further or alternative conditions, or substitute such shorter period (either unconditionally or subject to conditions) as may be thought fit;

(c) in lieu of confirming or imposing a period of interim suspension or interim prohibition, may accept from the Defendant in terms satisfactory to the Chairman of the Panel an undertaking in writing to continue to be suspended from practice or to continue not to accept or carry out any public access instructions (subject in either case to such conditions and for such period as the Panel may agree) pending the disposal of any charges of professional misconduct by a Disciplinary Tribunal based on the conviction or convictions that have caused the referral to the Panel;

(d) shall set down in writing signed by the Chairman of the Panel the decision of the Panel and the terms of any interim suspension or interim prohibition confirmed or imposed under rule 20(b) above or undertaking accepted under rule 20(c) above. If the members of the Panel are not unanimous as to the decision the decision made shall be that of the majority of them. Any period of suspension or prohibition which is confirmed or imposed shall be recorded as set out in rule 12(d) above;

(e) shall, if a period of interim suspension or prohibition is confirmed, imposed or the subject of a written undertaking under rule 20(c) above:

(1) confirm or fix a time and date within the period of the interim suspension or prohibition, alternatively inform the Defendant that such a time and date will be confirmed or fixed by the Secretary of the PCC and notified to the Defendant not less than fourteen days prior to such date, when, unless a Disciplinary Tribunal shall in the meantime have disposed of any charges of professional misconduct based on the conviction or convictions that caused the referral to the Suspension Panel, a Suspension Panel shall be convened for the purpose of reviewing the matter;

(2) inform the Defendant of his right to request a Suspension Panel to review the matter prior to the date confirmed or fixed under (1) above as provided in rule 14 above;

(3) inform the Defendant that he is entitled to request an expedited hearing of any charges of professional misconduct by a Disciplinary Tribunal and, if so requested, the Chairman of the Panel may so direct;

(f) may, if it has not already been referred to a Disciplinary Tribunal, refer the matter to a Disciplinary Tribunal.

21.   Where the appeal concerns a direction made or undertaking accepted under rules 13(b) or (c) above, at the conclusion of the hearing the Appeal Panel:

(a) may confirm, remove or modify any direction previously given by the Suspension Panel, subject to such conditions as to the Defendant's practice as the Panel may think fit;

(b) in lieu of any direction under rule 21(a) above the Panel may accept one or more written undertakings in such terms and upon such conditions as the Panel may think fit as to the form of written notification to be given to any professional client or lay client and as to the conduct of the Defendant's practice;

(c) shall set down in writing signed by the Chairman of the Panel the decision of the Panel and the terms of any direction made or undertaking accepted under rules 21(a) or (b) above together with a copy or copies of the letter or letters approved as the form of notification to professional clients and lay clients;

(d) shall, if any direction is confirmed or modified or undertaking accepted under rule 21(b) above limited to any specified period:

(1) confirm or fix a time and date within that period, alternatively inform the Defendant that such a time and date will be fixed by the Secretary of the PCC and notified to the Defendant not less than fourteen days prior to the expiration of such period when, unless a Disciplinary Tribunal shall in the meantime have disposed of any charges of professional misconduct based on the criminal charge or charges that caused the referral to the Suspension Panel, a Suspension Panel shall be convened for the purpose of reviewing the matter;

(2) inform the Defendant of his right to request a Suspension Panel to review the matter prior to the date fixed in (1) above as provided in rule 14 above;

> (3) inform the Defendant that he is entitled to request an expedited hearing of any charges of professional misconduct by a Disciplinary Tribunal and, if so requested, the Chairman of the Panel may so direct;
>
> (e) may, if it has not already been referred to a Disciplinary Tribunal, refer the matter to a Disciplinary Tribunal.

22. A pending appeal to an Appeal Panel shall not operate as a stay of any period of interim suspension or interim prohibition or the terms of any direction or undertaking which is the subject of the appeal.

23. There shall be no right of appeal from the decision of an Appeal Panel.

Costs

24. A Suspension Panel and an Appeal Panel shall have no power to award costs.

Report and Publication of Decisions

25. As soon as practicable after the conclusion of a Suspension Panel hearing or an Appeal Panel hearing, the Secretary of the PCC shall confirm the decision to the Defendant in writing.

26. In any case where a period of interim suspension or prohibition is imposed or an undertaking from a Defendant is accepted as a consequence of which he is suspended from practice or prohibited from accepting or carrying out public access instructions (either unconditionally or subject to conditions) the Secretary of the PCC shall communicate brief details thereof in writing to the following:

    (a) the Lord Chancellor;

    (b) the Lord Chief Justice;

    (c) the Attorney General;

    (d) the Director of Public Prosecutions;

    (e) the President of the Council of the Inns of Court;

    (f) the Chairman of the Bar Council;

    (g) the Leaders of the six circuits;

    (h) the Chairman of the PCC;

    (i) the Defendant;

    (j) the Defendant's head of chambers;

    (k) the Treasurers of the Defendant's Inn of Call and of any other Inns of which he is a member;

    (l) such one or more press agencies or other publications, as the Chairman of the PCC may direct.

    Save in cases where interim suspension or interim prohibition is followed by a sentence of disbarment or suspension from practice or prohibition from accepting or carrying out any public access instructions imposed by a Disciplinary Tribunal, if a Defendant ceases for whatever reason to be suspended from practice or prohibited from accepting or carrying out any public access instructions the Secretary of the PCC shall communicate brief details of the circumstances in which the Defendant has ceased to be suspended from practice or prohibited from accepting or carrying out any public access instructions to all the persons and agencies to which brief details of the interim suspension had previously been communicated pursuant to this rule.

27.   In any case where a direction is made requiring notification of a criminal charge or charges to professional clients and lay clients or any undertaking is accepted under rules 13(c) and 21(b) above the Secretary of the PCC shall communicate brief details thereof in writing to the following:

(a)   the Lord Chancellor;

(b)   the Lord Chief Justice;

(c)   the Attorney General;

(d)   the Director of Public Prosecutions;

(e)   the President of the Council of the Inns of Court;

(f)   the Chairman of the Bar Council;

(g)   the Leaders of the six circuits;

(h)   the Chairman of the PCC;

(i)   the Defendant;

(j)   the Defendant's head of chambers.

Service of documents

28.   Regulation 30 of the Disciplinary Tribunals Regulations shall apply for the purposes of the service of any documents in connection with the procedures which are the subject of these Rules save that for the reference in Regulation 30(3) to the 'Directions Judge or the Chairman of the Disciplinary Tribunal' there shall be substituted the 'Chairman of the PCC'.

Transitional Provisions

29.   These Rules shall not be applied in respect of any conviction or charge prior to 1 February 2000.

ANNEXE O

FITNESS TO PRACTISE RULES

[Amended 14 July 2001]

Introduction

1. These Rules are supplemental to:

    (a) the Complaints Rules;

    (b) the Disciplinary Tribunals Regulations;

    (c) the Summary Procedure Rules; and

    (d) the Interim Suspension Rules;

    as approved from time to time and annexed to the Code of Conduct of the Bar of England and Wales.

2. These Rules prescribe the manner in which any question concerning whether a barrister is unfit to practise, as defined in these Rules, shall be processed.

Definitions

3. In these Rules:

    (a) 'the Commissioner' means the Complaints Commissioner;

    (b) 'Medical Panel' means a Medical Panel as provided for in rule 4 of these Rules;

    (c) 'Review Panel' means a Review Panel as provided for in rule 5 of these Rules;

    (d) 'the Defendant' means the barrister whose case is referred to a Medical Panel pursuant to the procedure prescribed by these Rules;

    (e) 'Medical Expert' means a medical expert appointed by the Bar Council for the purpose of serving on Medical and Review Panels;

    (f) 'Appointed Medical Advisor' means a medical expert appointed by the Bar Council for the purpose of performing medical (including psychiatric) examinations on barristers and advising Medical and Review panels;

    (g) 'Unfit to practise' when used to describe a barrister means that he is incapacitated by reason of ill health and:
    - (1) the barrister is suffering from serious incapacity due to his physical or mental condition (including any addiction); and
    - (2) as a result the barrister's fitness to practise is seriously impaired; and
    - (3) his suspension or the imposition of conditions is necessary for the protection of the public.

Composition of Panels

4. A Medical Panel shall consist of five members nominated by the Chairman of the PCC being:

    (a) a Chairman and two other barristers of at least ten years Call of whom the Chairman and at least one other shall be Queen's Counsel;

    (b) a Medical Expert;

    (c) a Lay Representative.

    Provided that:
    - (1) no barrister or Lay Representative shall be nominated to serve on a Panel which is to consider any case which may have been considered at any meeting of the PCC which he attended; and

(2) the proceedings of a Medical Panel shall be valid notwithstanding that one or more of the members other than the Chairman or Medical Expert or Lay Representative becomes unable to continue to act or disqualified from continuing to act, so long as the number of members present throughout the substantive hearing is not reduced below three and continues to include the Chairman and the Medical Expert and Lay Representative.

5.   A Review Panel shall consist of:

    (a) a Chairman and one other barrister nominated by the Chairman of the Bar;

    (b) a representative nominated by the Treasurer of the Defendant's Inn;

    (c) a Medical Expert;

    (d) a Lay Representative

Provided that no individual shall sit on both the Medical Panel and the Review Panel considering the same case.

Referral to a Medical Panel

6.   Where information in writing or a complaint in writing is received by the Bar Council about any barrister which raises a question whether the barrister is unfit to practise, the Commissioner shall consider whether to refer the case to a Medical Panel.

7.   The Commissioner shall refer a case to a Medical Panel if:

    (a) having been referred to him under rule 6 above the Commissioner considers a barrister may be unfit to practise; or

    (b) a complaint of professional misconduct or inadequate professional service has been referred to the Commissioner or the PCC during the investigation of which it appears that a barrister may be unfit to practise; or

    (c) in any other circumstances it appears to the Commissioner, the PCC or any other Disciplinary Panel or Tribunal that a barrister may be unfit to practise; or

    (d) a barrister requests the Commissioner in writing to refer his case to a Medical Panel.

8.   As soon as practicable after the decision has been made to refer a case to a Medical Panel, the Secretary of the PCC shall write to the Defendant notifying him of the decision, together with a copy of these Rules. The letter of notification shall:

    (a) contain a summary of the reasons why the case has been referred to a Medical Panel;

    (b) lay down a fixed time and date (normally not less than fourteen and not more than twenty-one days from the date of the letter) for a preliminary hearing of the Panel to take place. One alternative shall be given;

    (c) invite the Defendant to accept one or other of the dates proposed or to provide a written representation to the Chairman of the PCC, objecting to both dates with reasons and providing two further alternative dates not more than twenty-one days from the date of the letter of notification. Any such representation must be received by the Chairman of the PCC not more than fourteen days from the date of the letter of notification. The Chairman of the PCC shall consider any such representation and either confirm one of the original dates or re-fix the hearing. If no such representation is received within fourteen days of the date of the letter of notification the hearing shall take place at the time and date first fixed pursuant to rule 8(b) above. The Chairman's decision, which shall be notified in writing to the Defendant by the Secretary of the PCC, shall be final. Once fixed, a hearing date shall be vacated only in exceptional circumstances and with the agreement of the Chairman of the PCC;

(d) inform the Defendant that he is entitled to make representations in writing or orally, by himself or by another member of the Bar on his behalf, and that he may produce medical evidence, provided (but subject to the discretion of the Chairman of the Panel to consider any form of evidence placed before it) that a proof of such evidence shall have been submitted prior to the hearing;

(e) inform the Defendant that he may be invited to attend within a period of time upon an Appointed Medical Advisor nominated by the Panel to carry out an examination of the Defendant, and requested to authorise disclosure of his medical records;

(f) inform the Defendant of his right to appeal as provided in rule 18 below.

Procedure and Powers of Medical Panels

9. At any hearing of a Medical Panel the proceedings shall be governed by the rules of natural justice, subject to which:

(a) the procedure shall be informal, the details being at the discretion of the Chairman of the Panel;

(b) the Defendant shall be entitled to make representations in writing or orally, by himself or by another member of the Bar or a solicitor on his behalf, and may produce medical evidence, provided (but subject to the discretion of the Chairman of the Panel to consider any form of evidence placed before it) that a proof of such evidence shall have been submitted prior to the hearing;

(c) the attendance of the Defendant shall be required. Should he nevertheless fail to attend, the hearing may proceed in his absence, subject to the Panel being satisfied that this course is appropriate, that all relevant procedures requiring the Defendant's attendance have been complied with and that no acceptable explanation for the Defendant's absence has been provided. Should the Panel not be so satisfied, it shall have the power to adjourn the hearing;

(d) the hearing shall not be in public unless so requested by the Defendant and a record shall be taken electronically. The tape of the hearing shall be retained under the arrangements of the Secretary of the PCC for two years or until any charges of professional misconduct against the Defendant arising out of the case have been finally disposed of through the Bar Council's procedure for complaints and any appeal procedure has been exhausted whichever period is the longer;

(e) if it decides an adjournment is necessary for any reason, the Panel may adjourn the hearing for such period and to such time and place, and upon such terms, as it may think fit.

10. If the members of a Medical Panel are not unanimous as to any decision the decision made shall be that of the majority of them. If the members of the Panel are equally divided the decision shall be that which is the most favourable to the Defendant.

11. At the conclusion of a preliminary hearing of a Medical Panel, the Panel:

(a) may give directions for a full hearing of the Panel, including:
(1) a direction within a specified period of time an Appointed Medical Advisor nominated by the Panel shall carry out an examination of the Defendant; and

(2) a request to the Defendant to authorise disclosure of his medical records to such Appointed Medical Advisor;

(b) shall warn the Defendant that if he refuses any request made under rule 11(a) above any Panel hearing his case shall be entitled to draw such adverse inferences as it may think fit from such refusal;

(c) may direct that the barrister be suspended from practice or prohibited from accepting or carrying out any public access instructions (either unconditionally or subject to conditions) for a specified period which should not save in exceptional circumstances exceed 3 months pending the full hearing of the Panel, provided that no such period of interim suspension or prohibition should be imposed unless the Panel is satisfied that it is necessary to protect the public.

(d) in lieu of imposing a period of suspension or prohibition under (c) above may accept from the Defendant an undertaking in writing in terms satisfactory to the Panel (and subject to such conditions and for such a period as the Panel may agree) either:

(i)   immediately to be suspended from practice, or

(ii) not to accept or carry out any public access instructions,

pending the conclusion of the full hearing;

(e) may accept from the Defendant an undertaking or undertakings in writing in terms satisfactory to the Panel (and subject to such conditions and for such a period as the Panel may agree) as to the conduct of the Defendant's practice pending the conclusion of the full hearing;

(f) shall set down in writing signed by the Chairman of the Panel the decision of the Panel including the terms of any directions given under rule 11(a) above and the period and terms of any interim suspension or prohibition imposed under rule 11(c) above or undertaking accepted under rule 11(d) or (e) above.

(g) shall, if a period of interim suspension or prohibition is imposed under rule 11(c) above or a written undertaking is accepted under rule 11(d) above:

(1) fix a time and date within the period of suspension or prohibition imposed or to which the undertaking relates, alternatively inform the Defendant that such a time and date will be fixed by the Secretary of the PCC and notified to the Defendant not less than fourteen days prior to such date, when, unless a Medical Panel has concluded proceedings, a Panel shall be convened for the purpose of reviewing the matter;

(2) inform the Defendant of his right to request a Panel to review the matter prior to the date fixed in (1) above as provided in rule 15 below;

(3) inform the Defendant of his right of appeal as provided in rule 18 below;

(4) inform the Defendant that he is entitled to request an expedited full hearing of the Medical Panel and, if so requested, the Chairman of the Panel may so direct.

12.   If a Medical Panel shall decide to give directions under rule 11(a) above, as soon as practicable after the report of any examination requested has been carried out (or refused) and a summary of the case against the Defendant has been prepared on

behalf of the Panel, the Secretary of the PCC shall notify the Defendant. The letter of notification shall:

(a) contain:

    (1) the summary of the case against the Defendant;

    (2) a copy of any report produced by the Appointed Medical Advisor nominated to carry out an examination of the Defendant;

(b) lay down a fixed time and date (normally not less than fourteen and not more than twenty-one days from the date of the letter) for a full hearing of the Panel to take place. One alternative shall be given;

(c) invite the Defendant to accept one or other of the dates proposed or to provide a written representation to the Chairman of the PCC, objecting to both dates with reasons and providing two further alternative dates not more than twenty-one days from the date of the letter of notification. Any such representation must be received by the Chairman of the PCC not more than fourteen days from the date of the letter of notification. The Chairman of the PCC shall consider this representation and either confirm one of the original dates or re-fix the hearing. If no such representation is received within fourteen days of the date of the letter of notification the hearing shall take place at the time and date first fixed pursuant to rule 12(b) above. The Chairman's decision, which shall be notified in writing to the Defendant by the Secretary of the PCC, shall be final. Once fixed, a hearing date shall be vacated only in exceptional circumstances and with the agreement of the Chairman of the PCC;

(d) inform the Defendant of his right to appeal as provided in rule 18 below.

13. At any full hearing of a Medical Panel the provisions of rule 9 above shall apply but in addition the Defendant himself or by another member of the Bar shall be entitled to cross- examine any Appointed Medical Advisor whose report is in evidence before the Panel.

14. At the conclusion of a full hearing of a Medical Panel, the Panel:

(a) may decide to take no action;

(b) if satisfied that the Defendant is or may become unfit to practise shall have power to impose one or more of the penalties or conditions set out in rules 14(c), (d) and (e) below;

(c) may impose a period of interim suspension or interim prohibition from accepting or carrying out any public access instructions (either unconditionally or subject to conditions) of up to six months, but shall inform the Defendant that such period of interim suspension or interim prohibition shall be continued without any further decision of a Panel unless determined at a review of his case as provided in rule 15 below;

(d) may impose an indefinite period of suspension or prohibition from accepting or carrying out any public access instructions;

(e) may make the Defendant's right to continue to practise, or to resume practice after any period of suspension or prohibition from accepting or carrying out any public access instructions, subject to such conditions as the Panel may think fit, including, without prejudice to the generality of the foregoing:

    (1) a requirement that the Defendant should attend one or more Appointed Medical Advisors for regular examination whose report(s) should be made

available to the Chairman of the PCC and any Medical Panel or Review Panel when considering the case;

(2) a requirement that the Defendant should attend one or more clinics or hospitals as the Panel may decide for the purposes of treatment in respect of any physical or mental condition which the Panel may think is or may become a cause of the Defendant's Unfitness to practise;

(f) in lieu of imposing any penalty or condition under rule 14(b) above the Panel may accept from the Defendant one or more undertakings in writing satisfactory to the Panel referring to such period of suspension or prohibition and any conditions which the Panel would have imposed or made under rules 14(c), (d) and (e) above;

(g) shall inform the Defendant of his right to request a Panel to review his case as provided in rule 15 below;

(h) shall inform the Defendant of his right of appeal as provided in rule 18 below;

(i) shall inform the Defendant that to attempt to practise during a period of suspension or to accept or carry out any public access instructions during a period of prohibition or, if the Defendant's right to continue to practise is subject to one or more conditions, not to comply with any such condition, would be serious professional misconduct likely to result in a charge of professional misconduct and a hearing before a Disciplinary Tribunal;

(j) shall set down in writing signed by the Chairman of the Panel the decision of the Panel and the terms of any suspension imposed, conditions made, or undertakings accepted.

15.   At any time, after a period of suspension or prohibition imposed or undertaken under rules 14(d) or (f) above has expired, or in the event of a significant change in circumstances or other good reason, the Defendant may make a request in writing to the Chairman of the PCC for a Panel to be convened to review his case. Where a significant change in circumstances or good reason is relied upon the letter must set out the details of any such alleged change in circumstances or good reason. On receipt of such a letter the Chairman may in his discretion convene a Panel or refuse the request. In either case the Chairman shall inform the Defendant in writing of his decision but shall not be obliged to give reasons. The Chairman's decision shall be final.

16.   At any time during which a Defendant is subject to a period of suspension or prohibition or is practising subject to conditions made pursuant to these Rules the Chairman of the PCC may in his discretion convene a Panel to review that Defendant's case.

17.   When a case is referred for review to a Medical Panel under rules 15 or 16 above:

(a) there shall be a rehearing of the case by the Panel and the provisions of rules 9, 10 and 13 above shall apply save that copies of the report of any expert or any proof of evidence referred to at any previous hearing of a Medical Panel in respect of the same case may be referred to;

(b) unless agreed in writing between the Chairman of the Panel and the Defendant that any of the provisions contained in rules 8, 11 and 12 shall not apply, there shall be a preliminary as well as a full hearing of the Panel and the provisions contained in rules 8, 11, 12 and 14 above shall apply thereto.

18. A Defendant may by letter served on the Secretary of the PCC not more than fourteen days after the date of the relevant decision of a Medical Panel give notice of his wish to appeal against the decision.

Appeals

19. As soon as practicable after receipt of a letter in accordance with rule 18 above the Secretary of the PCC shall convene a Review Panel and write to the Defendant notifying him of a fixed time and date (normally not less than fourteen and not more than twenty-one days from the date of receipt of the letter) for the hearing to take place. The Defendant may make a written representation, addressed to the Chairman of the proposed Review Panel, objecting to the date with reasons and providing two further alternative dates. Any such representation must be received by the Chairman of the Review Panel not more than fourteen days from the date of the letter of notification. The Chairman shall consider any such representation and either confirm the original date or re-fix the hearing. If no such representation is received within fourteen days of the date of the letter of notification the hearing shall take place at the time and place originally notified to the Defendant. The Chairman's decision, which shall be notified in writing to the Defendant by the Secretary of the PCC, shall be final. Once fixed, a hearing date shall be vacated only in exceptional circumstances and with the agreement of the Chairman of the Review Panel.

20. The proceedings before a Review Panel shall be by way of a rehearing and the provisions of rules 9 and 13 above shall apply as if for references therein to the Medical Panel and the Chairman of the Medical Panel for the purposes of a full hearing of a Medical Panel there were substituted references respectively to the Review Panel and the Chairman of the Review Panel, save that copies of the report of any expert or any proof of evidence referred to at any hearing of a Medical Panel in respect of the same case may be referred to.

21. At the conclusion of the hearing, the Review Panel:

(a) may allow the appeal and decide to take no action;

(b) confirm the decision that is the subject of the appeal;

(c) may exercise any of the powers of a Medical Panel as set out in rules 14(c), (d), (e), and (f) above;

(d) shall inform the Defendant of his right to request a Medical Panel to review his case as provided in rule 15 above;

(e) shall inform the Defendant that to attempt to practise during a period of suspension or to attempt to accept or carry out any public access instructions during a period of prohibition or, if the Defendant's right to continue to practise is subject to one or more conditions, not to comply with any such condition, would be serious professional misconduct likely to result in a charge of professional misconduct and a hearing before a Disciplinary Tribunal;

(f) shall set down in writing signed by the Chairman of the Panel the decision of the Panel and the terms of any suspension or prohibition imposed, conditions made, or undertakings accepted. If the members of the Panel are not unanimous as to the decision the decision shall be that of the majority of them.

22. A pending appeal to a Review Panel shall not operate as a stay of any period of suspension or any conditions or the terms of any undertaking which is the subject of the appeal.

23. There shall be no right of appeal from the decision of a Review Panel.

Costs

24. A Medical Panel and a Review Panel shall have no power to award costs.

Confidentiality of medical reports

25. A Defendant's medical records and any report prepared for or submitted to a Medical Panel or a Review Panel shall not be used for any other purpose than is provided for in these Rules and shall not be disclosed to any other person or body without the consent in writing of the Defendant.

Report and Publication of Decisions

26. As soon as practicable after the conclusion of a Medical Panel hearing or a Review Panel hearing, the Secretary of the PCC shall confirm the decision to the Defendant in writing.

27. Unless the decision of a Medical Panel full hearing or a Review Panel hearing is to take no action and the Defendant is permitted to continue to practise without being subject to any conditions, the Secretary of the PCC shall communicate brief details thereof in writing to the following:

    (a) the Lord Chancellor;

    (b) the Lord Chief Justice;

    (c) the Attorney General;

    (d) the Director of Public Prosecutions;

    (e) the President of the Council of the Inns of Court;

    (f) the Chairman of the Bar Council;

    (g) the Leaders of the six circuits;

    (h) the Chairman of the PCC;

    (i) the Defendant;

    (j) the Defendant's head of chambers;

    (k) the Treasurers of the Defendant's Inn of Call and of any other Inns of which he is a member.

Service of documents

28. Regulation 30 of the Disciplinary Tribunals Regulations shall apply for the purposes of the service of any documents in connection with the procedures which are the subject of these Rules save that for the reference in Regulation 30(3) to the 'Directions Judge or the Chairman of the Disciplinary Tribunal' there shall be substituted the 'Chairman of the PCC'.

ANNEXE P

ADJUDICATION PANEL AND APPEALS RULES

Introduction

1. Adjudication Panels ('Panels') shall be appointed by the Professional Conduct and Complaints Committee ('the Committee') to determine complaints considered by the Committee not to raise a *prima facie* case of professional misconduct, but to raise a *prima facie* case that the barrister concerned has provided inadequate professional service to the complainant.

2. Panels shall consist of the Complaints Commissioner ('the Commissioner') as chairman, one lay member of the Committee and two barrister members of the Committee, at least one of whom shall be a Queen's Counsel.

3. Anything required by these Rules to be done or any discretion required to be exercised by, and any notice required to be given to, the Complaints Commissioner ('the Commissioner') or the Secretary of the Committee ('the Secretary'), may be done or exercised by, or given to, any person authorised by the Complaints Commissioner to act in his stead or by the Chief Executive of the Bar Council to act instead of the Secretary of the Committee (either prospectively or retrospectively and either generally or for a particular purpose).

Powers of Panels

4. The powers of a Panel shall be:

    (a) to consider any complaint referred to it pursuant to paragraph 28(e) of the Complaints Rules and to direct such investigations as they see fit in respect thereof

    (b) to dismiss any complaint without making a finding as to the existence or otherwise of inadequate professional service if they conclude that due to lapse of time, disputes of fact which cannot fairly be resolved by the Panel, or for any other reason it cannot fairly be determined

    (c) to determine whether the barrister concerned has provided inadequate professional service in respect of the matter complained of

    (d) to determine what remedy should be granted to the complainant in respect of such inadequate service.

Investigation and Procedure

5. When a complaint is referred to a Panel as set out in paragraph 4(a) above the Commissioner shall consider what, if any, further investigation is required to be made in order for the panel to deal fairly with the matters falling to it for decision, and the Secretary shall make such investigations as the Commissioner or the Panel direct to assist the deliberations of the panel, such as whether the complainant claims to have suffered financial loss as a result of the conduct complained of, and if so the exact nature and amount of that claimed loss and the evidence available to support the claim, and from the barrister the nature of the work he carried out for the complainant out of which the complaint arose, the fee rendered for such work, and whether or not such fee has been paid.

6. The Secretary shall, whether or not there are to be additional investigations under paragraph 5 above, notify both the barrister and the complainant of the matters that

the PCC has directed the panel to consider. As soon as practicable thereafter, he shall prepare a bundle of papers to be considered by the panel and shall copy those to the barrister and the complainant and shall invite their written comments within 14 days (which period may be extended with the permission of the Commissioner).

7. At the expiration of the time limit specified in paragraph 6 or on completion of any enquiries made under paragraph 5, the Secretary shall copy any further papers that are to be considered by the panel to the barrister and the complainant and shall set a date for the panel to meet. Both the barrister and the complainant shall be informed of the date of the hearing and the complainant shall be invited to make any further comments in writing which must arrive not less than seven days before the date of the hearing. Such comments shall be copied to the barrister and the panel.

8. The Panel may consider complaints and the results of any investigations in whatever manner they think fit, and may adjourn consideration of any complaint at any time, and for any reason and, in particular to enable the complainant to comment on any information provided by the barrister at the hearing which had not previously been disclosed by him.

9. Following such consideration, the Panel may decide:

    (a) that for any reason the complaint cannot fairly be determined by them, whereupon it shall dismiss the complaint and shall give notice in writing of its decision and the reasons for it to the barrister and the complainant

    (b) that the complainant has not established on the balance of probabilities that the barrister concerned has provided inadequate professional service to the complainant, whereupon it shall dismiss the complaint and shall give notice in writing of its decision and the reasons for it to the barrister and the complainant

    (c) that the complainant has so established, whereupon it shall consider what remedy should be granted to the complainant in respect of the service which it has found to have been inadequate.

10. Following a finding under paragraph 9(c) above, the Panel may:

    (a) determine that it is not appropriate to take any action in respect of the inadequate service,

    (b) direct the barrister to make a formal apology to the complainant for the inadequate service provided,

    (c) direct the barrister to repay or remit all or part of any fee rendered in respect of the inadequate service,

    (d) direct the barrister to pay compensation to the complainant in such sum as the panel shall direct not exceeding £5,000.

    In determining whether any sum is to be paid under paragraph (d) hereof, or in fixing the amount of such sum, the panel shall in particular have regard to any loss suffered by the complainant as a result of the inadequate professional service, the availability to the complainant of other forms of redress, to the gravity of the conduct complained of, and to the fee claimed by the barrister for the inadequate service.

11. Following any such finding as is mentioned in paragraph 9(c) hereof, the Panel shall give notice in writing to the barrister and to the complainant of the respects in which they have found the barrister to have provided inadequate professional

service, and the reasons for such finding, and of the remedy to be granted to the complainant under paragraph 10 above.

12. If the panel is not unanimous on any issue, the finding made shall be that of the majority of them. If the panel is equally divided, the burden of proof being on the complainant, the finding shall be that most favourable to the barrister.

13. Following such reopening or reconsideration, the panel may take any further or different action it thinks fit, as if the former decision had not been made.

14. Whether or not the panel shall have determined that the barrister has provided an inadequate professional service, it may refer any matter of policy which arises to the relevant Committee of the Bar Council.

15. No finding of an Adjudication Panel shall be publishable except:

    (a) by the Commissioner in any annual or other report on his work, in which case the identities of the parties shall so far as possible be concealed, unless the barrister concerned seeks that any finding be published. In that case the manner and extent of publication shall be at the discretion of the Commissioner; or

    (b) if the Adjudication Panel considers that the circumstances of the complaint are relevant to the barrister's capacity as a pupilmaster, it may notify the barrister's Inn of its concern in such manner as it sees fit.

Appeals

16. An appeal shall lie at the instance of a barrister against a finding that he has provided inadequate professional service, and against any decision as to the remedy to be granted to the complainant in respect of such inadequate service.

17. Any such appeal shall be heard and determined by a panel ('the Appeal Panel') consisting of not less than three or more than five past or present members of the Committee (or of the Professional Conduct Committee established under the rules in effect immediately before the coming into effect of these Rules) of whom at least one shall be a Queen's Counsel and shall chair the panel, at least one shall be a junior of more than five years' call and at least one shall be a lay representative. None of the members of the Appeal panel shall have been members of the tribunal which made any finding appealed against.

18. An appeal shall be made by the barrister sending to the Secretary within 28 days of the date of letter notifying him of the decision appealed against a notice stating the findings to be appealed against, the decision the barrister contends for, and the grounds of such appeal, accompanied by the sum of £100 payable to the Bar Council to defray expenses.

19. Service of notice of an appeal by a barrister shall operate as a stay of any order made in favour of the complainant.

20. On receipt of such a notice, the Secretary shall notify the Commissioner of the intended appeal, and shall afford him an opportunity to respond to the grounds of appeal stated in the notice. For the purpose of so responding the Commissioner may seek information or assistance from such persons and in such manner as he sees fit.

21. On such an appeal,

    (a) the procedure shall be informal, the details being at the discretion of the chairman of the Appeal Panel including whether or not there should be an oral hearing in relation to the appeal

(b) the barrister, the complainant and the Commissioner may attend or be represented

(c) the Appeal Panel may make such order as they think fit in relation to the complaint, including any order which the tribunal appealed from had the power to make, save that they may not make any order in relation to the costs of the appeal

(d) the Appeal Panel shall not allow the appeal unless they are satisfied that the tribunal appealed from reached a wrong decision on any question of law, made a finding of fact which was against the weight of the evidence or exercised any discretion granted to it on a wrong basis

(e) if the Appeal Panel allows an appeal, in whole or in part, it may in its discretion direct the refund to the barrister of the sum deposited under paragraph 18 above

(f) whether or not the appeal is allowed, the Appeal Panel may refer any issue of policy which arises to the relevant Committee of the Bar Council.

Definitions

22. In these Rules unless the context otherwise requires

(a) Any term defined in the Code of Conduct shall carry the same meaning as it does in the Code of Conduct.

(b) 'The Complaints Rules' shall mean the rules prescribing the manner in which complaints are to be considered set out in Annex J to the Code of Conduct, and any term defined in the Complaints Rules shall carry the same meaning as it does in those Rules.

(c) Any reference to a person includes any natural person, legal person and/or firm. Any reference to the masculine gender includes the feminine and the neuter, and any reference to the singular includes the plural, and in each case *vice versa*.

Commencement and Transitional Arrangements

23. In relation to any adjudication panel or appeal arising out of a complaint which had been referred to a panel before 31 October 2004, these Rules shall not apply but the Adjudication Panel and Appeals Rules in force immediately before that date shall apply to that panel or appeal.

ANNEXE Q

THE CODE OF CONDUCT FOR LAWYERS IN THE EUROPEAN COMMUNITY

1   PREAMBLE

1.1   The Function of the Lawyer in Society

In a society founded on respect for the rule of law the lawyer fulfils a special role. His duties do not begin and end with the faithful performance of what he is instructed to do so far as the law permits. A lawyer must serve the interests of justice as well as those whose rights and liberties he is trusted to assert and defend and it is his duty not only to plead his client's cause but to be his adviser.

A lawyer's function therefore lays on him a variety of legal and moral obligations (sometimes appearing to be in conflict with each other) towards:

the client;

the courts and other authorities before whom the lawyer pleads his client's cause or acts on his behalf;

the legal profession in general and each fellow member of it in particular; and

the public for whom the existence of a free and independent profession, bound together by respect for rules made by the profession itself, is an essential means of safeguarding human rights in face of the power of the state and other interests in society.

1.2   The Nature of Rules of Professional Conduct

1.2.1   Rules of professional conduct are designed through their willing acceptance by those to whom they apply to ensure the proper performance by the lawyer of a function which is recognised as essential in all civilised societies. The failure of the lawyer to observe these rules must in the last resort result in a disciplinary sanction.

1.2.2   The particular rules of each Bar or Law Society arise from its own traditions. They are adapted to the organisation and sphere of activity of the profession in the Member State concerned and to its judicial and administrative procedures and to its national legislation. It is neither possible nor desirable that they should be taken out of their context nor that an attempt should be made to give general application to rules which are inherently incapable of such application.

The particular rules of each Bar and Law Society nevertheless are based on the same values and in most cases demonstrate a common foundation.

1.3   The Purpose of the Code

1.3.1   The continued integration of the European Union and European Economic Area and the increasing frequency of the cross-border activities of lawyers within the European Economic Area have made necessary in the public interest the statement of common rules which apply to all lawyers from the Community whatever Bar or Law Society they belong to in relation to their cross-border practice. A particular purpose of the statement of those rules is to mitigate the difficulties which result from the application of 'double deontology' as set out in Article 4 of the E.C. Directive 77/249 of 22nd March 1977.

1.3.2   The organisations representing the legal profession through the CCBE propose that the rules codified in the following articles:

— be recognised at the present time as the expression of a consensus of all the Bars and Law Societies of the European Union and European Economic Area;

— be adopted as enforceable rules as soon as possible in accordance with national or EEA procedures in relation to the cross-border activities of the lawyer in the European Union and European Economic Area;

— be taken into account in all revisions of national rules of deontology or professional practice with a view to their progressive harmonisation.

They further express the wish that the national rules of deontology or professional practice be interpreted and applied whenever possible in a way consistent with the rules in this Code.

After the rules in this Code have been adopted as enforceable rules in relation to his cross-border activities the lawyer will remain bound to observe the rules of the Bar or Law Society to which he belongs to the extent that they are consistent with the rules in this Code.

1.4   Field of Application Ratione Personae

The following rules shall apply to lawyers of the European Union and European Economic Area as they are defined by the Directive 77/249 of 22nd March 1977.

1.5   Field of Application Ratione Materiae

Without prejudice to the pursuit of a progressive harmonisation of rules of deontology or professional practice which apply only internally within a Member State, the following rules shall apply to the cross-border activities of the lawyer within the European Union and European Economic Area. Cross-border activities shall mean:-

(a) all professional contacts with lawyers of Member States other than his own; and

(b) the professional activities of the lawyer in a Member State other than his own, whether or not the lawyer is physically present in that Member State.

1.6   Definitions

In these rules:

'Home Member State' means the Member State of the Bar or Law Society to which the lawyer belongs.

'Host Member State' means any other Member State where the lawyer carries on cross-border activities.

'Competent authority' means the professional organisation(s) or authority(ies) of the Member State concerned responsible for the laying down of rules of professional conduct and the administration of discipline of lawyers.

2   GENERAL PRINCIPLES

2.1   Independence

2.1.1   The many duties to which a lawyer is subject require his absolute independence, free from all other influence, especially such as may arise from his personal interests or external pressure. Such independence is as necessary to trust in the process of justice as the impartiality of the judge. A lawyer must therefore avoid any impairment of his independence and be careful not to compromise his professional standards in order to please his client, the court or third parties.

2.1.2   This independence is necessary in non-contentious matters as well as in litigation. Advice given by a lawyer to his client has no value if it is given only to ingratiate himself, to serve his personal interests or in response to outside pressure.

2.2   Trust and Personal Integrity

Relationships of trust can only exist if a lawyer's personal honour, honesty and integrity are beyond doubt. For the lawyer these traditional virtues are professional obligations.

2.3   Confidentiality

2.3.1   It is of the essence of a lawyer's function that he should be told by his client things which the client would not tell to others, and that he should be the recipient of other information on a basis of confidence. Without the certainty of confidentiality there cannot be trust. Confidentiality is therefore a primary and fundamental right and duty of the lawyer.

The lawyer's obligation of confidentiality serves the interest of the administration of justice as well as the interest of the client. It is therefore entitled to special protection by the State.

2.3.2   A lawyer shall respect the confidentiality of all information that becomes known to him in the course of his professional activity.

2.3.3   The obligation of confidentiality is not limited in time.

2.3.4   A lawyer shall require his associates and staff and anyone engaged by him in the course of providing professional services to observe the same obligation of confidentiality.

2.4   Respect for the Rules of Other Bars and Law Societies

Under the laws of the European Union and the European Economic Area a lawyer from an- other Member State may be bound to comply with the rules of the Bar or Law Society of the host Member State. Lawyers have a duty to inform themselves as to the rules which will affect them in the performance of any particular activity.

Members of organisations of CCBE are obliged to deposit their Code of Conduct at the Secretariat of CCBE so that any lawyer can get hold of the copy of the current Code from the Secretariat.

2.5   Incompatible Occupations

2.5.1   In order to perform his functions with due independence and in a manner which is consistent with his duty to participate in the administration of justice a lawyer is excluded from some occupations.

2.5.2   A lawyer who acts in the representation or the defence of a client in legal proceedings or before any public authorities in a host Member State shall there observe the rules regarding incompatible occupations as they are applied to lawyers of the host Member State.

2.5.3   A lawyer established in a host Member State in which he wishes to participate directly in commercial or other activities not connected with the practice of the law shall respect the rules regarding forbidden or incompatible occupations as they are applied to lawyers of that Member State.

2.6   Personal Publicity

2.6.1   A lawyer should not advertise or seek personal publicity where this is not permitted.

In other cases a lawyer should only advertise or seek personal publicity to the extent and in the manner permitted by the rules to which he is subject.

2.6.2   Advertising and personal publicity shall be regarded as taking place where it is permitted, if the lawyer concerned shows that it was placed for the purpose of reaching clients or potential clients located where such advertising or personal publicity is permitted and its communication elsewhere is incidental.

2.7   The Client's Interests

Subject to due observance of all rules of law and professional conduct, a lawyer must always act in the best interests of his client and must put those interests before his own interests or those of fellow members of the legal profession.

2.8   Limitation of Lawyer's Liability towards his client

To the extent permitted by the law of the Home member State and the Host member State, the lawyer may limit his liabilities towards his client in accordance with rules of the Code of Conduct to which he is subject.

3   RELATIONS WITH CLIENTS

3.1   Acceptance and Termination of Instructions

3.1.1   A lawyer shall not handle a case for a party except on his instructions. He may, however, act in a case in which he has been instructed by another lawyer who himself acts for the party or where the case has been assigned to him by a competent body.

The lawyer should make reasonable efforts to ascertain the identity, competence and authority of the person or body who instructs him when the specific circumstances show that the identity, competence and authority are uncertain.

3.1.2   A lawyer shall advise and represent his client promptly conscientiously and diligently. He shall undertake personal responsibility for the discharge of the instructions given to him. He shall keep his client informed as to the progress of the matter entrusted to him.

3.1.3   A lawyer shall not handle a matter which he knows or ought to know he is not competent to handle, without co-operating with a lawyer who is competent to handle it.

A lawyer shall not accept instructions unless he can discharge those instructions promptly having regard to the pressure of other work.

3.1.4   A lawyer shall not be entitled to exercise his right to withdraw from a case in such a way or in such circumstances that the client may be unable to find other legal assistance in time to prevent prejudice being suffered by the client.

3.2   Conflict of Interest

3.2.1   A lawyer may not advise, represent or act on behalf of two or more clients in the same matter if there is a conflict, or a significant risk of a conflict, between the interests of those clients.

3.2.2   A lawyer must cease to act for both clients when a conflict of interests arises between those clients and also whenever there is a risk of a breach of confidence or where his independence may be impaired.

3.2.3   A lawyer must also refrain from acting for a new client if there is a risk of a breach of confidences entrusted to the lawyer by a former client or if the knowledge which the lawyer possesses of the affairs of the former client would give an undue advantage to the new client.

3.2.4 Where lawyers are practising in association, paragraphs 3.2.1 to 3.2.3 above shall apply to the association and all its members.

3.3 Pactum de Quota Litis

3.3.1 A lawyer shall not be entitled to make a pactum de quota litis.

3.3.2 By 'pactum de quota litis' is meant an agreement between a lawyer and his client entered into prior to the final conclusion of a matter to which the client is a party, by virtue of which the client undertakes to pay the lawyer a share of the result regardless of whether this is represented by a sum of money or by any other benefit achieved by the client upon the conclusion of the matter.

3.3.3 The pactum de quota litis does not include an agreement that fees be charged in proportion to the value of a matter handled by the lawyer if this is in accordance with an officially approved fee scale or under the control of the competent authority having jurisdiction over the lawyer.

3.4 Regulation of Fees

3.4.1 A fee charged by a lawyer shall be fully disclosed to his client and shall be fair and reasonable.

3.4.2 Subject to any proper agreement to the contrary between a lawyer and his client fees charged by a lawyer shall be subject to regulation in accordance with the rules applied to members of the Bar or Law Society to which he belongs. If he belongs to more than one Bar or Law Society the rules applied shall be those with the closest connection to the contract between the lawyer and his client.

3.5 Payment on Account

If a lawyer requires a payment on account of his fees and/or disbursements such payment should not exceed a reasonable estimate of the fees and probable disbursements involved.

Failing such payment, a lawyer may withdraw from the case or refuse to handle it, but subject always to paragraph 3.1.4 above.

3.6 Fee Sharing with Non-Lawyers

3.6.1 Subject as after-mentioned a lawyer may not share his fees with a person who is not a lawyer except where an association between the lawyer and the other person is permitted by the laws of the Member State to which the lawyer belongs.

3.6.2 The provisions of 6.1 above shall not preclude a lawyer from paying a fee, commission or other compensation to a deceased lawyer's heirs or to a retired lawyer in respect of taking over the deceased or retired lawyer's practice.

3.7 Cost Effective Resolution and Availability of Legal Aid

3.7.1 The lawyer should at all times strive to achieve the most cost effective resolution of the client's dispute and should advise the client at appropriate stages as to the desirability of attempting a settlement and/or a reference to alternative dispute resolution.

3.7.2 A lawyer shall inform his client of the availability of legal aid where applicable.

3.8   Clients' Funds

3.8.1   When lawyers at any time in the course of their practice come into possession of funds on behalf of their clients or third parties (hereinafter called 'clients' funds') it shall be obligatory:

3.8.1.1   That clients' funds shall always be held in an account in a bank or similar institution subject to supervision of Public Authority and that all clients' funds received by a lawyer should be paid into such an account unless the client explicitly or by implication agrees that the funds should be dealt with otherwise.

3.8.1.2   That any account in which the clients' funds are held in the name of the lawyer should indicate in the title or designation that the funds are held on behalf of the client or clients of the lawyer.

3.8.1.3   That any account or accounts in which clients' funds are held in the name of the lawyer should at all times contain a sum which is not less than the total of the clients' funds held by the lawyer.

3.8.1.4   That all funds shall be paid to clients immediately or upon such conditions as the client may authorise.

3.8.1.5   That payments made from clients' funds on behalf of a client to any other person including

(a) payments made to or for one client from funds held for another client and

(b) payment of the lawyer's fees,

be prohibited except to the extent that they are permitted by law or have the express or implied authority of the client for whom the payment is being made.

3.8.1.6   That the lawyer shall maintain full and accurate records, available to each client on request, showing all his dealings with his clients' funds and distinguishing clients' funds from other funds held by him.

3.8.1.7   That the competent authorities in all Member States should have powers to allow them to examine and investigate on a confidential basis the financial records of lawyers' clients' funds to ascertain whether or not the rules which they make are being complied with and to impose sanctions upon lawyers who fail to comply with those rules.

3.8.2   Subject as after-mentioned, and without prejudice to the rules set out in 3.8.1 above, a lawyer who holds clients' funds in the course of carrying on practice in any Member State must comply with the rules relating to holding and accounting for clients' funds which are applied by the competent authorities of the Home Member State.

3.8.3   A lawyer who carries on practice or provides services in a Host Member State may with the agreement of the competent authorities of the Home and Host Member States concerned comply with the requirements of the Host Member State to the exclusion of the requirements of the Home Member State. In that event he shall take reasonable steps to inform his clients that he complies with the requirements in force in the Host Member State.

3.9   Professional Indemnity Insurance

3.9.1   Lawyers shall be insured at all times against claims based on professional negligence to an extent which is reasonable having regard to the nature and extent of the risks which each lawyer may incur in his practice.

3.9.2   When a lawyer provides services or carries out practice in a Host Member State, the following shall apply.

3.9.2.1   The lawyer must comply with any Rules relating to his obligation to insure against his professional liability as a lawyer which are in force in his Home Member State.

3.9.2.2   A lawyer who is obliged so to insure in his home Member State and who provides services or carries out practice in any Host Member State shall use his best endeavours to obtain insurance cover on the basis required in his home Member State extended to services which he provides or practice which he carries out in a Host Member State.

3.9.2.3   A lawyer who fails to obtain the extended insurance cover referred to in paragraph 3.9.2.2 above or who is not obliged so to insure in his home Member State and who provides services or carries out practice in a Host Member State shall in so far as possible obtain insurance cover against his professional liability as a lawyer whilst acting for clients in that Host Member State on at least an equivalent basis to that required of lawyers in the Host Member State.

3.9.2.4   To the extent that a lawyer is unable to obtain the insurance cover required by the foregoing rules, he shall inform such of his clients as might be affected.

3.9.2.5   A lawyer who carries out practice or provides services in a Host Member State may with the agreement of the competent authorities of the Home and Host Member States concerned comply with such insurance requirements as are in force in the Host Member State to the exclusion of the insurance requirements of the Home Member State. In this event he shall take reasonable steps to inform his clients that he is insured according to the requirements in force in the Host Member State.

4   RELATIONS WITH THE COURTS

4.1   Applicable Rules of Conduct in Court

A lawyer who appears, or takes part in a case, before a court or tribunal in a Member State must comply with the rules of conduct applied before that court or tribunal.

4.2   Fair Conduct of Proceedings

A lawyer must always have due regard for the fair conduct of proceedings. He must not, for example, make contact with the judge without first informing the lawyer acting for the opposing party or submit exhibits, notes or documents to the judge without communicating them in good time to the lawyer on the other side unless such steps are permitted under the relevant rules of procedure. To the extent not prohibited by law a lawyer must not divulge or submit to the court any proposals for settlement of the case made by the other party or its lawyers without the express consent by the other party's lawyer.

4.3   Demeanour in Court

A lawyer shall while maintaining due respect and courtesy towards the court defend the interest of his client honourably and fearlessly without regard to his own interests or to any consequences to himself or to any other person.

4.4   False or Misleading Information

A lawyer shall never knowingly give false or misleading information to the court.

4.5   Extension to Arbitrators Etc.

The rules governing a lawyer's relations with the courts apply also to his relations with arbitrators and any other persons exercising judicial or quasi-judicial functions, even on an occasional basis.

5   RELATIONS BETWEEN LAWYERS

5.1   Corporate Spirit of the Profession

5.1.1   The corporate spirit of the profession requires a relationship of trust and co-operation between lawyers for the benefit of their clients and in order to avoid unnecessary litigation and other behaviour harmful to the reputation of the profession. It can, however, never justify setting the interests of the profession against those of the client.

5.1.2   A lawyer should recognise all other lawyers of Member States as professional colleagues and act fairly and courteously towards them.

5.2   Co-operation among Lawyers of Different Member States

5.2.1   It is the duty of a lawyer who is approached by a colleague from another Member State not to accept instructions in a matter which he is not competent to undertake. He should in such case be prepared to help his colleague to obtain the information necessary to enable him to instruct a lawyer who is capable of providing the service asked for.

5.2.2   Where a lawyer of a Member State co-operates with a lawyer from another Member State, both have a general duty to take into account the differences which may exist between their respective legal systems and the professional organisations competences and obligations of lawyers in the Member States concerned.

5.3   Correspondence Between Lawyers

5.3.1   If a lawyer sending a communication to a lawyer in another Member State wishes it to remain confidential or without prejudice he should clearly express this intention when communicating the document.

5.3.2   If the recipient of the communication is unable to ensure its status as confidential or without prejudice he should return it to the sender without revealing the contents to others.

5.4   Referral Fees

5.4.1   A lawyer may not demand or accept from another lawyer or any other person a fee, commission or any other compensation for referring or recommending the lawyer to a client.

5.4.2   A lawyer may not pay anyone a fee, commission or any other compensation as a consideration for referring a client to himself.

5.5   Communication with Opposing Parties

A lawyer shall not communicate about a particular case or matter directly with any person whom he knows to be represented or advised in the case or matter by another lawyer, without the consent of that other lawyer (and shall keep the other lawyer informed of any such communications).

5.6   Change of Lawyer

5.6.1   A lawyer who is instructed to represent a client in substitution for another lawyer in relation to a particular matter should inform that other lawyer and, subject to 5.6.2 below, should not begin to act until he has ascertained that arrangements have been made for the settlement of the other lawyer's fees and disbursements. This duty does not, however, make the new lawyer personally responsible for the former lawyer's fees and disbursements.

5.6.2   If urgent steps have to be taken in the interests of the client before the conditions in 5.6.1 above can be complied with, the lawyer may take such steps provided he informs the other lawyer immediately.

5.7   Responsibility for Fees

In professional relations between members of Bars of different Member States, where a lawyer does not confine himself to recommending another lawyer or introducing him to the client but himself entrusts a correspondent with a particular matter or seeks his advice, he is personally bound, even if the client is insolvent, to pay the fees, costs and outlays which are due to the foreign correspondent. The lawyers concerned may, however, at the outset of the relationship between them make special arrangements on this matter. Further, the instructing lawyer may at any time limit his personal responsibility to the amount of the fees, costs and outlays incurred before intimation to the foreign lawyer of his disclaimer of responsibility for the future.

5.8   Training Young Lawyers

In order to improve trust and co-operation amongst lawyers of different Member States for the clients' benefit there is a need to encourage a better knowledge of the laws and procedures in different Member States. Therefore when considering the need for the profession to give good training to young lawyers, lawyers should take into account the need to give training to young lawyers from other Member States.

5.9   Disputes Amongst Lawyers in Different Member States

5.9.1   If a lawyer considers that a colleague in another Member State has acted in breach of a rule of professional conduct he shall draw the matter to the attention of his colleague.

5.9.2   If any personal dispute of a professional nature arises amongst lawyers in different Member States they should if possible first try to settle it in a friendly way.

5.9.3   A lawyer shall not commence any form of proceedings against a colleague in another Member State on matters referred to in 5.9.1 or 5.9.2 above without first informing the Bars or Law Societies to which they both belong for the purpose of allowing both Bars or Law Societies concerned an opportunity to assist in reaching a settlement.

ANNEXE R

THE PUPILLAGE FUNDING AND ADVERTISING REQUIREMENTS 2003

Funding

1. The members of a set of chambers must pay to each non-practising chambers pupil by the end of each month of the non-practising six months of his pupillage no less than:

   (a) £833.33; plus

   (b) such further sum as may be necessary to reimburse expenses reasonably incurred by the pupil on:
       (i) travel for the purposes of his pupillage during that month; and
       (ii) attendance during that month at courses which he is required to attend as part of his pupillage.

2. The members of a set of chambers must pay to each practising chambers pupil by the end of each month of the practising six months of his pupillage no less than:

   (a) £833.33; plus

   (b) such further sum as may be necessary to reimburse expenses reasonably incurred by the pupil on:
       (i) travel for the purposes of his pupillage during that month; and
       (ii) attendance during that month at courses which he is required to attend as part of his pupillage; less

   (c) such amount, if any, as the pupil may receive during that month from his practice as a barrister; and less

   (d) such amounts, if any, as the pupil may have received during the preceding months of his practising pupillage from his practice as a barrister, save to the extent that the amount paid to the pupil in respect of any such month was less than the total of the sums provided for in sub-paragraphs (a) and (b) above.

3. The members of a set of chambers may not seek or accept repayment from a chambers pupil of any of the sums required to be paid under paragraphs 1 and 2 above, whether before or after he ceases to be a chambers pupil, save in the case of misconduct on his part.

Advertising

4. All vacancies for pupillages must be advertised on a website designated by the Bar Council and the following information must be provided:

   (a) The name and address of chambers.

   (b) The number of tenants.

   (c) A brief statement of the work undertaken by chambers e.g. 'predominately criminal'.

   (d) The number of pupillage vacancies.

   (e) The level of award.

   (f) The procedure for application.

   (g) The minimum educational or other qualification required.

   (h) The date of closure for the receipt of applications.

   (i) The date by which the decisions on the filling of vacancies will be made.

Application

5. The requirements set out in paragraphs 1 to 4 above:

    (a) apply in the case of pupillages commencing on or after 1st January 2003;

    (b) do not apply in the case of pupils who qualified for call to the Bar pursuant to regulations 35 (solicitors), 36 (other qualified lawyers) or 55 (teachers of the law of England and Wales of experience and distinction) of the Consolidated Regulations;

    (c) do not apply in the case of pupils who are undertaking a period of pupillage in a set of chambers as part of a pupillage training programme offered by another organisation that is authorised by the Bar Council to take pupils;

    (d) do not apply in the case of pupils who have completed both the non-practising and the practising six months of pupillage;

    (e) save as provided in paragraph 3 above, do not apply in respect of any period after a pupil ceases, for whatever reason, to be a chambers pupil; and

    (f) may be waived in part or in whole by the Pupillage Funding Committee.

6. For the purposes of these requirements:

    (a) 'chambers pupil' means, in respect of any set of chambers, a pupil undertaking the non-practising or practising six months of pupillage with a pupil-master or pupil- masters who is or are a member or members of that set of chambers;

    (b) 'non-practising chambers pupil' means a chambers pupil undertaking the nonpractising six months of pupillage;

    (c) 'practising chambers pupil' means a chambers pupil undertaking the practising six months of pupillage;

    (d) 'month' means calendar month commencing on the same day of the month as that on which the pupil commenced the non-practising or practising six months pupillage, as the case may be;

    (e) any payment made to a pupil by a barrister pursuant to paragraph 805 of the Code of Conduct shall constitute an amount received by the pupil from his practice as a barrister; and

    (f) the following travel by a pupil shall not constitute travel for the purposes of his pupillage:
        (i)   travel between his home and chambers; and
        (ii) travel for the purposes of his practice as a barrister.

SECTION 3

Miscellaneous Guidance

This section contains miscellaneous guidance, advice and information issued by the Bar Council. It does not form part of the Code.

INDEX

Pupillage Guidelines

Written Standards for the Conduct of Professional Work

Guidance on Preparation of Witness Statements

Guidance on Preparation of Defence Case Statements

Guidance on Holding Out as a Barrister

The Equality Code for the Bar

USEFUL WEB LINKS

There is a wealth of other guidance available from the following sources. In particular, you should ensure that you consult the Bar Council's website regularly and rely upon it as the most recent version of available guidance.

www.legaleducation.org.uk — this site will enable you to access the Consolidated Regulations of the Inns of Court, which are the rules governing qualification as a barrister.

www.barcouncil.org.uk — this is the Bar Council's website.

www.cps.gov.uk — the Crown Prosecution Service website, a useful source of guidance in relation to prosecution work and relationship between counsel and the CPS.

PUPILLAGE GUIDELINES

PART I — ADMINISTRATION

A Applications for Pupillage

1. **General**

(a) All chambers and other training organisations authorised by the Bar Council to take pupils must have selection procedures for pupils in which applicants are recruited through fair and open competition and on the basis of merit.

(b) All pupils must be recruited in accordance with the Equality Code or an employer's equal opportunities policy and other guidance issued by the Bar Council.

2. **Advertisement of Vacancies**

(a) All vacancies for pupillage in chambers must be advertised in accordance with the Pupillage Funding & Advertising Requirements.

(b) All vacancies for pupillage in organisations other than chambers are expected to be advertised in accordance with the Pupillage Funding & Advertising Requirements.

3. **Selection Procedures**

(a) Chambers and other organisations authorised by the Bar Council to take pupils must establish and follow selection procedures that ensure that pupils are selected through fair and open competition and on the basis of merit.

(b) In particular it is recommended that:

(i) selection criteria must be relevant and applied consistently to all applicants;

(ii) short listing and other selection decisions must be undertaken by at least two people;

(iii) applicants who are selected for interview must be sent a copy of the chambers' pupillage policy document prior to attending for interview;

(iv) all selectors should be familiar with the contents of the Equality Code.

(c) Records of all applicants and documentation relating to selection decisions should be kept for a period of at least one year. They should indicate the manner in which applications are disposed of and, where known, the ethnic origin and sex of each applicant.

4. **Registration**

(a) All chambers and other organisations authorised by the Bar Council to take pupils should ensure that each pupil has registered his pupillage with the Bar Council in accordance with Regulation 42 and Schedule 14, part 1 of the Consolidated Regulations before the pupillage commences.

(b) All pupils must be assigned a named pupil supervisor before the pupillage is registered with the Bar Council.

(c) Each organisation must ensure that a pupil supervisor to whom a pupil is assigned is entitled to act as a pupil supervisor under CR47.1, that is that he is entered on the register of approved Pupil Supervisors kept by the Bar Council, that his practice is and has been for the previous two years his primary occupation and that his principal place of practice is a chambers or office which is also the principal place of practice of at least one other barrister or member of another authorised body who is of at least three years standing.

(d) Each organisation must ensure that no more than one pupil is assigned to a pupil supervisor at a time, unless the pupil supervisor has obtained the prior approval of the Joint Regulations Committee.

B   Funding of Pupillage

1. All pupillages in chambers must be funded in accordance with the Pupillage Funding & Advertising Requirements.

C   Documentation and Records

1. **Pupillage Policy Document**

    (a) Every set of chambers or other organisation authorised by the Bar Council to take pupils must prepare a document or documents setting out its policies in relation to:

    - the number and type of pupillages on offer
    - recruitment of pupils
    - the roles and duties of pupils
    - the roles and duties of pupil supervisors
    - the general pattern of pupillage (e.g. whether it is served with one pupil supervisor etc)
    - the check list(s) used during pupillage
    - arrangements for funding, including payment of expenses
    - procedures for providing pupils with an objective assessment of their progress at regular intervals throughout pupillage
    - complaints and grievances by pupils and pupil supervisors

    (b) Every set of chambers which takes pupils should also include in its pupillage policy document its policies in relation to:

    - chambers policy on payment of devilling and work completed for other members of chambers
    - chambers policy on the payment of clerks fees and rent during the practising period of pupillage
    - the method for fairly distributing briefs and other work amongst working pupils
    - policy and procedure for the recruitment of tenants and when prospective tenants will be notified of tenancy decisions

    (c) All pupils should be given a copy of the pupillage policy document when they are shortlisted for interview and reminded of it at the start of the pupillage.

2. **Check lists**

    (a) All chambers or organisations authorised by the Bar Council to take pupils must ensure that all pupils use a check list in a form either generally or specially approved by the Education & Training Department of the Bar Council.

    (b) Completed check lists must be signed and dated by the pupil supervisor.

3. **Monitoring of Pupillage**

    (a) All chambers and organisations authorised by the Bar Council to take pupils must comply with the Bar Council's monitoring of pupillage scheme.

(b) Chambers and other organisations taking pupils are required to submit a pupillage return every year and to submit a copy of the pupillage policy document or documents and completed check lists when requested to do so by the Bar Council or a review panel.

PART II — CONDUCT OF PUPILLAGE

1. **Training**

   (a) Chambers and other organisations authorised by the Bar Council to take pupils should ensure that each pupil has a copy of the Pupillage File, Good Practice in Pupillage guide and the appropriate checklist by no later than the end of the first week of pupillage.

   (b) A pupil may only exercise a right of audience as a barrister in his practising six months of pupillage provided that he has completed or been exempted from the non-practising six months of pupillage and has been given permission from his pupil supervisor or head of chambers/training principal.

   (c) Pupil supervisors must ensure that the pupil has the opportunity to do all such work and gain all such experience as is appropriate for a person commencing practice in the type of work done by the pupil supervisor and in any event so as to enable the pupil to complete the check list, in particular
       (i) To ensure that the pupil has an understanding and appreciation of the operation in practice of rules of conduct and etiquette at the Bar
       (ii) To ensure that the pupil has gained sufficient practical experience of advocacy to be able to competently prepare and present a case
       (iii) To ensure that the pupil has gained sufficient practical experience of conferences and negotiation to be able to conduct the same competently
       (iv) To ensure that the pupil has gained sufficient practical experience in the undertaking of legal research and the preparation of drafts and opinions to be able to undertake the same competently

   (d) The pupil supervisor must ensure that the pupil is provided with, and retains, the appropriate check list, and completes it conscientiously and accurately. The pupil supervisor must sign and date the check list and should ensure that it is retained by chambers for a minimum of three years.

   (e) The pupil supervisor must give the pupil time off to attend the compulsory advocacy training and Advice to Counsel courses and should ensure that he or she has completed the courses satisfactorily.

2. **Distribution of Work in Chambers**

   (a) The distribution of briefs among practising pupils should be carried out in a manner fair to all pupils.

   (b) Sets of chambers in which advocacy work by practising pupils is a regular occurrence should establish a system for the purpose of regulating the distribution of briefs or instructions among pupils. The system should be made known to pupils at the commencement of pupillage. Heads of chambers should ensure that the distribution of work to working pupils is reviewed regularly. The distribution to pupils of unnamed work arriving in chambers and of work returned between members of chambers should be monitored.

3. **Certification**

    (a) Provided that the period of pupillage has been satisfactorily completed, the pupil must provide a pupil with a certificate in accordance with Consolidated Regulation 52.

    (b) If a pupil supervisor is not satisfied that the pupil has satisfactorily completed pupillage and he will not sign the certificate, he must notify the pupil of his or her options i.e. a certificate may be accepted from the pupil supervisor's Head of Chambers, the person designated by the Head of Chambers as the person in charge of pupillage, or another person acceptable to the Masters of the Bench and the Bar Council. If a pupil remains unable to obtain a relevant certificate the pupil may appeal to (a) the Masters of the Bench of the relevant Inn and then (b) the Joint Regulations Committee (Consolidated Regulation 52).

    (c) Pupil supervisors should familiarise themselves with the Equality Code for the Bar, the Pupillage File and the guide to Good Practice in Pupillage.

    (d) If the pupil supervisor leaves chambers he or she should where possible make arrangements for the pupil.

4. **Monitoring**

    (a) Chambers and other organisations authorised by the Bar Council to take pupils must have complaints and grievance procedures.

    (b) Chambers must have a policy in the event of chambers dissolving in relation to current pupils and students who have been made offers of pupillage.

    (c) All pupillage training organisations should put systems in place to ensure that checklists are adequately completed, signed off and retained until they are requested by the Bar Council.

    (d) At the end of each period of pupillage, a pupil supervisor's certificate of satisfactory completion of pupillage must be signed and submitted to the Bar Council.

    (e) At the end of each year, the head of chambers or training principal must submit to the Bar Council an annual return in the form prescribed by the Bar Council.

    (f) The pupillage policy document, annual pupillage return and completed checklists must be made available to the Bar Council on request, for the purposes of monitoring of pupillage.

    (g) Any pupil taken on as a tenant or employed barrister at the end of pupillage must have been issued with a full qualification certificate by the Bar Council.

WRITTEN STANDARDS FOR THE CONDUCT OF PROFESSIONAL WORK

GENERAL STANDARDS

1 Introduction

1.1 These Standards are intended as a guide to the way in which a barrister should carry out his work. They consist in part of matters which are dealt with expressly in the Code of Conduct and in part of statements of good practice. They must therefore be read in conjunction with the Code of Conduct, and are to be taken into account in determining whether or not a barrister has committed a disciplinary offence. They apply to employed barristers as well as to barristers in independent practice, except where this would be inappropriate. In addition to these General Standards, there are Standards which apply specifically to the conduct of criminal cases.

2 General

2.1 The work which is within the ordinary scope of a barrister's practice consists of advocacy, drafting pleadings and other legal documents and advising on questions of law. A barrister acts only on the instructions of a professional client, and does not carry out any work by way of the management, administration or general conduct of a lay client's affairs, nor the management, administration or general conduct of litigation nor the receipt or handling of clients' money.

2.2 It is a fundamental principle which applies to all work undertaken by a barrister that a barrister is under a duty to act for any client (whether legally aided or not) in cases within his field of practice. The rules which embody this principle and the exceptions to it are set out in paragraphs 303, 601, 602, 603, 604 and 605 of the Code of Conduct.

3 Acceptance of Work

3.1 As soon as practicable after receipt of any brief or instructions a barrister should satisfy himself that there is no reason why he ought to decline to accept it.

3.2 A barrister is not considered to have accepted a brief or instructions unless he has had an opportunity to consider it and has expressly accepted it.

3.3 A barrister should always be alert to the possibility of a conflict of interests. If the conflict is between the interests of his lay client and his professional client, the conflict must be resolved in favour of the lay client. Where there is a conflict between the lay client and the Legal Aid Fund, the conflict must be resolved in favour of the lay client, subject only to compliance with the provisions of the Legal Aid Regulations.

3.4 If after a barrister has accepted a brief or instructions on behalf of more than one lay client, there is or appears to be a conflict or a significant risk of a conflict between the interests of any one or more of such clients, he must not continue to act for any client unless all such clients give their consent to his so acting.

3.5 Even if there is no conflict of interest, when a barrister has accepted a brief or instructions for any party in any proceedings, he should not accept a brief or instructions in respect of an appeal or further stage of the proceedings for any other party without obtaining the prior consent of the original client.

3.6 A barrister must not accept any brief or instructions if the matter is one in which he has reason to believe that he is likely to be a witness. If, however, having accepted a brief or instructions, it later appears that he is likely to be a witness in the case on a material question of fact, he may retire or withdraw only if he can do so without jeopardising his client's interests.

3.7 A barrister should not appear as a barrister:

(a) in any matter in which he is a party or has a significant pecuniary interest;

(b) either for or against any local authority, firm or organisation of which he is a member or in which he has directly or indirectly a significant pecuniary interest;

(c) either for or against any company of which he is a director, secretary or officer or in which he has directly or indirectly a significant pecuniary interest.

3.8 Apart from cases in which there is a conflict of interests, a barrister must not accept any brief or instructions if to do so would cause him to be otherwise professionally embarrassed: paragraph 603 of the Code of Conduct sets out the general principles applicable to such situations.

4 Withdrawal from a Case and Return of Brief or Instructions

4.1 When a barrister has accepted a brief for the defence of a person charged with a serious criminal offence, he should so far as reasonably practicable ensure that the risk of a conflicting professional engagement does not arise.

4.2 The circumstances in which a barrister must withdraw from a case or return his brief or instructions are set out in paragraph 608 of the Code of Conduct; the circumstances in which he is permitted to do so are set out in paragraph 609 the circumstances in which he must not do so are set out in paragraph 610.

5 Conduct of Work

5.1 A barrister must at all times promote and protect fearlessly and by all proper and lawful means his lay client's best interests.

5.2 A barrister must assist the Court in the administration of justice and, as part of this obligation and the obligation to use only proper and lawful means to promote and protect the interests of his client, must not deceive or knowingly or recklessly mislead the Court.

5.3 A barrister is at all times individually and personally responsible for his own conduct and for his professional work both in Court and out of Court.

5.4 A barrister must in all his professional activities act promptly, conscientiously, diligently and with reasonable competence and must take all reasonable and practicable steps to ensure that professional engagements are fulfilled. He must not undertake any task which:

(a) he knows or ought to know he is not competent to handle;

(b) he does not have adequate time and opportunity to prepare for or perform; or

(c) he cannot discharge within a reasonable time having regard to the pressure of other work.

5.5 A barrister must at all times be courteous to the Court and to all those with whom he has professional dealings.

5.6 In relation to instructions to advise or draft documents, a barrister should ensure that the advice or document is provided within such time as has been agreed with the professional client, or otherwise within a reasonable time after receipt of the relevant instructions. If it becomes apparent to the barrister that he will not be able to do the work within that time, he must inform his professional client forthwith.

5.7   Generally, a barrister should ensure that advice which he gives is practical, appropriate to the needs and circumstances of the particular client, and clearly and comprehensibly expressed.

5.8   A barrister must exercise his own personal judgment upon the substance and purpose of any advice he gives or any document he drafts. He must not devise facts which will assist in advancing his lay client's case and must not draft any originating process, pleading, affidavit, witness statement or notice of appeal containing:

    (a) any statement of fact or contention (as the case may be) which is not supported by his lay client or by his brief or instructions;

    (b) any contention which he does not consider to be properly arguable;

    (c) any allegation of fraud unless he has clear instructions to make such an allegation and has before him reasonably credible material which as it stands establishes a prima facia case of fraud; or

    (d) in the case of an affidavit or witness statement, any statement of fact other than the evidence which in substance according to his instructions, the barrister reasonably believes the witness would give if the evidence contained in the affidavit or witness statement were being given viva voce.

5.9   A barrister should be available on reasonable notice for a conference prior to the day of hearing of any case in which he is briefed; and if no such conference takes place then the barrister should be available for a conference on the day of the hearing. The venue of a conference is a matter for agreement between the barrister and his professional clients.

5.10   A barrister when conducting proceedings at Court:

    (a) is personally responsible for the conduct and presentation of his case and must exercise personal judgment upon the substance and purpose of statements made and questions asked;

    (b) must not, unless asked to so by the Court or when appearing before a tribunal where it his duty to do so, assert a personal opinion of the facts or the law;

    (c) must ensure that the Court is informed of all relevant decisions and legislative provisions of which he is aware, whether the effect is favourable or unfavourable towards the contention for which he argues, and must bring any procedural irregularity to the attention of the Court during the hearing and not reserve such matter to be raised on appeal;

    (d) must not adduce evidence obtained otherwise than from or through his professional client or devise facts which will assist in advancing his lay client's case;

    (e) must not make statements or ask questions which are merely scandalous or intended or calculated only to vilify, insult or annoy either a witness or some other person;

    (f) must if possible avoid the naming in open Court of third parties whose character would thereby be impugned;

    (g) must not by assertion in a speech impugn a witness whom he has had an opportunity to cross-examine unless in cross-examination he has given the witness an opportunity to answer the allegation;

    (h) must not suggest that a victim, witness or other person is guilty of crime, fraud or misconduct or make any defamatory aspersion on the conduct of any other person or attribute to another person the crime or conduct of which his lay client is accused unless such allegations go to a matter in issue (including the credibility of the witness) which is material to his lay client's case, and which appear to him to be supported by reasonable grounds.

5.11   A barrister must take all reasonable and practicable steps to avoid unnecessary expense or waste of the Court's time. He should, when asked, inform the Court of the probable length of his case; and he should also inform the Court of any developments which affect information already provided.

5.12   In Court a barrister's personal appearance should be decorous, and his dress, when robes are worn, should be compatible with them.

6

6.1   Witnesses

6.1.1   The rules which define and regulate the barrister's functions in relation to the preparation of evidence and contact with witnesses are set out in paragraphs 704, 705, 706, 707 and 708 of the Code of Conduct.

6.1.2   There is no longer any rule which prevents a barrister from having contact with any witness.

6.1.3   In particular, there is no longer any rule in any case (including contested cases in the Crown Court) which prevents a barrister from having contact with a witness whom he may expect to call and examine in chief, with a view to introducing himself to the witness, explaining the court's procedure (and in particular the procedure for giving evidence), and answering any questions on procedure which the witness may have.

6.1.4   It is a responsibility of a barrister, especially when the witness is nervous, vulnerable or apparently the victim of criminal or similar conduct, to ensure that those facing unfamiliar court procedures are put as much at ease as possible.

6.1.5   Unless otherwise directed by the Court or with the consent of the representative for the opposing side or of the Court, a barrister should not communicate directly or indirectly about the case with any witness, whether or not the witness is his lay client, once that witness has begun to give evidence until it has been concluded.

6.2   Discussing the Evidence with Witnesses

6.2.1   Different considerations apply in relation to contact with witnesses for the purpose of interviewing them or discussing with them (either individually or together) the substance of their evidence or the evidence of other witnesses.

6.2.2   Although there is no longer any rule which prevents a barrister from having contact with witnesses for such purposes a barrister should exercise his discretion and consider very carefully whether and to what extent such contact is appropriate, bearing in mind in particular that it is not the barrister's function (but that of his professional client) to investigate and collect evidence.

6.2.3   The guiding principle must be the obligation of counsel to promote and protect his lay client's best interests so far as that is consistent with the law and with counsel's overriding duty to the court (Code of Conduct paragraphs 302, 303).

6.2.4   A barrister should be alert to the risks that any discussion of the substance of a case with a witness may lead to suspicions of coaching, and thus tend to diminish the value of the witness's evidence in the eyes of the court, or may place the barrister in a position of professional embarrassment, for example if he thereby becomes himself a witness in the case. These dangers are most likely to occur if such discussion takes place:

(a) before the barrister has been supplied with a proof of the witness's evidence; or

(b) in the absence of the barrister's professional client or his representative.

A barrister should also be alert to the fact that, even in the absence of any wish or intention to do so, authority figures do subconsciously influence lay witnesses. Discussion of the substance of the case may unwittingly contaminate the witness's evidence.

6.2.5   There is particular danger where such discussions:

(a) take place in the presence of more than one witness of fact; or

(b) involve the disclosure to one witness of fact of the factual evidence of another witness.

These practices have been strongly deprecated by the courts as tending inevitably to encourage the rehearsal or coaching of witnesses and to increase the risk of fabrication or contamination of evidence: *R* v *Arif* (1993) May 26; *Smith New Court Securities Ltd* v *Scrimgeour Vickers (Asset Management) Ltd* [1992] BCLC 1104, [1994] 1 WLR 1271.

That is not to suggest that it is always inappropriate to disclose one witness' evidence to another. If the witness is one to be called by the other party, it is almost inevitable that a witness' attention must be drawn to discrepancies between the two statements. Discretion is, however, required, especially where the evidence of independent witnesses is involved.

6.2.6   Whilst there is no rule that any longer prevents a barrister from taking a witness statement in civil cases (for cases in the Crown Court see below), there is a distinction between the settling of a witness statement and taking a witness statement. It is not appropriate for a barrister who has taken witness statements, as opposed to settling witness statements prepared by others, to act as counsel unless he is a junior member of the team of Counsel and will not be examining the witness or there are exceptional circumstances, because it risks undermining the independence of the barrister as an advocate. Exceptional circumstances would include:

(a) the witness is a minor one;

(b) Counsel has no choice but to take a proof and this is the only practical course in the interests of justice — this would apply, for instance, where a witness appears unexpectedly at Court and there is no one else competent to take the statement.

The Cab-rank Rule does not require a barrister to agree to undertake the task of taking witness statements.

6.2.7   There is no rule which prevents a barrister from exchanging common courtesies with the other side's witnesses. However, a barrister should not discuss the substance of the case or any evidence with the other side's witnesses except in rare and exceptional circumstances and then only with the prior knowledge of his opponent.

6.3   Criminal Cases in the Crown Court

6.3.1   Contested criminal cases in the Crown Court present peculiar difficulties and may expose both barristers and witnesses to special pressures. As a general principle, therefore, with the exception of the lay client, character and expert witnesses, it is wholly inappropriate for a barrister in such a case to interview any potential witness. Interviewing includes discussing with any such witness the substance of his evidence or the evidence of other such witnesses.

6.3.2   As a general principle, prosecuting counsel should not confer with an investigator witness unless he has also discharged some supervisory responsibility in the investigation and should not confer with investigators or receive factual instructions directly from them on matters about which there is or may be a dispute.

6.3.3   There may be extraordinary circumstances in which a departure from the general principles set out in paragraphs 6.3.1 and 6.3.2 is unavoidable. An example of such circumstances is afforded by the decision in *Fergus* (1994) 98 Cr App R 313.

6.3.4   Where any barrister has interviewed any potential witness or any such witness has been interviewed by another barrister, that fact shall be disclosed to all other parties in the case before the witness is called. A written record must also be made of the substance of the interview and the reason for it.

7   Documents

7.1   A barrister should not obtain or seek to obtain a document, or knowledge of the contents of a document, belonging to another party other than by means of the normal and proper channels for obtaining such documents or such knowledge.

7.2   If a barrister comes into possession of a document belonging to another party by some means other than the normal and proper channels (for example, if the document has come into his possession in consequence of a mistake or inadvertence by another person or if the document appears to belong to another party, or to be a copy of such a document, and to be privileged from discovery or otherwise to be one which ought not to be in the possession of his professional or lay client) he should:

(a)   where appropriate make enquiries of his professional client in order to ascertain the circumstances in which the document was obtained by his professional or lay client; and

(b)   unless satisfied that the document has been properly obtained in the ordinary course of events at once return the document unread to the person entitled to possession of it.

7.3.1   If having come into possession of such a document the barrister reads it before he realises that he ought not to, and would be embarrassed in the discharge of his duties by his knowledge of the contents of the document, then provided he can do so without prejudice to his lay client he must return his brief or instructions and explain to his professional client why he has done so.

7.3.2   If, however, to return his brief or instructions would prejudice his lay client (for example, by reason of the proximity of the trial) he should not return his brief or instructions and should, unless the Court otherwise orders, make such use of the document as will be in his client's interests. He should inform his opponent of his knowledge of the document and of the circumstances, so far as known to him, in which the document was obtained and of his intention to use it. In the event of objection to the use of such document it is for the Court to determine what use, if any, may be made of it.

7.4   If during the course of a case a barrister becomes aware of the existence of a document which should have been but has not been disclosed on discovery he should advise his professional client to disclose it forthwith; and if it is not then disclosed, he must withdraw from the case.

8   Administration of Practice

8.1   A barrister must ensure that his practice is properly and efficiently administered in accordance with the provisions of paragraph 304 of the Code of Conduct.

8.2   A barrister should ensure that he is able to provide his professional client with full and proper details of and appropriate justification for fees which have been incurred, and a proper assessment of any work to be done, so that both the lay client and the professional client are able to determine the level of any financial commitment which has been incurred or may be incurred.

STANDARDS APPLICABLE TO CRIMINAL CASES

9   Introduction

9.1   These standards are to be read together with the General Standards and the Code of Conduct. They are intended as a guide to those matters which specifically relate to practice in the criminal Courts. They are not an alternative to the General Standards, which apply to all work carried out by a barrister. Particular reference is made to those paragraphs in the General Standards relating to the general conduct of a case (5.8), conduct in Court (5.10), discussion with witnesses (6.1, 6.2) and the use of documents belonging to other parties (7.1, 7.2, 7.3), which are not repeated in these standards.

10   Responsibilities of Prosecuting Counsel

10A   The Standards and principles contained in this paragraph apply as appropriate to all practising barristers, whether in independent practice or employed and whether appearing as counsel in any given case or exercising any other professional capacity in connection with it.

10.1 Prosecuting counsel should not attempt to obtain a conviction by all means at his command. He should not regard himself as appearing for a party. He should lay before the Court fairly and impartially the whole of the facts which comprise the case for the prosecution and should assist the Court on all matters of law applicable to the case.

10.2 Prosecuting counsel should bear in mind at all times whilst he is instructed:

(i)   that he is responsible for the presentation and general conduct of the case;

(ii) that he should use his best endeavours to ensure that all evidence or material that ought properly to be made available is either presented by the prosecution or disclosed to the defence.

10.3 Prosecuting counsel should, when instructions are delivered to him, read them expeditiously and, where instructed to do so, advise or confer on all aspects of the case well before its commencement.

10.4 In relation to cases tried in the Crown Court, prosecuting counsel:

(a) should ensure, if he is instructed to settle an indictment, that he does so promptly and within due time, and should bear in mind the desirability of not overloading an indictment with either too many defendants or too many counts, in order to present the prosecution case as simply and as concisely as possible;

(b) should ask, if the indictment is being settled by some other person, to see a copy of the indictment and should then check it;

(c) should decide whether any additional evidence is required and, if it is, should advise in writing and set out precisely what additional evidence is required with a view to serving it on the defence as soon as possible;

(d) should consider whether all witness statements in the possession of the prosecution have been properly served on the defendant in accordance with the Attorney-General's Guidelines;

(e) should eliminate all unnecessary material in the case so as to ensure an efficient and fair trial, and in particular should consider the need for particular witnesses and exhibits and draft appropriate admissions for service on the defence;

(f) should in all Class 1 and Class 2 cases and in other cases of complexity draft a case summary for transmission to the Court.

10.5   Paragraphs 6 to 6.3.4 of the Written Standards for the Conduct of Professional Work refer.

10.6   Prosecuting counsel should at all times have regard to the report of Mr Justice Farquharson's Committee on the role of Prosecuting Counsel which is set out in *Archbold*. In particular, he should have regard to the following recommendations of the Farquharson Committee:

(a) Where counsel has taken a decision on a matter of policy with which his professional client has not agreed, it would be appropriate or him to submit to the Attorney-General a written report of all the circumstances, including his reasons for disagreeing with those who instructed him;

(b) When counsel has had an opportunity to prepare his brief and to confer with those instructing him, but at the last moment before trial unexpectedly advises that the case should not proceed or that pleas to lesser offences should be accepted, and his professional client does not accept such advice, counsel should apply for an adjournment if instructed to do so;

(c) Subject to the above, it is for prosecuting counsel to decide whether to offer no evidence on a particular count or on the indictment as a whole and whether to accept pleas to a lesser count or counts.

10.7   It is the duty of prosecuting counsel to assist the Court at the conclusion of the summingup by drawing attention to any apparent errors or omissions of fact or law.

10.8   In relation to sentence, prosecuting counsel:

(a) should not attempt by advocacy to influence the Court with regard to sentence: if, however, a defendant is unrepresented it is proper to inform the Court of any mitigating circumstances about which counsel is instructed;

(b) should be in a position to assist the Court if requested as to any statutory provisions relevant to the offence or the offender and as to any relevant guidelines as to sentence laid down by the Court of Appeal;

(c) should bring any such matters as are referred to in (b) above to the attention of the Court if in the opinion of prosecuting counsel the Court has erred;

(d) should bring to the attention of the Court any appropriate compensation, forfeiture and restitution matters which may arise on conviction, for example pursuant to sections 35–42 of the Powers of Criminal Courts Act 1973 and the Drug Trafficking Offences Act 1986;

(e) should draw the attention of the defence to any assertion of material fact made in mitigation which the prosecution believes to be untrue: if the defence persist in that assertion, prosecuting counsel should invite the Court to consider requiring the issue to be determined by the calling of evidence in accordance with the decision of the Court of Appeal in *R* v *Newton* (1983) 77 Cr App R 13.

11   Responsibilities of Defence Counsel

11.1   When defending a client on a criminal charge, a barrister must endeavour to protect his client from conviction except by a competent tribunal and upon legally admissible evidence sufficient to support a conviction for the offence charged.

11.2   A barrister acting for the defence:

(a) should satisfy himself, if he is briefed to represent more than one defendant, that no conflict of interest is likely to arise;

(b) should arrange a conference and if necessary a series of conferences with his professional and lay clients;

(c) should consider whether any enquiries or further enquiries are necessary and, if so, should advise in writing as soon as possible;

(d) should consider whether any witnesses for the defence are required and, if so, which;

(e) should consider whether a Notice of Alibi is required and, if so, should draft an appropriate notice;

(f) should consider whether it would be appropriate to call expert evidence for the defence and, if so, have regard to the rules of the Crown Court in relation to notifying the prosecution of the contents of the evidence to be given;

(g) should ensure that he has sufficient instructions for the purpose of deciding which prosecution witnesses should be cross-examined, and should then ensure that no other witnesses remain fully bound at the request of the defendant and request his professional client to inform the Crown Prosecution Service of those who can be conditionally bound;

(h) should consider whether any admissions can be made with a view to saving time and expense at trial, with the aim of admitting as much evidence as can properly be admitted in accordance with the barrister's duty to his client;

(i) should consider what admissions can properly be requested from the prosecution;

(j) should decide what exhibits, if any, which have not been or cannot be copied he wishes to examine, and should ensure that appropriate arrangements are made to examine them as promptly as possible so that there is no undue delay in the trial.

(k) should as to anything which he is instructed to submit in mitigation which casts aspersions on the conduct or character of a victim or witness in the case, notify the prosecution in advance so as to give prosecuting Counsel sufficient opportunity to consider his position under paragraph 10.8(e).

11.3   A barrister acting for a defendant should advise his lay client generally about his plea. In doing so he may, if necessary, express his advice in strong terms. He must, however, make it clear that the client has complete freedom of choice and that the responsibility for the plea is the client's.

11.4   A barrister acting for a defendant should advise his client as to whether or not to give evidence in his own defence but the decision must be taken by the client himself.

11.5

11.5.1   Where a defendant tells his counsel that he did not commit the offence with which he is charged but nevertheless insists on pleading guilty to it for reasons of his own, counsel should:

(a) advise the defendant that, if he is not guilty, he should plead not guilty but that the decision is one for the defendant; counsel must continue to represent him but only after he has advised what the consequences will be and that what can be submitted in mitigation can only be on the basis that the client is guilty.

(b) explore with the defendant why he wishes to plead guilty to a charge which he says he did not commit and whether any steps could be taken which would enable him to enter a plea of not guilty in accordance with his profession of innocence.

11.5.2   If the client maintains his wish to plead guilty, he should be further advised:

(a) what the consequences will be, in particular in gaining or adding to a criminal record and that it is unlikely that a conviction based on such a plea would be overturned on appeal;

(b) that what can be submitted on his behalf in mitigation can only be on the basis that he is guilty and will otherwise be strictly limited so that, for instance, counsel will not be able to assert that the defendant has shown remorse through his guilty plea.

11.5.3   If, following all of the above advice, the defendant persists in his decision to plead guilty

(a) counsel may continue to represent him if he is satisfied that it is proper to do so;

(b) before a plea of guilty is entered counsel or a representative of his professional client who is present should record in writing the reasons for the plea;

(c) the defendant should be invited to endorse a declaration that he has given unequivocal instructions of his own free will that he intends to plead guilty even though he maintains that he did not commit the offence(s) and that he understands the advice given by counsel and in particular the restrictions placed on counsel in mitigating and the consequences to himself; the defendant should also be advised that he is under no obligation to sign; and

(d) if no such declaration is signed, counsel should make a contemporaneous note of his advice.

12   Confessions of Guilt

12.1   In considering the duty of counsel retained to defend a person charged with an offence who confesses to his counsel that he did commit the offence charged, it is essential to bear the following points clearly in mind:

(a) that every punishable crime is a breach of common or statute law committed by a person of sound mind and understanding;

(b) that the issue in a criminal trial is always whether the defendant is guilty of the of- fence charged, never whether he is innocent;

(c) that the burden of proof rests on the prosecution.

12.2   It follows that the mere fact that a person charged with a crime has confessed to his counsel that he did commit the offence charged is no bar to that barrister appearing or continuing to appear in his defence, nor indeed does such a confession release the barrister from his imperative duty to do all that he honourably can for his client.

12.3   Such a confession, however, imposes very strict limitations on the conduct of the defence, a barrister must not assert as true that which he knows to be false. He must not connive at, much less attempt to substantiate, a fraud.

12.4   While, therefore, it would be right to take any objections to the competency of the Court, to the form of the indictment, to the admissibility of any evidence or to the evidence admitted, it would be wrong to suggest that some other person had committed the offence charged, or to call any evidence which the barrister must know to be false having regard to the confession, such, for instance, as evidence in support of an alibi. In other words, a barrister must not (whether by calling the defendant or otherwise) set up an affirmative case inconsistent with the confession made to him.

12.5   A more difficult question is within what limits may counsel attack the evidence for the prosecution either by cross-examination or in his speech to the tribunal charged with the decision of the facts. No clearer rule can be laid down than this, that he is entitled to test the evidence given by each individual witness and to argue that the evidence taken as a whole is insufficient to amount to proof that the defendant is guilty of the offence charged. Further than this he ought not to go.

12.6   The foregoing is based on the assumption that the defendant has made a clear confession that he did commit the offence charged, and does not profess to deal with the very difficult questions which may present themselves to a barrister when a series of inconsistent statements are made to him by the defendant before or during the proceedings; nor does it deal with the questions which may arise where statements are made by the defendant which point almost irresistibly to the conclusion that the defendant is guilty but do not amount to a clear confession. Statements of this kind may inhibit the defence, but questions arising on them can only be answered after careful consideration of the actual circumstances of the particular case.

13   General

13.1   Both prosecuting and defence counsel:

(a) should ensure that the listing officer receives in good time their best estimate of the likely length of the trial (including whether or not there is to be a plea of guilty) and should ensure that the listing officer is given early notice of any change of such estimate or possible adjournment;

(b) should take all reasonable and practicable steps to ensure that the case is properly prepared and ready for trial by the time that it is first listed;

(c) should ensure that arrangements have been made in adequate time for witnesses to attend Court as and when required and should plan, so far as possible, for sufficient witnesses to be available to occupy the full Court day;

(d) should, if a witness (for example a doctor) can only attend Court at a certain time during the trial without great inconvenience to himself, try to arrange for that witness to be accommodated by raising the matter with the trial Judge and with his opponent;

(e) should take all necessary steps to comply with the Practice Direction (Crime: Tape Recording of Police Interviews) [1989] 1 WLR 631.

13.2 If properly remunerated (paragraph 502 of the Code), the barrister originally briefed in a case should attend all plea and directions hearings. If this is not possible, he must take all reasonable steps to ensure that the barrister who does appear is conversant with the case and is prepared to make informed decisions affecting the trial.

14 Video Recordings

14.1 When a barrister instructed and acting for the prosecution or the defence of an accused has in his possession a copy of a video recording of a child witness which has been identified as having been prepared to be admitted in evidence at a criminal trial in accordance with Section 54 of the Criminal Justice Act 1991, he must have regard to the following duties and obligations:

(a) Upon receipt of the recording, a written record of the date and time and from whom the recording was received must be made and a receipt must be given.

(b) The recording and its contents must be used only for the proper preparation of the prosecution or defence case or of an appeal against conviction and/or sentence, as the case may be, and the barrister must not make or permit any disclosure of the recording or its contents to any person except when, in his opinion, it is in the interests of his proper preparation of that case.

(c) The barrister must not make or permit any other person to make a copy of the recording, nor release the recording to the accused, and must ensure that:
   (i) when not in transit or in use, the recording is always kept in a locked or secure place, and:
   (ii) when in transit, the recording is kept safe and secure at all times and is not left unattended, especially in vehicles or otherwise.

(d) Proper preparation of the case may involve viewing the recording in the presence of the accused. If this is the case, viewing should be done:
   (i) if the accused is in custody, only in the prison or other custodial institution where he is being held, in the presence of the barrister and/or his instructing solicitor.
   (ii) if the accused is on bail, at the solicitor's office or in counsel's chambers or elsewhere in the presence of the barrister and/or his instructing solicitor.

(e) The recording must be returned to the solicitor as soon as practicable after the conclusion of the barrister's role in the case. A written record of the date and time despatched and to whom the recording was delivered for despatch must be made.

15 Attendance of Counsel at Court

15.1 Prosecuting counsel should be present throughout the trial, including the summing-up and the return of the jury. He may not absent himself without leave of the Court; but, if two or more barristers appear for the prosecution, the attendance of one is sufficient.

15.2

15.2.1   Defence counsel should ensure that the defendant is never left unrepresented at any stage of his trial.

15.2.2   Where a defendant is represented by one barrister, that barrister should normally be present throughout the trial and should only absent himself in exceptional circumstances which he could not reasonably be expected to foresee and provided that:

(a) he has obtained the consent of the professional client (or his representative) and the lay client; and

(b) a competent deputy takes his place.

15.2.3   Where a defendant is represented by two barristers, neither may absent himself except for good reason and then only when the consent of the professional client (or his representative) and of the lay client has been obtained, or when the case is legally aided and the barrister thinks it necessary to do so in order to avoid unnecessary public expense.

15.2.4   These rules are subject to modification in respect of lengthy trials involving numerous defendants. In such trials, where after the conclusion of the opening speech by the prosecution defending counsel is satisfied that during a specific part of the trial there is no serious possibility that events will occur which will relate to his client, he may with the consent of the professional client (or his representative) and of the lay client absent himself for that part of the trial. He should also inform the judge. In this event it is his duty:

(a) to arrange for other defending counsel to guard the interests of his client;

(b) to keep himself informed throughout of the progress of the trial and in particular of any development which could affect his client; and

(c) not to accept any other commitment which would render it impracticable for him to make himself available at reasonable notice if the interests of his client so require.

15.3.1   If during the course of a criminal trial and prior to final sentence the defendant voluntarily absconds and the barrister's professional client, in accordance with the ruling of the Law Society, withdraws from the case, then the barrister too should withdraw. If the trial judge requests the barrister to remain to assist the Court, the barrister has an absolute discretion whether to do so or not. If he does remain, he should act on the basis that his instructions are withdrawn and he will not be entitled to use any material contained in his brief save for such part as has already been established in evidence before the Court. He should request the trial judge to instruct the jury that this is the basis on which he is prepared to assist the Court.

15.3.2   If for any reason the barrister's professional client does not withdraw from the case, the barrister retains an absolute discretion whether to continue to act. If he does continue, he should conduct the case as if his client were still present in Court but had decided not to give evidence and on the basis of any instruction he has received. He will be free to use any material contained in his brief and may cross-examine witnesses called for the prosecution and call witnesses for the defence.

16 Appeals

16.1

16.1.1   Attention is drawn to the Guide to Proceedings in the Court of Appeal Criminal Division ('the Guide') which is set out in full its original form at (1983) 77 Cr App R 138 and is summarised in a version amended in April 1990 Volume 1 of *Archbold* at 7–173 to 7–184.

16.1.2   In particular when advising after a client pleads guilty or is convicted, defence counsel is encouraged to follow the procedures set out at paragraphs 1.2 and 1.4 of the Guide.

16.2   If his client pleads guilty or is convicted, defence counsel should see his client after he has been sentenced in the presence of his professional client or his representative. He should then proceed as follows:

(a) if he is satisfied that there are no reasonable grounds of appeal he should so advise orally and certify in writing. Counsel is encouraged to certify using the form set out in Appendix 1 to the Guide. No further advice is necessary unless it is reasonable for a written advice to be given because the client reasonably requires it or because it is necessary e.g. in the light of the circumstances of the conviction, any particular difficulties at trial, the length and nature of the sentence passed, the effect thereof on the defendant or the lack of impact which oral advice given immediately after the trial may have on the particular defendant's mind.

(b) if he is satisfied that there are more reasonable grounds of appeal or if his view is a provisional one or if he requires more time to consider the prospects of a successful appeal he should so advise orally and certify in writing. Counsel is encouraged to certify using the form set out in Appendix 1 to the Guide. Counsel should then furnish written advice to the professional client as soon as he can and in any event within 14 days.

16.3   Counsel should not settle grounds of appeal unless he considers that such grounds are properly arguable, and in that event he should provide a reasoned written opinion in sup- port of such grounds.

16.4   In certain cases counsel may not be able to perfect grounds of appeal without a transcript or other further information. In this event the grounds of appeal should be accompanied by a note to the Registrar setting out the matters on which assistance is required. Once such transcript or other information is available, counsel should ensure that the grounds of appeal are perfected by the inclusion of all necessary references.

16.5   Grounds of Appeal must be settled with sufficient particularity to enable the Registrar and subsequently the Court to identify clearly the matters relied upon.

16.6   If at any stage counsel is of the view that the appeal should be abandoned, he should at once set out his reasons in writing and send them to his professional client.

GUIDANCE ON PREPARATION OF WITNESS STATEMENTS

PREPARING WITNESS STATEMENTS FOR USE IN CIVIL PROCEEDINGS

DEALINGS WITH WITNESSES

GUIDANCE FOR MEMBERS OF THE BAR

[Amended 3 February 2001]

Introduction

1. The purpose of this paper, which has the approval of the Professional Standards Committee of the General Council of the Bar, is to offer guidance to members of the Bar instructed to prepare or settle a witness statement and as to dealings with witnesses. Guidance already exists for practice in some Courts, notably Appendix 4 to the Chancery Guide, Part H1 of the Commercial Court Guide and CPR Part 32 and PD 32, paragraphs 17 to 25 to which attention is drawn. The intention is that this paper should be consistent with that guidance.

2. This guidance is not applicable to criminal proceedings. Attention is drawn to the Guidance Note 'Written Standards for the Conduct of Professional Work' in Section 3 of the Code of Conduct.

Witness statements

3. The cardinal principle that needs to be kept in mind when drafting or settling a witness statement is that, when the maker enters the witness box, he or she will swear or affirm that the evidence to be given will be the truth, the *whole truth* and nothing but the truth. In most civil trials almost the first question in chief (and not infrequently the last) will be to ask the witness to confirm, to the best of his belief, the accuracy of the witness statement. It is therefore critical that the statement is one that accurately reflects, to the best of Counsel's ability, the witness's evidence.

4. Witnesses often misunderstand the function of those drafting and settling witness statements. The function of Counsel is to understand the relevant evidence that a witness can give and to assist the witness to express that evidence in the witness's own words. It is important it is made clear to the witness (by reminder to the professional client or the witness, if seen by Counsel) that the statement once approved is *the witness's* statement. Ultimately it is the witness's responsibility to ensure that the evidence he gives is truthful. It is good practice to remind witnesses expressly of this from time to time, especially where Counsel is assisting the witness to formulate in his own words a particular aspect of the evidence or putting forward a particular piece of drafting for the witness's consideration (which is expressly permitted by the proviso to Rule 704 of the Code of Conduct).

5. It is not Counsel's duty to vet the accuracy of a witness's evidence.[1] We all may doubt the veracity of our clients and witnesses occasionally. Counsel is, of course, entitled and it may often be appropriate to draw to the witness's attention other evidence which appears to conflict with what the witness is saying and is entitled to indicate that a Court may find a particular piece of evidence difficult to accept. But if the witness maintains the evidence, it should be recorded in the witness statement. If it is decided to call the witness, it will be for the Court to judge the correctness of the witness's evidence.

---

[1] If para. 6 of Appendix 4 of the Chancery Guide suggests otherwise, the PSC respectfully disagrees. The position would, of course, be different if to Counsel's knowledge the witness statement contained untruths: see *ZYX Music GmbH v King* [1995] 3 All ER 1.

6.   It follows that the statement:

(i)   Must accurately reflect the witness's evidence. Rule 704 of the Code of Conduct states:

'A barrister must not devise facts which will assist in advancing the lay client's case and must not draft any . . . witness statement [or] affidavit . . . containing:

. . .

(d)   in the case of a witness statement or affidavit any statement of fact other than the evidence which in substance according to his instructions the barrister reasonably believes the witness would give if the evidence contained in the witness statement or affidavit were being given in oral examination;[2]

provided that nothing in this paragraph shall prevent a barrister drafting a document containing specific factual statements or contentions included by the barrister subject to confirmation of their accuracy by the lay client or witness.'

(ii)   Must not contain any statement which Counsel knows the witness does not believe to be true. Nor should the witness be placed under any pressure to provide other than a truthful account of his evidence.

(iii)   Must contain all the evidence which a witness could reasonably be expected to give in answer to those questions which would be asked of him in examination-in-chief. The witness statement should not be drafted or edited so that it no longer fairly reflects the answers which the witness would be expected to give in response to oral examination-in-chief in accordance with the witness's oath or affirmation. Although it is not the function of a witness statement to answer such questions as might be put in cross-examination, great care should be exercised when excluding any material which is thought to be unhelpful to the party calling the witness and no material should be excluded which might render the statement anything other than the truth, the whole truth and nothing but the truth. While it is permissible to confine the scope of examination-in-chief to part only of the evidence which a witness could give, that is always subject to Counsel's overriding duty to assist the Court in the administration of justice and not to deceive or knowingly or recklessly to mislead the Court (Rule 302 of the Code of Conduct). Consequently, it would be improper to exclude material whose omission would render untrue or misleading anything which remains in the statement. It would also be improper to include fact A while excluding fact B, if evidence-in-chief containing fact A but excluding fact B could not have been given consistently with the witness's promise to tell the truth, the whole truth and nothing but the truth. Whether it is wise and in the client's interest in any given case to exclude unfavourable material which can properly be excluded is a matter of judgment.

(iv)   Save for formal matters and uncontroversial facts, should be expressed if practicable in the witness's own words. This is especially important when the statement is dealing with the critical factual issues in the case — e.g. the accident or the disputed conversation. Thus the statement should reflect the witness's own description of events. It should not be drafted or edited so as to massage or obscure the witness' real evidence.

---

[2] CPR Part 32.4(1).

(v) Must be confined to admissible evidence that the witness can give, including permissible hearsay.[3] Inadmissible hearsay, comment and argument should be excluded.

(vi) Should be succinct and exclude irrelevant material. Unnecessary elaboration is to be avoided. It is not the function of witness statements to serve as a commentary on the documents in the trial bundles. Nor are they intended to serve as another form of written argument.

7. Sometimes it becomes apparent, after a witness statement has been served, that the witness's recollection has altered. This may happen if the witness sees or hears how another witness puts the facts in a witness statement served by another party. Where Counsel learns that the witness has materially changed his evidence—

(i) He should consider with, and if necessary advise, his professional or BarDirect[4] client whether, in the circumstances, a correction to the original statement needs to be made in order to avoid another party being unfairly misled.

(ii) Where a correction to the original statement is appropriate, this should be done by recording the changed evidence in an additional witness statement and serving it on the other parties (and if appropriate filing it at court). If this is impracticable, e.g. because it occurs very shortly before the hearing, the other parties should be informed of the change immediately and the statement should be corrected at an early stage in court.

(iii) The underlying principle is that it is improper for a litigant to mislead the court or another party to the litigation.[5]

(iv) If a lay or BarDirect client refuses to accept Counsel's advice that disclosure of a correction should be made, Counsel's duty is to withdraw from further acting for the client.

Formalities

8. A witness statement:

(i) Should be expressed in the first person;

(ii) Should state the full name of the witness and the witness's place of residence or, if the statement is made in a professional, business or other occupational capacity, the address at which he works, the position he holds and the name of the firm or employer;

(iii) Should state the witness's occupation or if he has none his description;

(iv) Should state if the witness is a party to the proceedings or is an employee of such a party;

(v) Should usually be in chronological sequence divided into consecutively numbered paragraphs each of which should, so far as possible, be confined to a distinct portion of the evidence;

(vi) Must indicate which of the statements in it are made from the witness's own knowledge and which are matters of information and belief, indicating the source for any matters of information and belief;

---

[3] 32PD, para. 18.2 requires the witness to indicate which of the statements are matters of information and belief and the source for any such matters.

[4] Note that under the 8th Edition of the Code, 'BarDirect' is now termed 'licensed access'.

[5] On the duty to make disclosure of material changes of evidence and new documents, see generally *Vernon v Bosley (No. 2)* [1999] QB 18.

(vii) Must include a statement by the witness that he believes that the facts stated in it are true;

(viii) Must be signed by the witness or, if the witness cannot read or sign it, must contain a certificate made by an authorised person as to the witness's approval of the statement as being accurate;[6]

(ix) Must have any alterations initialled by the witness or by the authorised person;

(x) Should give in the margin the reference to any document or documents mentioned;

(xi) Must be dated.

There are further formal requirements in 32PD, paras 17–19, relating to intitulement, exhibits, pagination, production and presentation, to which attention is directed.

Dealings with Witnesses

Counsel seeing witnesses.[7]

9. The old rules preventing Counsel from seeing a witness, other than the client, have been progressively relaxed over recent years. The current position in civil proceedings can be summarised as follows:

(i) There is no longer any rule which prevents a barrister from having contact with any witness. Indeed, in taking witness statements and generally, it is the responsibility of a barrister, especially when the witness is nervous, vulnerable or apparently the victim of criminal or similar conduct, to ensure that those facing unfamiliar court procedures are put as much at ease as possible.

(ii) Although there is no longer any rule which prevents a barrister from having contact with witnesses, a barrister should exercise his discretion and consider very carefully whether and to what extent such contact is appropriate, bearing in mind in particular that it is not the barrister's function (but that of his professional client) to investigate and collect evidence.

(iii) The guiding principle must be the obligation of Counsel to promote and protect his lay client's best interests so far as that is consistent with the law and with Counsel's overriding duty to the Court (Code of Conduct paragraphs 302, 303). Often it will be in the client's best interests that Counsel should meet witnesses whose evidence will be of critical importance in the case, so as to be able to form a view as to the credibility of their evidence and to advise the lay client properly;

(iv) A barrister should be alert to the risks that any discussion of the substance of a case with a witness may lead to suspicions of coaching, and thus tend to diminish the value of the witness's evidence in the eyes of the court, or may place a barrister in a position of professional embarrassment, for example, if he thereby becomes himself a witness in the case. These dangers are most likely to occur if such discussion takes place:

(a) before the barrister has been supplied with a proof of the witness's evidence; or

(b) in the absence of the barrister's professional client or his representative.

---

[6] See 32PD, para. 21.

[7] This is largely taken from guidance Note 'Written Standards for the Conduct of Professional Work' in Section 3 of the Code of Conduct approved by the Lord Chancellor's Advisory Committee on Legal Education and Conduct and the designated judges.

(v)   Rule 705 of the Code of Conduct provides that a barrister must not rehearse practise or coach a witness in relation to his evidence. This does not prevent Counsel giving general advice to a witness about giving evidence e.g. speak up, speak slowly, answer the question, keep answers as short as possible, ask if a question is not understood, say if you cannot remember and do not guess or speculate. Nor is there any objection to testing a witness's recollection robustly to ascertain the quality of his evidence or to discussing the issues that may arise in cross-examination. By contrast, mock cross-examinations or rehearsals of particular lines of questioning that Counsel proposes to follow are not permitted. What should be borne in mind is that there is a distinction, when interviewing a witness, between questioning him closely in order to enable him to present his evidence fully and accurately or in order to test the reliability of his evidence (which is permissible) and questioning him with a view to encouraging the witness to alter, massage or obscure his real recollection (which is not). The distinction was neatly drawn by Judge Francis Finch in *In Re Eldridge*[8] in 1880, where he said:

> While a discreet and prudent attorney may very properly ascertain from witnesses in advance of the trial what they in fact do know and the extent and limitations of their memory, as guide for his own examinations, he has no right legal or moral, to go further. His duty is to extract the facts from the witness, not to pour them into him; to learn what the witness does know, not to teach him what he ought to know.'

At the risk of stating the obvious, this is a difficult area calling for the exercise of careful judgment.

(vi)   A barrister should also be alert to the fact that, even in the absence of any wish or intention to do so, authority figures do subconsciously influence lay witnesses. Discussion of the substance of the case may unwittingly contaminate the witness's evidence.

(vii)   There is particular danger where such discussions:

(a)   take place in the presence of more than one witness of fact; or

(b)   involve the disclosure to one witness of fact of the factual evidence of another witness.

These practices have been strongly deprecated by the courts as tending inevitably to encourage the rehearsal or coaching of witnesses and to increase the risk of fabrication or contamination of evidence: *R v Arif* (1993) 26 May; *Smith New Court Securities Ltd* v *Scrimgeour Vickers (Asset Management) Ltd* [1994] 1 WLR 1271.

(viii)   That is not to suggest that it is always inappropriate to disclose one witness's evidence to another. If conflicting witness statements have been obtained from different witnesses or served by the other side, it may be appropriate or necessary for a witness to be further questioned about, or have his attention drawn to, discrepancies between statements. Discretion is, however, required, especially where the evidence of independent witnesses is involved.

(ix)   Whilst there is no rule that any longer prevents a barrister from taking a witness statement in civil cases, there is a distinction between the settling of a witness statement and taking a witness statement. Save in exceptional circumstances, it is not appropriate for a barrister who has taken witness

---

[8] New York Court of Appeals; 37 NY 161, 171.

statements, as opposed to settling witness statements prepared by others, to act as Counsel in that case because it risks undermining the independence of the barrister as an advocate. Exceptional circumstances would include:

(a)   The witness is a minor one;

(b)   Counsel has no choice but to take the proof and this is the only practical course in the interests of justice — this would apply, for instance, where a witness appears unexpectedly at Court and there is no one else competent to take the statement;

(c)   Counsel is a junior member of a team of Counsel and will not be examining the witness.

The Cab Rank rule does not require a barrister to agree to undertake the task of taking witness statements.

(x)   A barrister should be prepared to exchange common courtesies with the other side's witnesses. However, a barrister should only discuss the substance of the case or any evidence with the other side's witnesses in rare and exceptional circumstances and then only with the prior knowledge of his opponent.

16 January, 2001

GUIDANCE ON PREPARATION OF DEFENCE CASE STATEMENTS

THE PREPARATION OF DEFENCE CASE STATEMENTS PURSUANT TO THE
CRIMINAL PROCEDURE AND INVESTIGATIONS ACT 1996

GUIDANCE ON THE DUTIES OF COUNSEL

(As approved by the PCCC on 24 September 1997)

1. It is becoming increasingly common for solicitors to instruct counsel to draft or settle Defence Case Statements, required under section 5 of the Criminal Procedure and Investigations Act 1996. Often these instructions are given to counsel with no or little previous involvement in the case shortly before the expiry of the time limit.

2. The relevant legislation is set out at §12–56 *et seq.* of the 2002 edition of *Archbold*. In summary, however:

    (i) The time limit for compliance is short — 14 days from service of prosecution material or a statement that there is none. The permitted grounds for an extension of time are limited;[1]

    (ii) The contents of the Defence Case Statement are obviously of great importance to the defendant. An inaccurate or inadequate statement of the defence could have serious repercussions for the defendant, if the trial judge permits 'appropriate' comment;

    (iii) Whilst it will be the natural instinct of most defence counsel to keep the Defence Case Statement short, a short and anodyne statement may be insufficient to trigger any obligation on the prosecution to give secondary disclosure of prosecution material.

3. Normally it will be more appropriate for instructing solicitors to draft the Defence Case Statement, since typically counsel will have had little involvement at this stage.

4. However, there is nothing unprofessional about counsel drafting or settling a Defence Case Statement, although it must be appreciated that there is no provision in the current regulations for graduated fees allowing for counsel to be paid a separate fee for his work. This most unsatisfactory situation (which has arisen, as a result of the 1996 Act, since the graduated fees regulations were negotiated) is being addressed urgently by the Fees and Legal Aid Committee. A barrister has no obligation to accept work for which he will not be paid. The absence of a fee will justify refusal of the instructions of counsel who are not to be retained for the trial and are simply asked to do no more than draft or settle the Defence Case Statement. Where counsel is retained for the trial, Rule 502(b) of the Code of Conduct deems instructions in a legally aided matter to be at a proper fee and counsel would not be justified in refusing to draft or settle a Defence Case Statement on the sole ground that there is no separate fee payable for this work.

5. Many members of the Bar will nevertheless feel that, in the interests of their lay client and or of good relations with instructing solicitors, they cannot refuse work, even where they would otherwise be entitled to do so. Those who do so need to recognise

---

[1] See the Defence Disclosure Time Limit Regulations 1997 made pursuant to the Act: [Paragraph 12–94 of Archbold, 2002 edition].

the crucial importance of:

(i)   Obtaining all prosecution statements and documentary exhibits;

(ii)   Getting instructions from the lay client, from a properly signed proof and preferably a conference. Those instructions need to explain the general nature of the defence, to indicate the matters on which issue is taken with the prosecution and to give an explanation of the reason for taking issue. They must also give details of any alibi defence, sufficient to give the information required by Section 5(7) of the 1996 Act;

(iii) Getting statements from other material witnesses;

(iv)   Ensuring that the client realises the importance of the Defence Case Statement and the potential adverse consequences of an inaccurate or inadequate statement;

(v)   Getting proper informed approval for the draft from the client. This is particularly important, given the risks of professional embarrassment if the client seeks to disown the statement during the course of the trial, perhaps when the trial is not going well or when under severe pressure in cross-examination. Counsel ought to insist on getting written acknowledgement from the lay client that:

(a) he understands the importance of the accuracy and adequacy of the Defence Case Statement for his case;

(b) he has had the opportunity of considering the contents of the statement carefully and approves it.

This may often mean having a conference with the lay client to explain the Defence Case Statement and to get informed approval, although in straightforward cases where counsel has confidence in the instructing solicitor, this could be left to the solicitor. Where the latter course is taken, a short written advice (which can be in a standard form) as to the importance of obtaining the written acknowledgement before service of the statement should accompany the draft Defence Case Statement. A careful record should be kept of work done and advice given.

(vi)   If there is inadequate time, counsel should ask the instructing solicitor to apply for an extension of time. This needs to be considered at a very early stage, since the application must be made before the expiry of the time limit.

6.   It follows that counsel ought not to accept any instructions to draft or settle a Defence Case Statement unless given the opportunity and adequate time to gain proper familiarity with the case and to comply with the fundamental requirements set out above. In short, there is no halfway house. If instructions are accepted, then the professional obligations on counsel are considerable.

GUIDANCE ON HOLDING OUT AS A BARRISTER

CODE OF CONDUCT: 7th EDITION

NON-PRACTISING BARRISTERS OFFERING LEGAL SERVICES

The new 7th edition of the Code of Conduct sets out the conditions which barristers must satisfy in order to be entitled to practise. The Code also contains the rules of conduct which practising barristers, be they in independent practice or employment, must observe. This note provides guidance for barristers who have not satisfied the conditions required to practise as a barrister or who for other reasons wish to supply legal services other than as practising barristers.

The Code does not prohibit non-practising barristers from supplying legal services. It merely prevents them, in connection with the supply of such services, from holding themselves out as barristers and from exercising rights which they have as barristers.

Holding Out as a Barrister

The restriction on holding out prevents non-practising barristers who are supplying or offering to supply legal services from using the title 'barrister' or otherwise conveying the impression that they are practising as barristers. It is not possible to provide a comprehensive list of the circumstances which might amount to 'holding out' but it is hoped that the following examples will give an idea of what is prohibited.

- Describing oneself as a barrister in any printed material used in connection with the provision of legal services: in particular in advertising or publicity, on a card or letterhead, or on premises.

- Describing oneself as a barrister to clients or prospective clients.

- Indicating to opposing parties or their representatives (e.g. in correspondence) that one is a barrister.

- Describing oneself as a barrister or as 'counsel', wearing robes, or sitting in a place reserved for counsel, in court.

- Using other descriptions in such contexts which imply that the individual is a barrister (e.g. membership of an Inn of Court).

These examples are not exhaustive.

Exercising Rights as a Barrister

Non-practising barristers may not exercise any rights that they have by reason of being barristers, the most obvious example being rights of audience. This means that such a barrister may not appear as an advocate in any court or tribunal unless it is one in which lay representatives are permitted to appear or unless the barrister has a right of audience by virtue of some other qualification (e.g. as a solicitor).

There are other rights which a practising barrister may exercise but a non-practising barrister may not. For example, section 22 of the Solicitors Act 1974 prohibits an unqualified person from preparing for reward any instrument relating to real or personal estate, or to any legal proceeding. Section 23 contains a similar prohibition against preparing papers for probate. It would not be permissible for a non-practising barrister to charge for preparing such an instrument or papers.

What Is Not Prohibited

The Code does not prohibit non-practising barristers from describing themselves as barristers when they are not supplying legal services. In particular, the following activities are excluded from the definition of 'legal services' in the Code.

- Lecturing or teaching law.
- Writing or editing law books, articles or reports.
- Reading for libel.
- Acting as an arbitrator or mediator.
- Acting as an honorary legal adviser to a charity.

In connection with those activities (and in other circumstances where the barrister is not supplying legal services at all) it is perfectly permissible to use the title 'barrister'.

There may be occasions on which it is unavoidable for non-practising barristers who are supplying or offering to supply legal services to disclose that they are qualified as barristers. These might include, for example, job applications or enquiries by clients as to the barrister's background. In these cases there is no objection to indicating that you have qualified as a barrister but, particularly if the issue arises in the course of conversation with clients, it should be made clear that you are not practising as a barrister, are not able to exercise any rights as a barrister and are not subject to the rules that practising barristers have to obey.

There is no prohibition on non-practising barristers who are in silk using the title QC.

The Equality and Diversity Code
for the Bar

CONTENTS

Section 2: Legal and Regulatory Framework

FOREWORD

The Bar of England and Wales continues to lead the way among professions in its practical approach to equality and diversity within the Bar. This concern with fair treatment and respect for individual dignity is especially important in a profession whose own task is to uphold people's rights without fear or favour.

This edition of the Equality Code has been updated to take into account increasing awareness in discrimination issues and developing law, including disability legislation. Although it cannot provide comprehensive guidance to the law, it does provide practical guidance on implementation of good equal opportunities practices in areas where equality and diversity issues are most likely to arise. It places greater emphasis on:

- practice development for pupils and junior tenants
- access to good quality work
- flexible working, including maternity and paternity leave

For those accessing the document electronically, there are hyperlinks to relevant legal provisions, codes of practice, model policies and guidance.

The profession was consulted about the first draft, and the final version incorporates many of the suggestions received. The Bar Council unanimously approved the Equality Code at its meeting on 17 July 2004.

The Bar Council's Equality and Diversity Advisers are willing to provide advice and guidance, and can provide information about planned training courses and briefings.

This Code is the result of much effort by experts in the field. We urge you to draw upon that expertise.

THE RT HON LORD
GOLDSMITH QC
ATTORNEY GENERAL

STEPHEN IRWIN QC

CHAIRMAN
GENERAL COUNCIL OF THE BAR

INTRODUCTION

The purpose of the Code

This new Equality and Diversity Code is designed to assist barristers and their employees to apply good equal opportunities practice in the development and running of Chambers. The advice is primarily for barristers in self-employed practice as employed barristers will be bound by their individual company/organisation's policies and rules for implementation. All barristers are required to comply with the broad obligations not to discriminate, as set out in paragraphs 305 and 404 of the Code of Conduct and in the anti-discrimination statutes. It is intended to be a practical guide rather than a legal handbook but seeks to reflect and give effect to the requirements of the law

Why does equality of opportunity matter?

Equality of opportunity is **fair, commercially advantageous, necessary for compliance with non-discrimination law and constitutionally important**.

Barristers advise and represent clients from an increasingly diverse range of backgrounds. They remain the largest pool for recruitment to the judiciary. It is in the best interests of both the public and the Bar that those of the highest ability and talent are attracted to the profession. Recent statistics for entry to the Bar are encouraging but retention remains an issue of concern. Cultures and practices which may deter those of high ability from remaining within the profession or from achieving their full potential must be identified and, where possible eliminated. Public confidence and support for the Bar can only be enhanced by systems which are seen as open and fair.

Barristers need to be able to recognise their own prejudices and to be aware of the assumptions which they make in evaluating others. They must learn how to ensure that prejudices and assumptions do not influence their treatment of others in the work context. Diversity training will assist barristers in understanding the cultures and sensitivities of others. Systems, such as fair recruitment processes, policies on flexible working and monitoring, will help to ensure that working practices really are achieving equality. Accreditation through schemes such as the Legal Services Commission's Quality Mark now require that good equal opportunities practices are applied.

The application of good equal opportunities practices will minimise the risk of breaches of discrimination law for which awards may now be substantial. But the commercial advantages go further. They entail the retention of an excellent pool of talent. Barristers in the early stages of their professional lives may be supported in their work by rent concessions and training. If they then leave Chambers because, for example, childcare commitments limit their earning capacity for a few years and a period of flexible working cannot be accommodated, their value is lost. They may be potential major contributors to Chambers whose value is lost by short-term considerations.

The Bar has a constitutional role in ensuring the independence of advocates before the Courts and in order to maintain confidence in that role, its own practices must be and be seen to be fair.

The Bar Council has now adopted a policy of 'mainstreaming' equal opportunities and Chambers are encouraged to do the same. This means that the furtherance of equal opportunity objectives and the potential for discrimination should be considered in relation to all policies, practices and decisions where equal opportunities issues may arise: for example, not just recruitment but also matters such as distribution of work, allocation of rooms, fees, the location and timing of meetings and Chambers entertaining.

Using the Code

The Code begins with a guide in Section 1 to the key areas (known as 'Action Areas') where good equal opportunities practice should be implemented. This is where practical guidance may be found, on the key areas of recruitment, maternity and fair access to work. Section 1 also includes a guide to the new statutory provisions on service provision to disabled clients.

Section 2 outlines the legal and regulatory framework which underpins the requirement not to discriminate. The duty not to discriminate is to be found not only in statute and regulations but also in the Bar's Code of Conduct. The key concepts of anti-discrimination law are summarised and some common misconceptions are clarified.

In each Section, the reader will find Links to regulatory provisions, statutory Codes of Practice, model policies and guidance on good practice. For those reading the Code in its paper version rather than electronically, Section 3 contains Annexes with further guidance on good equal opportunities practice, such as the Bar Council Maternity, Paternity and Flexible Working Policy guidance on Monitoring and on the role of an Equal Opportunities Officer in chambers. The Equality and Diversity Advisers of the Bar Council are available to provide further assistance. References to 'Heads of Chambers' in the text include all management structures with overall responsibility for running chambers.

SECTION 1: ACTION AREAS

A. RECRUITMENT: PUPILS AND TENANTS

General Guidance

1.1   The same broad principles apply to the recruitment of pupils, starter tenants, established practitioners and staff. Discrimination by barristers on the ground of sex, race, disability, sexual orientation and religion or belief in recruitment is unlawful. Discrimination on the ground of age is professional misconduct.

Advertisement

1.2   Vacancies should be advertised. A failure to advertise vacancies for pupils or tenants places Chambers and individual barristers at risk of allegations of indirect discrimination. It is good practice to include in advertisements:

- encouragement of applications from groups which are under-represented in Chambers;
- a statement of compliance with the Equality and Diversity Code;
- a statement indicating preparedness to make reasonable adjustments for disabled candidates.

Where Chambers use agencies or head hunters they should ensure that Chamber's equality policy is included in the instructions given to the agency.

Application Forms

1.3   An application form is generally preferable to curriculum vitae. An application form enables the assessment of candidates to be made on a clearly defined comparative basis by reference to specific qualities which are relevant to Chambers' selection criteria.

Chambers are reminded that reasonable adjustments may need to be made for disabled candidates at the application stage of the recruitment process when, for example, application forms may have to be provided in a particular format.

Selection Criteria

1.4   Candidates for pupillage or tenancy should be selected using selection criteria. Selection criteria should be objective and should relate to the work to be done.

- selection criteria enable Chambers to focus on the qualities which they require from the successful candidate.
- they reduce the opportunity for decisions to be influenced by stereotyping or unwitting prejudice.
- selection criteria may be designed so that a higher score is attributed to criteria to which greater importance is attached.
- chambers should avoid criteria that are subjective, such as personality-based attributes or behavioural attributes that cannot fairly be tested at interview.
- it is good practice to provide candidates with selection criteria in advance of the interview.

They promote a consistent and objective approach to candidates by selectors.

Short Listing

1.5   Short listing should be carried out by more than one person and by reference to relevant selection criteria which should be determined in advance of the recruitment process. It is good practice to draft a job or post description and a person specification to assist in identifying the relevant criteria and enable application forms to be drafted in a way which allows candidates to address the criteria. Where shortlisters cannot agree, it may be necessary for a committee to moderate short-listing decisions.

Selection Committees

1.6   All recruitment decisions Chambers make, except for sole practices, should be made by a number of selectors, except in sole practices. Selection committees should, so far as possible, include persons of different age, gender and social, racial or cultural background. They should not include any relative or close friend of the candidates. No candidate should feel that he or she is so remote from the interviewing committee as to be denied a fair prospect of success.

1.7   Where final decisions as to recruitment are made by Chambers or designated members of Chambers rather than the selection committee, no single member of Chambers should be permitted to veto a decision and any challenge to a recommendation of the selection committee should be by reference to the selection criteria and on grounds which are substantiated.

Training

1.8   Members of selection committees should be familiar with this Code and the applicable procedures and selection criteria. It is recommended that at least one member of each selection committee should be trained in fair selection methods.

Interviews

1.9   Interviews should be planned in advance and structured so that each candidate may demonstrate his or her abilities and qualities by reference to each selection criterion. Chambers should ensure that any reasonable adjustment required for a disabled candidate has been made so that disabled candidates are not disadvantaged at interview.

1.10   Interviews should be of sufficient length to enable informed decisions to be made and to minimise the potential prejudices involved in 'gut feeling'.

1.11   It is not essential to ask each candidate identical questions, but a planned sequence of topics is recommended.

1.12   Irrelevant questions, such as personal questions in relation to family and personal background should be avoided. However, disabled candidates should be asked what, if any, adjustments may be needed to enable the candidate to practise as a barrister.

1.13   Selectors should score candidates individually on an agreed scale and should then compare scores with others on the panel so as to seek to reach a consensus. Scores should not be adjusted to reflect personal preference.

1.14   Standard exercises either in written form or by way of oral presentation may be a useful aid to arriving at objective assessments of candidates. In relation to pupils and starter tenants, such exercises should be designed in such a way that any area of law covered is one which should be equally familiar to all candidates. Alternatively, a topic may be chosen which requires no prior specialist legal knowledge but is designed to test analytical or advocacy skills.

Record-Keeping

1.15   Candidates who have been rejected may want an explanation for their rejection.If good records are kept, reasons for rejection are generally easily explained in the event of a request or even legal challenge. If explanations for rejection can be given, this should enhance confidence in the recruitment system.

Monitoring and Review

1.16   Candidates should be asked to complete monitoring forms so as to enable Chambers to review their performance by reference to reliable statistics. Monitoring enables Chambers to self-check. It may be that prejudices and attitudes of which selectors are not even conscious are influencing decisions. Monitoring enables these possibilities to be recognised and examined. Where there are significant discrepancies between proportions of <u>applicants</u> from a particular group and proportions of <u>successful candidates</u> from a particular group, recruitment practices may need to be reviewed with a view to redressing observed discrepancies and to achieving diversity in Chambers. If there are no such discrepancies, statistics may support the objectivity of a particular process in the event of a challenge.

1.17   All documents relating to exercises should be retained for two years and statistics should be prepared by reference to gender, race, disability and age of the number of persons applying, being short-listed and being recruited.

Recruitment of Pupils

1.18   This guidance is in addition to the matters set out at paragraphs 1.1 to 1.7 above.

Pupillage Policy

1.19   Chambers should have a pupillage policy which includes a pupillage selection procedure. The pupillage selection procedure should be made available to candidates for pupillage and should be reviewed regularly.

Advertising Pupillages

1.20   Pupillages must be advertised on a website designated by the Bar Council, save in the exceptional circumstances set out in paragraph 5 of the Pupillage Funding and Advertising Requirements 2003 in Annexe R to the Code of Conduct. Subject to those exceptions, all pupillages must be advertised including supplementary or late vacancies and vacancies for candidates who intend to practise outside the UK (see para 404.2 (c) of the Code of Conduct).

Private Arrangements

1.21   Private arrangements to take pupils should not be made, save where the requirement to advertise is disapplied or waived pursuant to paragraph 5 of the Pupillage Funding and Advertising Requirements 2003 (see para 1.20 above). Private arrangements are contrary to good equal opportunities practice and the Bar Council will not register pupillages by private arrangement. They breach the requirement in the Code of Conduct that pupillages must be advertised.

References

1.22   Where references are sought, a standard form should be used. Alternatively, referees should be directed as to the selection criteria being applied and the type of information which is sought from them.

Recruitment of Starter Tenants

1.23   This section is in addition to paragraphs 1.1 to 1.17 above.

1.24   Every Chambers, which recruits starter tenants, should have a policy in relation to the recruitment of starter tenants. The policy should be made available to members of Chambers and to pupils when they begin their pupillage. Pupils should be informed as to when their Chambers will identify any vacancies for starter tenants and how pupils will be assessed for any vacancies identified.

1.25   Chambers should identify, preferably at a specified time each year, how many starter tenants they wish to recruit. Chambers should, so far as possible with the assistance of the senior clerk, practice director or similar, determine the quantity and the nature of work available, or potentially available, for starter tenants.

1.26   Starter tenancies should be advertised where Chambers do not recruit from among their own pupils.

1.27   Many Chambers prefer to consider their own pupils for starter tenancies and some recruit all pupils with a view to a tenancy. This is not objectionable provided that pupillage selection procedures have been fair and non-discriminatory.

1.28   Whichever approach is taken, the following guidance is recommended:
- all candidates for starter tenancies should be assessed according to an objective and transparent system of assessment, which may include an interview, and against the same criteria;
- assessments in relation to the candidates' demonstrated abilities and potential should be obtained from a wide range of sources by reference to relevant criteria;
- the sources will include records of any formal assessments of pupils conducted during their pupillage, assessments by barristers for whom the candidates have carried out work, including but not confined, to pupil supervisors, and feedback from instructing solicitors by whom candidates have been instructed;
- all comments provided in relation to candidates should be considered solely by reference to the agreed selection criteria.

1.29   Chambers should aim to identify ability and potential with objectivity, filtering out so far as possible the subjective loyalties and favouritisms which may be felt by individual members of Chambers (in particular pupil supervisors) to particular pupils and the converse, such as subjective dislikes based on personal prejudice, whether conscious or unwitting.

1.30   Candidates for starter tenancies should be assessed by a committee of at least three members of Chambers, wherever possible excluding pupil supervisors who have supervised any of the candidates.

1.31   The decision to offer a starter tenancy should be made either by the committee as a whole or, on recommendation by the committee, by all or a substantial proportion of the members of Chambers.

Recruitment of Established Practitioners

1.32   Reference is made to the general guidance at paragraphs 1.1 to 1.17 above.

1.33   Vacancies for established practitioners should be advertised.

1.34   Exceptionally, Chambers may identify or may be approached by individuals or groups of established practitioners with particular experience or expertise in the field(s) in which the Chambers practises. In those circumstances, it may be legitimate to recruit without advertisement provided that such recruitment can be justified both in terms of Chambers' real business needs and in terms of the skills of those recruited. Chambers should be aware that recruitment of this nature may give rise to allegations of discrimination.

Mini-Pupillages

1.35 Where Chambers are unable to offer mini-pupillages to all who apply, Chambers should organise their mini-pupillages in such a way as to ensure equality of opportunity, so far as practicable, by applying objective criteria. Where mini-pupillages are assessed, the same or equivalent assessment materials should be provided to all candidates, who should be assessed by at least two assessors applying the same criteria.

B. FAIR ACCESS TO WORK

Allocation of Work in Chambers

1.36 The opportunities for barristers to develop a successful practice in their areas of interest are frequently affected by the range and quality of work on which they are instructed in the early stages of their careers and even in pupillage. Paragraph 404(2) of the Code of Conduct requires that Chambers take all reasonable steps to ensure that the affairs of Chambers are conducted in a manner which is fair and equitable for all barristers. This responsibility extends to the fair distribution of work amongst pupils and members of Chambers. Pupils and tenants are entitled to equality of opportunity in terms of being able to experience the full range of work and training undertaken by Chambers.

1.37 Pupils and junior tenants should be afforded the opportunity to develop their practices in a fair and equal manner. Discriminatory and stereotyped career assumptions may exist and procedures should be in place to ensure that patterns of instruction and briefing are transparent and open to scrutiny.

1.38 Chambers should have in place effective procedures for the monitoring of work allocation and for responding to (and rectifying where appropriate) complaints and concerns about work allocation. There should be procedures in place for ensuring the fair distribution of work, particularly un-named work and for providing support and guidance in respect of practice development and marketing.

1.39 The onus is on Chambers rather than on the individual pupil or barrister to ensure that there is fair access to work.

1.40 Chambers should ensure that its clerks use the clerks' room software to best advantage so that regular breakdowns of work are undertaken. Analysis should include the amount of work done, the type of work, fees earned and received and solicitors instructing. As a guideline, in respect of pupils and junior tenants, breakdowns should be produced at three monthly intervals. This information should be discussed with the pupil or junior tenant as part of their individual practice development, as well as being used to monitor Chambers' internal work distribution procedures and instructing solicitors' briefing practices.

1.41 One or more members of Chambers or appropriate practice manager should be responsible for overseeing the monitoring of work and should meet with the Senior Clerk on a regular basis in order to compare and review the work distribution data so as to ensure that work is distributed in a manner which is fair.

1.42   Chambers should be particularly aware of issues relating to the distribution of any un-named work coming into Chambers, and the redistribution of work between members of Chambers and pupils and junior tenants. These in particular should be systematically monitored to ensure that any disparities in allocation are identified and rectified.

1.43   Chambers should use the work distribution data to ascertain whether any instructing organisations or solicitors exhibit briefing practices which tend to favour a particular group. Any such trend should be considered by a designated member or members of Chambers to see if there is any underlying discriminatory practice.

1.44   If briefing practices are identified which disadvantage a particular group (for example allocating sex and child abuse cases predominantly to female practitioners) these should be addressed through the clerks' room. If the issue cannot be resolved through the clerks' room, it may need to be addressed by the Head of Chambers and the solicitor(s) involved.

1.45   Any unequal or unfair treatment of pupils and members of Chambers in the allocation of work should be treated as a serious matter and dealt with appropriately so that it does not recur.

1.46   Chambers should ensure that all clerks are fully briefed on the need to distribute work in a fair and non-discriminatory manner and to monitor work allocation. Clerks, and in particular those involved in the distribution and monitoring of work allocation, should be provided with equality and diversity training.

1.47   Chambers should seek to ensure, where possible, that instructions and briefs are not delivered by solicitors at such times as to preclude those with childcare and other dependent care commitments from being eligible for that work (for example, where a brief is not delivered until Friday afternoon for a trial on Monday). Late delivery of briefs may also disadvantage disabled barristers who may require the Court to make adjustments for them which cannot be made on the morning of a trial or hearing. Any solicitor who insists on a directly discriminatory allocation of work should be reported to his or her professional disciplinary body. The work should be refused.

Practice Development

1.48   Chambers should arrange regular feedback sessions for working pupils and practice development meetings for tenants. The purpose of these meetings is to enable discussion of the allocation of work, work opportunity and development of individual practices.

1.49   Chambers are encouraged to set up mentoring schemes whereby a junior tenant may be a pupil's 'mentor' and a junior tenant may be linked to a more senior member of Chambers who can offer advice and guidance regarding practice development in a mentoring role. This will be relevant also to barristers returning to practice following a career break.

Marketing of Barristers and Pupils

1.50   Marketing strategies for tenants and pupils should take into account equal opportunities considerations. For example, socialising after work in the pub may provide an effective means of 'networking' for those who do not have childcare commitments or substantial student debts or both. Socialising in the pub may exclude pupils and junior tenants whose religious beliefs preclude the drinking of alcohol.

Chambers should be sensitive to these issues and should ensure that marketing and networking activities are organised so that all pupils and tenants can, so far as practicable, be equally involved.

1.51   Chambers should encourage pupils and junior tenants to take part in Chambers' seminars and lectures, attend outside seminars and lectures, write or contribute to articles in professional publications, become involved in professional organisations connected to their line of work and become involved with any legal advice or support centres or organisations.

1.52   The organisation of regular 'Practice Group Meetings' within Chambers is encouraged as a means of discussing individual and Chambers' issues and as a means of integrating pupils and members of Chambers.

C. MATERNITY, PATERNITY AND PARENTAL LEAVE

Written Policies

1.53   All Chambers of more than one tenant should have a written policy on maternity, paternity, parental leave and flexible working. This policy should contain particulars of:

- the member's right to return to Chambers after a specified period of leave;
- the extent of the periods of leave offered free of Chambers' rent and expenses;
- the manner in which the rent and expenses to be waived, deducted or reimbursed in respect of a period of leave will be calculated;
- the member's entitlement to work part-time or flexibly or to take a career break for childcare or other reasons;
- the procedure for dealing with grievances under the policy;
- Chambers' commitment regularly to review the effectiveness of the policy.

Period of Leave Free of Rent and Chambers' Expenses

1.54   The Maternity, Paternity and Flexible Working Policy approved by the Bar Council recommends that Chambers should offer their members taking maternity leave or leave following adoption, a minimum period of six months' free of Chambers' rent and expenses. This rent-free period should apply irrespective of whether the Chambers' rent is calculated as a percentage of fees earned or is a flat rate payment. The mechanics of calculation will be a matter for individual Chambers depending upon how rent is paid. For women paying a percentage of receipts, one option is to base the calculation of the rent free period on average earnings over the preceding twelve months. The rent-free period could be applied during the six months after the woman has returned to Chambers as this would be a time of relatively low income. Policies may need to cover matters such as clerks' fees, mortgage repayments and any contributions payable in respect of one-off investments, as appropriate.

1.55   The Maternity, Paternity and Flexible Working Policy approved by the Bar Council recommends that members of Chambers should be offered a minimum of one month's leave free of Chambers' rent and expenses following the birth or adoption of a child by their partner, where they have or share responsibility for that child and so that they can discharge that responsibility.

1.56   These recommended minimum periods of leave are not intended to discourage Chambers from adopting a more generous policy.

Right to Return to Chambers

1.57   The Bar Council recommends that a woman should have the right to return to her Chambers as a tenant following the birth or adoption of a child. The right to return should continue for a guaranteed period of at least a year. During that period, she should be able to return to Chambers without the need to re-apply for admission. Chambers are encouraged to offer a longer period of leave.

1.58   The recommendation in paragraph 1.57 should also be applied to a man who adopts and is the principal carer of the adopted child.

Assistance to Return to Chambers and to Work During Maternity Leave or Career Break

1.59   Chambers are encouraged to respond positively to members' wishes to work during their maternity leave or any career break. Chambers' written policy should set out how Chambers plan to assist their members to keep in touch with Chambers and with practice developments during any period of leave and to return to practice. Invitations to training events, social occasions and information on Chambers' business should be passed on to members on maternity leave or a career break and Chambers should endeavour to consult with them in relation to major Chambers' decisions which may affect the member's practice.

Grievance Procedures, Monitoring and Review

1.60   Chambers should adopt procedures which enable members to raise concerns about the Chambers' maternity, paternity and flexible working policy and its application. There should be one or more Chambers Equal Opportunity Officers (see para 2.14 below) who can respond to queries about the policy and provide reports on its effectiveness and value. The policy should be circulated to all members, clerks and staff of chambers so that they understand the policy and their role in relation to it.

D. FLEXIBLE AND PART-TIME WORKING AND CAREER BREAKS

Bar Council Recommendations

1.61   All Chambers of more than one tenant should have written policies permitting members of Chambers (female or male) to take career breaks, work flexible hours, part-time or partly from home to enable them to manage their family responsibilities and remain in practice. Such policies should reflect, in particular, the needs of the primary carer in relation to childcare responsibilities.

Written Policy

1.62   Chambers' arrangements for the payment of rent should not constitute disincentives to flexible working. Earnings related arrangements for the payment of rent may be preferable to fixed rates. A policy of fixed rent without any qualification is potentially indirectly discriminatory against women because it is likely to impact on a greater proportion of women than men (see para 2.16.b where indirect discrimination is explained). Rent arrangements need to reflect the economic effect on the individual and the Chambers, as do arrangements such as desk space and any capital benefit obtained from mortgage repayments on property acquired by a set of Chambers.

1.63   Members of Chambers working on flexible working arrangements should be included in Chambers' business and in Chambers' continuing professional development, marketing and social activities in the same way as full-time working members of Chambers.

Advantages of Flexible Working

1.64   Flexible working arrangements should assist in retaining some of the dispropor-
tionately high number of women who leave the Bar, including those who leave
after having children. This is a loss to the Bar because the presence of women at
senior levels broadens the profession's diversity, increases the number of women in
the pool for judicial appointment and strengthens and enhances the profession's
marketability. It is also a loss to Chambers in terms of the wasted investment in
training and the gap left in seniority.

1.65   The availability of flexible working arrangements is likely to increase commitment
to Chambers and the profession and improve morale.

1.66   The Bar has always accommodated flexible working: allowing barristers to combine
practice at the Bar with part-time judicial appointments, writing, academic or
political appointments. Flexible working for reasons associated with child care or
other domestic responsibilities can and should be treated in a similar way. Barristers
are already accustomed to working in teams and returning work to their colleagues
when they are unavailable.

1.67   The arrangements which any particular Chambers puts in place will need to reflect
the nature of the membership and the work undertaken. Systems such as telephone
conferencing, and e-mail should be used to best advantage to enable members of
Chambers to conduct their practices from home where desired. Different working
patterns may suit different individuals: for example, working during school term
times only for a parent with children of school age.

1.68   Individual practitioners should recognise that reduced working hours will have an
economic effect on their Chambers and should themselves be proactive in seeking
to agree fair arrangements for rent and the use of Chambers resources, including
accommodation, with their Chambers. Rental arrangements should be agreed and
understood before any period of flexible working commences.

E. HARASSMENT

What is Harassment?

1.69   Harassment is any form of unwanted conduct which has the aim or effect of dimin-
ishing a person's dignity or creating a humiliating or offensive environment for
that person. The fact that one person may be able to ignore or deal comfortably
with certain behaviour does not mean that it is acceptable if directed at another.
A single incident may constitute harassment if it is sufficiently serious. The motive
or intention of the perpetrator is normally irrelevant (see para 2.18 in relation to
harassment which also constitutes unlawful discrimination).

1.70   There is now a criminal offence of intentional harassment. It covers harassment on
any ground. The Act defines harassment as the use of 'threatening, abusive or insulting words or behaviour; or disorderly behaviour' or displays of writing, signs or other
visible representation which is threatening, abusive or insulting, and includes
harassment at the workplace. Harassment amounting to physical or sexual assault
is also a serious criminal offence and victims should be encouraged to report it to
the police.

Policy

1.71   All Chambers should have a harassment policy, which sets out a clear summary of
the type of behaviour which is unacceptable in the working environment and the
procedures for dealing with complaints about such behaviour. The policy should

apply to all members and employees of Chambers, squatters and pupils and personal copies should be provided.

1.72 Complaints of harassment are sensitive and Chambers should adopt policies which enable them to react quickly and appropriately if a complaint is raised. It becomes much more difficult to deal with complaints effectively where there is delay.

Guidance

1.73 Harassment causes distress. It can lead to impaired work performance, sickness, and even to recipients leaving Chambers altogether. Many recipients of harassment are afraid to complain. They fear that their complaint will be trivialised or that they will be subject to ridicule or reprisals or that nothing will be done.

1.74 Examples of behaviour which may amount to harassment based on sex, race, disability, religion or sexual orientation include:
- physical assault, including sexual assault;
- demands for sexual favours in return for career advancement;
- unnecessary physical contact;
- exclusion from social networks and activities;
- isolation;
- bullying;
- compromising suggestions or invitations;
- suggestive remarks or looks;
- display of offensive materials, including on computer screen;
- tasteless jokes or verbal abuse;
- offensive remarks or ridicule;
- dealing inappropriately with complaints of harassment.

1.75 By undertaking certain specific steps, Chambers should be able to alleviate the problems of harassment in the context of work related relationships. In particular, the following is recommended:
- a policy statement which makes it clear that harassment will not be tolerated or condoned and that employees, members of Chambers, pupils and others temporarily in chambers such as mini — pupils have a right to complain if it occurs;
- effective communication of the policy to all those to whom it applies;
- active promotion of the policy by people in managerial positions;
- training for those in managerial and supervisory roles on how to keep the working environment free of harassment and how to deal with it should it occur;
- the provision of informal means of resolving harassment in the first instance;
- the designation of an adviser to assist employees and others subjected to harassment;
- a formal complaints procedure, which should be monitored and reviewed;
- an independent, objective, sensitive and fair procedure for internal investigations of complaints; and
- a principle of treating violations of the harassment policy as a disciplinary offence.

1.76 Often victims of harassment just want the harassment to stop and do not wish to see the harasser disciplined. There are various informal methods by which

Chambers can deal with complaints of harassment, including:

- telling the harasser that their behaviour is unacceptable and asking them to stop immediately (if the recipient feels able to challenge the harasser directly or indirectly in this way);
- seeking the help and advice of the Inns' Student Officers where the harassment occurs in an Inn of Court or at an Inn's sponsored event;
- seeking the help and advice of the Bar Council's Equality and Diversity Advisers directly or by calling the confidential telephone number 020 7611 1310;
- seeking the help and advice of pupil supervisors or other members of Chambers.

Formal Resolution Options

1.77   Where informal methods fail to resolve the issue, or where the harassment complained of is of a more serious nature to begin with, one or more of the following formal methods of resolution may be appropriate:

- the initiation of Chambers' formal complaints or grievance procedure;
- contacting the relevant Inn to make a formal complaint where the complaint concerns a sponsor or pupil supervisor or something occurring at an Inn sponsored event;
- a complaint to the Professional Conduct Committee which has in place a special protocol for dealing with complaints of harassment;
- initiation of the Bar Council's mediation procedure in confidence through the Bar Council's EDAs. The Mediation Panel is made up of individual members of the Bar who have received training in harassment mediation. The role of the panel is to advise the complainant and, with his or her permission, to mediate between the parties, without necessarily finding fault or blame and without the imposition of sanctions;
- in extreme cases, the complainant might consider whether a complaint should be made to the police where the act complained of amounts to a criminal offence or whether a complaint of unlawful discrimination might be brought in a County Court or employment tribunal.

F. COMPLAINTS AND GRIEVANCES

Complaints Handled Internally

1.78   The Bar Council recommends that all Chambers should have a written grievance procedure and that this should include procedures for handling complaints of discrimination and harassment. The procedure should be brought to the attention of every pupil, tenant and Chambers' employee.

1.79   It is important for a person who has a complaint about discrimination, particularly where harassment is alleged, to have access to someone who can give them sympathetic advice and, if necessary, counselling. This should take place in an atmosphere of total confidentiality.

1.80   Complaints and grievances should be dealt with promptly, objectively and fairly.

1.81   In order to assist in the effective resolution of grievances within Chambers it is recommended that, in addition to the formal procedure, Chambers should nominate one or two members of Chambers to act as informal advisers to potential complainants, and to assist, when asked, in the informal resolution of grievances.

1.82 Barristers who have paid their voluntary subscriptions and their clerks may also approach the Bar Council Arbitration and Conciliation Service to resolve disputes between barristers themselves and between barristers and their clerks.

1.83 Chambers' employees are able to raise complaints through the new statutory grievance procedures which, together with statutory dismissal and disciplinary procedures, are an implied term of all contracts of employment in all Chambers regardless of size or number of employees.

1.84 When a complaint is made, in the interests of all concerned, confidentiality should be maintained throughout any investigatory process as far as possible and as appropriate in the circumstances. Names of complainants must not be released (save to those conducting the investigation and to the person complained against) without their consent.

Formal Procedures

1.85 Formal grievance procedures should include:
- the allocation of responsibility for investigating complaints to at least two members of Chambers, including one senior member, each of whom should be familiar with the Code of Conduct and the Equality and Diversity Code for the Bar. In the event of a conflict of interest, provision should be made for the involvement of additional members of Chambers, or other nominated persons;
- names of Chambers' informal advisers;
- an undertaking that complainants will not be victimised or suffer detriment because of a complaint made in good faith;
- an undertaking that all procedures will, as far as practicable, be confidential;
- a requirement for the complaint to be made in writing;
- a time limit within which a written response should be delivered;
- the range of remedial actions where complaints are substantiated;
- identification of the relevant Bar Council Committees and external bodies to which complaints may be addressed;
- an indication of opportunities for support and counselling provided by the associations and groups for women lawyers, members of minority ethnic groups, disabled people, lesbians or gay men, the Pupil Barristers' Group or the Mature Entrants' Group. Confidential assistance may also be sought from the Equal Opportunities Officers at the Bar Council.

Complaints of Unfair Work Allocation

1.86 By establishing regular monitoring and reviews of allocation of work, Chambers should reduce the need for formal complaints by providing a regular opportunity to identify and remedy problems. Where there is a complaint about the distribution of work from a pupil or tenant, the complaints procedure set out above should apply. A set period during which more detailed monitoring of the distribution of work will take place, may be included as a step in the investigation of the complaint.

Complaints of Harassment

1.87 See paragraphs 1.73 to 1.77 above.

Remedies

1.88   Where, following investigation of a complaint, actual or potential discrimination has been identified, remedial action should be taken immediately. This may include all or some of the following:

- a re-evaluation of the applications and/or another interview with another panel (eg for a complaint from an unsuccessful applicant for pupillage, tenancy or a job);
- a change of practice (eg in relation to unfair work allocation);
- implementation of a reasonable adjustment (in relation to a complaint from a disabled person);
- further advice, briefing or training for the members of selection panels, Chambers clerks and staff;
- advice and support to ensure that the complainant is not victimised as a consequence of making a complaint in good faith;
- disciplinary action.

1.89   A report on all complaints, and on the findings of the investigations, should be made to the Head of Chambers. Chambers should maintain confidential records of all complaints and records of meetings. These should be reviewed annually to ensure that the procedures are working effectively.

1.90   Chambers may be required to explain how they investigated any complaint that is taken to the Bar Council or other external body. An analysis of any complaints received will also be useful in identifying problem areas, training needs or scope for further action when Chambers review their procedures.

Complaints Made to External Bodies

1.91   Any individual (member of Chambers, pupil, employee or client) may complain about the conduct of an individual barrister to the Professional Conduct and Complaints Committee of the Bar Council, or to the Inn about a pupil supervisor.

1.92   Where an individual has a statutory complaint of unlawful discrimination, the complaint may be pursued through the employment tribunals or County Court as appropriate.

G. SERVICE PROVISION

Service provision to disabled clients

Introduction

1.93   This section will focus on the practical issues connected with service delivery, as it relates to disability, within the context of the legislative framework. It is designed to assist Chambers and individual barristers to comply with the disability legislation and generally to improve the services offered to disabled people by the Bar.

1.94   Disability is not always visible and many disabled people choose not to disclose their disability. Disability encompasses, for example, certain musculo-skeletal problems, circulatory conditions and mental illness.

1.95   Barristers are likely to come into professional contact with many disabled people including lay and professional clients, colleagues, pupils, members of the judiciary, witnesses and staff within the judicial system.

Obligations Under the Disability Discrimination Act 1995 ('DDA')

Who are the Clients to Whom Duties are Owed?

1.96   Obligations are owed to 'disabled' persons. The term 'disabled' receives a statutory definition in section 1 of the DDA. The disabled person may be the lay client or any person from the instructing solicitors. The duties under this code will also apply to other persons to whom the barrister or set of Chambers provide services or come into contact (such as witnesses in a case).

Who Owes the Duties?

1.97   A set of Chambers will be a 'service provider' for the purposes of the provisions of the DDA dealing with discrimination in the provision of services. A set of chambers will therefore owe duties under section 19 of the DDA both to the lay client and to the professional client. An individual barrister will also be a service provider and will therefore owe duties as such under the DDA.

What are the Duties?

1.98   The DDA makes it is unlawful for a barrister or set of Chambers to discriminate against a disabled person:
- by refusing to provide (or deliberately not providing) any service which it provides (or is prepared to provide) to members of the public; or
- in the standard of service which it provides to the disabled person or the manner in which it provides that service; or
- in the terms on which it provides a service to the disabled person (section 19 DDA).

1.99   Pro bono cases remain part of service provision and are subject to exactly the same duties as paid cases. Providing conference facilities at Chambers is also deemed to be the provision of a service.

1.100   It is also unlawful for service providers such as a set of Chambers or an individual barrister to discriminate in failing to comply with a duty to make reasonable adjustments (section 21 DDA).

1.101   The following are the duties owed by a service provider to a disabled person:
- not to discriminate against the disabled person by treating the disabled person less favourably for a reason related to the disabled person's disability (section 20(1));
- not to discriminate against the disabled person by failing to comply with a duty to make a reasonable adjustment causing the disabled person to find it either impossible or unreasonably difficult to use the service provider's services for example by failing to remove, alter or avoid physical features which make it impossible or unreasonably difficult for the disabled person to use the service;
- not to victimise any person (whether disabled or not) by treating them less favourably because they brought proceedings, gave evidence or information or made allegations relating to the DDA.

1.102   It is possible to justify discrimination against a disabled person but only in certain limited circumstances, defined in the DDA.

Less Favourable Treatment

1.103   A service provider discriminates against a disabled person if, for a reason which relates to the disabled person's disability, it treats the disabled person less favourably than it treats (or would treat) others to whom the reason does not (or would not) apply and it cannot show that the treatment in question is justified (section 20(1) DDA).

It is not necessary that the barrister knows that the person is a disabled person for less favourable treatment to occur.

1.104 It is unlawful to refuse to serve a disabled person or deliberately not serve the disabled person for a reason relating to the disabled person's disability (section 19(1)(a) DDA).

1.105 It is unlawful to provide service of a lower standard or in a worse manner to a person for a reason relating to or the disabled person's disability (section 19(1)(c) DDA).

1.106 It is unlawful to provide a disabled person with a service on worse terms (for example by charging more) for a reason relating to that person's disability (section 19(1)(d) DDA).

1.107 Chambers should note that the DDA does not prohibit positive action in favour of disabled people (see para 2.2 for distinction between positive action and positive discrimination). The protection of the DDA confers positive advantages on disabled people in certain respects.

The Duty to Make Reasonable Adjustments

1.108 As a service provider, a set of Chambers is required to make reasonable adjustments in several areas unless it can show that the failure to make a reasonable adjustment is justified.

1.109 The duty to make reasonable adjustments is owed to disabled people at large and not just individual disabled people. Barristers and Chambers therefore should not wait until a disabled person wants to use their services before investigating the need to make reasonable adjustments. It is recommended that barristers and Chambers should look at adjustments that they can make on an ongoing basis (whether or not they currently provide services to disabled people). The idea is to anticipate the requirements of disabled people and in order to do this effectively consultation should take place with existing disabled clients or disabled potential clients. Whilst this may not be possible to do on an individual basis, barristers and Chambers should consider consulting organisations of disabled persons to obtain their views.

1.110 The law requires reasonable adjustments to be made in the following areas:
- changing practices, policies and procedures;
- providing auxiliary aids and services;
- adjusting a physical feature by either removing the feature or altering it or ensuring that it can be avoided, or providing services by alternative means.

1.111 The service provider has a duty to take reasonable steps to change the policy, practice or procedure which makes it impossible or unreasonably difficult for disabled people to make use of its services.

1.112 When considering whether the services of a barrister or Chambers are unreasonably difficult for disabled people to use, account should be taken of whether the time, inconvenience, effort, discomfort or loss of dignity entailed in using the service would be considered unreasonable by other people if they had to endure similar difficulties. There may be unreasonable difficulty, for example, where a client in a wheelchair has to be carried up three steps to a conference room.

1.113 It is sensible to try to anticipate the needs of disabled clients rather than acting in a wholly reactive way. Consultation with organisations of disabled people about the needs of a group which may use the services of Chambers will help to give

Chambers an idea of the kind of adjustments that it may need to make. Similarly an individual barrister should consider consulting such organisations if he or she anticipates working with a disabled person on a particular case. Chambers and individual barristers should therefore indicate that reasonable adjustments will be made on request if this will assist disabled people to use their services.

1.114   Chambers or a barrister may discriminate unlawfully even if they do not know that a client is disabled. It is worthwhile remembering that not all disabilities are visible. What is important is not to act on assumptions, but to be prepared to ask in advance what reasonable adjustments can be made to ensure that the service of Chambers or the barrister can be used without the disabled person being put to unreasonable difficulty. If it is not reasonable to anticipate a particular requirement the barrister will not act unlawfully if he or she does not anticipate it.

1.115   The duty to make reasonable adjustments is a continuing duty, and it may be necessary to make more than one adjustment. The best approach is to consider what changes can be made in practical terms to ensure that the disabled person can use the barrister's or Chambers' services without unreasonable difficulty. The disabled person should be consulted about what he or she believes is the best solution. That view is not going to be conclusive and the barrister will have to consider what is a reasonable step to have to take in order to achieve this end.

1.116   In deciding whether it is reasonable to take any particular step, consideration could be given to whether it would be effective in overcoming the difficulty that disabled people face in accessing the services of Chambers or the barrister. Consider whether it would be practicable to take the step, and the financial and other costs of making the adjustment. Some steps which are suggested would cause disruption. A certain amount of disruption can be required but not a disproportionate amount. Chambers and barristers are entitled to take account of financial and other resources as well as the amount of resources already spent on making adjustments.

1.117   What needs to be borne in mind is the ultimate aim of rendering services accessible without unreasonable difficulty. Making adjustments for one group of disabled people will not absolve the Chambers from making different adjustments for different disabled people.

1.118   Providing access to Chambers for any purpose is also covered. Both the set of Chambers and also the Inns of Court may owe duties to members of the public attending Chambers. If the Inns of Court do not provide a reasonable means of access to Chambers through the common parts so that access through them remains impossible or unreasonably difficult for disabled people (which may result from difficulties in obtaining planning permission), the Chambers may have duties to provide a reasonable means of avoiding the physical feature which is causing the difficulty. In those circumstances, Chambers will also have a duty to provide a reasonable alternative method of making its services available to disabled persons. For example a Chambers which does not have wheelchair access may have to consider holding conferences with a wheelchair user away from Chambers.

1.119   If Chambers decides to make adjustments to its premises these should be drawn to the attention of disabled people (for example by a sign). Similarly if it is the intention of Chambers to make its services accessible by providing auxiliary aids, this should be made known.

1.120 It will be exceptionally rare for a Chambers or a barrister not to have to make any adjustments that would render services accessible to disabled persons. It is strongly recommended that a periodic audit be conducted by a nominated person in Chambers who should be mandated to discuss matters with individual barristers.

1.121 There is no obligation on Chambers or a barrister to take any steps which would fundamentally alter the nature of its service.

1.122 When a barrister or Chambers complies with the duty to make reasonable adjustments they are not entitled to pass on any additional costs of compliance solely to disabled clients.

1.123 The duty to make adjustments may affect the Chambers' policies (what it intends to do), its policies (how it plans to go about providing its services) and its practices (what it actually does when providing services).

1.124 The barrister or set of Chambers must take reasonable steps to provide auxiliary aids including equipment or services if these would facilitate disabled people using its services. An auxiliary aid may be the provision of a special piece of equipment but it is more likely, in the case of barrister services, simply to be the provision of some extra assistance to disabled people.

1.125 The obligation is to take such steps as it is reasonable for the barrister or Chambers to take in all the circumstances of the case to make it services accessible to disabled people. Therefore consideration needs to be given to the size and resources of the Chambers (or the resources of the individual barrister) as well as the cost of providing the auxiliary service.

1.126 The Disability Rights Commission (DRC) Code of Practice gives examples of the kind of auxiliary services or aids that may be appropriate for people with hearing disability (para 5.23 and following) and visual impairments (para 5.26 and following).

Adjustments to Physical Features

1.127 In terms of physical features it is advisable that an access audit should be carried out on a Chambers' premises. During this the views of people with different disabilities or those representing them should be sought, as this may help in identifying barriers and developing solutions. The best approach to removing the effect of physical features on accessibility is to alter the physical feature itself so as to create an inclusive environment. Removal of physical barriers will be preferable to alternative arrangements. There is an inherent loss of dignity for the disabled person in having to use some alternative route for example. It is only if it is not reasonable to remove the physical feature, or to alter it, that such alternative route adjustments should be made.

1.128 The DRC Code contains specific guidance on how the building regulations and leases affect reasonable adjustment duties. What needs to be borne in mind is that the duty to make adjustments will still arise in respect of any access issues and regardless of whether no physical adjustments are required or permitted.

1.129 Adjustments to physical features may require the consent of the landlord. Regulations provide that it is reasonable for the service provider to have to request consent but that it is not automatically reasonable for the service provider to have to make an alteration just because consent has been given. In essence the landlord may not unreasonably refuse consent to a reasonable alteration which is necessary to comply with the duty to make adjustments. The landlord is entitled to attach reasonable conditions to the consent. Detailed guidance is given in the DRC's Code concerning these regulations and the obtaining of consent (see para 1.126 above).

Justification

1.130   Both less favourable treatment and a failure to make reasonable adjustments may be justified on specific grounds which are set out in section 20(4) of the DDA provided that the discrimination is not direct discrimination. The Chambers or the barrister must reasonably believe that one or more of the following conditions are satisfied:

- the service provider is not obliged to do anything which would endanger the health or safety of any person;
- the disabled person is incapable of entering into an enforceable agreement, or of giving an informed consent, and for that reason the treatment is reasonable in that case;
- (in relation to refusing to provide, or deliberately not providing, any service) the treatment is necessary because the Chambers or barrister would otherwise be unable to provide the service to members of the public;
- (in relation to the standard of service or the terms on which it is provided) the treatment is necessary in order for the Chambers or barrister to be able to provide the service to the disabled person or to other members of the public.
- (In relation to the terms on which the service is provided) the difference in the terms on which the services provided to the disabled person and those on which it is provided to other members of the public reflects the greater cost to the provider of services in providing the service to the disabled person. However any increase in the cost of providing a service to the disabled person resulting from compliance with the duty to make reasonable adjustments disregarded for this purpose.

Other Areas of Potentially Discriminatory Service Provision

1.131   Discrimination by barristers as service providers on the ground of race or sex is unlawful. Discrimination on any other ground covered in paragraph 305 of the Code of Conduct is prohibited.

1.132   Examples of discriminatory service provision include the following:

- the racial or sexual harassment of a professional or lay client;
- a refusal to accept instructions to act on behalf of individuals or groups defined by their race, sex, sexuality, religion or belief;
- providing a service that is inappropriate (eg timing of conferences with clients with childcare responsibilities)
- failing to take account of the religious needs of clients in relation to dress, food and drink or religious observance;
- asking irrelevant questions based upon assumptions about client's sexuality.

1.133   Chambers should ensure that their members are equipped to provide an appropriate level of service for their clients by arranging diversity training for members of chambers and chambers staff. Clients whose first language is not English may have particular needs for interpreters and the Bar Council has produced a guidance document on this subject.

H. Staff in Chambers

1.134   Practice Management for the Bar sets out standards and guidelines covering the main areas of practice management. This includes recruitment and a section on personnel management which states the recommended standards for managing staff together with detailed guidance on their implementation. The comprehensive guidance in Practice Management is not replicated in this document. The recommendations for good practice set out here in earlier chapters are equally applicable to chambers staff and many of them explicitly include chambers staff.

1.135   Recruitment of chambers' staff should follow the recommendations relating to pupillage and tenancy recruitment wherever appropriate, for example open advertisements, clear and objective selection criteria and panel interviews.

1.136   It is important to ensure that all equal opportunity policy initiatives developed in Chambers cover staff as well as members of Chambers whenever appropriate. The Equal Opportunities Commission, Commission for Racial Equality and Disability Rights Commission have all developed Codes of Practice in recruitment.

Maternity, Paternity, Parental Leave

1.137   A policy for staff will differ markedly from a policy for members. Chambers should set out their policy for staff on maternity, paternity and parental leave and flexible working. This should, at least, meet the minimum legislative requirements. These provide for:

- time off for ante-natal care;
- Periods of paid and unpaid maternity leave for women following childbirth;
- paternity leave and pay for fathers;
- adoption leave and pay for individuals who adopt or one partner of a couple who jointly adopt;
- paternity leave and pay for the other member of the couple;
- parental leave for up to 13 weeks for parents with children (including adopted) under the age of six. This is extended to eighteen if the child is disabled.
- a reasonable amount of unpaid time off to deal with an emergency situation.

Complaints and Grievances

1.138   Chambers should have a written complaints and grievance procedure for staff which includes procedures covering complaints of discrimination and harassment. These should provide for both formal and informal routes for making complaints. Chambers should nominate an 'approachable' person in chambers to act as an informal adviser to staff. For further information see Action Area F.

SECTION 2: LEGAL & REGULATORY FRAMEWORK

Statutory Regulation

2.1   Barristers owe a legal duty not to discriminate on grounds of race, sex, disability, sexual orientation or religion or belief and a duty not to discriminate indirectly or to victimize in:

- the recruitment of staff and the selection of pupils and tenants;
- the terms, opportunities for training or gaining experience, benefits and services for prospective or current members of staff, pupils and tenants;
- the termination of service of staff or the termination of pupillage or tenancy, including pressure to leave;
- subjecting staff, pupils or tenants to detrimental treatment.

2.2   Discrimination following termination of the relationship between barristers and staff, pupils or tenants may be unlawful where there is sufficient connection between the relationship and the discriminatory act complained of, for example in the provision of references or post-employment benefits.

2.3   It is unlawful for barristers to discriminate against lay or professional clients in the provision of services on grounds of sex or race or for reasons relating to disability.

2.4   Discrimination 'on racial grounds' encompasses nationality, race, colour and ethnic origins.

2.5   Sex discrimination encompasses not only gender but also marital status, pregnancy and gender reassignment. Discrimination on grounds of pregnancy is a particular type of sex discrimination where no comparator is required, so that it is no defence to a claim based on pregnancy that a man absent by reason of sickness would have been treated in a similar fashion.

2.6   Many of the duties apply to barristers' clerks as they apply to barristers.

2.7   Disability is a legal concept defined in the DDA. It includes not only obvious visible disability but may include conditions such as manic depression or other mental impairment. Particular rules are made in respect of progressive conditions such as cancer. There is a positive duty to make reasonable adjustments to accommodate a disabled person, such as providing communications equipment or alterations to premises.

2.8   Age discrimination will be outlawed as from 2006.

2.9   The relevant statutory provisions are to be found in the Sex Discrimination Act 1975, Race Relations Act 1976, Disability Discrimination Act 1995, Employment Equality (Sexual Orientation) Regulations 2003, Employment Equality (Religion and Belief) Regulations 2003, Disability Discrimination Act 1995 (Amendment) Regulations 2003; EU Equal Treatment, Race Discrimination and Framework Employment Directives.

Bar Code of Conduct

2.10   Paragraph 305 of the Code of Conduct prohibits discrimination directly or indirectly by a practising barrister in relation to:

- any other person including a lay or professional client, another barrister, a pupil or student member of an Inn of Court

on the following grounds:

- race, colour, ethnic or national origin, nationality, citizenship, sex, sexual orientation, marital status, disability, religion or political persuasion.

2.11   To the extent that discrimination *in the provision of services* is not unlawful (for example, where discrimination is on grounds of sexual orientation or religious belief), the Code of Conduct makes such discrimination a matter of professional misconduct.

2.12   Discrimination on grounds of age in relation to pupillage and tenancy selection is prohibited unless it can be shown to be objectively and reasonably justifiable (para 305(ii)).

2.13   The Code of Conduct, paragraph 403 requires a barrister to have regard to this code, which is likely to be taken into account by Courts, tribunals and disciplinary panels in deciding whether discrimination has occurred.

2.14   Paragraph 404.2(d) of the Code of Conduct[1] requires that Chambers

   a. appoint at least one Equal Opportunity Officer; and

   b. have a written equal opportunities policy made available to all members of Chambers and staff and to the Bar Council when requested, which shall set out the policy adopted by the Chambers in relation to each of the Action Areas in the Equality and Diversity Code and shall have regard to the recommendations in the Equality and Diversity Code;

   c. shall not hold itself out as offering pupillages until the steps set out in a. and b. above have been complied with.

2.15   The Pupillage and Funding Requirements 2003, set out in Annexe R of the Code of Conduct, require that

2.16   all vacancies for pupillage are advertised on a website designated by the Bar Council, subject to limited exceptions.

Bar Council Equal Opportunity Policy Statement

2.17   The Bar Council, in pursuit of its constitutional function to represent the interests of the Bar and its statutory functions under the Courts and Legal Services Act 1990, will promote equality of opportunity irrespective of race, colour, ethnic or national origin, nationality, citizenship, sex, marital status, sexual orientation, disability, age, religion or political persuasion.

   In accordance with the Code of Conduct of the Bar of England and Wales, discrimination by a barrister is professional misconduct and the Bar Council will take disciplinary action against any barrister or employee of the Bar Council found to have discriminated.

   The Bar Council will monitor the effectiveness of its policy and the achievement of its objectives.

Key Concepts

2.18   Unlawful discrimination generally falls into one of three categories:

   a. Direct discrimination: where one person is treated less favourably than another was or would be treated in the same or similar circumstances because of a particular characteristic identified in the anti-discrimination legislation (gender, race, disability, sexual orientation or religion or belief);

   b. Indirect discrimination: where an apparently neutral provision, criterion or practice has a disadvantageous impact upon a particular group and where the provision, criterion or practice is not a proportionate means of achieving a legitimate aim (for example, holding an internal Chambers training seminar at a time when a particular group of members will find it difficult to attend and when

---

[1] This amendment to para 404 is awaiting the Department for Constitutional Affairs' approval.

the meeting could reasonably be held at some other time which would not exclude any particular group);

Victimisation: where a person is treated less favourably because he or she has brought proceedings under the anti-discrimination legislation, given evidence or information relating to proceedings or has alleged that unlawful discrimination has occurred (or is suspected of intending to do any of the above).

2.19   It is not a defence to claims for direct discrimination and victimisation that there was no intention to discriminate or that the discrimination was justified, save that discrimination for a reason related to disability can be justified if the reason for the treatment is substantial and material. This defence of justification has been applied very narrowly by the courts. In relation to indirect discrimination, treatment may be justified if it can be shown that it is a proportionate means of achieving a legitimate aim but the lack of an intention to discriminate is not a defence.

2.20   Discriminatory treatment may amount to harassment. Harassment is any form of unwanted conduct which is intended to, or which creates the effect of, violating a person's dignity or which creates an intimidating, hostile, degrading, humiliating or offensive environment for that person. The fact that one person may be able to ignore or deal comfortably with certain behaviour does not mean that it is acceptable if directed at another. A single incident may constitute harassment if it is sufficiently serious. The motive or intention of the perpetrator may be (but is not invariably) relevant. Where harassment is on a ground identified in the anti-discrimination legislation, it will be unlawful. There is a new free-standing definition of harassment contained in various regulations the relevant provisions are the Race Relations Act 1976 (Amendment) Regulations 2003; the Employment Equality (Sexual Orientation) Regulations 2003; the Employment Equality (Religion or Belief) Regulations 2003; and the Disability Discrimination Act 1995 (Amendment) Regulations 2003.

2.21   Any 'detriment' on a prohibited ground and in a protected area (e.g. employment and provision of services) will amount to unlawful discrimination. Detrimental treatment includes any treatment which the complainant reasonably perceives as disadvantageous.

2.22   The concepts applicable under the Disability Discrimination Act 1995 ('the DDA') are in some respects different from other discrimination legislation. The DDA covers claims for direct discrimination which cannot be justified. Barristers and their clerks have a further duty under the DDA to make reasonable adjustments to ensure that a disabled person is not placed at a disadvantage.

Clarifying Some Common Misconceptions

2.23   Proof of discrimination does not depend on showing motive or bad faith. It is possible to discriminate without intending to discriminate. Even treatment which is well-intentioned may amount to discrimination.

2.24   There is no defence of 'joke' or 'banter'. Jokes and banter which cause offence may be discriminatory even though there was no intention to cause offence.

2.25   Discrimination which involves the more favourable treatment of a member of a disadvantaged group ('positive discrimination') is unlawful in relation to persons encompassed within the anti-discrimination legislation, save that a form of positive discrimination may be exercised in relation to disabled persons who may require particular adjustments to be made. Applications may be encouraged from groups which are under-represented in an organisation (this is known as 'positive action') but applicants from such groups cannot be positively advantaged in any selection process.

2.26   Individuals from the same protected group may commit acts of unlawful discrimination against each other: a woman may unlawfully discriminate against another woman, for example, or a barrister in one racial group against another member of that group.

2.27   Some common misconceptions can be dispelled by appropriate diversity training or by access to information such as that provided to judges by the Judicial Studies Board's Bench Book (see para 1.133).

How Does an Individual Prove Discrimination?

2.28   If there is a difference in treatment and a difference in the relevant identifying characteristic (eg gender) of two persons in the same or similar circumstances, an inference of unlawful discrimination may be drawn. It is rare for discriminatory attitudes to be expressed overtly and unlawful discrimination may take place without the perpetrator being conscious that he or she is discriminating. The inference drawing process is the method by which Courts and tribunals test whether there has been unlawful discrimination.

2.29   In looking at whether inferences should be drawn, Courts and tribunals look at factors such as whether there have been assumptions or stereotyping which have influenced the complainant's treatment.

Sometimes, an organisation may demonstrate a preference for individuals in their own image: 'people like us' or someone 'whose face fits' or who will 'fit in'. Ignorance of cultural difference may lead to the application of inappropriate evaluations of behaviour or attitude.

2.30   An explanation for the difference in treatment which is objectively adequate will usually prevent any inference arising. Good practice gives a large measure of protection. For example, if objective criteria have been applied to all candidates in a recruitment exercise by a panel of interviewers and a reasoned decision has been made and recorded, a Court or Tribunal is more likely to be persuaded that a decision has not been influenced by excessively subjective and discriminatory judgments.

2.31   Whilst the civil standard of proof applies in discrimination cases in the employment tribunal and County Court, the criminal standard of proof applies in disciplinary proceedings for breach of the Code of Conduct. In the employment tribunal and the Courts and employment tribunal in race, sex, religion or belief and sexual orientation discrimination cases, the burden of proof shifts to the employer/ respondent/defendant where an employee/applicant/claimant establishes facts from which unlawful discrimination could be inferred in the absence of an adequate explanation.

APPENDIX 2
ANSWERS TO PROBLEMS

The following are the answers to the problems set in the course of **Chapter 2** and **Chapter 5**. The problems in **Chapter 9** will be dealt with during the practitioner large group sessions.

2.1 Relationship with the court

2.1.1 Duties and responsibilities owed to the court

(1) Paragraph 708(c) makes it clear that you have no choice (in civil or criminal proceedings) but to bring the authority to the attention of the court, whether or not you believe that you can distinguish it by argument (see *Copeland v Smith and Another* [2000] 1 All ER 457).

(2) It would be impolite and embarrassing to interrupt counsel for the claimant or stand up and address the court on the point. Inform counsel for the claimant of his error as soon as practicable, either by passing a note or speaking to him or her as he or she is leaving or just outside the court. It is then for him or her, knowing his or her duty, to return to the court, apologise and put the matter right.

(3) Accept his or her ruling with good grace, carry on as best you can and, if your client is convicted, appeal. Once the judge has ruled you must accept it. Do not argue with the tribunal, whatever your feelings; remember your duty to be courteous to the court. Contrast this position with one where there has been a procedural irregularity in the proceedings (see para 708(d)).

2.1.3 Further duties

(1) Your views on the reason for the jump are largely irrelevant! The defence are entitled to see the note. You remain under a continuing duty to review questions of disclosure (s 7A of the Criminal Procedure and Investigations Act 1996). If you, at any time before the accused is acquitted or convicted, form the opinion that there is material that might undermine the prosecution case, or be reasonably expected to assist the accused's defence, then it must be disclosed to the accused as soon as reasonably practicable (subject to the court's ruling to the contrary). In these circumstances your duty would probably be to get the witness back to court if requested. If the note were very much older then it would be better for defence counsel to apply to reopen cross-examination and satisfy the judge that the information was

relevant (see also para 10.2, Standards Applicable to Criminal Cases in the Written Standards for the Conduct of Professional Work in Section 3, Miscellaneous Guidance).

(2) The principle is the same as that involved where the judge makes an error in summing-up (para 10.7, Standards Applicable to Criminal Cases in the Written Standards for the Conduct of Professional Work in Section 3, Miscellaneous Guidance). You are bound to draw the error to his or her attention. If he or she does not correct it, consider carefully whether you still want to adduce the evidence or otherwise take advantage of the ruling. What is the point of securing a conviction which will be overturned on appeal? See, further, *R v Langford* The Times, 12 January 2001.

(3) It would be quite wrong for you not to tell your opponent. You could be professionally embarrassed under para 603(f) and if so, must withdraw from the case under para 608(a). Even if, having taken instructions from the defendant, no objection is raised you should think very carefully before continuing to act. You might well feel inhibited in the conduct of your case. More importantly, you risk a possible complaint if the defendant is convicted.

2.1.4 Specific responsibilities of defence counsel

(1) From a practical point of view, it is to be hoped that you kept a careful note of what your client told you. Ideally that should have been copied to your instructing solicitor, or the account at least communicated to him or her at the time. In that way, the account should be in the defendant's proof of evidence in any event. If it was not in the proof when the brief was delivered you should have spotted and rectified the omission prior to the trial. Prior to the Criminal Justice and Public Order Act 1994, guidance was given in the case of *R v Jaquith*; *R v Emode* [1989] Crim LR 508 and 563, CA. The basic rule is still the same: you should not give evidence unless it is absolutely necessary. It is necessary if your client will suffer if you do not and there is no other way. In this case your client may not be able to avoid the statutory inferences deriving from his silence *in interview*, but the suggestion of recent fabrication is obviously unfair. Your first move is to tell your opponent of the position (by interrupting him or her, if necessary), as discreetly as you can. If you have conducted yourself properly thus far, he or she will probably accept your word and withdraw the specific suggestion after you have agreed a formula about the date. Showing him or her your client's proof should be avoided if possible. If no agreement can be reached you must explain the situation to your clients (lay and professional) and may withdraw provided that your client's interests are not jeopardised (para 3.6, General Standards in Written Standards for the Conduct of Professional Work in Section 3, Miscellaneous Guidance). The trial will have to restart with fresh counsel so that you can give evidence. If you have a leader the trial can continue without you. If you are sure that withdrawal is the only proper course, do not be put off by any unsatisfactory compromise whether suggested by your opponent or the judge, merely to avoid a threat of wasted costs orders.

(2) Obviously if you have simply not put your case properly, you should immediately make that clear in front of the jury. Your client must not be prejudiced by your mistake and cannot be prejudiced by its correction. However, in the circumstances described here much will depend on what the judge has said. Most judges would

realize what has happened and simply smile to themselves or at prosecution counsel. If, however, the judge asks you: 'That is not how it was put, was it Mr or Ms Smith?' or 'You did not challenge the evidence of your client's presence, did you Mr or Ms Smith?', you can simply agree. If the judge asks, 'Mr or Ms Smith, what on earth is going on?', you can simply state that you have put the case according to your instructions. Do not engage in or rise to comments about whose 'fault' it is. If there is some explicit demand to know your client's instructions, you should politely but firmly refuse to answer such a question: 'Your Honour, it is not appropriate for me to answer that question...' If the judge presses the matter then ask him or her to send the jury out. In the absence of the jury you should point out that you cannot under any circumstances reveal your client's instructions and waive privilege without your client's consent (para 702). For the same reason you should not show your instructions to the judge.

(3) Paragraph 702 applies here. With regard to the first part of the problem, you are under no obligation to volunteer the information, but *you must not* refer to the defendant's character in any way which suggests that he or she has no previous convictions. In other words, you must never mislead the court (para 302). This is bound severely to restrict what may be said in mitigation and may have the effect of preventing any reference at all to character. You may then be faced by a penetrating question from the court, in which case (subject to your client's instructions, as to which see below) you would use a formula such as 'There is nothing further I can add.'. If you have not got clear instructions from your client, then ask for time to take some. From a practical point of view, as soon as you realize the police antecedents are incomplete (which ought to be before you go into court) you should explain the position to your client and obtain from him or her clear instructions as to whether he or she wishes you to disclose straight away, or only if asked, or not at all. Tactics will play a part in any advice you give. If the court puts the case over for reports then the information is likely to come out anyway. A virtue can be made in mitigation of the fact that disclosure has been made.

The answer to the second part of the question is the same, although your advice will almost inevitably be to make disclosure. The original sentencing court is likely to find out about the breach and may take the view, if the defendant is called back to that court, that the instant court imposed too lenient a sentence because it was not in possession of all the pertinent information.

2.2 Relationship with the lay client

(1) Distinguish between your duty and his or her rights. You must put in cross-examination all those instructions which are relevant and material to the defence. You are the arbiter of that (see para 708(a)). He or she is entitled to give evidence himself or herself and call witnesses who can give material evidence. You can only advise him or her. If he or she rejects your advice you must still pursue his or her case with vigour, but you must not make submissions you consider not to be properly arguable (see para 708(f)). (See paras 708(g) and (j) and 508, General Standards and 11.4, Standards Applicable to Criminal Cases in Written Standards for the Conduct of Professional Work in Section 3, Miscellaneous Guidance.)

(2) The first step is to obtain instructions from the client as to what really happened. Write this down and invite him or her to sign your note. This is to guard against him or her subsequently alleging that you acted improperly or contrary to his or her instructions. Explain to the client the consequences, if any, of this new information upon the conduct or likely outcome of his or her case. It may be you are now unable to pursue part of his or her claim/defence. You may be professionally embarrassed (see para 603). If this is so, inform your opponent and the court as soon as possible. You do not need to say why (para 702). Alternatively, it may be necessary to apply to amend your statement of case. Inform your opponent of your intention to do so and the extent of the amendment you will seek. Explain to the client the likely implications upon the question of costs. Ensure he or she understands the nature of the oath he or she will take in court and the necessity to give evidence in accordance with the truth of what he or she says actually happened. After the case, telephone your instructing solicitor and inform him or her of what took place. This may affect the future relationship between him or her and the lay client. Also consider whether any conflicts of interest exist (see para 703).

(3) Clients frequently react in emotional terms to losing in court, both in civil and criminal proceedings. They may threaten harm to others or even to themselves. Do not 'disappear' without speaking to your client after the case. Poor communication is often the cause of dissatisfied clients lodging a complaint with the Professional Conduct and Complaints Committee. It is important to spend some time with the client after the hearing of the case, explaining precisely what has happened, why it has happened and whether there are any grounds of appeal. Warn the client of the consequences both to him and others of either making or carrying out such threats. Do not repeat to any third party what the client has said unless your duty of confidentiality is being used to conceal a crime (see para 702).

2.3 Relationship with the professional client

2.3.1 Duties and responsibilities owed to the professional client

(1) You should not agree to supply such an opinion. It is a breach of the Code (para 307) if you compromise your professional standards in order to please your client or permit your absolute independence to be compromised.

It is a clear abuse of your position, and it is tantamount to fraud, to supply an opinion for publication to others which is at odds with your true opinion. In various individual situations it may be proper for you to write an opinion for your client which will be shown to a third party, in which you deal with the matter differently from an opinion given to the client for the client's consumption only, eg by omission of reference to privileged matters or to considerations or qualifications which do not ultimately alter the effect or emphasis of your conclusions, but it is an area fraught with technical difficulty and one in which you will always be wise to discuss the points of concern with your colleagues in chambers.

Note: In any case where a solicitor asks for your advice in general terms, or on a particular basis without sufficient details for the giving of definitive advice governing an individual case, if you have any reason to suspect that the opinion is for circulation to others than an individual client, you should carefully state the assumed facts or other basis on which you advise in the body of the opinion itself.

(2) Remember your duty to act fearlessly on behalf of your lay client without regard to any consequences to yourself (para 303(a)). You should make an application for the 'costs thrown away' to be paid by the defendant's solicitors irrespective of the extent of your personal or professional relationship with them. Otherwise your client will suffer loss through no fault of his or her own. It is for the court to determine the merits of your application.

2.3.3 Prosecuting counsel and the Crown Prosecution Service

Whilst para 10.6, Standards Applicable to Criminal Cases in Written Standards for the Conduct of Professional Work in Section 3, Miscellaneous Guidance gives some guidance, the problem is one of communication. You have given weight to factors which you consider important. The solicitor may have others, including the need to adopt a consistent approach to all cases. You should listen to his or her arguments and explain yours clearly to him or her. If you are unable to persuade him or her and you maintain your original opinion, you should consider withdrawing.

2.4 Relationship with other members of the profession

(1) Almost certainly no, particularly if there is an issue on liability. Your knowledge of the view taken by your colleague of the strength of the claimant's case gives you an unfair advantage, particularly if, on the papers before you, the claimant's case does not strike you as being so weak (see para 603(g)). It is only if liability is not in dispute that you could consider continuing. Even if you do not feel embarrassed you should disclose to your colleague what has happened and ensure that he or she feels that his or her case is not unfairly disadvantaged by your earlier discussion.

(2) The first step is to speak to your senior clerk. It is courteous to ask for a word with him or her in private, as it is likely to embarrass him or her if you question him or her in front of the junior clerks. Ask him or her for an explanation as to why this particular brief was given to the pupil when you have advised on the case previously. There may be a good reason, for example, the solicitor may have asked for a pupil to do the case for reasons of cost or he or she may have indicated to the clerk that the client was not happy with your previous advice and did not feel confident about you conducting his or her case. If no satisfactory explanation is forthcoming, ask your clerk what reason the solicitor was given for your unavailability. If you are satisfied that the clerk has deliberately lied to the professional client in order to stop your work, speak to the head of chambers about the matter. You should not 'retrieve' the brief from the pupil for the next day when the solicitor has already been informed that he or she is doing the case. At the very least, however, you should ensure that the situation does not recur.

5.7 Court etiquette: problems

(1) Don't panic. The first step is to telephone your clerk. Instruct him or her to contact the court and your solicitors to inform them of your delay and your expected time of arrival at court. On arrival at court, you must apologise to your client, instructing

solicitor and opponent. If you have kept the judge (and jury) waiting, it will be necessary to apologise in open court. Do not make excuses which are untrue such as 'my car broke down'. You have a duty to be candid no matter how embarrassed or concerned you are about the consequences (para 302). Punctuality is vital so do not make a habit of being late (para 701(a)). Having said that, most members of the Bar have had one experience of this!

(2) Unfortunately, this situation is a not uncommon one to face members of the Criminal Bar, known as 'double-courting'. Once the first case has finished you have no option but to hasten to the second court and make your apologies to the judge. Expect a reprimand from the judge, and possibly the consideration of a wasted costs order. This is a situation that ought not to have arisen: Written Standards for the Conduct of Professional Work in Section 3, Miscellaneous Guidance of the Code of Conduct provides at para 4.1 that 'When a barrister has accepted a brief for the defence of a person charged with a serious criminal offence, he should so far as reasonably practicable ensure that the risk of a conflicting professional engagement does not arise'. Both cases ought not to have been accepted. You should have discussed the matter with your clerk before going to court. It is sometimes difficult to have a discussion in which you are asking the clerk to alter something he or she has put into the diary. Remember, however, that you are responsible for the proper administration of your practice, and you will get the flak from the judge, not your clerk (para 306, and see *Wasted Costs Order (No 4 of 1993)* The Times, 21 April 1995).

Speak to your clerk on your return to chambers. Tell him or her what has occurred and try to ensure that it never happens again. In the event of a dispute with your clerk which cannot be resolved between you, consult your head of chambers.

INDEX